An American Primer

An American Primer

EDITED BY

DANIEL J. BOORSTIN

CHICAGO AND LONDON
THE UNIVERSITY OF CHICAGO PRESS

Collector's Edition

Standard Book Number: 226–06494–8

Library of Congress Catalog Card Number: 66–20576

THE UNIVERSITY OF CHICAGO PRESS, CHICAGO 60637

The University of Chicago Press, Ltd., London W.C.1

© 1966 by The University of Chicago

Published 1966

Second Impression 1969

Printed in the United States of America

Designed by John B. Goetz

17,712

Contents

☆ ☆

vi

CONTENTS

Thomas Alva Edison
On the Industrial Research Laboratory
1887

EDITED BY MATTHEW JOSEPHSON

In 1876 Thomas Alva Edison gave up his previous business of manufacturing telegraphic instruments and moved out to a quiet country retreat at Menlo Park, New Jersey. There he established himself in his own research laboratory devoted entirely to inventive work. Formerly it was only the cultivated devotees of pure science who possessed laboratories, and they used them for experiments touching the principles of natural science and aiming chiefly to add to the sum of human knowledge. Edison's was actually the world's first industrial research laboratory, intended for the uses of a free-lance inventor; and, in many ways, it was his most important invention. By virtue of this achievement alone he became a central figure in the new age of technology.

The modest wooden-frame structure at Menlo Park resembled a country meeting house without a steeple. It had a drafting room, a scientific library, and a big workroom equipped with various instruments of precision and with quantities of chemicals, minerals, wire, batteries, and induction coils; in outbuildings were a steam engine, a furnace, a forge, and some of the new-fangled electric dynamos. At the time only a very few of America's leading universities boasted such laboratory equipment (Edison's had cost some $40,000). Certainly no engineering or industrial concern possessed such a laboratory, or such an unusual staff as Edison's "twenty earnest men" who resided with him in the "village of science" at Menlo Park.

Edison called his all-purpose research laboratory an "invention factory." Some thought he was a braggart when he vowed that he would turn out a minor invention every ten days and some "big job" every six months. Soon he had forty-four different projects under way and was taking out as many as four hundred patents a year. The Edison Laboratory was notable not only for the great diversity of its products, but also for thoroughness of research and testing. Contrary to the once-prevalent notion about Edison's dislike of theoretical scientists, he employed several distinguished mathematical physicists and university-trained engineers on his staff, as well as clockmakers and machinists. In short Edison "made a business out of invention itself," as Werner Sombart wrote. He delivered inventions to order, though the time of delivery was somewhat unpredictable. In developing practical new products Edison worked closely with big industrialists, and also with such leading financiers as the Vanderbilts and Morgans; yet he did not work primarily for money, but "to invent more"—and he repeatedly lost whole fortunes doing it.

At the little Edison Laboratory, the first strangled cries of the infant phonograph were heard; the brilliant light of the Edison lamp shone forth; America's earliest full-scale electric locomotive rumbled over a small track outside; and the mysterious two-electrode vacuum bulb also put in its appearance, hinting at the future of electronics and radio. One of the Edison Laboratory's most famous employees, A. E. Kennelly, paid tribute to it as "the meeting ground of practical inventive experience and scientific discovery."

Menlo Park was abandoned after a decade, as Edison moved on to a larger stage. Henry Ford, who attributed much of his success in the mass production of automobiles to Edison's ideas, built an exact reproduction of the old laboratory for the Ford Institute at Dearborn, signalizing it as the birthplace of modern American technology.

A man of "pure act," Edison did not stop to write down his original ideas about the first laboratory. But these are well defined in a letter he wrote in 1887 when he had completed its replica (but tenfold enlarged) at West Orange, New Jersey, the second Edison Laboratory—now in the custody of the National Park Service as a National Monument. Edison's letter was addressed to J. Hood Wright of New York, a friendly financier who was one of the backers of the old Edison Electric Light Company; it was drafted by Edison in the pages of his laboratory notebook for 1887, and is written with his characteristic imagination and in his own outrageous orthography.

M Y LABORATORY will soon be completed. The dimensions are one building 250 ft long 50 wide & 3 stories [high] 4 other bldgs. 25 x 100 ft one story high all of brick. I will have the best equipped and largest Laboratory extant, and the facilities incomparably superior to any other for rapid & cheap development of an invention, & working it up into Commercial shape with models, patterns & special machinery. In fact there is no similar institution in Existence. We do our own castings forgings. Can build anything from a ladys watch to a Locomotive.

The Machine shop is sufficiently large to employ 50 men & 30 men can be worked in other parts of the works. Inventions that formerly took months & cost a large sum can now be done 2 or 3 days with very small expense, as I shall carry a stock of almost every conceivable material of every size and with the latest machinery a man will produce 10 times as much as in a laboratory which has but little material, not of a size, delays of days waiting for castings and machinery not universal or modern. . . .

You are aware from your long acquaintance with me that I do not fly any financial Kites, or speculate, and that the works which I control are well managed. In the early days of the shops it was necessary that I should largely manage them [alone], first because the art had to be created. 2nd. because I could get no men who were competent in such a new business. But as soon as it was possible I put other persons in charge. I am perfectly well aware of the fact that my place is in the Laboratory; but I think you will admit that I know how a shop should be managed & also know how to select men to manage them.

With this prelude I will come to business.

My ambition is to build up a great Industrial Works in the Orange Valley starting in a small way & gradually working up. The Laboratory supplying the perfected inventions, models, patterns & fitting up necessary special machinery in the factory for each invention.

My plan contemplates to working of only that class of inventions which requires but small investments. . . . Such a work in time could be running on 30 to 40 special things of so diversified nature that the average profit could scarcely be [varied] by competitors. Now Mr. Wright, do you think this is practicable. If so can you help me along with it.

The letter, dated November 14, 1887, is taken from Edison's notebooks, which are preserved at the Edison Laboratory, West Orange, New Jersey.

It was with a sure instinct that the American people, after 1877, made Thomas Alva Edison one of the greatest of their folk heroes. He appealed to them as one of the old-fashioned, self-taught, individualistic Yankee inventors who epitomized the practical genius acclaimed as our national trait. During the era after the Civil War when America was dominated by great acquisitors, he was above all creative: new industries, untold new wealth flowed from his many innovations. Finally, the rise of the former train-boy and tramp telegrapher from rags to riches was an enactment of the American Dream.

Renewed study of Edison's career has led historians to revise sharply the traditional concept of him as an "antiscientific" mechanical inventor. Today he appears rather as a transitional figure in nineteenth-century science who introduced important changes into the very method of invention. With Edison the crude, single-handed methods of earlier contrivers gave way to the more complex ones of skilled and specialized men, working no longer alone, but as groups or teams engaged in systematic research. The individualistic inventors had pursued their experiments at a workbench in a factory, or in an attic or barn equipped with few scientific tools. Edison, at an early stage of his career, saw that it required an amplitude of good instruments, a group of expert helpers, and a proper establishment in order to pursue scientific investigations for prospective inventions in organized fashion.

Gradually, in the 1890's, a few large industrial concerns in America followed Edison's lead and established laboratories where scientific workers were employed in research, usually subordinated to the corporation's needs. Among the first and most important of the corporate laboratories were those of the Bell System, Eastman Kodak, and General Electric. During World War I the number of such research centers was rapidly multiplied—Germany's industrial corporations were far ahead of us then—and the scope of their activities was greatly expanded, to include basic scientific research as an adjunct to practical inventive work. In 1927, in advanced old age, Edison visited the gigantic laboratory of the General Electric Company at Schenectady, New York. By then this was staffed with hundreds of technicians, among them some of the nation's leading theoretical scientists, such as Charles Steinmetz, Irving Langmuir, and W. D. Coolidge. Edison beheld scientific instruments and devices of a power and complexity that even he had scarcely imagined: "lightning bolts" discharging all of 120,000 volts; lamps of

100,000 candlepower; and vacuum tubes for long-distance radio transmission.

Since that time a deluge of technological invention has transformed the world we live in; whole armies of scientific workers pursue their investigations in thousands of elaborate research institutions located throughout the United States, which are operated at a cost of billions of dollars each year. Inventions, nuclear, industrial, or military, are "made to order" by technical organizations or teams, though time of development and perfection are still no more certain than they were in Edison's day. All this multifarious activity in industrial research derives its essential form and character from the little "invention factory" pioneered by Edison in 1876.

Andrew Carnegie
Wealth
1889

EDITED BY ROBERT H. BREMNER

"Wealth" first appeared in the North American Review for June, 1889. That year Andrew Carnegie celebrated his fifty-fourth birthday and the forty-first anniversary of his arrival in the United States. In 1889 Carnegie's fortune was approximately $30,000,000, his annual income about $1,850,000. He had been rich for twenty-five years and had every prospect of growing still richer.

Carnegie once admitted that if he had been free to choose he would hardly have selected a business career. But in 1848, in Allegheny City, Pennsylvania, a poor immigrant boy from Dunfermline, Scotland, could not choose his occupation. "What I could get to do," Carnegie recalled, "not what I desired, was the question." Characteristically he made the best of the situation. He came from artisan stock and, like his ancestors, went to work while still a boy. His forebears, in their apprenticeships, learned to weave cloth or cobble shoes. Carnegie, in his youthful employments, learned how to get along with people and how to make money work. Before turning thirty he had learned and earned enough to become his own master.

A great capitalist, with unusual talents for salesmanship and public relations, Carnegie had the outlook of a master craftsman. Except in youth he was not a hard worker. He made it a practice to employ skilled assistants and to keep himself free from routine. He lived well, took long vacations, and spent part of every day in reading and recreation. Like his grandfathers—one was nicknamed "Professor," the other called himself a "thinking cobbler"—Carnegie took it for granted that a man could practice a trade, such as steel-making, and still lead a vigorous intellectual life.

The years just before Carnegie wrote "Wealth" were among the most eventful in his career. In the 1880's Carnegie strengthened his position in the steel industry, began making large-scale benefactions, published three books, started contributing to periodicals, attempted to convert England to republicanism, became interested in the peace movement, and cultivated friendships with John Morley, Herbert Spencer, Matthew Arnold, and William Gladstone. In 1886 a near-fatal illness and the deaths of his beloved brother and strong-willed mother brought one phase of his life to a close. Another began in 1887 when, after a courtship of seven years, he married Louise Whitfield.

For twenty-five years before 1889 Carnegie had been making private resolutions about the disposition of his fortune. In 1868 he had proposed to limit his income to $50,000 a year, spend his surplus on benevolence, and, as soon as possible, "Cast business aside forever except for others." Mrs. Carnegie shared her husband's philanthropic interests and, in a marriage settlement, formally approved his intention to devote the bulk of his estate to charitable and educational purposes.

Carnegie wrote "Wealth" in the library of his house at 5 West 51 Street, New York City. He sent it to the North American Review in May, 1889. The editor, Allen Thorndyke Rice, on receiving the manuscript, called on Carnegie and asked him to read it aloud. Rice recommended only one change: Carnegie had estimated that $900 of each $1,000 spent on charities was wasted; he revised this figure at Rice's suggestion to $950.

THE PROBLEM of our age is the proper administration of wealth, so that the ties of brotherhood may still bind together the rich and poor in harmonious relationship. The conditions of human life have not only been changed, but revolutionized, within the past few hundred years. In former days there was little difference between the

The essay is reprinted as it originally appeared in the *North American Review*, CXLVIII (1889), 653–64.

dwelling, dress, food, and environment of the chief and those of his retainers. The Indians are to-day where civilized man then was. When visiting the Sioux, I was led to the wigwam of the chief. It was just like the others in external appearance, and even within the difference was trifling between it and those of the poorest of his braves. The contrast between the palace of the millionaire and the cottage of the laborer with us to-day measures the change which has come with civilization.

This change, however, is not to be deplored, but welcomed as highly beneficial. It is well, nay, essential for the progress of the race, that the houses of some should be homes for all that is highest and best in literature and the arts, and for all the refinements of civilization, rather than that none should be so. Much better this great irregularity than universal squalor. Without wealth there can be no Maecenas. The "good old times" were not good old times. Neither master nor servant was as well situated then as to-day. A relapse to old conditions would be disastrous to both—not the least so to him who serves—and would sweep away civilization with it. But whether the change be for good or ill, it is upon us, beyond our power to alter, and therefore to be accepted and made the best of. It is a waste of time to criticise the inevitable.

It is easy to see how the change has come. One illustration will serve for almost every phase of the cause. In the manufacture of products we have the whole story. It applies to all combinations of human industry, as stimulated and enlarged by the inventions of this scientific age. Formerly articles were manufactured at the domestic hearth or in small shops which formed part of the household. The master and his apprentices worked side by side, the latter living with the master, and therefore subject to the same conditions. When these apprentices rose to be masters, there was little or no change in their mode of life, and they, in turn, educated in the same routine succeeding apprentices. There was, substantially, social equality, and even political equality, for those engaged in industrial pursuits had then little or no political voice in the State.

But the inevitable result of such a mode of manufacture was crude articles at high prices. To-day the world obtains commodities of excellent quality at prices which even the generation preceding this would have deemed incredible. In the commercial world similar causes have produced similar results, and the race is benefited thereby. The poor enjoy what the rich could not before afford. What were the luxuries have become the necessaries of life. The laborer has now more comforts than the farmer had a few generations ago. The farmer has more luxuries than the landlord had, and is more richly clad and better housed. The landlord has books and pictures rarer, and appointments more artistic, than the King could then obtain.

The price we pay for this salutary change is, no doubt, great. We assemble thousands of operatives in the factory, in the mine, and in the counting-house, of whom the employer can know little or nothing, and to whom the employer is little better than a myth. All intercourse between them is at an end. Rigid Castes are formed, and, as usual, mutual ignorance breeds mutual distrust. Each Caste is without sympathy for the other, and ready to credit anything disparaging in regard to it. Under the law of competition, the employer of thousands is forced into the strictest economies, among which the rates paid to labor figure prominently, and often there is friction between the employer and the employed, between capital and labor, between rich and poor. Human society loses homogeneity.

The price which society pays for the law of competition, like the price it pays for cheap comforts and luxuries, is also great; but the advantages of this law are also greater still, for it is to this law that we owe our wonderful material development, which brings improved conditions in its train. But, whether the law be benign or not, we must say of it, as we say of the change in the conditions of men to which we have referred: It is here; we cannot evade it; no substitutes for it have been found; and while the law may be sometimes hard for the individual, it is best for the race, because it insures the survival of the fittest in every department. We accept and welcome, therefore, as conditions to which we must accommodate ourselves, great inequality of environment, the concentration of business, industrial and commercial, in the hands of a few, and the law of competition between these, as being not only beneficial, but essential for the future progress of the race. Having accepted these, it follows that there must be great scope for the exercise of special ability in the merchant and in the manufacturer who has to conduct affairs upon a great scale. That this talent for organization and management is rare among men is proved by the fact that it invariably secures for its possessor enormous rewards, no matter where or under what laws or conditions. The experienced in affairs always rate the MAN whose services can be obtained as a partner as not only the first consideration, but such as to render the question of his capital scarcely worth considering, for such men soon create capital; while, without the special talent required, capital soon takes wings. Such men become interested in firms or corporations using millions; and estimating only simple interest to be made upon the capital invested, it is inevitable that their income must exceed their expenditures, and that they must accumulate wealth. Nor is there any middle ground which such men can occupy, because the great manufacturing or commercial concern which does not earn at least interest upon its capital soon becomes bankrupt. It must either go forward or fall behind: to stand still is impossible. It is a condition essential for its successful operation that it should be thus far profitable, and even that, in addition to interest on capital, it should make profit. It is a law, as certain as any of the others named, that men possessed of this peculiar talent for affairs, under the free play of economic forces, must, of necessity, soon be in receipt of more revenue than can be judiciously expended upon themselves; and this law is as beneficial for the race as the others.

Objections to the foundations upon which society is based are not in order, because the condition of the race is better with these than it has been with any others which have been tried. Of the effect of any new substitutes proposed we cannot be sure. The Socialist or Anarchist who seeks to overturn present conditions is to be regarded as attacking the foundation upon which civilization itself rests, for civilization took its start from the day that the capable, industrious workman said to his incompetent and lazy fellow, "If thou dost not sow, thou shalt not reap," and thus ended primitive Communism by separating the drones from the bees. One who studies this subject will soon be brought face to face with the conclusion that upon the sacredness of property civilization itself depends—the right of the laborer to his hundred dollars in the savings bank, and equally the legal right of the millionaire to his millions. To those who propose to substitute Communism for this intense Individualism the answer, therefore, is: The race has tried that. All progress from that barbarous day to the present time has resulted from its displacement. Not evil, but good, has come to the race from the accumulation of wealth by those who have the ability and energy that produce it. But even if we admit for a moment that it might be better for the race to discard its present foundation, Individualism,—that it is a nobler ideal that man should labor, not for himself alone, but in and for a brotherhood of his fellows, and share with them all in common, realizing Swedenborg's idea of Heaven, where, as he says, the angels derive their happiness, not from the laboring for self, but for each other,

—even admit all this, and a sufficient answer is, This is not evolution, but revolution. It necessitates the changing of human nature itself—a work of eons, even if it were good to change it, which we cannot know. It is not practicable in our day or in our age. Even if desirable theoretically, it belongs to another and long-succeeding sociological stratum. Our duty is with what is practicable now; with the next step possible in our day and generation. It is criminal to waste our energies in endeavoring to uproot, when all we can profitably or possibly accomplish is to bend the universal tree of humanity a little in the direction most favorable to the production of good fruit under existing circumstances. We might as well urge the destruction of the highest existing type of man because he failed to reach our ideal as to favor the destruction of Individualism, Private Property, the Law of Accumulation of Wealth, the Law of Competition; for these are the highest results of human experience, the soil in which society so far has produced the best fruit. Unequally or unjustly, perhaps, as these laws sometimes operate, and imperfect as they appear to the Idealist, they are, nevertheless, like the highest type of man, the best and most valuable of all that humanity has yet accomplished.

We start, then, with a condition of affairs under which the best interests of the race are promoted, but which inevitably gives wealth to the few. Thus far, accepting conditions as they exist, the situation can be surveyed and pronounced good. The question then arises,—and, if the foregoing be correct, it is the only question with which we have to deal, —What is the proper mode of administering wealth after the laws upon which civilization is founded have thrown it into the hands of the few? And it is of this great question that I believe I offer the true solution. It will be understood that *fortunes* are here spoken of, not moderate sums saved by many years of effort, the returns from which are required for the comfortable maintenance and education of families. This is not *wealth*, but only *competence*, which it should be the aim of all to acquire.

There are but three modes in which surplus wealth can be disposed of. It can be left to the families of the decedent; or it can be bequeathed for public purposes; or, finally, it can be administered during their lives by its possessors. Under the first and second modes most of the wealth of the world that has reached the few has hitherto been applied. Let us in turn consider each of these modes. The first is the most injudicious. In monarchical countries, the estates and the greatest portion of the wealth are left to the first son, that the vanity of the parent may be gratified by the thought that his name and title are to descend to succeeding generations unimpaired. The condition of this class in Europe today teaches the futility of such hopes or ambitions. The successors have become impoverished through their follies or from the fall in the value of land. Even in Great Britain the strict law of entail has been found inadequate to maintain the status of an hereditary class. Its soil is rapidly passing into the hands of the stranger. Under republican institutions the division of property among the children is much fairer, but the question which forces itself upon thoughtful men in all lands is: Why should men leave great fortunes to their children? If this is done from affection, is it not misguided affection? Observation teaches that, generally speaking, it is not well for the children that they should be so burdened. Neither is it well for the state. Beyond providing for the wife and daughters moderate sources of income, and very moderate allowances indeed, if any, for the sons, men may well hesitate, for it is no longer questionable that great sums bequeathed oftener work more for the injury than for the good of the recipients. Wise men will soon conclude that, for the best interests of the members of their families and of the state, such bequests are an improper use of their means.

It is not suggested that men who have failed to educate their sons to earn a livelihood shall cast them adrift in poverty. If any man has seen fit to rear his sons with a view to their living idle lives, or, what is highly commendable, has instilled in them the sentiment that they are in a position to labor for public ends without reference to pecuniary considerations, then, of course, the duty of the parent is to see that such are provided for *in moderation*. There are instances of millionaires' sons unspoiled by wealth, who, being rich, still perform great services in the community. Such are the very salt of the earth, as valuable as, unfortunately, they are rare; still it is not the exception, but the rule, that men must regard, and, looking at the usual result of enormous sums conferred upon legatees, the thoughtful man must shortly say, "I would as soon leave to my son a curse as the almighty dollar," and admit to himself that it is not the welfare of the children, but family pride, which inspires these enormous legacies.

As to the second mode, that of leaving wealth at death for public uses, it may be said that this is only a means for the disposal of wealth, provided a man is content to wait until he is dead before it becomes of much good in the world. Knowledge of the results of legacies bequeathed is not calculated to inspire the brightest hopes of much post-humous good being accomplished. The cases are not few in which the real object sought by the testator is not attained, nor are they few in which his real wishes are thwarted. In many cases the bequests are so used as to become only monuments of his folly. It is well to remember that it requires the exercise of not less ability than that which acquired the wealth to use it so as to be really beneficial to the community. Besides this, it may fairly be said that no man is to be extolled for doing what he cannot help doing, nor is he to be thanked by the community to which he only leaves wealth at death. Men who leave vast sums in this way may fairly be thought men who would not have left it at all, had they been able to take it with them. The memories of such cannot be held in grateful rememberance, for there is no grace in their gifts. It is not to be wondered at that such bequests seem so generally to lack the blessing.

The growing disposition to tax more and more heavily large estates left at death is a cheering indication of the growth of a salutary change in public opinion. The State of Pennsylvania now takes—subject to some exceptions—one-tenth of the property left by its citizens. The budget presented in the British Parliament the other day proposes to increase the death-duties; and, most significant of all, the new tax is to be a graduated one. Of all forms of taxation, this seems the wisest. Men who continue hoarding great sums all their lives, the proper use of which for public ends would work good to the community, should be made to feel that the community, in the form of the state, cannot thus be deprived of its proper share. By taxing estates heavily at death the state marks its condemnation of the selfish millionaire's unworthy life.

It is desirable that nations should go much further in this direction. Indeed, it is difficult to set bounds to the share of a rich man's estate which should go at his death to the public through the agency of the state, and by all means such taxes should be graduated, beginning at nothing upon moderate sums to dependents, and increasing rapidly as the amounts swell, until of the millionaire's hoard, as of Shylock's, at least

> "—— The other half
> Comes to the privy coffer of the state."

This policy would work powerfully to induce the rich man to attend to the administration of wealth during his life, which is the end that society should always have in view, as being that by far most fruitful for the people. Nor need it be feared that this policy would sap the root of enterprise and render men less anxious to accumulate, for to the class whose ambition it is to leave great fortunes and be talked about after their death, it will attract even more attention, and, indeed, be a somewhat nobler ambition to have enormous sums paid over to the state from their fortunes.

There remains, then, only one mode of using great fortunes; but in this we have the true antidote for the temporary unequal distribution of wealth, the reconciliation of the rich and the poor—a reign of harmony —another ideal, differing, indeed, from that of the Communist in requiring only the further evolution of existing conditions, not the total overthrow of our civilization. It is founded upon the present most intense individualism, and the race is prepared to put it in practice by degrees whenever it pleases. Under its sway we shall have an ideal state, in which the surplus wealth of the few will become, in the best sense, the property of the many, because administered for the common good, and this wealth, passing through the hands of the few, can be made a much more potent force for the elevation of our race than if it had been distributed in small sums to the people themselves. Even the poorest can be made to see this, and to agree that great sums gathered by some of their fellow-citizens and spent for public purposes, from which the masses reap the principal benefit, are more valuable to them than if scattered among them through the course of many years in trifling amounts.

If we consider what results flow from the Cooper Institute, for instance, to the best portion of the race in New York not possessed of means, and compare these with those which would have arisen for the good of the masses from an equal sum distributed by Mr. Cooper in his lifetime in the form of wages, which is the highest form of distribution, being for work done and not for charity, we can form some estimate of the possibilities for the improvement of the race which lie embedded in the present law of the accumulation of wealth. Much of this sum, if distributed in small quantities among the people, would have been wasted in the indulgence of appetite, some of it in excess, and it may be doubted whether even the part put to the best use, that of adding to the comforts of the home, would have yielded results for the race, as a race, at all comparable to those which are flowing and are to flow from the

Cooper Institute from generation to generation. Let the advocate of violent or radical change ponder well this thought.

We might even go so far as to take another instance, that of Mr. Tilden's bequest of five millions of dollars for a free library in the city of New York, but in referring to this one cannot help saying involuntarily, How much better if Mr. Tilden had devoted the last years of his own life to the proper administration of this immense sum; in which case neither legal contest nor any other cause of delay could have interfered with his aims. But let us assume that Mr. Tilden's millions finally become the means of giving to this city a noble public library, where the treasures of the world contained in books will be open to all forever, without money and without price. Considering the good of that part of the race which congregates in and around Manhattan Island, would its permanent benefit have been better promoted had these millions been allowed to circulate in small sums through the hands of the masses? Even the most strenuous advocate of Communism must entertain a doubt upon this subject. Most of those who think will probably entertain no doubt whatever.

Poor and restricted are our opportunities in this life; narrow our horizon; our best work most imperfect; but rich men should be thankful for one inestimable boon. They have it in their power during their lives to busy themselves in organizing benefactions from which the masses of their fellows will derive lasting advantage, and thus dignify their own lives. The highest life is probably to be reached, not by such imitation of the life of Christ as Count Tolstoï gives us, but, while animated by Christ's spirit, by recognizing the changed conditions of this age, and adopting modes of expressing this spirit suitable to the changed conditions under which we live; still laboring for the good of our fellows, which was the essence of his life and teaching, but laboring in a different manner.

This, then, is held to be the duty of the man of Wealth: First, to set an example of modest, unostentatious living, shunning display or extravagance; to provide moderately for the legitimate wants of those dependent upon him; and after doing so to consider all surplus revenues which come to him simply as trust funds, which he is called upon to administer, and strictly bound as a matter of duty to administer in the manner which, in his judgment, is best calculated to produce the most beneficial results for the community—the man of wealth thus becoming the mere agent and trustee for his poorer brethren, bringing to their service his superior wisdom, experience, and ability to administer, doing for them better than they would or could do for themselves.

We are met here with the difficulty of determining what are moderate sums to leave to members of the family; what is modest, unostentatious living; what is the test of extravagance. There must be different standards for different conditions. The answer is that it is as impossible to name exact amounts of actions as it is to define good manners, good taste, or the rules of propriety; but, nevertheless, these are verities, well known although undefinable. Public sentiment is quick to know and to feel what offends these. So in the case of wealth. The rule in regard to good taste in the dress of men or women applies here. Whatever makes one conspicuous offends the canon. If any family be chiefly known for display, for extravagance in home, table, equipage, for enormous sums ostentatiously spent in any form upon itself,—if these be its chief distinctions, we have no difficulty in estimating its nature or culture. So likewise in regard to the use or abuse of its surplus wealth, or to generous, freehanded cooperation in good public uses, or to unabated efforts to accumulate and hoard to the last, whether they administer or bequeath. The verdict rests with best and most enlightened public sentiment. The community will surely judge, and its judgments will not often be wrong.

The best uses to which surplus wealth can be put have already been indicated. Those who would administer wisely must, indeed, be wise, for one of the serious obstacles to the improvement of our race is indiscriminate charity. It were better for mankind that the millions of the rich were thrown into the sea than so spent as to encourage the slothful, the drunken, the unworthy. Of every thousand dollars spent in so called charity to-day, it is probable that $950 is unwisely spent; so spent, indeed, as to produce the every evils which it proposes to mitigate or cure. A well known writer of philosophic books admitted the other day that he had given a quarter of a dollar to a man who approached him as he was coming to visit the house of his friend. He knew nothing of the habits of this beggar; knew not the use that would be made of this money, although he had every reason to suspect that it would be spent improperly. This man professed to be a disciple of Herbert Spencer; yet the quarter-dollar given that night will probably work more injury than all the money which its thoughtless donor will ever be able to give in true charity will do good. He only gratified his own feelings, saved himself from annoyance,—and this was probably one of the most selfish and very worst actions of his life, for in all respects he is most worthy.

In bestowing charity, the main consideration should be to help those who will help themselves; to provide part of the means by which those who desire to improve may do so; to give those who desire to rise the aids by which they may rise; to assist, but rarely or never to do all. Neither the individual nor the race is improved by alms-giving. Those worthy of assistance, except in rare cases, seldom require assistance. The really valuable men of the race never do, except in cases of accident or sudden change. Every one has, of course, cases of individuals brought to his own knowledge where temporary assistance can do genuine good, and these he will not overlook. But the amount which can be wisely given by the individual for individuals is necessarily limited by his lack of knowledge of the circumstances connected with each. He is the only true reformer who is as careful and as anxious not to aid the unworthy as he is to aid the worthy, and, perhaps, even more so, for in alms-giving more injury is probably done by rewarding vice than by relieving virtue.

The rich man is thus almost restricted to following the examples of Peter Cooper, Enoch Pratt of Baltimore, Mr. Pratt of Brooklyn, Senator Stanford, and others, who know that the best means of benefiting the community is to place within its reach the ladders upon which the aspiring can rise—parks, and means of recreation, by which men are helped in body and mind; works of art, certain to give pleasure and improve the public taste, and public institutions of various kinds, which will improve the general condition of the people;—in this manner returning their surplus wealth to the mass of their fellows in the forms best calculated to do them lasting good.

Thus is the problem of Rich and Poor to be solved. The laws of accumulation will be left free; the laws of distribution free. Individualism will continue, but the millionaire will be but a trustee for the poor; intrusted for a season with a great part of the increased wealth of the community, but administering it for the community far better than it could or would have done for itself. The best minds will thus have reached a stage in the development of the race in which it is clearly seen that there is no mode of disposing of surplus wealth creditable to thoughtful and earnest men into whose hands it flows save by using it year by year for the general good. This day already dawns. But a little while, and although, without incurring the pity of their fellows, men may die sharers in great business enterprises from which their capital cannot be or has not been withdrawn, and is left chiefly at death for public uses, yet the man who dies leaving behind him millions of available wealth, which was his to administer during life, will pass away "unwept, unhonored, and unsung," no matter to what uses he leaves the dross which he cannot take with him. Of such as these the public verdict will then be: "The man who dies thus rich dies disgraced."

Such, in my opinion, is the true Gospel concerning Wealth, obedience to which is destined some day to solve the problem of the Rich and the Poor, and to bring "Peace on earth, among men Good-Will."

In June, 1889, Mrs. Carnegie sent a copy of "Wealth" to Gladstone, with a note saying, "We think we have found the true path—it is the one we mean to tread—if it commends itself to you we shall be so happy." At Gladstone's request W. T. Stead reprinted the article in the Pall Mall Gazette, bestowing on it the name by which it has since been known, "The Gospel of Wealth." Subsequently published in England as a penny pamphlet, often reprinted, and widely commented on in newspapers and periodicals on both sides of the Atlantic, "The Gospel" won Carnegie greater fame than he had ever before enjoyed.

Carnegie continued his discussion of the creation and employment of wealth in "The Best Fields for Philanthropy" published in the North American Review in December, 1889. Again asserting that "great wealth must inevitably flow into the hands of the few exceptional managers of men," he offered more specific suggestions for putting private wealth to public use. Parks, concert halls, organs, baths, and church buildings struck him as suitable philanthropic projects. To large givers he particularly recommended the establishment or endowment of universities, technical institutes, museums, libraries, observatories, hospitals, medical schools and laboratories, "and other institutions connected with the alleviation of human suffering, and expecially with the prevention rather than the cure of human ills."

Contemporary critics found little to object to in Carnegie's advice to philanthropists. Both American and British commentators, however, disputed Carnegie's views on the origin of wealth. "Our great American fortunes," declared Albert Shaw in 1893, "are the products of social opportunities rather than the mere creative power of their holders." An

English clergyman, Hugh Price Hughes, writing in 1890, denied that millionaires were the natural results of industrial enterprise. Free trade, free land, and a progressive income tax, Hughes said, would prevent the accumulation of absurdly large and potentially dangerous private fortunes. Carnegie, as was his way, genially adopted many of his critics' arguments. In his later writings, while still praising the judgment and ability of "great administrators," he paid more attention to the social bases of wealth and in 1908 forthrightly stated: "The community created the millionaire's wealth."

After the Homestead strike of 1892, Carnegie's principles and practice of philanthropy, although still widely endorsed, were sometimes derided. In Socialism for Millionaires (1896) George Bernard Shaw observed, "We often give to public objects money that we should devote to raising wages . . . or substituting three eight-hour shifts for two twelve-hour ones." Carnegie's most persistent critic, Finley Peter Dunne's Mr. Dooley, mimicked the Gospel: "Him that giveth to th' poor, they say, lindeth to th' Lord; but in these days we look f'r quick returns on our invistmints." Confessing admiration and affection for his adversary, Mr. Dooley remarked in 1906 that Carnegie was giving in the way everyone would like to. "Ivry time he dhrops a dollar it makes a noise like a waither fallin' down stairs with a tray iv dishes."

The gospel of wealth, as Carnegie formulated it in 1889, required possessors of surplus wealth to dispose of their bounty during their own lives. In the 1890's Carnegie continued to emphasize, in word and deed, the donor's personal responsibility for selecting and supervising suitable objects of philanthropy. After 1901, when he retired from business with a capital of $250,000,000 and an annual income of $12,500,000, the letter of the gospel no longer sufficed. Conventional giving, even on the scale he had long practiced, failed to answer his problem. His wealth was too great for any one man to administer in a normal human lifetime. Carnegie's solution was the creation of a series of perpetual trusts for the support of education, scientific research, international peace, and other causes in which he was interested. To the largest of his foundations, the Carnegie Corporation of New York, he gave $125,000,000 and the undistributed portion of his estate, so that it could do in perpetuity what he had attempted in life: give wisely and productively for fostering cultural amenities, advancing knowledge, and promoting human welfare.

"Wealth" is a nineteenth-century document; the foundations which bear Carnegie's name and which have served as models for so many later ones are products of the twentieth century. As avid for success in philanthropy as in business, Carnegie was receptive to new ideas and, with the help of the distinguished guests he frequently entertained, he kept abreast of expert opinion in a variety of fields. The course he ultimately followed in philanthropy departed in important respects from the path he charted in 1889. By his later practice he amended and dignified the gospel proclaimed in "Wealth." Laboring, as he would have said, in the spirit of 1889, but laboring in a different manner, Carnegie devised and utilized methods of giving that were suited to his means, to the changed conditions of the age, and to the needs of the future.

People's Party Platform
1892

EDITED BY JOHN D. HICKS

The People's Party platform of 1892 was the culmination of a quarter-century of agrarian protest against the growing pre-eminence of industry over agriculture in the United States. The blessings of civilization, many farmers believed, had not been distributed equally between cities and country, but had fallen disporportionately to the cities. "Towns and cities flourish and 'boom,' and grow and 'boom,' and yet agriculture languishes." Since the Civil War, the farmers had stated their case through four successive organizations—the Grangers, the Greenbackers, the Farmers' Alliances, and finally the People's (or Populist) Party. Probably their troubles were due less to the evil machinations of railroads, bankers, middlemen, and manufacturers, whom they tended to blame, than to unforeseen forces set loose by the revolutionary use of new machines and new transportation facilities. But the farmers, particularly those who suffered most, in the South and West, would not believe it. Governmental betrayals, they insisted, had funneled their rightful profits into the coffers of the "plutocrats." Only if the people themselves took control of their government, and wrote and administered new laws, could these evils be corrected.

The ideas expressed in the platform of 1892 did not stem, therefore, from on-the-spot thinking by a single platform committee. These ideas had grown with the years, and the task of the committee was primarily one of lucid and orderly restatement. Probably the claim of Ignatius Donnelly that he had written nine-tenths of the platform was an

513

exaggeration, but that he was its principal draftsman can hardly be doubted. Two preceding conventions, one held at Cincinnati, May 20, 1891, and another at St. Louis, February 22, 1892, had adopted platforms from which the Omaha version was drawn, and Donnelly had played a major part in the writing of each. His famous Preamble, which was actually longer than the platform proper, he had read to the St. Louis convention in only a slightly different form. On that occasion the St. Paul Pioneer Press had promptly branded his words as a "stereotyped Donnellian wail of woe."

Donnelly was an orator and an agitator, an outstanding demagogue in an age of demagogues. He earnestly favored third-party action; he knew that the Populist conventions needed a stirring, emotional appeal to inspire them; and he provided exactly what in his judgment the situation required. In contrast to the actions of delegates at most nominating conventions, the Omaha delegates, at a session held by previous planning on the Fourth of July, went wild about their platform rather than about their candidates. According to one reporter, "When that furious and hysterical arraignment of the present times, that incoherent intermingling of Jeremiah and Bellamy, the platform, was adopted, the cheers and yells which rose like a tornado from four thousand throats and raged without cessation for thirty-four minutes, during which women shrieked and wept, men embraced and kissed their neighbors, locked arms, marched back and forth, and leaped upon tables and chairs in the ecstasy of their delirium,—this dramatic and historical scene must have told every quiet, thoughtful witness that there was something at the back of all this turmoil more than the failure of crops or the scarcity of ready cash."

ASSEMBLED upon the one hundred and sixteenth anniversary of the Declaration of Independence, the People's Party of America in their first National Convention, invoking upon their action the blessing of Almighty God, puts forth, in the name and on behalf of

The original of the People's Party platform of 1892 seems not to exist; nor are the official proceedings of the Omaha convention available, either in published or in unpublished form. *The People's Party Campaign Book* (Washington: National Watchman Publishing Company, 1892) appeared prior to the convention, and is the people of this country, the following preamble and declaration of principles:

[PREAMBLE]

The conditions which surround us best justify our co-operation. We meet in the midst of a nation brought to the verge of moral, political and material ruin. Corruption dominates the ballot box, the Legislatures, the Congress, and touches even the ermine of the Bench. The people are demoralized; most of the States have been compelled to isolate the voters at the polling places to prevent universal intimidation or bribery. The newspapers are largely subsidized or muzzled, public opinion silenced, business prostrated, our homes covered with mortgages, labor impoverished, and the land concentrating in the hands of the capitalists. The urban workmen are denied the right of organization for self-protection; imported pauperized labor beats down their wages; a hireling standing army, unrecognized by our laws, is established to shoot them down, and they are rapidly degenerating into European conditions. The fruits of the toil of millions are boldly stolen to build up colossal fortunes for a few, unprecedented in the history of mankind, and the possessors of these in turn despise the Republic and endanger liberty. From the same prolific womb of governmental injustice we breed the two great classes—tramps and millionaires.

The national power to create money is appropriated to enrich bond holders; a vast public debt, payable in legal tender currency, has been funded into gold-bearing bonds, thereby adding millions to the burdens of the people.

Silver, which has been accepted as coin since the dawn of history, has been demonetized to add to the purchasing power of gold by decreasing the value of all forms of property as well as human labor, and the supply of currency is purposely abridged to fatten usurers, bankrupt enterprise and enslave industry.

A vast conspiracy against mankind has been organized on two continents, and it is rapidly taking possession of the world. If not met

---

therefore of no help. The platform was published at once, however, in the various party journals, including the *National Economist*, VII (July 9, 1892), 257–58. It appears also in the *Tribune Almanac* for 1892, pp. 38–40, and in Edward McPherson, *A Handbook of Politics for 1892* (Washington: James J. Chapman, 1892). Since the McPherson version contains sections omitted in some of the others, and is relatively free from the typographical errors that disfigure the *National Economist* text, it is the one reproduced here.

and overthrown at once, it forebodes terrible social convulsions, the destruction of civilization, or the establishment of an absolute despotism.

We have witnessed, for more than a quarter of a century, the struggles of the two great political parties for power and plunder, while grievous wrongs have been inflicted upon the suffering people. We charge that the controlling influences dominating both these parties have permitted the existing dreadful conditions to develop without serious effort to prevent or restrain them.

OLD PARTIES TREATED AS ONE.

Neither do they now promise us any substantial reform. They have agreed together to ignore, in the coming campaign, every issue but one. They propose to drown the outcries of a plundered people with the uproar of a sham battle over the tariff, so that capitalists, corporations, national banks, rings, trusts, watered stock, the demonetization of silver and the oppressions of the usurers may all be lost sight of. They propose to sacrifice our homes, lives and children, on the altar of mammon; to destroy the multitude in order to secure corruption funds from the millionaires.

Assembled on the anniversary of the birthday of the nation, and filled with the spirit of the grand general and chieftain who established our independence, we seek to restore the Government of the Republic to the hands of the "plain people" with whose class it originated. We assert our purposes to be identical with the purposes of the National Constitution, to form a more perfect Union and establish justice, insure domestic tranquility, provide for the common defense, promote the general welfare and secure the blessings of liberty for ourselves and our posterity.

We declare that this Republic can only endure as a free government while built upon the love of the whole people for each other and for the nation; that it cannot be pinned together by bayonets; that the civil war is over and that every passion and resentment which grew out of it must die with it, and that we must be in fact, as we are in name, one united brotherhood of freedom.

FARMERS' DEMANDS.

Our country finds itself confronted by conditions for which there is no precedent in the history of the world; our annual agricultural productions amount to billions of dollars in value, which must within a few weeks or months be exchanged for billions of dollars' worth of commodities consumed in their production; the existing currency supply is wholly inadequate to make this exchange; the results are falling prices, the formation of combines and rings, the impoverishment of the producing class. We pledge ourselves that, if given power, we will labor to correct these evils by wise and reasonable legislation, in accordance with the terms of our platform.

We believe that the powers of government—in other words, of the people—should be expanded (as in the case of the postal service) as rapidly and as far as the good sense of an intelligent people and the teachings of experience shall justify, to the end that oppression, injustice and poverty, shall eventually cease in the land.

While our sympathies as a party of reform are naturally upon the side of every proposition which will tend to make men intelligent, virtuous and temperate, we nevertheless regard these questions—important as they are—as secondary to the great issues now pressing for solution, and upon which not only our individual prosperity, but the very existence of free institutions depend; and we ask all men to first help us to determine whether we are to have a Republic to administer, before we differ as to the conditions upon which it is to be administered; believing that the forces of reform this day organized will never cease to move forward, until every wrong is righted, and equal rights and equal privileges securely established for all the men and women of this country.

[PLATFORM]

We declare, therefore,

PERPETUAL LABOR UNION.

First—That the union of the labor forces of the United States this day consummated shall be permanent and perpetual; may its spirit enter into all hearts for the salvation of the Republic, and the uplifting of mankind.

WEALTH FOR WORKERS.

Second—Wealth belongs to him who creates it, and every dollar taken from industry without an equivalent is robbery. "If any will not work, neither shall he eat." The interests of rural and civic labor are the same; their enemies are identical.

517

OWNERSHIP OF RAILWAYS.

Third—We believe that the time has come when the railroad corporations will either own the people or the people must own the railroads; and should the Government enter upon the work of owning and managing all railroads, we should favor an amendment to the Constitution by which all persons engaged in the Government service shall be placed under a civil service regulation of the most rigid character, so as to prevent the increase of the power of the national administration by the use of such additional Government employes.

FINANCE.

1st. We demand a national currency, safe, sound and flexible, issued by the General Government only, a full legal tender for all debts public and private, and that without the use of banking corporations; a just, equitable and efficient means of distribution direct to the people at a tax not to exceed 2 per cent. per annum, to be provided as set forth in the Sub-Treasury plan of the Farmers' Alliance, or a better system; also by payments in discharge of its obligations for public improvements.

(A) We demand free and unlimited coinage of silver and gold at the present legal ratio of 16 to 1.

(B) We demand that the amount of circulating medium be speedily increased to not less than $50 per capita.

(C) We demand a graduated income tax.

(D) We believe that the money of the country should be kept as much as possible in the hands of the people, and hence we demand that all State and National revenues shall be limited to the necessary expenses of the Government, economically and honestly administered.

(E) We demand that Postal Savings Banks be established by the Government for the safe deposit of the earnings of the people and to facilitate exchange.

TRANSPORTATION.

2d. Transportation being a means of exchange and a public necessity, the government should own and operate the railroads in the interest of the people.

The telegraph and telephone, like the post office system, being a necessity for the transmission of news, should be owned and operated by the Government in the interest of the people.

LAND.

3d. The land, including all the natural sources of wealth, is the heritage of the people and should not be monopolized for speculative purposes, and alien ownership of land should be prohibited. All land now held by railroads and other corporations in excess of their actual needs, and all lands now owned by aliens, should be reclaimed by the Government and held for actual settlers only.

The following supplementary resolutions, not to be incorporated in the platform, came from the Committee on Resolutions and were adopted as follows:

THE SUPPLEMENTARY PLATFORM.

Whereas, Other questions having been presented for our consideration, we hereby submit the following, not as a part of the platform of the People's Party, but as resolutions expressive of the sentiment of this Convention:

1. *Resolved*, That we demand a free ballot and a fair count in all elections, and pledge ourselves to secure it to every legal voter without Federal intervention, through the adoption by the States of the unperverted Australian or secret ballot system.

2. That the revenue derived from a graduated income tax should be applied to the reduction of the burden of taxation now resting upon the domestic industries of this country.

3. That we pledge our support to fair and liberal pensions to ex-Union soldiers and sailors.

4. That we condemn the fallacy of protecting American labor under the present system, which opens our ports to the pauper and criminal classes of the world, and crowds out our wage-earners; and we denounce the present ineffective laws against contract labor, and demand the further restriction of undesirable immigration.

5. That we cordially sympathize with the efforts of organized workingmen to shorten the hours of labor, and demand a rigid enforcement of the existing eight-hour law on Government work, and ask that a penalty clause be added to the said law.

6. That we regard the maintenance of a large standing army of mercenaries, known as the Pinkerton system, as a menace to our liberties, and we demand its abolition; and we condemn the recent invasion of the Territory of Wyoming by the hired assassins of plutocracy, assisted by Federal officials.

7. That we commend to the favorable consideration of the people and to the reform press the legislative system known as the initiative and referendum.

8. That we favor a constitutional provision limiting the office of President and Vice-President to one term, and providing for the election of Senators of the United States by a direct vote of the people.

9. That we oppose any subsidy or national aid to any private corporation for any purpose.

10. That this convention sympathizes with the Knights of Labor, and their righteous contest with the tyrannical combine of clothing manufacturers of Rochester, and declare[s] it to be the duty of all who hate tyranny and oppression, to refuse to purchase the goods made by the said manufacturers, or to patronize any merchants who sell such goods.

Donnelly's Preamble set forth in lurid language the evils that he and other Populists believed American society had suffered from plutocratic domination. His indictment was new only in its phraseology; the ills he recounted were the ills of which reformers had long complained. Donnelly's vigorous denunciations set the pattern for many other protests that were to come later. Bryan's "cross of gold," Theodore Roosevelt's "malefactors of great wealth," and Franklin D. Roosevelt's "economic royalists" were in the same tradition. To this day anyone who speaks out firmly against monopolistic excesses is likely to be classified as a "neo-Populist"; indeed, if he does not take care, he is in danger of repeating some of Donnelly's well-worn phrases. And "new conservatives" who deplore departures from the old American tradition, however they choose to define it, reserve their greatest scorn for whatever they deem "populist," or "populistic."

The Populists sought, unsuccessfully as it turned out, to unite the forces of rural and urban labor in a great crusade to wrest control of the government from the hands of special interests. They were individualists, however, not socialists, and the rural element, which in the end had to go it alone without the aid of urban labor, consisted primarily of farmers who were, or who aspired to be, landowners, and therefore small capitalists. As such, they hoped for a better chance to get on in the world.

The only truly socialistic reform that the Populists demanded was government ownership and operation of the railroads and of the means of communication. But they could not hide their fear of big government, and, partly as a means of restraining it, they earnestly favored rigid civil service regulations for all governmental employees.

Many Populist proposals achieved a great measure of success after the People's Party itself had disappeared. For this result twentieth-century progressives, of whatever party, were primarily responsible. The post-Populist reformers were mainly urban and middle-class, but the unimportant status they occupied in society was due, they came to believe, to the unsavory behavior of the same overprivileged classes against whom the Populists had railed. Populist proposals often needed to be revamped for the purposes of later reformers, but the Populists were sometimes held to be right on diagnosis even when they erred on prescription. There was something wrong with banking and currency in the United States, as the Populists maintained, but a better answer than free silver or fiat money came with the Federal Reserve System. Grievances against the railroads might not best be remedied by public ownership, but the Progressives worked for and obtained a far greater degree of regulation than the nineteenth century had known. The reservation of government land for actual settlers only was hardly practicable, but the systematic conservation of natural resources certainly was. The subtreasury plan to establish federal depositories for imperishable farm products might not be immediately feasible, but a federal program of rural credits was presently adopted. Also, it can be argued that the Warehouse Act of 1916 constituted in effect the "better plan" for which the Populists were willing to settle as an alternative to the subtreasury, while Wallace's "ever normal granary" went far beyond their wildest dreams.

Other Populist proposals eventually were adopted, almost intact. Chief among these were the graduated income tax, the Australian ballot, certain restrictions on immigration, the eight-hour day, postal-savings facilities, the initiative and referendum, and the election of United States senators by direct vote of the people. The Populists did not originate all these reforms, but their platforms and orators took them up, popularized them, and passed them along to a later generation for enactment into law. Few platforms of any American political party have obtained a greater degree of affirmative legal response than the one the People's Party adopted in 1892.

Frederick Jackson Turner
The Significance of the Frontier in American History
1893

EDITED BY RAY ALLEN BILLINGTON

The American mood during the 1890's was one of restlessness, of vaguely sensed uncertainty. Farmers met in revival-like political conventions to demand financial heresies that sent chills of alarm through Wall Street; workers banded into newfangled labor unions to slow the wheels of industry with calamitous strikes; social critics such as Henry George, Edward Bellamy, Jacob A. Riis, and Henry Demarest Lloyd boldly revealed society's ills and proposed sweeping reform; thousands of the dispossessed marched to the polls under banners of socialism raised by Daniel De Leon and Eugene V. Debs; New England Brahmins joined the Immigration Restriction League to press for laws that would forever close America's gates to European immigrants. These were all manifestations of the deep-seated unrest that marked the closing of one chapter in the nation's history. The era of cheap lands and westward expansion was drawing to an end. The United States would no longer be the land of limitless opportunity for the downtrodden which it had been in the past.

One who sought to analyze the causes of this unrest was a young historian at the University of Wisconsin named Frederick Jackson Turner. Taking his cue from a pronouncement of the Director of the Census of 1890 that for the first time an unbroken frontier line no longer existed in the West, Turner asked himself: "How have three centuries of constant expansion altered the thought, the character, and the institutions of the American people?" Could the unique features of the nation's civilization result partly from the repeated "beginning over again" as society moved ever westward? And, if so, what would be its fate in the dawning era of closed-space existence?

To answer these questions, Turner drew upon his own background and on the intellectual stimulation he had received while a student at the University of Wisconsin and at the Johns Hopkins University. As a boy in the backwoods town of Portage, Wisconsin, he had seen men subduing the wilderness and had observed the mingling of peoples from many backgrounds which is natural in such communities. As a young man he had visited settlements of newly arrived Germans and had been fascinated by watching their adjustment to primitive conditions of life. As an undergraduate he had been taught by his able mentor, Professor William Francis Allen, that society was a constantly evolving organism, adjusting to environmental changes as did the plants and animals described by Charles Darwin. As a graduate student he had been introduced to the works of such European economists as Achille Loria and Walter Bagehot, who stressed social evolution and the influence of the land-quest on peoples.

Merging these memories and concepts, Turner fashioned a remarkable essay, "Problems in American History," which set forth in a few paragraphs the "frontier hypothesis" in germinal form. When this was published locally in 1892, his old Johns Hopkins professor, Herbert Baxter Adams, recognized its importance and encouraged him to expand his brief references into a full-blown discussion. This Turner did during the autumn of 1892; he read a rough draft of the paper to his friend Woodrow Wilson when Wilson visited Madison that December. The president of the University of Wisconsin, Charles Kendall Adams, himself a famous historian, suggested that the essay be read when the American Historical Association gathered in Chicago that summer to help commemorate the World's Columbian Exposition. There, on July 12, 1893, Frederick Jackson Turner presented his views to a wider audience for the first time.

IN A RECENT bulletin of the superintendent of the census for 1890 appear these significant words: "Up to and including 1880 the country had a frontier of settlement, but at present the unsettled area has been so broken into by isolated bodies of settlement that there can hardly be said to be a frontier line. In the discussion of its extent, its westward movement, etc., it cannot, therefore, any longer have a place in the census reports." This brief official statement marks the closing of a great historic movement. Up to our own day American history has been in a large degree the history of the colonization of the Great West. The existence of an area of free land, its continuous recession, and the advance of American settlement westward explain American development.

Behind institutions, behind constitutional forms and modifications, lie the vital forces that call these organs into life and shape them to meet changing conditions. The peculiarity of American institutions is the fact that they have been compelled to adapt themselves to the changes of an expanding people—to the changes involved in crossing a continent, in winning a wilderness, and in developing at each area of this progress, out of the primitive economic and political conditions of the frontier, the complexity of city life. Said Calhoun in 1817, "We are great, and rapidly —I was about to say fearfully—growing!" So saying, he touched the distinguishing feature of American life. All peoples show development: the germ theory of politics has been sufficiently emphasized. In the case of most nations, however, the development has occurred in a limited area; and if the nation has expanded, it has met other growing peoples whom it has conquered. But in the case of the United States we have a different phenomenon. Limiting our attention to the Atlantic coast, we have the familiar phenomenon of the evolution of institutions in a limited area, such as the rise of representative government; the differentiation of simple colonial governments into complex organs; the progress from primitive industrial society, without division of labor, up to manufacturing civilization. But we have in addition to this *a recurrence of the process of evolution in each Western area reached in the process of expansion.* Thus American development has exhibited not merely advance along a single line but a return to primitive conditions on a continually advancing frontier line, and a new development for that

The document is here printed as it first appeared in the *Proceedings of the Forty-first Annual Meeting of the State Historical Society of Wisconsin* (Madison, 1894), pp. 79–112.

area. American social development has been continually beginning over again on the frontier. This perennial rebirth, this fluidity of American life, this expansion westward with its new opportunities, its continuous touch with the simplicity of primitive society, furnish the forces dominating American character. The true point of view in the history of this nation is not the Atlantic coast, it is the Great West. Even the slavery struggle, which is made so exclusive an object of attention by writers like Professor von Holst, occupies its important place in American history because of its relation to westward expansion.

In this advance the frontier is the outer edge of the wave—the meeting point between savagery and civilization. Much has been written about the frontier from the point of view of border warfare and the chase, but as a field for the serious study of the economist and the historian it has been neglected.

What is the [American] frontier? It is not the European frontier—a fortified boundary line running through dense populations. The most significant thing about it is that it lies at the hither edge of free land. In the census reports it is treated as the margin of that settlement which has a density of two or more to the square mile. The term is an elastic one, and for our purpose does not need sharp definition. We shall consider the whole frontier belt, including the Indian country and the outer margin of the "settled area" of the census reports. This paper will make no attempt to treat the subject exhaustively; its aim is simply to call attention to the frontier as a fertile field for investigation, and to suggest some of the problems which arise in connection with it.

In the settlement of America we have to observe how European life entered the continent, and how America modified and developed that life, and reacted on Europe. Our early history is the study of European germs developing in an American environment. Too exclusive attention has been paid by institutional students to the Germanic origins, too little to the American factors. The frontier is the line of most rapid and effective Americanization. The wilderness masters the colonist. It finds him a European in dress, industries, tools, modes of travel, and thought. It takes him from the railroad car and puts him in the birch canoe. It strips off the garments of civilization, and arrays him in the hunting shirt and the moccasin. It puts him in the log cabin of the Cherokee and the Iroquois, and runs an Indian palisade around him. Before long he has gone to planting Indian corn and plowing with a sharp stick; he shouts the war cry and takes the scalp in orthodox Indian fashion. In short, at the frontier the environment is at first too strong for the man. He must accept the conditions which it furnishes, or perish, and so he fits himself into the Indian clearings and follows the Indian trails. Little by little he transforms the wilderness, but the outcome is not the old Europe, not simply the development of Germanic germs, any more than the first phenomenon was a case of reversion to the Germanic mark. The fact is that here is a new product that is American. At first the frontier was the Atlantic coast. It was the frontier of Europe in a very real sense. Moving westward, the frontier became more and more American. *As successive terminal moraines result from successive glaciations, so each frontier leaves its traces behind it, and when it becomes a settled area the region still partakes of the frontier characteristics.* Thus the advance of the frontier has meant a steady movement away from the influence of Europe, a steady growth of independence on American lines. And to study this advance, the men who grew up under these conditions, and the political, economic, and social results of it, is to study the really American part of our history.

THE STAGES OF FRONTIER ADVANCE

In the course of the seventeenth century the frontier was advanced up the Atlantic river courses, just beyond the fall line, and the tidewater region became the settled area. In the first half of the eighteenth century another advance occurred. Traders followed the Delaware and Shawnese Indians to the Ohio as early as the end of the first quarter of the century. Governor Spotswood of Virginia made an expedition in 1714 across the Blue Ridge. The end of the first quarter of the century saw the advance of the Scotch-Irish and the Palatine Germans up the Shenandoah Valley into the western part of Virginia, and along the Piedmont region of the Carolinas. The Germans in New York pushed the frontier of settlement up the Mohawk to German Flats. In Pennsylvania the town of Bedford indicates the line of settlement. Settlements had begun on New River, a branch of the Kanawha, and on the sources of the Yadkin and French Broad. The king attempted to arrest the advance by his proclamation of 1763 forbidding settlements beyond the sources of the rivers flowing into the Atlantic; but in vain. In the period of the Revolution the frontier crossed the Alleghenies into Kentucky and Tennessee, and the upper waters of the Ohio were settled. When the first census was taken in 1790, the continuous settled area was bounded by a line which ran near the coast of Maine, and included New England except a portion of

Vermont and New Hampshire, New York along the Hudson and up the Mohawk about Schenectady, eastern and southern Pennsylvania, Virginia well across the Shenandoah Valley, and the Carolinas and eastern Georgia. Beyond this region of continuous settlement were the small settled areas of Kentucky and Tennessee and the Ohio, with the mountains intervening between them and the Atlantic area, thus giving a new and important character to the frontier. The isolation of the region increased its peculiarly American tendencies, and the need for transportation facilities to connect it with the East called out important schemes of internal improvement, which will be noted farther on. The "West," as a self-conscious section, began to evolve.

From decade to decade distinct advances of the frontier occurred. By the census of 1820 the settled area included Ohio, southern Indiana and Illinois, southeastern Missouri, and about one-half of Louisiana. This settled area had surrounded Indian areas, and the management of these tribes became an object of political concern. The frontier region of the time lay along the Great Lakes, where Astor's American Fur Company operated in the Indian trade, and beyond the Mississippi, where Indian traders extended their activity even to the Rocky Mountains; Florida also furnished frontier conditions. The Mississippi River region was the scene of typical frontier settlements.

The rising steam navigation on Western waters, the opening of the Erie Canal, and the westward extension of cotton culture added five frontier states to the Union in this period. Grund, writing in 1836, declares: "It appears, then, that the universal disposition of Americans to emigrate to the western wilderness, in order to enlarge their dominion over inanimate nature, is the actual result of an expansive power, which is inherent in them, and which, by continually agitating all classes of society, is constantly throwing a large portion of the whole population on the extreme confines of the state, in order to gain space for its development. Hardly is a new state or territory formed before the same principle manifests itself again, and gives rise to a further emigration; and so it is destined to go on until a physical barrier must finally obstruct its progress."

In the middle of this century the line indicated by the present eastern boundary of Indian Territory, Nebraska, and Kansas marked the frontier of the Indian country. Minnesota and Wisconsin still exhibited frontier conditions, but the distinctive frontier of the period is found in California, where the gold discoveries had sent a sudden tide of adventurous miners, and in Oregon and the settlements in Utah. As the frontier had leaped over the Alleghenies, so now it skipped the Great Plains and the Rocky Mountains; and in the same way that the advance of the frontiersmen beyond the Alleghenies had caused the rise of important questions of transportation and internal improvement, so now the settlers beyond the Rocky Mountains needed means of communication with the East, and in the furnishing of these arose the settlement of the Great Plains and the development of still another kind of frontier life. Railroads, fostered by land grants, sent an increasing tide of immigrants into the far West. The United States Army fought a series of Indian wars in Minnesota, Dakota, and the Indian Territory.

By 1880 the settled area had been pushed into northern Michigan, Wisconsin, and Minnesota, along Dakota rivers, and into the Black Hills region, and was ascending the rivers of Kansas and Nebraska. The development of mines in Colorado had drawn isolated frontier settlements into that region, and Montana and Idaho were receiving settlers. The frontier was found in these mining camps and the ranches of the Great Plains. The superintendent of the census for 1890 reports, as previously stated, that the settlements of the West lie so scattered over the region that there can no longer be said to be a frontier line.

In these successive frontiers we find natural boundary lines which have served to mark and to affect the characteristics of the frontiers, namely: the "fall line"; the Allegheny Mountains; the Mississippi; the Missouri where its direction approximates north and south; the line of the arid lands, approximately the ninety-ninth meridian; and the Rocky Mountains. The fall line marked the frontier of the seventeenth century; the Alleghenies that of the eighteenth; the Mississippi that of the first quarter of the nineteenth; the Missouri that of the middle of this century (omitting the California movement); and the belt of the Rocky Mountains and the arid tract, the present frontier. Each was won by a series of Indian wars.

THE FRONTIER FURNISHES A FIELD FOR COMPARATIVE STUDY OF SOCIAL DEVELOPMENT

At the Atlantic frontier one can study the germs of processes repeated at each successive frontier. We have the complex European life, sharply precipitated by the wilderness into the simplicity of primitive conditions. The first frontier had to meet its Indian question, its question of the disposition of the public domain, of the means of intercourse with the older settlements, of the extension of political organization, of religious and educational activity. And the settlement of these and similar questions for one frontier served as a guide for the next. The American student need not go to the "prim little townships of Sleswick" for illustrations of the law of continuity and development. For example, he may study the origin of our land policies in the colonial land policy; he may see how the system grew by adapting the statutes to the customs of the successive frontiers. He may see how the mining experience in the lead regions of Wisconsin, Illinois, and Iowa was applied to the mining laws of the Sierras, and how our Indian policy has been a series of experimentations on successive frontiers. Each tier of new states has found, in the older ones, material for its constitutions. Each frontier has made similar contributions to American character, as will be discussed farther on.

But with all these similarities there are essential differences, due to the place element and the time element. It is evident that the farming frontier of the Misisssippi Valley presents different conditions from the mining frontier of the Rocky Mountains. The frontier reached by the Pacific Railroad, surveyed into rectangles, guarded by the United States Army, and recruited by the daily immigrant ship, moves forward at a swifter pace and in a different way than the frontier reached by the birch canoe or the pack horse. The geologist traces patiently the shores of ancient seas, maps their areas, and compares the older and the newer. It would be a work worth the historian's labors to mark these various frontiers and in detail compare one with another. Not only would there result a more adequate conception of American development and characteristics, but invaluable additions would be made to the history of society.

Loria, the Italian economist, has urged the study of colonial life as an aid in understanding the stages of European development, affirming that colonial settlement is for economic science what the mountain is for geology, bringing to light primitive stratifications. "America," he says, "has the key to the historical enigma which Europe has sought for centuries in vain, and the land which has no history reveals luminously the course of universal history." He is right. The United States lies like a huge page in the history of society. Line by line as we read from west to east we find the record of social evolution. It begins with the Indian and the hunter; it goes on to tell of the disintegration of savagery by the entrance of the trader, the pathfinder of civilization; we read the annals of the pastoral stage in ranch life; the exploitation of the soil by the raising of unrotated crops of corn and wheat in sparsely settled farming communities; the intensive culture of the denser farm settlement; and finally the manufacturing organization with city and factory system. This page is familiar to the student of census statistics, but how little of it has been used by our historians.

Each of these areas has had an influence in our economic and political history; the evolution of each into a higher stage has worked political transformations. But what constitutional historian has made any adequate attempt to interpret political facts by the light of these social areas and changes?

The Atlantic frontier was compounded of fisherman, fur-trader, miner, cattle-raiser, and farmer. Excepting the fisherman, each type of industry was on the march toward the West, impelled by an irresistible attraction. Each passed in successive waves across the continent. Stand at Cumberland Gap and watch the procession of civilization, marching single file—the buffalo, following the trail to the salt springs, the Indian, the fur-trader and hunter, the cattle-raiser, the pioneer farmer—and the frontier has passed by. Stand at South Pass in the Rockies a century later and see the same procession with wider intervals between. The unequal rate of advance compels us to distinguish the frontier into the trader's frontier, the rancher's frontier or the miner's frontier, and the farmer's frontier. When the mines and the cowpens were still near the fall line, the traders' pack trains were tinkling across the Alleghenies, and the French on the Great Lakes were fortifying their posts, alarmed by the British trader's birch canoe. When the trappers scaled the Rockies, the farmer was still near the mouth of the Missouri.

THE INDIAN TRADER'S FRONTIER

Why was it that the Indian trader passed so rapidly across the continent? What effects followed from the trader's frontier? The trade was coeval with American discovery. The Norsemen, Vespucius, Verrazano, Hudson, John Smith, all trafficked for furs. The Plymouth pilgrims settled in Indian cornfields, and their first return cargo was of beaver and lumber. The records of the various New England colonies show how steadily exploration was carried into the wilderness by this trade. What is true for New England is, as would be expected, even plainer for the rest of the colonies. All along the coast from Maine to Georgia the Indian trade opened up the river courses. Steadily the trader passed westward, utilizing the older lines of French trade. The Ohio, the Great Lakes, the Mississippi, the Missouri, and the Platte, the lines of westward advance, were ascended by traders. They found the passes in the Rocky Mountains and guided Lewis and Clark, Frémont, and Bidwell.

The explanation of the rapidity of this advance is bound up with the effects of the trader on the Indian. The trading post left the unarmed tribes at the mercy of those that had purchased firearms—a truth which the Iroquois Indians wrote in blood, and so the remote and unvisited tribes gave eager welcome to the trader. "The savages," wrote La Salle, "take better care of us French than of their own children; from us only can they get guns and goods." This accounts for the trader's power and the rapidity of his advance. Thus the disintegrating forces of civilization entered the wilderness. Every river valley and Indian trail became a fissure in Indian society, and so that society became honeycombed. Long before the pioneer farmer appeared on the scene, primitive Indian life had passed away. The farmers met Indians armed with guns. The trading frontier, while steadily undermining Indian power by making the tribes ultimately dependent on the whites, yet through its sale of guns gave to the Indian increased power of resistance to the farming frontier. French colonization was dominated by its trading frontier, English colonization by its farming frontier. There was an antagonism between the two frontiers as between the two nations. Said Duquesne to the Iroquois, "Are you ignorant of the difference between the king of England and the king of France? Go see the forts that our king has established and you will see that you can still hunt under their very walls. They have been placed for your advantage in places which you frequent. The English, on the contrary, are no sooner in possession of a place than the game is driven away. The forest falls before them as they advance, and the soil is laid bare so that you can scarce find the wherewithal to erect a shelter for the night."

And yet, in spite of this opposition of the interests of the trader and the farmer, the Indian trade pioneered the way for civilization. The buffalo trail became the Indian trail, and this became the trader's "trace;" the trails widened into roads, and the roads into turnpikes, and these in turn were transformed into railroads. The same origin can be shown for the railroads of the South, the far West, and the Dominion of Canada. The trading posts reached by these trails were on the sites of Indian villages which had been placed in positions suggested by nature;

and these trading posts, situated so as to command the water systems of the country, have grown into such cities as Albany, Pittsburg, Detroit, Chicago, St. Louis, Council Bluffs, and Kansas City. Thus civilization in America has followed the arteries made by geology, pouring an ever richer tide through them, until at last the slender paths of aboriginal intercourse have been broadened and interwoven into the complex mazes of modern commercial lines; the wilderness has been interpenetrated by lines of civilization, growing ever more numerous. It is like the steady growth of a complex nervous system for the originally simple, inert continent. If one would understand why we are today one nation rather than a collection of isolated states, he must study this economic and social consolidation of the country. In this progress from savage conditions lie topics for the evolutionist.

The effect of the Indian frontier as a consolidating agent in our history is important. From the close of the seventeenth century various intercolonial congresses have been called to treat with the Indians and establish common measures of defense. Particularism was strongest in colonies with no Indian frontier. This frontier stretched along the western border like a cord of union. The Indian was a common danger, demanding united action. Most celebrated of these conferences was the Albany Congress of 1754, called to treat with the Six Nations, and to consider plans of union. Even a cursory reading of the plan proposed by the Congress reveals the importance of the frontier. The powers of the general council and the officers were, chiefly, the determination of peace and war with the Indians, the regulation of Indian trade, the purchase of Indian lands, and the creation and government of new settlements as a security against the Indians. It is evident that the unifying tendencies of the Revolutionary period were facilitated by the previous co-operation in the regulation of the frontier. In this connection may be mentioned the importance of the frontier, from that day to this, as a military training school, keeping alive the power of resistance to aggression, and developing the stalwart and rugged qualities of the frontiersman.

THE RANCHER'S FRONTIER

It would not be possible in the limits of this paper to trace the other frontiers across the continent. Travelers of the eighteenth century found the "cowpens" among the canebrakes and peavine pastures of the South, and the "cow drivers" took their droves to Charleston, Philadelphia, and New York. Travelers at the close of the War of 1812 met droves of more

than a thousand cattle and swine from the interior of Ohio going to
Pennsylvania to fatten for the Philadelphia market. The ranges of the
Great Plains, with ranch and cowboy and nomadic life, are things of
yesterday and of today. The experience of the Carolina cowpens guided
the ranchers of Texas. One element favoring the rapid extension of the
rancher's frontier is the fact that in a remote country lacking transportation facilities the product must be in small bulk, or must be able to
transport itself, and the cattle-raiser could easily drive his product to
market. The effect of these great ranches on the subsequent agrarian
history of the localities in which they existed should be studied.

THE FARMER'S FRONTIER

The maps of the census reports show an uneven advance of the
farmer's frontier, with tongues of settlement pushed forward and with
indentations of wilderness. In part this is due to Indian resistance, in
part to the location of river valleys and passes, in part to the unequal
force of the centers of frontier attraction. Among the important centers
of attraction may be mentioned the following: fertile and favorably
situated soils, salt springs, mines, and army posts.

ARMY POSTS

The frontier army post, serving to protect the settlers from the
Indians, has also acted as a wedge to open the Indian country, and has
been a nucleus for settlement. In this connection mention should also
be made of the government military and exploring expeditions in
determining the lines of settlement. But all the more important
expeditions were greatly indebted to the earliest pathmakers, the Indian
guides, the traders and trappers, and the French voyageurs, who were
inevitable parts of governmental expeditions from the days of Lewis and
Clark. Each expedition was an epitome of the previous factors in
western advance.

SALT SPRINGS

In an interesting monograph Victor Hehn has traced the effect of salt
upon early European development and has pointed out how it affected
the lines of settlement and the form of administration. A similar study
might be made for the salt springs of the United States. The early
settlers were tied to the coast by the need of salt, without which they
could not preserve their meats or live in comfort. Writing in 1752,
Bishop Spangenburg says of a colony for which he was seeking lands in

North Carolina, "They will require salt & other necessaries which they can neither manufacture nor raise. Either they must go to Charleston, which is 300 miles distant . . . Or else they must go to Boling's Point in V^a on a branch of the James, & is also 300 miles from here . . . or else they must go down to Roanoke—I know not how many miles— where salt is brought up from the Cape Fear." This may serve as a typical illustration. An annual pilgrimage to the coast for salt thus became essential. Taking flocks or furs and ginseng root, the early settlers sent their pack trains after seeding time each year to the coast. This proved to be an important educational influence, since it was almost the only way in which the pioneer learned what was going on in the East. But when discovery was made of the salt springs of the Kanawha, and the Holston, and Kentucky, and central New York, the West began to be freed from dependence on the coast. It was in part the effect of finding these salt springs that enabled settlement to cross the mountains.

From the time the mountains rose between the pioneer and the seaboard, a new order of Americanism arose. The West and the East began to get out of touch with each other. The settlements from the sea to the mountains kept connection with the rear and had a certain solidarity. But the overmountain men grew more and more independent. The East took a narrow view of American advance, and nearly lost these men. Kentucky and Tennessee history bears abundant witness to the truth of this statement. The East began to try to hedge and limited westward expansion. Though Webster could declare that there were no Alleghenies in his politics, yet in politics in general they were a very solid factor.

LAND

The exploitation of the beasts took hunter and trader to the West, the exploitation of the grasses took the rancher West, and the exploitation of the virgin soil of the river valleys and prairies attracted the farmer. Good soils have been the most continuous attraction to the farmer's frontier. The land hunger of the Virginians drew them down the rivers into Carolina, in early colonial days; the search for soils took the Massachusetts men to Pennsylvania and to New York. As the Eastern lands were taken up, migration flowed across them to the West. Daniel Boone, the great backwoodsman, who combined the occupations of hunter, trader, cattle-raiser, farmer, and surveyor—learning, probably

534

from the traders, of the fertility of the lands on the upper Yadkin, where the traders were wont to rest as they took their way to the Indians—left his Pennsylvania home with his father, and passed down the Great Valley road to that stream. Learning from a trader of its game and the rich pastures of Kentucky, he pioneered the way for the farmers to that region. Thence he passed to the frontier of Missouri, where his settlement was long a landmark on the frontier. Here again he helped to open the way for civilization, finding salt licks, and trails, and land. His son was among the earliest trappers in the passes of the Rocky Mountains, and his party are said to have been the first to camp on the present site of Denver. His grandson, Colonel A. J. Boone of Colorado, was a power among the Indians of the Rocky Mountains, and was appointed an agent by the government. Kit Carson's mother was a Boone. Thus this family epitomizes the backwoodsman's advance across the continent.

The farmer's advance came in a distinct series of waves. In Peck's *New Guide to the West*, published in Cincinnati in 1837, occurs this suggestive passage:

Generally, in all the western settlements, three classes, like the waves of the ocean, have rolled one after the other. First, comes the pioneer, who depends for the subsistence of his family chiefly upon the natural growth of vegetation, called the "range," and the proceeds of hunting. His implements of agriculture are rude, chiefly of his own make, and his efforts directed mainly to a crop of corn and a "truck patch." The last is a rude garden for growing cabbage, beans, corn for roasting ears, cucumbers and potatoes. A log cabin and, occasionally, a stable and corn-crib, and a field of a dozen acres, the timber girdled or "deadened," and fenced, are enough for his occupancy. It is quite immaterial whether he ever becomes the owner of the soil. He is the occupant for the time being, pays no rent, and feels as independent as the "lord of the manor." With a horse, cow, and one or two breeders of swine, he strikes into the woods with his family, and becomes the founder of a new county, or perhaps state. He builds his cabin, gathers around him a few other families of similar tastes and habits, and occupies till the range is somewhat subdued, and hunting a little precarious, or, which is more frequently the case, till neighbors crowd around, roads, bridges, and fields annoy him, and he lacks elbow room. The pre-emption law enables him to dispose of his cabin and corn-field to the next class of emigrants, and, to employ his own figures, he "breaks for the high timber," "clears out for the New Purchase," or migrates to Arkansas, or Texas, to work the same process over.

The next class of emigrants purchase the lands, add field to field, clear out the roads, throw rough bridges over the streams, put up hewn log houses, with

535

glass windows, and brick or stone chimneys, occasionally plant orchards, build mills, school-houses, court-houses, etc., and exhibit the picture and forms of plain, frugal, civilized life.

Another wave rolls on. The men of capital and enterprise come. The "settler" is ready to sell out, and take the advantage of the rise of property—push farther into the interior, and become, himself, a man of capital and enterprise in turn. The small village rises to a spacious town or city; substantial edifices of brick, extensive fields, orchards, gardens, colleges and churches are seen. Broadcloths, silks, leghorns, crapes, and all the refinements, luxuries, elegancies, frivolities and fashions are in vogue. Thus wave after wave is rolling westward:—the real *Eldorado* is still farther on.

A portion of the two first classes remain stationary amidst the general movement, improve their habits and condition and rise in the scale of society.

The writer has traveled much amongst the first class—the real pioneers. He has lived many years in connection with the second grade; and now the third wave is sweeping over large districts of Indiana, Illinois and Missouri. Migration has become almost a habit in the West. Hundreds of men can be found, not over fifty years of age, who have settled for the fourth, fifth or sixth time on a new spot. To sell out, and remove only a few hundred miles, makes up a portion of the variety of backwoods life and manners.

Omitting those of the pioneer farmers who move from the love of adventure, the advance of the more steady farmer is easy to understand. Obviously the immigrant was attracted by the cheap lands of the frontier, and even the native farmer felt their influence strongly. Year by year the farmers who lived on soil, whose returns were diminished by unrotated crops, were offered the virgin soil of the frontier at nominal prices. Their growing families demanded more lands, and these were dear. The competition of the unexhausted, cheap, and easily tilled prairie lands compelled the farmer either to go West and continue the exhaustion of the soil on a new frontier or to adopt intensive culture. Thus the census of 1890 shows, in the Northwest, many counties in which there is an absolute, or a relative, decrease of population. These states have been sending farmers to advance the frontier on the plains, and have themselves begun to turn to intensive farming and to manufacture. A decade before this, Ohio had shown the same transition stage. Thus the demand for land and the love of wilderness freedom drew the frontier ever onward.

Having now roughly outlined the various kinds of frontiers, and their modes of advance, chiefly from the point of view of the frontier itself, we may next inquire what were the influences on the East and on the

Old World. A rapid enumeration of some of the more noteworthy effects is all that I have time for.

COMPOSITE NATIONALITY

First, we note that the frontier promoted the formation of a composite nationality for the American people. The coast was preponderantly English, but the later tides of continental immigration flowed across to the free lands. This was the case from the early colonial days. The Scotch-Irish and the Palatine Germans, or "Pennsylvania Dutch," furnished dominant elements in the stock of the colonial frontier. With these peoples were also the freed indented servants, or redemptioners, who at the expiration of their time of service passed to the frontier. Governor Alexander Spotswood of Virginia writes in 1717, "The Inhabitants of our frontiers are composed generally of such as have been transported hither as Servants, and being out of their time, and settle themselves where Land is to be taken up and that will produce the necessarys of Life with little Labour." Very generally these redemptioners were of non-English stock. In the crucible of the frontier the immigrants were Americanized, liberated, and fused into a mixed race, English in neither nationality nor characteristics. The process has gone on from the early days to our own. Burke and other writers in the middle of the eighteenth century believed that Pennsylvania was threatened with the "danger of being wholly foreign in language, manners, and perhaps even inclinations." The German and Scotch-Irish elements in the frontier of the South were only less great. In the middle of the present century the German element in Wisconsin was already so considerable that leading publicists looked to the creation of a German state out of the commonwealth by concentrating their colonization. Such examples teach us to beware of misinterpreting the fact that there is a common English speech in America into a belief that the stock is also English.

INDUSTRIAL INDEPENDENCE

In another way the advance of the frontier decreased our dependence on England. The coast, particularly of the South, lacked diversified industries and was dependent on England for the bulk of its supplies. In the South there was even a dependence on the Northern colonies for articles of food. Governor James Glen of South Carolina writes in the

537

middle of the eighteenth century: "Our trade with New York and Philadelphia was of this sort, draining us of all the little money and bills that we could gather from other places, for their bread, flowr, beer, hams, bacon, and other things of their produce, all which except beer, our new townships begin to supply us with, which are settled with very industrious and consequently thriving Germans. This no doubt diminishes the number of shipping, and the appearance of our trade, but is far from being a detriment to us."

Before long the frontier created a demand for merchants. As it retreated from the coast it became less and less possible for England to bring her supplies directly to the consumer's wharfs, and carry away staple crops; and staple crops began to give way to diversified agriculture for a time. The effect of this phase of the frontier action upon the northern section is perceived when we realize how the advance of the frontier aroused seaboard cities like Boston, New York, and Baltimore to engage in rivalry for what Washington called "the extensive and valuable trade of a rising empire."

EFFECTS ON NATIONAL LEGISLATION

The legislation which most developed the powers of the national government, and played the largest part in its activity, was conditioned on the frontier. Writers have discussed the subjects of tariff, land, and internal improvement as pendants to the slavery question. But when American history comes to be rightly viewed it will be seen that the slavery question is an incident. In the period from the end of the first half of the present century to the close of the Civil War, slavery rose to primary but far from exclusive importance. But this does not justify Professor von Holst, to take an example, in treating our constitutional history in its formative period down to 1828 in a single volume, giving six volumes chiefly to the history of slavery from 1828 to 1861, under the title of a *Constitutional History of the United States.* The growth of nationalism and the evolution of American political institutions were dependent on the advance of the frontier. Even so recent a writer as Rhodes, in his *History of the United States since the Compromise of 1850,* has treated the legislation called out by the western advance as incidental to the slavery struggle.

This is a wrong perspective. The pioneer needed the goods of the coast, and so the grand series of internal improvements and railroad legislation began, with potent nationalizing effects. But the West was not content with bringing the farm to the factory. Under the lead of Clay—"Harry of the West"—protective tariffs were passed, with the cry of bringing the factory to the farm.

THE PUBLIC DOMAIN

The public domain has been a force of profound importance in the nationalization and development of the government. The effects of the struggle of the landed and the landless states, and of the Ordinance of 1787, need no discussion. Administratively the frontier called out some of the highest and most vitalizing activities of the general government. The purchase of Louisiana was perhaps the constitutional turning point in the history of the republic, inasmuch as it afforded both a new area for national legislation, and the occasion of the downfall of the policy of strict construction. But the purchase of Louisiana was called out by frontier needs and demands. As frontier states accrued to the Union, the national power grew. In a speech on the dedication of the Calhoun monument, Mr. Lamar explained: "In 1789 the states were the creators of the federal government; in 1861 the federal government was the creator of a large majority of the states."

When we consider the public domain from the point of view of the sale and disposal of the public lands, we are again brought face to face with the frontier. The policy of the United States in dealing with its lands is in sharp contrast with the European system of scientific administration. Efforts to make this domain a source of revenue, and to withhold it from emigrants in order that settlement might be compact, were in vain. The jealousy and the fears of the East were powerless in the face of the demands of the frontiersmen. John Quincy Adams was obliged to confess: "My own system of administration, which was to make the national domain the inexhaustible fund for progressive and unceasing internal improvement, has failed." The reason is obvious; systems of administration were not what the West demanded; it wanted land. Adams states the situation as follows:

"The slave-holders of the South have bought the co-operation of the Western country by the bribe of the Western lands, abandoning to the new Western States their own proportion of this public property, and aiding them in the design of grasping all the lands into their own hands. Thomas H. Benton was the author of this system, which he brought forward as a substitute for the American system of Mr. Clay, and to supplant him as the leading statesman of the West. Mr. Clay, by his tariff compromise with Mr. Calhoun, abandoned his own American system. At the same time he brought forward

539

a plan for distributing among all the States of the Union the proceeds of the sales of the public lands. His bill for that purpose passed both houses of Congress, but was vetoed by President Jackson, who, in his annual message of December, 1832, formally recommended that all the public lands should be gratuitously given away to individual adventurers and to the States in which the lands are situated."

"No subject," said Henry Clay, "which has presented itself to the present, or perhaps any preceding, congress, is of greater magnitude than that of the public lands." When we consider the far-reaching effects of the government's land policy upon political, economic, and social aspects of American life, we are disposed to agree with him. But this legislation was framed under frontier influences, and under the lead of Western statesmen like Benton and Jackson. Said Senator Scott of Indiana in 1841: "I consider the pre-emption law merely declaratory of the custom or common law of the settlers."

NATIONAL TENDENCIES OF THE FRONTIER

It is safe to say that the legislation with regard to land, tariff, and internal improvements—the American system of the nationalizing Whig Party—was conditioned on frontier ideas and needs. But it was not merely in legislative action that the frontier worked against the sectionalism of the coast. The economic and social characteristics of the frontier worked against sectionalism. The men of the frontier had closer resemblances to the Middle region than to either of the other sections. Pennsylvania had been the seed plot of frontier emigration, and, although she passed on her settlers along the Great Valley into the west of Virginia and the Carolinas, yet the industrial society of these Southern frontiersmen was always more like that of the Middle region than like that of the tidewater portion of the South, which later came to spread its industrial type throughout the South.

The Middle region, entered by New York harbor, was an open door to all Europe. The tidewater part of the South represented typical Englishmen, modified by a warm climate and servile labor, and living in baronial fashion on great plantations; New England stood for a special English movement—Puritanism. The Middle region was less English than the other sections. It had a wide mixture of nationalities, a varied society, the mixed town and county system of local government, a varied economic life, many religious sects. In short, it was a region mediating between New England and the South, and the East and the West. It

540

represented that composite nationality which the contemporary United States exhibits, that juxtaposition of non-English groups, occupying a valley or a little settlement, and presenting reflections of the map of Europe in their variety. It was democratic and nonsectional, if not national; "easy, tolerant, and contented;" rooted strongly in material prosperity. It was typical of the modern United States. It was least sectional not only because it lay between North and South but also because with no barriers to shut out its frontiers from its settled region, and with a system of connecting waterways, the Middle region mediated between East and West as well as between North and South. Thus it became the typically American region. Even the New Englander, who was shut out from the frontier by the Middle region, tarrying in New York or Pennsylvania on his westward march, lost the acuteness of his sectionalism on the way.

Until the spread of cotton culture into the interior gave homogeneity to the South, the western part of it showed tendencies to fall away from the faith of the fathers into internal improvement legislation and nationalism. In the Virginia convention of 1829–30, called to revise the constitution, Mr. Leigh, of Chesterfield, one of the tidewater counties, declared:

"One of the main causes of discontent which led to this convention, that which had the strongest influence in overcoming our veneration for the work of our fathers, which taught us to contemn the sentiments of Henry and Mason and Pendleton, which weaned us from our reverence for the constituted authorities of the state, was an overweening passion for internal improvement. I say this with perfect knowledge; for it has been avowed to me by gentlemen from the West over and over again. And let me tell the gentleman from Albemarle (Mr. Gordon) that it has been another principal object of those who set this ball of revolution in motion, to overturn the doctrine of state rights, of which Virginia has been the very pillar, and to remove the barrier she has interposed to the interference of the federal government in that same work of internal improvement, by so reorganizing the legislature that Virginia, too, may be hitched to the federal car."

It was this nationalizing tendency of the West that transformed the democracy of Jefferson into the national republicanism of Monroe and the democracy of Andrew Jackson. The West of the War of 1812, the West of Clay, and Benton, and Harrison, and Andrew Jackson, shut off by the Middle states and the mountains from the coast sections, had a solidarity of its own with national tendencies. On the tide of the Father of Waters, North and South met and mingled into a nation. Interstate migration went steadily on—a process of cross-fertilization of ideas and institutions. The fierce struggle of the sections over slavery on the western frontier does not diminish the truth of this statement; it proves the truth of it. Slavery was a sectional trait that would not down, but in the West it could not remain sectional. It was the greatest of frontiersmen who declared: "I believe this government cannot endure permanently half slave and half free. It will become all of one thing, or all of the other." Nothing works for nationalism like intercourse within the nation. Mobility of population is death to localism, and the Western frontier worked irresistibly in unsettling population. The effects reached back from the frontier and affected profoundly the Atlantic Coast, and even the Old World.

GROWTH OF DEMOCRACY

But the most important effect of the frontier has been in the promotion of democracy here and in Europe. As has been pointed out, the frontier is productive of individualism. Complex society is precipitated by the wilderness into a kind of primitive organization based on the family. The tendency is anti-social. It produces antipathy to control, and particularly to any direct control. The tax-gatherer is viewed as a representative of oppression. Professor Osgood, in an able article, has pointed out that the frontier conditions prevalent in the colonies are important factors in the explanation of the American Revolution, where individual liberty was sometimes confused with absence of all effective government. The same conditions aid in explaining the difficulty of instituting a strong government in the period of the confederacy. The frontier individualism has from the beginning promoted democracy.

The frontier states that came into the Union in the first quarter of a century of its existence came in with democratic suffrage provisions, and had reactive effects of the highest importance upon the older states whose peoples were being attracted there. It was *western* New York that forced an extension of suffrage in the constitutional convention of that state in 1821; and it was *western* Virginia that compelled the tidewater region to put a more liberal suffrage provision in the constitution framed in 1830, and to give to the frontier region a more nearly proportionate representation with the tidewater aristocracy. The rise of democracy as an effective force in the nation came in with Western preponderance under Jackson and William Henry Harrison, and it meant the triumph of the frontier—with all of its good and with all of its evil elements.

542

An interesting illustration of the tone of frontier democracy in 1830 comes from the debates in the Virginia convention already referred to. A representative from western Virginia declared: "But, sir, it is not the increase of population in the West which this gentleman ought to fear. It is the energy which the mountain breeze and western habits impart to those emigrants. They are regenerated, politically I mean, sir. They soon become *working politicians*; and the difference, sir, between a *talking* and a *working* politician is immense. The Old Dominion has long been celebrated for producing great orators; the ablest metaphysicians in policy; men that can split hairs in all abstruse questions of political economy. But at home, or when they return from congress, they have negroes to fan them asleep. But a Pennsylvania, a New York, an Ohio, or a western Virginia statesman, though far inferior in logic, metaphysics and rhetoric to an old Virginia statesman, has this advantage, that when he returns home he takes off his coat and takes hold of the plough. This gives him bone and muscle, sir, and preserves his republican principles pure and uncontaminated."

So long as free land exists, the opportunity for a competency exists, and economic power secures political power. But the democracy born of free land, strong in selfishness and individualism, intolerant of administrative experience and education, and pressing individual liberty beyond its proper bounds, has its dangers as well as its benefits. Individualism in America has allowed a laxity in regard to governmental affairs which has rendered possible the spoils system, and all the manifest evils that follow from the lack of a highly developed civic spirit. In this connection may be noted also the influence of frontier conditions in permitting lax business honor, inflated paper currency, and wildcat banking. The colonial and Revolutionary frontier was the region whence emanated many of the worst forms of an evil currency. The West in the War of 1812 repeated the phenomenon on the frontier of that day, while the speculation and wildcat banking of the period of the crisis of 1837 occurred on the new frontier belt of the next tier of states. Thus each one of the periods of lax financial integrity coincides with periods when a new set of frontier communities had arisen, and coincides in area with these successive frontiers, for the most part. The recent Populist agitation is a case in point. Many a state that now declines any connection with the tenets of the Populists itself adhered to such ideas in an earlier stage of the development of the state. A primitive society can hardly be expected to show the intelligent appreciation of the complexity of business interests in a developed society. The continual recurrence of these areas of paper-money agitation is another evidence that the frontier can be isolated and studied as a factor in American history of the highest importance.

ATTEMPTS TO CHECK AND REGULATE THE FRONTIER

The East has always feared the result of an unregulated advance of the frontier, and has tried to check and guide it. The English authorities would have checked settlement at the headwaters of the Atlantic tributaries and allowed the savages to enjoy their deserts in quiet lest the peltry trade should decrease. This called out Burke's splendid protest:

"[If] you stopped your grants, what would be the consequence? The people would occupy without grants. They have already so occupied in many places. You cannot station garrisons in every part of these deserts. If you drive the people from one place, they will carry on their annual tillage, and remove with their flocks and herds to another. Many of the people in the back settlements are already little attached to particular situations. Already they have topped the Appalachian mountains. From thence they behold before them an immense plain, one vast, rich, level meadow; a square of five hundred miles. Over this they would wander without a possibility of restraint; they would change their manners with their habits of life; would soon forget a government by which they were disowned; would become hordes of English Tartars; and, pouring down upon your unfortified frontiers a fierce and irresistible cavalry, become masters of your governors and your counselors, your collectors and comptrollers, and of all the slaves that adhered to them. Such would, and in no long time must, be the effect of attempting to forbid as a crime, and to suppress as an evil, the command and blessing of Providence, 'Increase and multiply.' Such would be the happy result of an endeavor to keep as a lair of wild beasts that earth which God by an express charter has given to the children of men."

But the English government was not alone in its desire to limit the advance of the frontier, and guide its destinies. Tidewater Virginia and South Carolina gerrymandered those colonies to ensure the dominance of the coast in their legislatures. Washington desired to settle a state at a time in the Northwest; Jefferson would have reserved from settlement the territory of his Louisiana purchase north of the thirty-second parallel, in order to offer it to the Indians in exchange for their settlements east of the Mississippi. "When we shall be full on this side," he writes, "we may lay off a range of states on the western bank from the head to the mouth, and so range after range, advancing compactly as we multiply." Madison went so far as to argue to the French minister that the United States had no interest in seeing population extend itself on the right bank of the Mississippi, but should rather fear it. When the Oregon question was under debate, in 1824, Smyth of Virginia would have drawn an unchangeable line for the limits of the United States at the outer limit of two tiers of states beyond the Mississippi, complaining that the seaboard states were being drained of the flower of their population by the bringing of too much land into market. Even Thomas Benton, the man of widest views of the destiny of the West, at this stage of his career declared that along the ridge of the Rocky Mountains "the western limits of the republic should be drawn, and the statue of the fabled god Terminus should be raised upon its highest peak, never to be thrown down." But the attempts to limit our boundaries, to restrict land sales and settlement, and to deprive the West of its share of political power were all in vain. Steadily that frontier of settlement advanced and carried with it individualism, democracy, and nationalism, and powerfully affected the East and the Old World.

MISSIONARY ACTIVITY

The most effective efforts of the East to regulate the frontier came through its educational and religious activity, exerted by interstate migration and by organized societies. Speaking in 1835, Dr. Lyman Beecher declared: "It is equally plain that the religious and political destiny of our nation is to be decided in the West," and he pointed out that the population of the West "is assembled from all the states of the Union, and from all the nations of Europe, and is rushing in like the waters of the flood, demanding for its moral preservation the immediate and universal action of those institutions which discipline the mind, and arm the conscience and the heart. And so various are the opinions and habits, and so recent and imperfect is the acquaintance, and so sparse are the settlements of the West, that no homogeneous public sentiment can be formed to legislate immediately into being the requisite institutions. And yet they are all needed immediately, in their utmost perfection and power. A nation is being 'born in a day'. . . . But what will become of the West, if her prosperity rushes up to such a majesty of power, while those great institutions linger which are necessary to form the mind, and the conscience, and the heart of that vast world. It must not be permitted. . . . let no man at the East quiet himself, and dream of liberty, whatever may become of the West. . . . Her destiny is our destiny."

With this appeal to the conscience of New England, he adds appeals to her fears lest other religious sects anticipate her own. The New England preacher and schoolteacher left their mark on the West. The dread of Western emancipation from New England's political and economic control was paralleled by fears lest the West cut loose from her religion. Commenting in 1850 on reports that settlement was rapidly extending northward in Wisconsin, the editor of the *Home Missionary* writes: "We scarcely know whether to rejoice or to mourn over this extension of our settlements. While we sympathize in whatever tends to increase the physical resources and prosperity of our country, we cannot forget that with all these dispersions into remote and still remoter corners of the land, the supply of the means of grace is becoming relatively less and less." Acting in accordance with such ideas, home missions were established and Western colleges were erected. As seaboard cities like Philadelphia, New York, and Baltimore strove for the mastery of Western trade, so the various denominations strove for the possession of the West. Thus an intellectual stream from New England sources fertilized the West. On the other hand, the contest for power and the expansive tendency furnished to the various sects by the existence of a moving frontier must have had important results on the character of religious organization in the United States. The religious aspects of the frontier make a chapter in our history which needs study.

INTELLECTUAL TRAITS

From the conditions of frontier life came intellectual traits of profound importance. The works of travelers along each frontier from colonial days onward describe for each certain traits, and these traits have, while softening down, still persisted as survivals in the place of their origin, even when a higher social organization succeeded. The result is that to the frontier the American intellect owes its striking characteristics. That coarseness and strength combined with acuteness and inquisitiveness, that practical, inventive turn of mind, quick to find expedients, that masterful grasp of material things, lacking in the artistic but powerful to effect great ends, that restless, nervous energy, that dominant individualism, working for good and for evil, and withal that buoyancy and exuberance which comes with freedom, these are traits of

546

the frontier, or traits called out elsewhere because of the existence of the frontier. Since the days when the fleet of Columbus sailed into the waters of the New World, America has been another name for opportunity, and the people of the United States have taken their tone from the incessant expansion which has not only been open but has even been forced upon them. He would be a rash prophet who should assert that the expansive character of American life has now entirely ceased. Movement has been its dominant fact, and, unless this training has no effect upon a people, the American intellect will continually demand a wider field for its exercise. But never again will such gifts of free land offer themselves. For a moment at the frontier the bonds of custom are broken, and unrestraint is triumphant. There is not *tabula rasa.* The stubborn American environment is there with its imperious summons to accept its conditions; the inherited ways of doing things are also there; and yet, in spite of environment, and in spite of custom, each frontier did indeed furnish a new field of opportunity, a gate of escape from the bondage of the past; and freshness, and confidence, and scorn of older society, impatience of its restraints and its ideas, and indifference to its lessons, have accompanied the frontier. What the Mediterranean Sea was to the Greeks, breaking the bond of custom, offering new experiences, calling out new institutions and activities, that, and more, the ever retreating frontier has been to the United States directly, and to the nations of Europe more remotely. And now, four centuries from the discovery of America, at the end of a hundred years of life under the Constitution, the frontier has gone, and with its going has closed the first period of American history.

No single interpretation of America's past has been more enthusiastically received at the time—or more violently rejected later—than Frederick Jackson Turner's "frontier hypothesis." For more than a generation after its initial statement in 1893 it remained the creed of nearly every American historian. There was a reason for this; Turner's explanation of the nation's uniqueness admirably fitted the popular mood during the first quarter of the twentieth century. The frontier thesis was a flattering formula; it assured the people that the mighty nation of which they were so proud was their own creation, and not a mere importation from

Europe. It was a nationalistic formula; Americans could learn that the institutions responsible for this greatness—democracy, individualism, freedom—were uniquely their own. It was a democratic formula; citizens in that day of political Progressivism could glory in the fact that the humble as well as the mighty had shaped the destiny of the United States. It was an optimistic formula; America's greatness had been achieved by individual effort which would continue to inspire progress in the future. So the nation embraced the frontier thesis as the gospel, and rewrote its textbooks to glorify the pioneer above the industrialist or the immigrant.

This was dangerous, as Turner recognized, for he was a better historian than some of his disciples and realized that no single force was responsible for such a complex social organism as the United States. The tide of reaction set in shortly after his death in 1932. Again the time was ripe for such a change. Scholars, readjusting their concepts to the terrible new world created by the Great Depression, began to wonder whether the United States had ever been the land of limitless opportunity pictured by frontier historians, just as they questioned the role of pioneer individualism in a land where cooperative effort seemed essential for economic rehabilitation. Others bridled against Turner's agrarian emphasis in a day when factories, cities, and class conflicts shaped the course of events.

So critics leaped to the attack during the 1930's and 1940's. Some quarreled with Turner's loose terminology and exact definitions, insisting that his very vagueness invalidated his hypothesis. Others singled out special areas for criticism, denying that the frontier had ever served as a safety valve for discontented easterners, or that it had fostered democracy. Still others damned the Turnerites for focusing undue attention on a single causal force, maintaining that industrialization, urbanization, and social unrest had always been more important than westward expansion in shaping the national character. Even more devastating was the charge that the frontier hypothesis had helped plunge the United States into its state of chaos. By stressing the uniqueness of the national experience, critics insisted, Turner's thesis had engendered an isolationist spirit that hindered the international cooperation needed to lift the country from depression and foster the one-world ideal of the twentieth century.

In the end these critics went too far, and once more in the 1950's and 1960's the pendulum began to swing in the other direction. A new generation of scholars, sensibly paying less attention to Turner's state-

548

ment of the frontier hypothesis than to the hypothesis itself, launched investigations that have restored this challenging thesis to its rightful place in American historiography. Some, using the techniques of sociologists, political scientists, and statisticians, have concluded that the pioneering experience did stimulate the growth of democratic institutions differing from those of Europe. Others, drawing on findings of economists, have agreed that a frontier safety valve had operated to influence the pattern of labor organization during the nineteenth century. Still others have demonstrated that comparative studies of frontier and nonfrontier countries suggested that expansion did stimulate innovation, mobility, and the blurring of class lines, just as Turner had postulated.

Whatever the results of the scholarly in-fighting, Turner's theories have become part of the nation's folklore and have altered the diplomatic and political behavior of the United States. Expansionist-minded diplomats, fastening on the Turnerian doctrine that the perennial rebirth of society on new frontiers has rekindled the democratic spirit, have argued for half a century that new territories must be acquired or the national heritage surrendered. Imperialists used this argument in demanding territorial acquisitions after the Spanish-American War; men of such differing beliefs as J. P. Morgan and Woodrow Wilson agreed that the extension of American authority abroad would foster both economic growth and democracy; Franklin D. Roosevelt insisted that the export of the nation's democratic institutions was a necessary prelude to the better world that would emerge from World War II; his successor advanced the "Truman Doctrine" as a device to expand and defend the frontiers of democracy throughout the world. Belief in the superiority of American democratic institutions was older than Turner, but his insistence that these institutions owed their greatness to the frontier experience was a significant force in their acceptance and propagation.

Domestic policy in the United States has similarly been altered by popular belief in the Turnerian doctrine. Progressive statesmen, agreeing that the end of the frontier closed the door on those who sought to rehabilitate themselves by exploiting nature's virgin resources, have through the twentieth century acted on the belief that the federal government must supply Americans with the opportunity and security formerly provided by free land. This was the philosophy that underlay the New Nationalism of Theodore Roosevelt, the New Freedom of Woodrow Wilson, the New Deal of Franklin D. Roosevelt, and the Fair

Deal of Harry Truman. "Our last frontier has long since been reached," declared Franklin Roosevelt. "Equality of opportunity as we have known it no longer exists. Our task now is not the discovery or exploitation of natural resources or necessarily producing more goods. It is the sober, less dramatic business . . . of distributing wealth and products more equitably, of adapting existing economic organizations to the service of the people. The day of enlightened administration has come." A still later president, John F. Kennedy, signaled his approval of these beliefs by adopting "the New Frontier" as a slogan for his Administration. And President Lyndon B. Johnson has proclaimed his predecessor's "frontier" as only the borderland of the "Great Society." In such programs Frederick Jackson Turner's essay endures today, as part of the public consciousness of the United States.

Richard Warren Sears
Cheapest Supply House on Earth
1894

EDITED BY JOHN E. JEUCK

Mail-order selling and the money-back guaranty are widely identified with Richard Warren Sears, not because the founder of Sears, Roebuck and Company originated either, but because he exploited them most successfully by his compelling advertising copy and his success in achieving enormous catalogue circulations. Motivated initially by a search for profits and prosperity, Sears exhausted himself in a continuing search for the "right proposition," which he defined in terms of a merchandise offering, price, advertising copy, and circulation plan that would generate sales.

Sears sketched out his copy for the cover and the pages of the 1894 mail-order catalogue in the closing days of the Columbian Exposition Year, 1893. Whether he planned and wrote the copy in his sparely furnished office in Minneapolis' Globe Building, or in a Van Buren Street loft in Chicago, is not clear, since his mail-order company was then operating from both cities—moving finally to Chicago only in January, 1895. Indeed, Sears may have planned his "Book of Bargains" while en route between the two cities—or in the midnight hours at home or in his hotel. His mail-order business had become (and long remained) the absorbing interest of his life, second only to his devotion to his family, whose demands appear to have been modest compared to the excitement and the profit of the avalanche of orders which the mails brought in the wake of Sears's advertising efforts.

Separated by great distances from the market he sought to serve, Richard Sears was conscious of the need to promise "satisfaction or your money back," both to overcome the understandable reluctance of customers to buy without comparing merchandise, and to counter the campaigns waged against mail order by local merchants throughout the land. "YOU TAKE NO RISK," Sears spelled out his general guaranty, " . . . whether you send part or full amount of cash with your order, as we ALWAYS REFUND MONEY where goods are not found perfectly satisfactory." Lest the distant farmers fail to be satisfied with even that promise, Sears tried further to reassure them by referring his unseen prospects to their neighbors, the express companies, and the Union National Bank of Minneapolis.

The catalogue of 1894 was significant in several respects. It was the largest (322 pages) yet issued; it was the first to make any pretense toward offering a "complete" line of goods; it was only the second catalogue using the new title "Sears, Roebuck and Company," and the earliest to list the new Chicago location. Also the cover of the 1894 catalogue appears to have been the first to be printed in color. Although catalogues were to vary in price to the customer, the company advertised the 1894 catalogue as free for the writing, a practice that Sears later was to adopt as policy. The catalogue was also one of the last to reflect the unfettered personality of Richard Sears. From 1895, catalogues increasingly reflected the expanding size and dignity of the growing corporation and the trend toward "truth in advertising" with more accurate and detailed descriptions of merchandise.

[Cover]

CHEAPEST SUPPLY HOUSE ON EARTH
OUR TRADE REACHES AROUND THE WORLD.

SEARS, ROEBUCK AND CO.

Globe Building   149 W. Van Buren
Minneapolis, Minn.   Chicago, Ill.

CONSUMER'S GUIDE
FOR
1894.

[page 3]

OUR COMBINED CATALOGUE.

PRESERVE THIS BOOK.   IT'S A MONEY SAVER.

TO OUR PATRONS:

Again we come to you, and we honestly believe, with the grandest collection of Bargains ever printed in one volume. *This is a Book of Bargains; a Money Saver for Everyone.* It is not our aim to include in this book and confuse you with a great variety of goods on which we can save you no money, but it has been our aim to include goods on which you can make a great saving. By a comparison of our prices with those of any thoroughly reliable house, you will see at once *you can save money* on everything you buy from us. It would be useless for us to include in this book a lot of goods at prices which with transportation charges added would cost you as much as you could buy the same article for in your local market. *We have studied to avoid this* by offering you only such goods as we are in a position to buy from the manufacturers direct and in such quantities as enables us to deliver them to you for as little or less money than they would cost your local dealer.

The advertising copy reprinted here—cover and pages 3 and 4—comes from the Sears, Roebuck and Company catalogue of 1894.

OUR OLD FRIENDS AND PATRONS

Will remember us as originally an *Exclusive Watch House, and later, Watches, Diamonds, Jewelry and Silverware,* and we believe we can modestly claim what is universally conceded that we honestly earned and have since maintained the reputation of being *The* LARGEST WATCH *and* JEWELRY HOUSE *in the* WORLD selling goods direct to the consumer. *Our daily average sales of Watches have been over 400, Jewelry and Silverware in proportion,* while in the *Diamond* business our sales have almost from the very start *exceeded that of any firm in America* selling direct to the consumer.

WE HAVE ADDED MANY NEW LINES

And we shall hope for the same support in our new departure that has been so liberally accorded us in the past. *We have studied* to carefully and honestly represent every article so that when it reaches you, its appearance will almost universally be *better* than the description we give.

ABOUT OUR RELIABILITY.

We are authorized and incorporated under the laws of the State of Minnesota, with a cash capital paid in full of $75,000.00. We refer you to The Union National Bank of Minneapolis, and you are at liberty, if you choose, to send your money to them with instructions not to turn it over to us unless they know us to be perfectly reliable. We refer to any Express Company doing business in Minneapolis or Chicago—Adams, American, United States, Great Northern or Northern Pacific, or you can very likely find people in your own locality who know of us. *Ask your nearest Express Agent* about us; most any Express Agent can tell you about us. *Every Express Agent* in the United States knows of our reputation, as they have delivered our goods, and must, in most cases, know what our customers think of us.

WHERE WE SELL GOODS.

Almost Everywhere! There isn't a town in the Union where we haven't sold goods, our goods go into every city, town and hamlet in every state, as well as most every country on the globe. *Don't think* you live too far away. Our biggest trade is in Pennsylvania; 2d, New York; 3d, Illinois; 4th, Ohio, and so on, according to the population of the several states. *Distance cuts no figure. We can serve you anywhere,*

554

anytime. Freight rates are low. Express rates are low. We have *Special facilities for Shipping* and in many cases *Special rates.*

WE AIM TO MAKE CUSTOMERS

Of Everyone by treating every customer in such a manner as to insure their always remaining a customer. WE CAN'T AFFORD TO LOSE A CUSTOMER, and by instructing our employes to treat every customer at a distance exactly as they would like to be treated were they in a customer's place, and rigidly enforcing this rule, we have grown into one of the first institutions of the country and our patrons far and near are talking in our favor and thus adding new customers daily.

WHO WE SELL.

We sell the consumer, by that we mean we deal direct with the party who buys for his own use, thus saving you the middle man's profit. Anyone can buy from us; there is no restriction. Our terms and conditions are the most liberal ever offered. We make it very easy to buy of us.

Read our Terms, Conditions, etc., on next page.

Very truly,

SEARS, ROEBUCK & CO.

Globe Building, Minneapolis, Minn. 149 West Van Buren Street, Chicago, Ills.

ADDRESS US AT EITHER PLACE.

[page 4]

TERMS, CONDITIONS OF SHIPMENT, ETC.

The terms and conditions of Shipment will usually be found under each description, but in all cases, unless otherwise specified, CASH IN FULL MUST ACCOMPANY YOUR ORDER. We have tried in all cases to make our terms as liberal as possible, and by comparison you will find we offer terms not given by any other house in existence. On account of weight and bulk some goods can not be sent by express or C.O.D., but so far as we can, we send C.O.D., subject to examination to anyone.

OUR WATCHES, DIAMONDS AND JEWELRY we continue sending C.O.D. to any one anywhere, subject to examination. No MONEY IN ADVANCE. *Prepay all Express Charges on Watches,* excepting a few special cheap watches on which we require cash in full and do not pay charges as explained under each description. UNDERSTAND, *Diamonds, Watches and Jewelry* will be sent to anyone, No MONEY IN ADVANCE. *No other House on Earth* handling the fine line we do give such liberal terms.

PIANOS AND ORGANS we will send to anyone and allow TEN DAYS TRIAL FREE, subject to the conditions fully explained in Catalogue pages.

GUNS AND REVOLVERS we will send to anyone anywhere C.O.D., subject to examination, on receipt of 50c to $3.00 as a guarantee of good faith. For full particulars read GUN PAGES.

HARNESS. We send Harness C.O.D., subject to examination to any one, on receipt of $1.00 as a Guarantee. For particulars read HARNESS PAGES.

SILVERWARE. Some Silverware we send C.O.D., subject to examination, *No Money in Advance.* For particulars see SILVERWARE PAGES.

CLOTHING. We send Clothing C.O.D., subject to examination on VERY LIBERAL TERMS. For particulars see CLOTHING DEPARTMENT.

BICYCLES. C.O.D.; subject to examination on receipt of ONE DOLLAR.

BABY CARRIAGES. C.O.D., subject to examination on receipt of TWO DOLLARS.

FULL PARTICULARS as to TERMS OF SALE, CONDITION OF SHIPMENT, *Etc.,* will be found under the *General Descriptions throughout this Book,* and in most cases will be found *more liberal* than is offered by any other concern.

YOU TAKE NO RISK in ordering of us whether you send part or full amount of cash with your order, as we ALWAYS REFUND MONEY where goods are not found perfectly satisfactory.

HOW TO ORDER.

ALWAYS WRITE YOUR ORDERS PLAINLY: Order Everything by Number; Always sign your Name plainly and in full; Always give the Name of your nearest Express Office or Railroad Station to which you wish goods shipped. If goods are to be sent by Express, give Name of Express company, or Name of Railroad company if to be sent by freight. Goods Can Not Be Sent by Mail C.O.D. Anything to be sent by mail must be paid for in Advance.

IF YOU DON'T FIND WHAT YOU WANT in this Book, write us. We may have the very thing in stock; if we haven't, we can no doubt get it for you at a great saving. *Don't hesitate to write us* at any time. *We are always at your service.*

Your obedient servants,

SEARS, ROEBUCK & CO.,

Globe Building, Minneapolis, Minn.   149 West Van Buren St., Chicago, Ill.

ADDRESS US AT EITHER PLACE.

By the turn of the century, Sears, Roebuck and Company had out-stripped Montgomery Ward in sales, and Richard Sears was a rich man. His living standards were modest and his interest in added wealth, though real, had become secondary. The excitement of generating orders sustained his consuming interest in the catalogue until he resigned from the company in 1908. By then it was the largest mail-order business in the world, with sales in 1907 of more than $50 million. Since that time, when the enterprise was still limited almost entirely to the rural market, Sears, Roebuck and Company has become the world's largest general merchandise house, with sales of some $5 billion in 1963 made through the catalogue and more than 700 retail stores located in the United States, Canada, Venezuela, Brazil, Colombia, Mexico, Peru, Costa Rica, Puerto Rico, El Salvador, and Panama.

Excepting the Bible, the Sears catalogue has probably the widest circulation of any book in the world. Currently, the various editions of the big "wish book" number more than 50 million copies annually. It is found not only in households, but in libraries, schools, offices, army camps, and embassies throughout the world—on both sides of the "iron" and "bamboo curtains." The catalogue is one of the best-read titles in USIA libraries throughout the world.

The overriding purpose of the catalogue is—and always has been—to sell merchandise. But its side effects have been impressive. Company president Robert E. Wood observed in the company's 1937 catalogue: "We conceive of this company not only as a great retail organization but as a great public institution as well." General Wood's statement is not extravagant. The catalogue is not only a source book for theater costumes and set designers, but a sharer with Henry Ford's "tin lizzie" in the distinction of forming the substance of much American humor. On the larger stage of international politics, it is reported that President Franklin Roosevelt once remarked that Soviet propaganda might profitably be countered by bombing the Russians with Sears, Roebuck catalogues (Life Magazine, Nov. 11, 1957). And the one-time chief of the Associated Press Moscow Bureau, Eddy Gilmore, is authority for the assertion that "Two innocent enough articles of American life—the Sears Roebuck catalogue and the phonograph record—are the most powerful pieces of foreign propaganda in Russia. The catalogue comes first" (Liberty Magazine, Jan. 18, 1947).

At home, the mail-order catalogue changed the face of retail trade in rural America—and, at a later date, contributed greatly to the establishment of more efficient distribution in the cities as well. Initially, the catalogue served to break down the monopoly of local retailers throughout the land. The extent to which it furnished a standard of prices and values on farms and in villages and hamlets is evident in the enormous editorial attack it received from small-town newspapers during their crusades to defend local merchants against the mail-order business. Perhaps the largest "book burnings" in the United States were the fires made by irate merchants who burned the catalogues in the public square. (A recent echo of the use of the catalogue as an instrument of protest was the 1962 campaign of the National Farmers Organization to persuade midwestern farmers to pile Sears catalogues up in front of Sears stores to protest against the Committee for Economic Development's published report on agricultural policy.)

Launched on the final quarter of its first centennial, the Sears catalogue continues as a standard of value. Catalogue prices are used to construct a "cost of living" index by professional economists. Writing in the fall of 1957, a journalist noted: "Only recently has the catalogue been intentionally used as a weapon in the cold war. This spring Radio Free Europe started beaming a series of broadcasts from Munich to Poland, Hungary, Czechoslovakia, Rumania and Bulgaria, describing in detail what the American worker is able to buy with his wages. The price of every item in the Sears catalogue from 'A' (abdominal bands) to 'Z' (zircon rings) is now being beamed behind the Iron Curtain" (Life Magazine, Nov. 11, 1957). Having survived numerous attacks by competing merchants, the catalogue has remained an object of study by its competitors.

Louis H. Sullivan
The Tall Office Building Artistically Considered
1896

EDITED BY CARL W. CONDIT

When the first multistory office buildings began to rise in New York after the Civil War, the architects were clearly baffled by the formal and functional problems that they presented. The architects sought solutions either in irrelevant aesthetic concepts or in historical or even pseudomystical principles that had no architectural reference. Most of the results strike us today as ludicrous. It was not simply that the architects fell back on styles derived from the past, for in the hands of imaginative designers eclecticism could and did lead to distinguished works of architecture. The trouble, rather, was that the architects fled from the essential utilitarian, structural, and geometric facts of the high office building. Again and again they sought to deny its height, its iron and steel structure, and its repetitive internal character by overloading the exterior of the building with lavish ornamental detail that bore no relation to the internal divisions and structure. In extreme cases a single building could be made to look like as many as six different buildings piled one above the other, each badly done in itself and each unrelated to the rest.

Sullivan's essay is directed precisely against this architectural refusal to face the facts. His paper is a document of prime importance in architectural aesthetics, and because of the unprecedented problem to which he addressed himself, it is revolutionary for the development of building form in our mechanized industrial society. The positive program which he offers has many of the features of an urgent manifesto (a

560

characteristic intensified by his overblown and rather turgid rhetoric), but it is equally a description of the new architectural practice that had arisen in Chicago in the 1880's. William Le Baron Jenney and John Wellborn Root had already understood the problem of the multistory building and by 1890 had produced solutions which are among the first masterpieces of modern architecture. Yet Sullivan was the logical spokesman for the new style emerging in Chicago. He had received international attention for his Transportation Building at the Columbian Exposition of 1893, had given the leading paper at the annual meeting of the American Institute of Architects in 1894, and had been elected to the Institute's Board of Directors in 1895. The exact circumstances under which he wrote the essay are unknown, but it seems reasonable to conclude that the editors of Lippincott's first suggested the paper. It was to be his only article in a magazine of general interest.

In the five years preceding the publication of the paper in 1896, Sullivan and his engineering partner Dankmar Adler enjoyed a number of major commissions, three of which offered the architect opportunities to realize the principles he had already formulated in his mind. All three were epoch-making buildings, and two still stand today among the best we have produced—the Wainwright in St. Louis (1890–91), the Garrick Theater in Chicago (1891–92; demolished in 1961), and the Guaranty in Buffalo (1894–95). Sullivan's designs for these buildings reveal the two essential aspects of the program developed in his essay. The first is the highly empirical approach, presented in the clear and exact description of the demands posed by the tall office building and the planning elements necessary to satisfy them. The assumption underlying this description is summed up in Sullivan's assertion that "every problem contains and suggests its own solution." The second aspect seems antithetical to the first and offers the most difficult problem in understanding Sullivan's work. It is subjective and emotional, imbued with a romantic naturalism and a sense of wonder before the new technical possibilities. Sullivan wanted to do more than present the facts of a building. He was compelled to celebrate his powerful feelings for the new technology of steel construction and to search for a form that would seem at once organic in the naturalistic sense and expressive of his own inner, nonrational responses to techniques. Thus his celebrated idea that form follows function must be understood in the context of highly charged feeling that expresses itself in descriptions of the tall building as "a proud and soaring thing," or as offering "the most stupendous" and "magnificent" opportunity "to the proud spirit of man." Sullivan's search for the union of emotional expressiveness and scientific reason is the dominant one that occupies the creative architect in the mid-twentieth century.

THE ARCHITECTS of this land and generation are now brought face to face with something new under the sun—namely, that evolution and integration of social conditions, that special grouping of them, that results in a demand for the erection of tall office buildings.

It is not my purpose to discuss the social conditions; I accept them as the fact, and say at once that the design of the tall office building must be recognized and confronted at the outset as a problem to be solved—a vital problem, pressing for a true solution.

Let us state the conditions in the plainest manner. Briefly, they are these: offices are necessary for the transaction of business; the invention and perfection of the high-speed elevators make vertical travel, that was once tedious and painful, now easy and comfortable; development of steel manufacture has shown the way to safe, rigid, economical constructions rising to a great height; continued growth of population in the great cities, consequent congestion of centers and rise in value of ground, stimulate an increase in number of stories; these successfully piled one upon another, react on ground values—and so on, by action and reaction, interaction and inter-reaction. Thus has come about that form of lofty construction called the "modern office building." It has come in answer to a call, for in it a new grouping of social conditions has found a habitation and a name.

Up to this point all in evidence is materialistic, an exhibition of force, of resolution, of brains in the keen sense of the word. It is the joint product of the speculator, the engineer, the builder.

Problem: How shall we impart to this sterile pile, this crude, harsh, brutal agglomeration, this stark, staring exclamation of eternal strife, the graciousness of those higher forms of sensibility and culture that rest on the lower and fiercer passions? How shall we proclaim from the dizzy height of this strange, weird, modern housetop the peaceful evangel of sentiment, of beauty, the cult of a higher life?

This is the problem; and we must seek the solution of it in a process

The essay is reprinted as it originally appeared in *Lippincott's Magazine*, LVII (March, 1896), 403–9.

analogous to its own evolution—indeed, a continuation of it—namely, by proceeding step by step from general to special aspects, from coarser to finer considerations.

It is my belief that it is of the very essence of every problem that it contains and suggests its own solution. This I believe to be natural law. Let us examine, then, carefully the elements, let us search out this contained suggestion, this essence of the problem.

The practical conditions are, broadly speaking, these:

Wanted—1st, a story below-ground, containing boilers, engines of various sorts, etc.—in short, the plant for power, heating, lighting, etc. 2nd, a ground floor, so called, devoted to stores, banks, or other establishments requiring large area, ample spacing, ample light, and great freedom of access. 3rd, a second story readily accessible by stairways—this space usually in large subdivisions, with corresponding liberality in structural spacing and expanse of glass and breadth of external openings. 4th, above this an indefinite number of stories of offices piled tier upon tier, one tier just like another tier, one office just like all the other offices—an office being similar to a cell in a honeycomb, merely a compartment, nothing more. 5th, and last, at the top of this pile is placed a space or story that, as related to the life and usefulness of the structure, is purely physiological in its nature—namely, the attic. In this the circulatory system completes itself and makes its grand turn, ascending and descending. The space is filled with tanks, pipes, valves, sheaves, and mechanical etcetera that supplement and complement the force-originating plant hidden below-ground in the cellar. Finally, or at the beginning rather, there must be on the ground floor a main aperture or entrance common to all the occupants or patrons of the building.

This tabulation is, in the main, characteristic of every tall office building in the country. As to the necessary arrangements for light courts, these are not germane to the problem, and as will become soon evident, I trust need not be considered here. These things, and such others as the arrangement of elevators, for example, have to do strictly with the economics of the building, and I assume them to have been fully considered and disposed of to the satisfaction of purely utilitarian and pecuniary demands. Only in rare instances does the plan or floor arrangement of the tall office building take on an aesthetic value, and this usually when the lighting court is external or becomes an internal feature of great importance.

As I am here seeking not for an individual or special solution, but for a true normal type, the attention must be confined to those conditions that, in the main, are constant in all tall office buildings, and every mere incidental and accidental variation eliminated from the consideration, as harmful to the clearness of the main inquiry.

The practical horizontal and vertical division or office unit is naturally based on a room of comfortable area and height, and the size of this standard office room as naturally predetermines the standard structural unit, and, approximately, the size of window openings. In turn, these purely arbitrary units of structure form in an equally natural way the true basis of the artistic development of the exterior. Of course the structural spacings and openings in the first or mercantile story are required to be the largest of all; those in the second or quasi-mercantile story are of a somewhat similar nature. The spacings and openings in the attic are of no importance whatsoever (the windows have no actual value), for light may be taken from the top, and no recognition of a cellular division is necessary in the structural spacing.

Hence it follows inevitably, and in the simplest possible way, that if we follow our natural instincts without thought of books, rules, precedents, or any such educational impedimenta to a spontaneous and "sensible" result, we will in the following manner design the exterior of our tall office building—to wit:

Beginning with the first story, we give this a main entrance that attracts the eye to its location, and the remainder of the story we treat in a more or less liberal, expansive, sumptuous way—a way based exactly on the practical necessities, but expressed with a sentiment of largeness and freedom. The second story we treat in a similar way, but usually with milder pretension. Above this, throughout the indefinite number of typical office tiers, we take our cue from the individual cell, which requires a window with its separating pier, its sill and lintel, and we, without more ado, make them look all alike because they are all alike. This brings us to the attic, which, having no division into office-cells, and no special requirement for lighting, gives us the power to show by means of its broad expanse of wall, and its dominating weight and character, that which is the fact—namely, that the series of office tiers has come definitely to an end.

This may perhaps seem a bald result and a heartless, pessimistic way of stating it, but even so we certainly have advanced a most characteristic stage beyond the imagined sinister building of the speculator-engineer-builder combination. For the hand of the architect is now definitely felt in the decisive position at once taken, and the suggestion of a thoroughly sound, logical, coherent expression of the conditions is becoming apparent.

When I say the hand of the architect, I do not mean necessarily the accomplished and trained architect. I mean only a man with a strong, natural liking for buildings, and a disposition to shape them in what seems to his unaffected nature a direct and simple way. He will probably tread an innocent path from his problem to its solution, and therein he will show an enviable gift of logic. If he have some gift for form in detail, some feeling for form purely and simply as form, some love for that, his result in addition to its simple straightforward naturalness and completeness in general statement, will have something of the charm of sentiment.

However, thus far the results are only partial and tentative at best; relatively true, they are but superficial. We are doubtless right in our instinct but we must seek a fuller justification, a finer sanction, for it.

I assume now that in the study of our problem we have passed through the various stages of inquiry, as follows: 1st, the social basis of the demand for tall office buildings; 2nd, its literal material satisfaction; 3rd, the elevation of the question from considerations of literal planning, construction, and equipment, to the plane of elementary architecture as a direct outgrowth of sound, sensible building; 4th, the question again elevated from an elementary architecture to the beginnings of true architectural expression, through the addition of a certain quality and quantity of sentiment.

But our building may have all these in a considerable degree and yet be far from that adequate solution of the problem I am attempting to define. We must now heed the imperative voice of emotion.

It demands of us, what is the chief characteristic of the tall office building? And at once we answer, it is lofty. This loftiness is to the artist-nature its thrilling aspect. It is the very open organ-tone in its appeal. It must be in turn the dominant chord in his expression of it, the true excitant of his imagination. It must be tall, every inch of it tall. The force and power of altitude must be in it, the glory and pride of exaltation must be in it. It must be every inch a proud and soaring thing, rising in sheer exultation that from bottom to top it is a unit without a single dissenting line—that it is the new, the unexpected, the eloquent peroration of most bald, most sinister, most forbidding conditions.

The man who designs in this spirit and with the sense of responsibility to the generation he lives in must be no coward, no denier, no bookworm, no dilettante. He must live of his life and for his life in the fullest, most consummate sense. He must realize at once and with the grasp of inspiration that the problem of the tall office building is one of the most stupendous, one of the most magnificent opportunities that the Lord of Nature in His beneficence has ever offered to the proud spirit of man.

That this has not been perceived—indeed, has been flatly denied—is an exhibition of human perversity that must give us pause.

One more consideration. Let us now lift this question into the region of calm, philosophic observation. Let us seek a comprehensive, a final solution: let the problem indeed dissolve.

Certain critics, and very thoughtful ones, have advanced the theory that the true prototype of the tall office building is the classical column, consisting of base, shaft and capital—the moulded base of the column typical of the lower stories of our building, the plain or fluted shaft suggesting the monotonous, uninterrupted series of office-tiers, and the capital the completing power and luxuriance of the attic.

Other theorizers, assuming a mystical symbolism as a guide, quote the many trinities in nature and art, and the beauty and conclusiveness of such trinity in unity. They aver the beauty of prime numbers, the mysticism of the number three, the beauty of all things that are in three parts—to wit, the day, subdividing into morning, noon, and night; the limbs, the thorax, and the head, constituting the body. So they say, should the building be in three parts vertically, substantially as before, but for different motives.

Others, of purely intellectual temperament, hold that such a design should be in the nature of a logical statement; it should have a beginning, a middle, and an ending, each clearly defined—therefore again a building, as above, in three parts vertically.

Others, seeking their examples and justification in the vegetable kingdom, urge that such a design shall above all things be organic. They quote the suitable flower with its bunch of leaves at the earth, its long graceful stem, carrying the gorgeous single flower. They point to the pine-tree, its massy roots, its lithe, uninterrupted trunk, its tuft of green high in the air. Thus, they say, should be the design of the tall office building: again in three parts vertically.

Others still, more susceptible to the power of a unit than to the grace of a trinity, say that such a design should be struck out at a blow, as though by a blacksmith or by mighty Jove, or should be thought-born, as was Minerva, full grown. They accept the notion of a triple division as permissible and welcome, but non-essential. With them it is a subdivision of their unit: the unit does not come from the alliance of the three; they accept it without murmur, provided the subdivision does not disturb the sense of singleness and repose.

All of these critics and theorists agree, however, positively, unequivocally, in this, that the tall office building should not, must not, be made a field for the display of architectural knowledge in the encyclopaedic sense; that too much learning in this instance is fully as dangerous, as obnoxious, as too little learning; that miscellany is abhorrent to their sense; that the sixteen-story building must not consist of sixteen separate, distinct and unrelated buildings piled one upon the other until the top of the pile is reached.

To this latter folly I would not refer were it not the fact that nine out of every ten tall office buildings are designed in precisely this way in effect, not by the ignorant, but by the educated. It would seem indeed, as though the "trained" architect, when facing this problem, were beset at every story, or at most, every third or fourth story, by the hysterical dread lest he be in "bad form"; lest he be not bedecking his building with sufficiency of quotation from this, that, or the other "correct" building in some other land and some other time; lest he be not copious enough in the display of his wares; lest he betray, in short, a lack of resource. To loosen up the touch of this cramped and fidgety hand, to allow the nerves to calm, the brain to cool, to reflect equably, to reason naturally, seems beyond him; he lives, as it were, in a waking nightmare filled with the disjecta membra of architecture. The spectacle is not inspiriting.

As to the former and serious views held by discerning and thoughtful critics, I shall, with however much of regret, dissent from them for the purpose of this demonstration, for I regard them as secondary only, non-essential, and as touching not at all upon the vital spot, upon the quick of the entire matter, upon the true, the immovable philosophy of the architectural art.

This view let me now state, for it brings to the solution of the problem a final, comprehensive formula.

All things in nature have a shape, that is to say, a form, an outward semblance, that tells us what they are, that distinguishes them from ourselves and from each other.

Unfailingly in nature these shapes express the inner life, the native quality, of the animal, tree, bird, fish, that they present to us; they are so characteristic, so recognizable, that we say, simply, it is "natural" it should be so. Yet the moment we peer beneath this surface of things, the moment we look through the tranquil reflection of ourselves and the clouds above us, down into the clear, fluent, unfathomable depth of nature, how startling is the silence of it, how amazing the flow of life, how absorbing the mystery. Unceasingly the essence of things is taking shape in the matter of things, and this unspeakable process we call birth and growth. Awhile the spirit and the matter fade away together, and it is this that we call decadence, death. These two happenings seem jointed and interdependent, blended into one like a bubble and its iridescence, and they seem borne along upon a slowly moving air. This air is wonderful past all understanding.

Yet to the steadfast eye of one standing upon the shore of things, looking chiefly and most lovingly upon that side on which the sun shines and that we feel joyously to be life, the heart is ever gladdened by the beauty, the exquisite spontaneity, with which life seeks and takes on its forms in an accord perfectly responsive to its needs. It seems ever as though the life and the form were absolutely one and inseparable, so adequate is the sense of fulfillment.

Whether it be the sweeping eagle in his flight or the open apple-blossom, the toiling work-horse, the blithe swan, the branching oak, the winding stream at its base, the drifting clouds, over all the coursing sun, form ever follows function, and this is the law. Where function does not change form does not change. The granite rocks, the ever-brooding hills, remain for ages; the lightning lives, comes into shape, and dies in a twinkling.

It is the pervading law of all things organic, and inorganic, of all things physical and metaphysical, of all things human and all things superhuman, of all true manifestations of the head, of the heart, of the soul, that the life is recognizable in its expression, that form ever follows function. This is the law.

Shall we, then, daily violate this law in our art? Are we so decadent, so

CARL W. CONDIT

imbecile, so utterly weak of eyesight, that we cannot perceive this truth so simple, so very simple? Is it indeed a truth so transparent that we see through it but do not see it? Is it really then, a very marvelous thing, or is it rather so commonplace, so everyday, so near a thing to us, that we cannot perceive that the shape, form, outward expression, design or whatever we may choose, of the tall office building should in the very nature of things follow the functions of the building, and that where the function does not change, the form is not to change?

Does this not readily, clearly, and conclusively show that the lower one or two stories will take on a special character suited to the special needs, that the tiers of typical offices, having the same unchanging function, shall continue in the same unchanging form, and that as to the attic, specific and conclusive as it is in its very nature, its function shall equally be so in force, in significance, in continuity, in conclusiveness of outward expression? From this results, naturally, spontaneously, unwittingly, a three-part division, not from any theory, symbol, or fancied logic.

And thus the design of the tall office building takes its place with all other architectural types made when architecture, as has happened once in many years, was a living art. Witness the Greek temple, the Gothic cathedral, the medieval fortress.

And thus, when native instinct and sensibility shall govern the exercise of our beloved art; when the known law, the respected law, shall be that form ever follows function; when our architects shall cease struggling and prattling handcuffed and vainglorious in the asylum of a foreign school; when it is truly felt, cheerfully accepted, that this law opens up the airy sunshine of green fields, and gives to us a freedom that the very beauty and sumptuousness of the outworking of the law itself as exhibited in nature will deter any sane, any sensitive man from changing into license, when it becomes evident that we are merely speaking a foreign language with a noticeable American accent, whereas each and every architect in the land might, under the benign influence of this law, express in the simplest, most modest, most natural way that which it is in him to say; that he might really and would surely develop his own characteristic individuality, and that the architectural art with him would certainly become a living form of speech, a natural form of utterance, giving surcease to him and adding treasures small and great to the growing art of his land; when we know and feel that Nature is our friend, not our implacable enemy—that an afternoon in the country, an

569

hour by the sea, a full open view of one single day, through dawn, high noon, and twilight, will suggest to us so much that is rhythmical, deep, and eternal in the vast art of architecture, something so deep, so true, that all the narrow formalities, hard-and-fast rules, and strangling bonds of the schools cannot stifle it in us—then it may be proclaimed that we are on the high-road to a natural and satisfying art, an architecture that will soon become a fine art in the true, the best sense of the word, an art that will live because it will be of the people, for the people, and by the people.

Sullivan's essay was widely read during the decade following its publication in Lippincott's Magazine. We may assume this not only from the circulation which Lippincott's enjoyed among readers of serious periodical literature, but also from the fact that the paper was twice reprinted within ten years. Before the end of the century the architect's reputation had grown to national proportions. The great majority of his commissions came from Chicago, but in the decade of the 1890's he was designing buildings to be erected in New York, New Orleans, and Seattle, as well as in the cities of the Great Lakes and midwestern regions. He was acknowledged as the leading architect and philosopher of the Chicago movement; elsewhere, he was at least listened to with considerable respect. Yet the subsequent history of his brave and original document provides a clue to the fate of Sullivan's work and ideas. The two reprintings that followed within a few years of the original publication indicate that its ideas met an early acclaim. The reprinting of 1922, however, can only be regarded as a belated and ironic memorial to its author, now nearing death, poverty-stricken, forgotten by everyone save a few friends in the city he had made architecturally famous.

The influence of "The Tall Office Building" has been as ambiguous as the architect's interpretation was bound to be. The three-part vertical division that Sullivan proposed for the skyscraper was perfectly rational and was quickly accepted by many architects of the new office towers. This much was simple logic and provided an obviously sensible answer to the main utilitarian questions. But the ambiguity arose over the rival claims of functionalism and soaring height. The skyscraper architects of New York, who set the national pace, were unwilling to follow the organic principles of the Chicago school, preferring instead the eclectic approach of the nineteenth century. Within these limits, however, they were enthusiastic about exploring the possibilities of great height and found many ways to adapt the historical systems of ornament to an emphatic verticalism. The eclectic phase reached its culmination in Cass Gilbert's vivid design for the Woolworth Tower in New York (1911–13). In the skyscraper boom of the 1920's the derivative elements were gradually refined away until the architects reached the pure verticalism of Raymond Hood's Daily News Building in New York (1930), or Graham, Anderson, Probst and White's Field Building in Chicago (1934). But in these extreme forms we can see the confusion between creating true organic design and an obsession with stretching out height itself.

On the functional side Sullivan's ideas were brilliantly illustrated in a body of industrial and warehouse architecture that reached levels of remarkable power in the hands of the gifted Chicago architects. This strictly empirical approach spread from Chicago to other industrial centers. A highly refined factory architecture arose from the demands of the automotive industry in Detroit, where Albert Kahn transformed industrial requirements into the elegant and simple geometry of the modern curtain-wall factory. The high point of this development came with the power houses and other subsidiary buildings of the Tennessee Valley Authority, especially those erected during the hydroelectric phase of construction (1933–45). But even at the best this is technical and empirical form, and clearly does not possess the emotional expressiveness that Sullivan thought indispensable.

The question, then, of the precise influence of Sullivan's essay is not one that can be answered in clear-cut terms. If we consider in their entirety the norms that he laid down, we are forced to conclude that at least for the first third of the twentieth century American architecture was unprepared to explore fully the path he had opened. In the 1930's the new European ideas of Gropius and Le Corbusier began to gain headway in the United States. When large-scale building was resumed after the long hiatus of the Depression and World War II, the imported forms and associated technical innovations were in the ascendant. The revival of Sullivan's principles in commercial and public building did not come until the mid-century decade, and even now they appear in the work of only a small group of architects. The essential problem, again, is to avoid the two extremes of a mechanistic functionalism and a capricious self-expression—to find, in short, an organic union of technological necessities and emotional power. The most striking revival of Sullivan's program has come in Chicago itself, chiefly under the leadership of Mies van der Rohe and the Chicago office of Skidmore, Owings and Merrill. This work combines the clear statement of physical laws as they are embodied in scientific building technology with great dignity and power derived from the spatial and geometric possibilities of steel framing. In the delicate vertical tracery of van der Rohe's high buildings, especially, one finds the proud and soaring quality that so excited Sullivan's imagination. In the East, Louis I. Kahn has designed buildings which reveal a greater measure of the uninhibited emotionalism that Sullivan loved. Kahn possesses a remarkable faculty for combining a rational plan with a plastic self-expression of a highly personal but disciplined nature.

The contemporary Chicago work is close in actual appearance to that of the original Chicago school, while Kahn's designs seem remote from it in visual impact. Each offers us examples of varying degrees of emphasis in the prescription that Sullivan set forth, one tending toward the public and anonymous, the other toward the subjective and nonrational. But it is impossible to argue that the ideas presented in "The Tall Office Building" form the immediate basis for this body of work, or for any other comparable to it. Men as different in background, training, and talent as the German van der Rohe and the Philadelphian Kahn are not likely to have found in a Sullivan paper of 1896 the exclusive source of their inspiration. This underlying identity of thought and performance, surviving precariously for seventy years, tells us something more profound about the building arts of our time. Stripped of their rhetorical decoration and their peculiar emotional bias, Sullivan's key ideas are permanently valid and long ago entered into the mainstream of contemporary culture, where they eventually gained wide currency among the creative spirits of modern building.

William Jennings Bryan
"Cross of Gold" Speech
1896

EDITED BY RICHARD HOFSTADTER

William Jennings Bryan's "Cross of Gold" speech, delivered at the Democratic National Convention in Chicago on July 9, 1896, was probably the most effective speech in the history of American party politics. Bryan, then only thirty-six, had come to Chicago as a leader of the Nebraska delegation, but with the avowed intention of vaulting from this relatively obscure role into the presidential nomination. He was, to be sure, widely known in the party and had for some time been soliciting the support of delegates. He was also known in Congress as an eloquent speaker. But his hopes for the nomination seemed laughable to those to whom he confided them. He went to the convention with hardly any assets other than his fine voice and the outlines of this speech glimmering in his head, and he swept the convention by storm.

The great issue before the convention was whether the party should take its place behind President Cleveland and the conservative Democrats in a continued defense of the gold standard or yield to the fervent demand of the South and West for free coinage of silver at 16 to 1 as the remedy for depressed prices, unemployment, and the blight of depression. The question of the monetary standard, an important issue for twenty years, had come to a head with the panic and depression of 1893; it had been subjected to a continuous and heated debate since the summer of that year, when Cleveland, in a hard-fought defense of the

573

Treasury's gold reserve, had pushed through Congress the repeal of the Sherman Silver Purchase Act of 1890.

The circumstances under which the debate took place put Bryan in a favorable position. It is true that his first efforts at the convention were not auspicious. He had hardly arrived before he was engaged in a hard struggle, finally successful, to seat his Nebraska delegation against the opposition of gold delegates. He was unable to win serious consideration for the position of temporary chairman, which he had hoped to gain as a means of putting himself in a prominent spot, and a growing general awareness of his candidacy made him unthinkable as permanent chairman. Bryan hoped that he might still become chairman of the Committee on Resolutions, but this post he wisely yielded to the claims of the veteran silver Senator James K. Jones of Arkansas. Bryan himself, as a member of this committee, drafted the silver plank that touched off the great debate. His first stroke of good fortune came when Senator Jones asked him to conduct the defense of the platform. His second came when Senator "Pitchfork Ben" Tillman of South Carolina, who was eager to have time for a long speech, asked to be the first speaker among the silver advocates, thus leaving Bryan as the last, and possibly climactic, orator. His third came from the character of Tillman's speech itself, a rancorous performance so ill-conceived that its sectional aspersions had to be repudiated from the floor by other silver spokesmen. When Bryan rose to speak, therefore, he was left as the only effective spokesman of the silver cause. Three gold advocates had spoken with some persuasiveness, but they had poor voices, and at times were almost inaudible. The crowd leaned back in relief when Bryan began. He spoke in a splendidly calm and conciliatory manner, and his large, melodious voice could be heard without effort throughout the hall.

The speech itself was hardly an improvisation. In three years of debating and lecturing on the silver issue, Bryan had had ample opportunity to polish his arguments, to pick up and experiment with key phrases. Only a few days before, he had given a speech at Crete, Nebraska, which was a kind of dress rehearsal of some portions of the speech. In his Memoirs (still the best account of the occasion) he noted that his speech was extemporaneous only "in so far as the arrangement was concerned. No new arguments had been advanced and therefore no new answers were required."

No one dares quarrel with the simple strategy of Bryan's speech. Perceiving that the money question, faced head-on, was a thicket of *technicalities already all too familiar and well-argued, and that the members of his audience were not open to further persuasion on the merits of the issue, Bryan offered a speech designed to set the right tone —first, to soften the worst asperities of the family quarrel, but then firmly to assert the justice of the silver case and rally its adherents not around a sectional interest but on the common grounds of humanity.*

MR. CHAIRMAN AND GENTLEMEN OF THE CONVENTION:

I WOULD be presumptuous, indeed, to present myself against the distinguished gentlemen to whom you have listened if this were a mere measuring of abilities; but this is not a contest between persons. The humblest citizen in all the land, when clad in the armor of a righteous cause, is stronger than all the hosts of error. I come to speak to you in defense of a cause as holy as the cause of liberty—the cause of humanity.

When this debate is concluded, a motion will be made to lay upon the table the resolution offered in commendation of the administration, and also the resolution offered in condemnation of the administration. We object to bringing this question down to the level of persons. The individual is but an atom; he is born, he acts, he dies; but principles are eternal; and this has been a contest over a principle.

Never before in the history of this country has there been witnessed such a contest as that through which we have just passed. Never before in the history of American politics has a great issue been fought out as this issue has been, by the voters of a great party. On the fourth of March, 1895, a few Democrats, most of them members of Congress, issued an address to the Democrats of the nation, asserting that the money question was the paramount issue of the hour; declaring that a majority of the Democratic party had the right to control the action of the party on this paramount issue; and concluding with the request that the believers in the free coinage of silver in the Democratic party should organize, take charge of, and control the policy of the Democratic party. Three months later, at Memphis, an organization was perfected, and the silver Democrats went forth openly and courageously proclaiming their

The speech is taken from Bryan's book *The First Battle* (Chicago: W. B. Conkey Company, 1896), pp. 199–206. Brackets appear in the original.

belief, and declaring that, if successful, they would crystallize into a platform the declaration which they had made. They began the conflict. With a zeal approaching the zeal which inspired the crusaders who followed Peter the Hermit, our silver Democrats went forth from victory unto victory until they are now assembled, not to discuss, not to debate, but to enter up the judgment already rendered by the plain people of this country. In this contest brother has been arrayed against brother, father against son. The warmest ties of love, acquaintance and association have been disregarded; old leaders have been cast aside when they have refused to give expression to the sentiments of those whom they would lead, and new leaders have sprung up to give direction to this cause of truth. Thus has the contest been waged, and we have assembled here under as binding and solemn instructions as were ever imposed upon representatives of the people.

We do not come as individuals. As individuals we might have been glad to compliment the gentleman from New York [Senator Hill] but we know that the people for whom we speak would never be willing to put him in a position where he could thwart the will of the Democratic party. I say it was not a question of persons; it was a question of principle, and it is not with gladness, my friends, that we find ourselves brought into conflict with those who are now arrayed on the other side.

The gentleman who preceded me [ex-Governor Russell] spoke of the State of Massachusetts; let me assure him that not one present in all this convention entertains the least hostility to the people of the State of Massachusetts, but we stand here representing people who are the equals, before the law, of the greatest citizens in the State of Massachusetts. When you [turning to the gold delegates] come before us and tell us that we are about to disturb your business interests, we reply that you have disturbed our business interests by your course.

We say to you that you have made the definition of a business man too limited in its application. The man who is employed for wages is as much a business man as his employer; the attorney in a country town is as much a business man as the corporation counsel in a great metropolis; the merchant at the cross-roads store is as much a business man as the merchant of New York; the farmer who goes forth in the morning and toils all day—who begins in the spring and toils all summer—and who by the application of brain and muscle to the natural resources of the country creates wealth, is as much a business man as the man who goes upon the board of trade and bets upon the price of grain; the miners who go down a thousand feet into the earth, or climb two thousand feet upon the cliffs, and bring forth from their hiding places the precious metals to be poured into the channels of trade are as much business men as the few financial magnates who, in a back room, corner the money of the world. We come to speak for this broader class of business men.

Ah, my friends, we say not one word against those who live upon the Atlantic coast, but the hardy pioneers who have braved all the dangers of the wilderness, who have made the desert to blossom as the rose—the pioneers away out there [pointing to the West], who rear their children near to Nature's heart, where they can mingle their voices with the voices of the birds—out there where they have erected schoolhouses for the education of their young, churches where they praise their Creator, and cemeteries where rest the ashes of their dead—these people, we say, are as deserving of the consideration of our party as any people in this country. It is for these that we speak. We do not come as aggressors. Our war is not a war of conquest; we are fighting in the defense of our homes, our families, and posterity. We have petitioned, and our petitions have been scorned; we have entreated, and our entreaties have been disregarded; we have begged, and they have mocked when our calamity came. We beg no longer; we entreat no more; we petition no more. We defy them.

The gentleman from Wisconsin has said that he fears a Robespierre. My friends, in this land of the free you need not fear that a tyrant will spring up from among the people. What we need is an Andrew Jackson to stand, as Jackson stood, against the encroachments of organized wealth.

They tell us that this platform was made to catch votes. We reply to them that changing conditions make new issues; that the principles upon which Democracy rests are as everlasting as the hills, but that they must be applied to new conditions as they arise. Conditions have arisen, and we are here to meet those conditions. They tell us that the income tax ought not to be brought in here; that it is a new idea. They criticize us for our criticism of the Supreme Court of the United States. My friends, we have not criticized; we have simply called attention to what you already know. If you want criticisms, read the dissenting opinions of the court. There you will find criticisms. They say that we passed an unconstitutional law; we deny it. The income tax law was not unconstitutional when it was passed; it was not unconstitutional when it went before the Supreme Court for the first time; it did not become unconstitutional until one of the judges changed his mind, and we cannot be expected to know when a judge will change his mind. The income tax is just. It simply intends to put the burdens of government justly upon the backs of the people. I am in favor of an income tax. When I find a man who is not willing to bear his share of the burdens of the government which protects him, I find a man who is unworthy to enjoy the blessings of a government like ours.

They say that we are opposing national bank currency; it is true. If you will read what Thomas Benton said, you will find he said that, in searching history, he could find but one parallel to Andrew Jackson; that was Cicero, who destroyed the conspiracy of Cataline and saved Rome. Benton said that Cicero only did for Rome what Jackson did for us when he destroyed the bank conspiracy and saved America. We say in our platform that we believe that the right to coin and issue money is a function of government. We believe it. We believe that it is a part of sovereignty, and can no more with safety be delegated to private individuals than we could afford to delegate to private individuals the power to make penal statutes or levy taxes. Mr. Jefferson, who was once regarded as good Democratic authority, seems to have differed in opinion from the gentleman who has addressed us on the part of the minority. Those who are opposed to this proposition tell us that the issue of paper money is a function of the bank, and that the Government ought to go out of the banking business. I stand with Jefferson rather than with them, and tell them, as he did, that the issue of money is a function of government, and that the banks ought to go out of the governing business.

They complain about the plank which declares against life tenure in office. They have tried to strain it to mean that which it does not mean. What we oppose by that plank is the life tenure which is being built up in Washington, and which excludes from participation in official benefits the humbler members of society.

Let me call your attention to two or three important things. The gentleman from New York says that he will propose an amendment to the platform providing that the proposed change in our monetary system shall not affect contracts already made. Let me remind you that there is no intention of affecting those contracts which according to present laws are made payable in gold; but if he means to say that we cannot change our monetary system without protecting those who have loaned money before the change was made, I desire to ask him where, in law or in morals, he can find justification for not protecting the debtors when the act of 1873 was passed, if he now insists that we must protect the creditors.

He says he will also propose an amendment which will provide for the suspension of free coinage if we fail to maintain the party within a year. We reply that when we advocate a policy which we believe will be successful, we are not compelled to raise a doubt as to our own sincerity by suggesting what we shall do if we fail. I ask him, if he would apply his logic to us, why he does not apply it to himself. He says he wants this country to try to secure an international agreement. Why does he not tell us what he is going to do if he fails to secure an international agreement? There is more reason for him to do that than there is for us to provide against the failure to maintain the parity. Our opponents have tried for twenty years to secure an international agreement, and those are waiting for it most patiently who do not want it at all.

And now, my friends, let me come to the paramount issue. If they ask us why it is that we say more on the money question than we say upon the tariff question, I reply that, if protection has slain its thousands, the gold standard has slain its tens of thousands. If they ask us why we do not embody in our platform all the things that we believe in, we reply that when we have restored the money of the Constitution all other necessary reforms will be possible; but that until this is done there is no other reform that can be accomplished.

Why is it that within three months such a change has come over the country? Three months ago, when it was confidently asserted that those who believe in the gold standard would frame our platform and nominate our candidates, even the advocates of the gold standard did not think that we could elect a president. And they had good reason for their doubt, because there is scarcely a State here today asking for the gold standard which is not in the absolute control of the Republican party. But note the change. Mr. McKinley was nominated at St. Louis upon a platform which declared for the maintenance of the gold standard until it can be changed into bimetallism by international agreement. Mr. McKinley was the most popular man among the Republicans, and three months ago everybody in the Republican party prophesied his election. How is it today? Why, the man who was once pleased to think that he looked like Napoleon—that man shudders today when he remembers that he was nominated on the anniversary of the battle of Waterloo. Not only that, but as he listens he can hear with ever-increasing distinctness the sound of the waves as they beat upon the lonely shores of St. Helena.

Why this change? Ah, my friends, is not the reason for the change evident to any one who will look at the matter? No private character, however pure, no personal popularity, however great, can protect from the avenging wrath of an indignant people a man who will declare that he is in favor of fastening the gold standard upon this country, or who is willing to surrender the right of self-government and place the legislative control of our affairs in the hands of foreign potentates and powers.

We go forth confident that we shall win. Why? Because upon the paramount issue of this campaign there is not a spot of ground upon which the enemy will dare to challenge battle. If they tell us that the gold standard is a good thing, we shall point to their platform and tell them that their platform pledges the party to get rid of the gold standard and substitute bimetallism. If the gold standard is a good thing, why try to get rid of it? I call your attention to the fact that some of the very people who are in this convention today and who tell us that we ought to declare in favor of international bimetallism—thereby declaring that the gold standard is wrong and that the principle of bimetallism is better—these very people four months ago were open and avowed advocates of the gold standard, and were then telling us that we could not legislate two metals together, even with the aid of all the world. If the gold standard is a good thing, we ought to declare in favor of its retention and not in favor of abandoning it; and if the gold standard is a bad thing why should we wait until other nations are willing to help us to let go? Here is the line of battle, and we care not upon which issue they force the fight; we are prepared to meet them on either issue or on both. If they tell us that the gold standard is the standard of civilization, we reply to them that this, the most enlightened of all the nations of the earth, has never declared for a gold standard and that both the great parties this year are declaring against it. If the gold standard is the standard of civilization, why, my friends, should we not have it? If they come to meet us on that issue we can present the history of our nation. More than that; we can tell them that they will search the pages of history in vain to find a single instance where the common people of any land have ever declared themselves in favor of the gold standard. They can find where the holders of the fixed investments have declared for a gold standard, but not where the masses have.

Mr. Carlisle said in 1878 that this was a struggle between "the idle holders of idle capital" and "the struggling masses, who produce the wealth and pay the taxes of the country;" and, my friends, the question we are to decide is: Upon which side will the Democratic party fight; upon the side of "the idle holders of idle capital" or upon the side of "the struggling masses?" That is the question which the party must answer first, and then it must be answered by each individual hereafter. The sympathies of the Democratic party, as shown by the platform, are on the side of the struggling masses who have ever been the foundation of the Democratic party. There are two ideas of government. There are those who believe that, if you will only legislate to make the well-to-do prosperous, their prosperity will leak through on those below. The Democratic idea, however, has been that if you legislate to make the masses prosperous, their prosperity will find its way up through every class which rests upon them.

You come to us and tell us that the great cities are in favor of the gold standard; we reply that the great cities rest upon our broad and fertile prairies. Burn down your cities and leave our farms, and your cities will spring up again as if by magic; but destroy our farms and the grass will grow in the streets of every city in the country.

My friends, we declare that this nation is able to legislate for its own people on every question, without waiting for the aid or consent of any other nation on earth; and upon that issue we expect to carry every State in the Union. I shall not slander the inhabitants of the fair State of Massachusetts nor the inhabitants of the State of New York by saying that, when they are confronted with the proposition, they will declare that this nation is not able to attend to its own business. It is the issue of 1776 over again. Our ancestors, when but three millions in number, had the courage to declare their political independence of every other nation; shall we, their descendants, when we have grown to seventy millions, declare that we are less independent than our forefathers? No, my friends, that will never be the verdict of our people. Therefore, we care not upon what lines the battle is fought. If they say bimetallism is good, but that we cannot have it until other nations help us, we reply that, instead of having a gold standard because England has, we will restore bimetallism, and then let England have bimetallism because the United States has it. If they dare to come out in the open field and defend the gold standard as a good thing, we will fight them to the uttermost.

Having behind us the producing masses of this nation and the world, supported by the commercial interests, the laboring interests, and the toilers everywhere, we will answer their demand for a gold standard by saying to them: You shall not press down upon the brow of labor this crown of thorns, you shall not crucify mankind upon a cross of gold.

"The audience," Bryan recalled of the immediate response to his address, "acted like a trained choir—in fact, I thought of a choir as I noticed how instantaneously and in unison they responded to each point made." He remembered, also, that they "seemed to rise and sit down as one man." When his last words had echoed through the hall, the convention dissolved in an uproar that went on for an hour. Although many of the eastern gold men sat immobile, there were some, even among them, who rose to bellow their appreciation of Bryan's performance. The next day he was nominated on the fifth ballot. Without influential backers or large funds, with the aid only of his golden tongue, his political shrewdness, and a few strokes of luck, he had won his objective. He had come to Chicago with $100, and when he and Mrs. Bryan checked out of their modest quarters in the Clifton House, he held the presidential nomination of his party and still had $40 in his pocket.

Immediate reactions to Bryan were mixed. Mark Hanna, Republican campaign manager, gleefully noted that "He's talking Silver all the time, and that's where we've got him." Hanna realized, as Bryan and his followers apparently did not, that "Free Silver" meant little to urban workingmen. Republican orators campaigned on the theme that America needed not an increase of coin, but an increase of confidence; not more money in circulation, but more jobs for the workers. Many Populist reformers saw in Bryan's nomination the wreckage of the farmer-labor alliance for which they had hoped. "Free silver is the cow-bird of the reform movement," claimed Henry Demarest Lloyd. "It waited till the nest had been built by the sacrifices and labor of others, and then it laid its eggs in it, pushing out the others which it smashed on the ground." When the Populist Party dutifully echoed the Democratic nomination, many urban radicals deserted. Lloyd proved correct. Although Bryan waged a vigorous campaign, every state east of the Mississippi and north of the Ohio went to McKinley. Within four years the issue of "Free Cuba" replaced "Free Silver" in national politics. Bryan had unconsciously prophesied the political crucifixion of agrarian Populism in his "Cross of Gold" speech.

If the issues of the speech soon died out as meaningful propaganda, the attitudes of mind which it represented lived on. Agrarian rhetoric championed the prohibition movement of later years, fought the battles of fundamentalist religion versus the forces of evolution in the famous Scopes trial (1925), and eventually lobbied successfully in New Deal days to establish the principle of parity price levels for agriculture. Commercial farmers eventually were subsidized by the products of the industrial America that Bryan once had denounced. Populism, as portrayed in the "Cross of Gold" speech, was only another episode in the well-established tradition of American entrepreneurial radicalism. Bryan's address marked the first tentative step in the direction of effective agrarian organization.

The speech has become a standard point of reference in the history of the American political mind, the one document to which historians of the silver controversy have been sure to refer, and a set piece of American oratory. Also, it remains significant in reconstructing the emotional content of agrarian complaints against the new American industrial order. On another occasion, Bryan argued that "the great political questions are in their final analysis great moral questions." Bryanism and Populism were cries of moral outrage against both the real and the imagined evils of urban America. A major issue of the "Cross of Gold" speech was who should control the government, the urban or the rural, the financial or the agrarian interests? In today's terms, the controversy is the "one man, one vote" problem. Does the city rule, or do "upstate" and "downstate" areas dominate our political life? The early sentiments voiced by Bryan remain active. Many people today share in the spirit of Vachel Lindsay's bombastic rhetoric:

> Prairie avenger, mountain lion,
> Bryan, Bryan, Bryan, Bryan,
> Gigantic troubadour, speaking like a siege gun,
> Smashing Plymouth Rock with his boulders from the West.

In the short run, Bryan and the Populists were defeated. But in the long run, the crusade given impetus by the "Cross of Gold" speech marches on.

William Allen White
What's the Matter with Kansas?
1896

EDITED BY WALTER JOHNSON

It was hot—hot as only Kansas can be under the unrelenting August sun. Politics were boiling as well in Emporia, Kansas. The nomination of thirty-six-year-old William Jennings Bryan as the Democratic-Populist candidate for the Presidency was being assailed by the twenty-eight-year-old editor of the Emporia Gazette as a threat to true "Americanism."

Bryan voiced the protests of an older rural America against the increasing dominance of a new industrial-urban society. Until the closing decade of the nineteenth century, a fairly democratic society had been able to maintain itself largely as a result of the unlimited resources of a land of plenty. All that had been needed was freedom for the individual to exploit these rich resources. But by the stormy nineties, pioneer America had disappeared. And unlimited freedom for the individual in this changed situation now often meant the exploitation of others, an exploitation that was to be seen in its starkest form in the slums, the poverty, and the unemployment of the heartbreaking years from 1893 to 1896.

The silver-tongued orator of the Platte contended that, if democracy were to survive, the federal government must regulate the menace to freedom by a minority in order to guarantee that all would still have equality of opportunity. To William Allen White—imbued with the beliefs of the Gospel of Wealth that governments existed only to protect property and that unemployment, poverty, and slums were individual

584

responsibilities—the Democratic-Populist ticket of Bryan meant the destruction of the American way of life. "In this American government," he wrote in an editorial, "paternalism plays no part. It is every man for himself. It is a free for all, and in the end the keenest, most frugal, and most industrious win."

All that summer of '96 White argued with Vernon L. Parrington, then teaching at the College of Emporia, who tried to explain that urban-industrialism had altered the American scene and that new ideas were necessary to cope with the new situations. White was adamant. As he denounced the Democrats and the Populists in his daily editorials, they retaliated by parading through Emporia's dusty streets carrying signs picturing William Allen White as a jackass.

Then, one day in mid-August, as White was returning from the Post Office, a group of Populists began to argue with him. The thermometer stood at 107 that morning. The red-faced editor was in no mood to debate the campaign in the stifling heat, but the Populists were incensed over the Gazette's editorials. Finally he broke away, with his brain—and his emotions—sizzling. When he reached the Gazette office, the editorial page needed more copy. He sat down at his old roll-top desk and, with his big pen scratching across the paper, he ridiculed Bryan, the Democrats, and the Populists in slashing, picturesque language.

TODAY the Kansas department of agriculture sent out a statement which indicates that Kansas has gained less than two thousand people in the past year. There are about 125,000 families in the state, and there were about 10,000 babies born in Kansas, and yet so many people have left the state that the natural increase is cut down to less than 2,000 net.

This has been going on for eight years.

If there had been a high brick wall around the state eight years ago, and not a soul had been admitted or permitted to leave, Kansas would be a half million souls better off than she is today. And yet the nation has increased in population. In five years ten million people have been

---

The text is taken from the *Emporia Gazette*, August 16, 1896.

added to the national population, yet instead of gaining a share of this—say, half a million—Kansas has apparently been a plague spot and, in the very garden of the world, has lost population by the ten thousands every year.

Not only has she lost population, but she has lost wealth. Every moneyed man in the state who could get out without great loss has gone. Every month in every community sees someone who has a little money pick up and leave the state. This has been going on for eight years. Money is being drained out all the time. In towns where ten years ago there were three or four or half a dozen money-lending concerns, stimulating industry by furnishing capital, there is now none, or one or two that are looking after the interests and principal already outstanding.

No one brings any money into Kansas any more. What community knows over one or two men who have moved in with more than $5,000 in the past three years. And what community cannot count half a score of men in that time who have left, taking all the money they could scrape together.

Yet the nation has grown rich. Other states have increased in population and wealth—other neighboring states. Missouri has gained nearly two million, while Kansas has been losing half a million. Nebraska has gained in wealth and in population while Kansas has gone downhill. Colorado has gained in every way, while Kansas has lost in every way since 1888.

What is the matter with Kansas?

There is no substantial city in the state. Every big town save one has lost in population. Yet Kansas City, Omaha, Lincoln, St. Louis, Denver, Colorado Springs, Sedalia, Des Moines, the cities of the Dakotas, St. Paul and Minneapolis—all cities and towns in the West, have steadily grown.

Take up the Government Blue Book and you will see that Kansas is virtually off the map. Two or three little scabby consular places in yellow fever stricken communities that do not aggregate ten thousand dollars a year is all the recognition Kansas has. Nebraska draws about one hundred thousand dollars; little old North Dakota draws fifty thousand dollars; Oklahoma doubles Kansas; Missouri leaves her a thousand miles behind; Colorado is almost seven times greater than Kansas—the whole west is ahead of Kansas.

Take it by any standard you please, Kansas is not in it.

Go east and you hear them laugh at Kansas; go west and they sneer at her; go south and they "cuss" her; go north and they have forgotten her. Go into any crowd of intelligent people gathered anywhere on the globe, and you will find the Kansas man on the defensive. The newspaper columns and magazines once devoted to praise of the state, to boastful facts and startling figures concerning her resources, are now filled with cartoons, jibes and Pefferian speeches. Kansas just naturally isn't in the civilized world. She has traded places with Arkansas and Timbuctoo.

What's the matter with Kansas?

We all know; yet here we are at it again. We have an old mossback Jacksonian who snorts and howls because there is a bathtub in the State house; we are running that old jay for governor. We have another shabby, wild-eyed, rattle-brained fanatic who has said openly in a dozen speeches that "the rights of the user are paramount to the rights of the owner"; we are running him for chief justice, so that capital will come tumbling over itself to get into the state. We have raked the ash heap of human failure in the state and found an old hoop skirt of a man who has failed as a businessman, who has failed as an editor, who has failed as a preacher, and we are going to run him for congressman-at-large. He will help the looks of the Kansas delegation in Washington. Then we have discovered a kid without a law practice and have decided to vote for him as attorney general. Then, for fear some hint that the state had become respectable might percolate through the civilized portions of the nation, we have decided to send three or four harpies out lecturing, telling the people that Kansas is raising hell and letting the corn go to weeds.

Oh, this is a state to be proud of! We are a people who can hold up our heads! What we need here is less money, less capital, fewer white shirts and brains, fewer men with business judgment, and more of these fellows who boast that they are "just ordinary old clodhoppers, but that they know more in a minute about finance than John Sherman"; we need more men who are "posted," who can bellow about the crime of '73, who hate prosperity, and who think that because a man believes in national honor, that he is a tool of Wall street. We have had a few of them—some hundred fifty thousand—but we want more.

We need several thousand gibbering idiots to scream about the "Great Red Dragon" of Lombard street. We don't need population, we don't need wealth, we don't need well-dressed men on the streets; we don't need standing in the nation; we don't need cities on these fertile prairies; you bet we don't! What we are after is the money power.

Because we have become poorer and ornerier and meaner than a spavined, distempered mule, we, the people of Kansas, propose to kick; we don't care to build up, we wish to tear down.

"There are two ideas of government," said our noble Bryan at Chicago. "There are those who believe that if you just legislate to make the well-to-do prosperous, their prosperity will leak through on those below. The Democratic idea has been that if you legislate to make the masses prosperous their prosperity will find its way up and through every class and rest upon us."

That's the stuff! Give the prosperous man the dickens! Legislate the thriftless into ease, whack the stuffing out of the creditors and tell the debtor who borrowed money five years ago when money in circulation was more general than it is now, that the contraction of currency gives him a right to repudiate.

Whoop it up for the ragged trousers; put the lazy, greasy fizzle, who can't pay his debts on an altar and bow down and worship him. Let the state ideal be high. What we need is not the respect of our fellow men, but a chance to get something for nothing.

Oh, yes, Kansas is a great state. Here are people fleeing from it by the score every day, capital going out of the state by the hundreds of dollars; and every industry except farming paralyzed, and that crippled, because its products have to go across the ocean before they can find a laboring man at work who can afford to buy them. Let's don't stop this year. Let's drive all the decent, self-respecting men out of the state. Let's keep the old clodhoppers who know it all. Let's encourage the man who is "posted". He can talk, and what we need is not mill hands to eat our meat, nor factory hands to eat our wheat, nor cities to oppress the farmer by consuming his butter and eggs and chickens and produce; what Kansas needs is men who can talk, who have large leisure to argue the currency question while their wives wait at home for that nickel's worth of bluing.

What's the matter with Kansas?

Nothing under the shining sun. She is losing wealth, population and standing. She has got her statesmen, and the money power is afraid of her. Kansas is all right. She has started in to raise hell, as Mrs. Lease advised, and she seems to have an over-production. But that doesn't matter. Kansas never did believe in diversified crops. Kansas is all right. There is absolutely nothing wrong with Kansas. "Every prospect pleases and only man is vile."

White's biting, sarcastic language in "What's the Matter with Kansas?" expressed views held by millions of his fellow citizens. H. H. Kohlsaat, publisher of the Chicago Times-Herald and Evening Post, reprinted the editorial, explaining to his readers: "This is one of the most bitterly ironical arraignments of the shiftless spirit that has handicapped that rich state." The New York Sun followed suit and then Mark Hanna, chairman of the Republican National Committee, had it distributed across the nation as a campaign document. And White was deeply flattered when his political idol, Thomas B. Reed, speaking in the House of Representatives, wrote him on September 17, 1896: "Would you have the goodness to present to the author of 'The Matter With Kansas' my personal thanks. I have not seen as much sense in one column in a dozen years."

Yet in just a few years the young conservative editor of the Emporia Gazette was to become a loyal supporter and publicist of Theodore Roosevelt's attack on the "malefactors of great wealth." And he would join T. R. in 1912 to do battle for the Lord and the Bull Moose party. Roosevelt's New Nationalism—profoundly influenced by Herbert Croly's book, The Promise of American Life—was a far more comprehensive demand for enlarging the power of the federal government to regulate the economy than that of Bryan and the Populists. As White himself said many years later: "All we Progressives did was catch the Populists in swimming and steal all their clothing except the frayed underdrawers of Free Silver."

The Progressive Era from 1901 to World War I was a period of rapid readjustment in American attitudes. Under the leadership of Theodore Roosevelt, Woodrow Wilson, Senator Robert M. La Follette, Governor Hiram Johnson, and a host of others, and influenced by the "muckrake" writings of Lincoln Steffens, Ida Tarbell, and Ray Stannard Baker, and by the novels of Winston Churchill, Upton Sinclair, and William Allen White, millions of middle-class citizens became convinced that unlimited freedom for the individual to amass great wealth and wield immense political power had become a threat to the continuation of American democracy. To counteract private power on a scale unheard of before in the United States, these progressive-minded citizens supported the expansion of governmental power to curb the misuse of private power.

Although the now-famous editor of the Emporia Gazette no longer believed in the ideas of the Gospel of Wealth as he had expressed them in "What's the Matter with Kansas?" many of these ideas survived the

Progressive Era and occupied a prominent place in the decade of the 1920's. Certainly Calvin Coolidge, who epitomized the political thinking of the prosperous twenties, found the Gospel of Wealth most congenial, as did the large majority of citizens who supported him.

But another economic depression—even more serious than that of the 1890's—shook the faith of the majority in the doctrine of strictly limited governmental power. Nevertheless, despite the social and political changes of the era of the New Deal, some Americans have continued to have a deep, abiding faith in many of the ideas of the Gospel of Wealth and a contempt for social legislation. Such legislation, in their opinion, transports "the thriftless into ease," it "whacks the stuffings out of the creditors," and offers a "chance to get something for nothing." It is significant that, until his death in 1944, William Allen White received thousands of requests yearly for copies of his famed editorial—requests which were invariably met from the large stack of reprints in the Gazette office.

During the 1950's a number of writers—both of a conservative and a liberal bent—charged the Populists with being, among other things, irrational, anti-intellectual, antiforeign, and anti-Semitic demagogues. William Allen White never accused the Populists of being anti-Jewish or antiforeign, but such phrases as "old mossback Jacksonian who snorts and howls," "shabby, wild-eyed, rattle-brained fanatic," and "gibbering idiots" helped shape a mythology about the Populists which some later writers have embellished.

Contempt for the unsuccessful, so blatantly expressed in "What's the Matter with Kansas?" has been a deep current in American thinking. The followers of Theodore Roosevelt, Woodrow Wilson, Franklin D. Roosevelt, Harry S Truman, and John F. Kennedy have been willing through governmental legislation and regulation to help protect people from exploitation and to aid the victims of unforeseen economic disasters to regain the opportunity to forge ahead. But they have not been inclined, any more than their conservative opponents, to put "the lazy, greasy fizzle who can't pay his debts on an altar and bow down and worship him."

Although William Allen White's scathing editorial is an overdrawn picture of the Populists, it reflects much of the thinking of the 1890's. And its belief in the value of hard work, in the necessity of individual initiative, and in the importance of being successful are still deeply ingrained in the American conscience.

Oliver Wendell Holmes, Jr.
The Path of the Law
1897

EDITED BY LON L. FULLER

"The Path of the Law" was originally an oration in the sense that term bore when it could be used without irony or hint of disparagement. It was indeed, in the language of the time, an elegant oration. The date was January 8, 1897; the occasion was the dedication of a new building of the Boston University School of Law. Holmes was then fifty-five and had been a member of the Supreme Judicial Court of Massachusetts for fourteen years. Some five years later President Theodore Roosevelt appointed him to the Supreme Court of the United States, where he served for thirty years. It has truly been said of him that he is the only American jurist who competes with John Marshall for the superlative. There can be no doubt that the most familiar summing up of his thought is to be found in "The Path of the Law."

The course of Holmes's intellectual development prior to "The Path of the Law" makes it plain that "The Path" is best understood as a reaction against two strains of legal thought current in Holmes's time which he found thoroughly uncongenial.

The first of these reveals its influence quite plainly in the animadversions against "logic" with which Part II of "The Path" is sprinkled. During the period from about 1870 to 1920, it was quite common to encounter in legal discussions statements like these: An offer is by its very nature revocable. It would be a violation of logic to permit a person who is not a party to a contract to sue on it. The legal nature of a claim to damages does not permit an assignment of it. Holmes himself once described this method by saying that the schools "take their premises on inspiration and then use logic as the only tool to develop the results."

The other object of Holmes's intellectual aversion lay in the "will theory," a theory that tended to rest legal responsibility not on what a defendant did, but on what he "willed." Thus, a contractual promisor was held to his promise because he "willed" to be held, or a criminal was punished because he "willed" an evil act. Holmes saw in this kind of reasoning a confusion of morality and law, and he set about in Part I to remove that confusion.

A remarkable amalgam of abstract logic and the will theory can be found in the writings of Christopher Columbus Langdell, Dean of the Harvard Law School from 1870 to 1895. In Langdell's day it had been pretty well established, for sound commercial reasons, that the posted acceptance of an offer to enter a contract is effective at the moment of posting, and before it reaches the mind, or even the mail slot, of the offeror. Since this rule imposed a contract on the parties before their wills had been brought together by a completed circuit, Langdell condemned the rule as a violation of proper legal reasoning. In response to an argument that the rule in question best served "the purposes of substantial justice, and the interests of contracting parties as understood by themselves," Langdell replied, "The true answer to this argument is, that it is irrelevant," though, to be sure, he continued with a half-hearted and highly abstract attempt to demonstrate that the rule in question did in fact serve badly the needs of commerce.

To the mental torment that such an argument was certain to inflict on Holmes, there was added another dimension. Having taught himself German, Holmes became exposed to the Teutonic version of Langdellian logic. In this version, what might in an American have been dismissed as an innocent naiveté, appeared now clothed with a cosmic profundity that made it doubly offensive to one of Holmes's skeptical temper.

One influence that probably shaped Holmes's thought affirmatively was the positivistic philosophy of science associated with the names of Bacon, Comte, Mach, Poincaré, and Pearson. There is certainly a close affinity between Holmes's predictive theory of law and a view that asks of the scientist not that he understand nature, but that he simply set about observing and charting her regularities. Holmes himself, after reading Pearson's Grammar of Science, wrote to Pollock that it "hits my way of thinking better than books of philosophy." But this acquaintance with

Pearson came some nine years after "The Path of the Law." Since there is no evidence that Holmes was ever a close student of the philosophy of science, it seems likely that we are dealing not with anything like a direct influence, but with independent expressions of a generally prevailing intellectual mood.

It was no accident that Holmes seized the occasion he did for presenting the thoughts of "The Path of the Law." A friend, Melville M. Bigelow, had been a leading figure in the creation of the Boston University School of Law. With Holmes he shared a tough, Darwinian approach to social phenomena. Bigelow's general conception of law was expressed in 1906 in a book with a curious but significant title, Centralization in the Law. This book urged a "scientific method in law and education." It declared:

The conception of law which the Faculty of the Boston University Law School stands for is that the law is the expression, more or less deflected by opposition, of the dominant force in society. . . . It follows from the view that law is the resultant of actual, conflicting forces in society, that the notion of abstract, eternal principles as a governing power, with their author the external sovereign, must go.

The transition from this passage to Holmes's own words is an easy one.

I

WHEN we study law we are not studying a mystery but a well known profession. We are studying what we shall want in order to appear before judges, or to advise people in such a way as to keep them out of court. The reason why it is a profession, why people will pay lawyers to argue for them or to advise them, is that in societies like ours the command of the public force is intrusted to the judges in certain cases, and the whole power of the state will be put forth, if necessary, to carry out their judgments and decrees. People want to know under what circumstances and how far they will run the risk of

---

"The Path of the Law" first appeared in print as an article in the *Harvard Law Review*, X (1897), 457 ff. As it appears here it has been abridged by about one half. Commentators have remarked that the article is really divided into two distinct parts; Roman numerals have been inserted to make this division plain. In Holmes's own words, the first part deals with "the limits of the law," the second with "the forces which determine its content and its growth."

coming against what is so much stronger than themselves, and hence it becomes a business to find out when this danger is to be feared. The object of our study, then, is prediction, the prediction of the incidence of the public force through the instrumentality of the courts.

The means of the study are a body of reports, of treatises, and of statutes, in this country and in England, extending back for six hundred years, and now increasing annually by hundreds. In these sibylline leaves are gathered the scattered prophecies of the past upon the cases in which the axe will fall. These are what properly have been called the oracles of the law. Far the most important and pretty nearly the whole meaning of every new effort of legal thought is to make these prophecies more precise, and to generalize them into a thoroughly connected system. The process is one, from a lawyer's statement of a case, eliminating as it does all the dramatic elements with which his client's story has clothed it, and retaining only the facts of legal import, up to the final analyses and abstract universals of theoretic jurisprudence. The reason why a lawyer does not mention that his client wore a white hat when he made a contract, while Mrs. Quickly would be sure to dwell upon it along with the parcel gilt goblet and the sea-coal fire, is that he foresees that the public force will act in the same way whatever his client had upon his head. It is to make the prophecies easier to be remembered and to be understood that the teachings of the decisions of the past are put into general propositions and gathered into text-books, or that statutes are passed in a general form. The primary rights and duties with which jurisprudence busies itself again are nothing but prophecies. One of the many evil effects of the confusion between legal and moral ideas, about which I shall have something to say in a moment, is that theory is apt to get the cart before the horse, and to consider the right or the duty as something existing apart from and independent of the consequences of its breach, to which certain sanctions are added afterward. But, as I shall try to show, a legal duty so called is nothing but a prediction that if a man does or omits certain things he will be made to suffer in this or that way by judgment of the court;—and so of a legal right. . . .

I wish, if I can, to lay down some first principles for the study of this body of dogma or systematized prediction which we call the law, for men who want to use it as the instrument of their business to enable them to prophesy in their turn, and, as bearing upon the study, I wish to point out an ideal which as yet our law has not attained.

The first thing for a business-like understanding of the matter is to understand its limits, and therefore I think it desirable at once to point out and dispel a confusion between morality and law, which sometimes rises to the height of conscious theory, and more often and indeed constantly is making trouble in detail without reaching the point of consciousness. You can see very plainly that a bad man has as much reason as a good one for wishing to avoid an encounter with the public force, and therefore you can see the practical importance of the distinction between morality and law. A man who cares nothing for an ethical rule which is believed and practised by his neighbors is likely nevertheless to care a good deal to avoid being made to pay money, and will want to keep out of jail if he can.

I take it for granted that no hearer of mine will misinterpret what I have to say as the language of cynicism. The law is the witness and external deposit of our moral life. Its history is the history of the moral development of the race. The practice of it, in spite of popular jests, tends to make good citizens and good men. When I emphasize the difference between law and morals I do so with reference to a single end, that of learning and understanding the law. For that purpose you must definitely master its specific marks, and it is for that that I ask you for the moment to imagine yourselves indifferent to other and greater things.

I do not say that there is not a wider point of view from which the distinction between law and morals becomes of secondary or no importance, as all mathematical distinctions vanish in presence of the infinite. But I do say that that distinction is of the first importance for the object which we are here to consider,—a right study and mastery of the law as a business with well understood limits, a body of dogma enclosed within definite lines. I have just shown the practical reason for saying so. If you want to know the law and nothing else, you must look at it as a bad man, who cares only for the material consequences which such knowledge enables him to predict, not as a good one, who finds his reasons for conduct, whether inside the law or outside of it, in the vaguer sanctions of conscience. The theoretical importance of the distinction is no less, if you would reason on your subject aright. The law is full of phraseology drawn from morals, and by the mere force of language continually invites us to pass from one domain to the other without perceiving it, as we are sure to do unless we have the boundary constantly before our minds. The law talks about rights, and duties, and malice, and intent, and negligence, and so forth, and nothing is easier, or, I may say, more common in legal reasoning, than to take these words in their moral sense, at some stage of the argument, and so to drop into fallacy. For instance, when we speak of the rights of man in a moral sense, we mean to mark the limits of interference with individual freedom which we think are prescribed by conscience, or by our ideal, however reached. Yet it is certain that many laws have been enforced in the past, and it is likely that some are enforced now, which are condemned by the most enlightened opinion of the time, or which at all events pass the limit of interference as many consciences would draw it. Manifestly, therefore, nothing but confusion of thought can result from assuming that the rights of man in a moral sense are equally rights in the sense of the Constitution and the law. No doubt simple and extreme cases can be put of imaginable laws which the statute-making power would not dare to enact, even in the absence of written constitutional prohibitions, because the community would rise in rebellion and fight; and this gives some plausibility to the proposition that the law, if not a part of morality, is limited by it. But this limit of power is not coextensive with any system of morals. For the most part it falls far within the lines of any such system, and in some cases may extend beyond them, for reasons drawn from the habits of a particular people at a particular time. I once heard the late Professor Agassiz say that a German population would rise if you added two cents to the price of a glass of beer. A statute in such a case would be empty words, not because it was wrong, but because it could not be enforced. No one will deny that wrong statutes can be and are enforced, and we should not all agree as to which were the wrong ones.

The confusion with which I am dealing besets confessedly legal conceptions. Take the fundamental question, What constitutes the law? You will find some text writers telling you that it is something different from what is decided by the courts of Massachusetts or England, that it is a system of reason, that it is a deduction from principles of ethics or admitted axioms or what not, which may or may not coincide with the decisions. But if we take the view of our friend the bad man we shall find that he does not care two straws for the axioms or deductions, but that he does want to know what the Massachusetts or English courts are likely to do in fact. I am much of his mind. The prophecies of what the courts will do in fact, and nothing more pretentious, are what I mean by the law.

Take again a notion which as popularly understood is the widest conception which the law contains;—the notion of legal duty, to which already I have referred. We fill the word with all the content which we draw from morals. But what does it mean to a bad man? Mainly, and in the first place, a prophecy that if he does certain things he will be subjected to disagreeable consequences by way of imprisonment or compulsory payment of money. But from his point of view, what is the difference between being fined and being taxed a certain sum for doing a certain thing? That his point of view is the test of legal principles is shown by the many discussions which have arisen in the courts on the very question whether a given statutory liability is a penalty or a tax. On the answer to this question depends the decision whether conduct is legally wrong or right, and also whether a man is under compulsion or free. Leaving the criminal law on one side, what is the difference between the liability under the mill acts or statutes authorizing a taking by eminent domain and the liability for what we call a wrongful conversion of property where restoration is out of the question? In both cases the party taking another man's property has to pay its fair value as assessed by a jury, and no more. What significance is there in calling one taking right and another wrong from the point of view of the law? It does not matter, so far as the given consequence, the compulsory payment, is concerned, whether the act to which it is attached is described in terms of praise or in terms of blame, or whether the law purports to prohibit it or to allow it. . . .

Nowhere is the confusion between legal and moral ideas more manifest than in the law of contract. Among other things, here again the so called primary rights and duties are invested with a mystic significance beyond what can be assigned and explained. The duty to keep a contract at common law means a prediction that you must pay damages if you do not keep it,—and nothing else. If you commit a tort, you are liable to pay a compensatory sum. If you commit a contract, you are liable to pay a compensatory sum unless the promised event comes to pass, and that is all the difference. . . .

I have spoken only of the common law, because there are some cases in which a logical justification can be found for speaking of civil liabilities as imposing duties in an intelligible sense. These are the relatively few in which equity will grant an injunction, and will enforce it by putting the defendant in prison or otherwise punishing him unless he complies with the order of the court. But I hardly think it advisable to shape general theory from the exception, and I think it would be better to cease troubling ourselves about primary rights and sanctions altogether, than to describe our prophecies concerning the liabilities commonly imposed by the law in those inappropriate terms. . . .

. . . Morals deal with the actual internal state of the individual's mind, what he actually intends. From the time of the Romans down to now, this mode of dealing has affected the language of the law as to contract, and the language used has reacted upon the thought. We talk about a contract as a meeting of the minds of the parties, and thence it is inferred in various cases that there is no contract because their minds have not met; that is, because they have intended different things or because one party has not known of the assent of the other. Yet nothing is more certain than that parties may be bound by a contract to things which neither of them intended, and when one does not know of the other's assent. Suppose a contract is executed in due form and in writing to deliver a lecture, mentioning no time. One of the parties thinks that the promise will be construed to mean at once, within a week. The other thinks that it means when he is ready. The court says that it means within a reasonable time. The parties are bound by the contract as it is interpreted by the court, yet neither of them meant what the court declares that they have said. In my opinion no one will understand the true theory of contract or be able even to discuss some fundamental questions intelligently until he has understood that all contracts are formal, that the making of a contract depends not on the agreement of two minds in one intention, but on the agreement of two sets of external signs,—not on the parties' having *meant* the same thing but on their having *said* the same thing. . . .

II

So much for the limits of the law. The next thing which I wish to consider is what are the forces which determine its content and its growth. You may assume, with Hobbes and Bentham and Austin, that all law emanates from the sovereign, even when the first human beings to enunciate it are the judges, or you may think that law is the voice of the Zeitgeist, or what you like. It is all one to my present purpose. Even if every decision required the sanction of an emperor with despotic power and a whimsical turn of mind, we should be interested none the less, still with a view to prediction, in discovering some order, some rational explanation, and some principle of growth for the rules which he laid down. In every system there are such explanations and principles to be found. It is with regard to them that a second fallacy comes in, which I think it important to expose.

The fallacy to which I refer is the notion that the only force at work in the development of the law is logic. In the broadest sense, indeed, that notion would be true. The postulate on which we think about the universe is that there is a fixed quantitative relation between every phenomenon and its antecedents and consequents. If there is such a thing as a phenomenon without these fixed quantitative relations, it is a miracle. It is outside the law of cause and effect, and as such transcends our power of thought, or at least is something to or from which we cannot reason. The condition of our thinking about the universe is that it is capable of being thought about rationally, or, in other words, that every part of it is effect and cause in the same sense in which those parts are with which we are most familiar. So in the broadest sense it is true that the law is a logical development, like everything else. The danger of which I speak is not the admission that the principles governing other phenomena also govern the law, but the notion that a given system, ours, for instance, can be worked out like mathematics from some general axioms of conduct. . . .

This mode of thinking is entirely natural. The training of lawyers is a training in logic. The processes of analogy, discrimination, and deduction are those in which they are most at home. The language of judicial decision is mainly the language of logic. And the logical method and form flatter that longing for certainty and for repose which is in every human mind. But certainty generally is illusion, and repose is not the destiny of man. Behind the logical form lies a judgment as to the relative worth and importance of competing legislative grounds, often an inarticulate and unconscious judgment, it is true, and yet the very root and nerve of the whole proceeding. . . . We do not realize how large a part of our law is open to reconsideration upon a slight change in the habit of the public mind. No concrete proposition is self-evident, no matter how ready we may be to accept it, not even Mr. Herbert Spencer's. Every man has a right to do what he wills, provided he interferes not with a like right on the part of his neighbors.

Why is a false and injurious statement privileged, if it is made honestly in giving information about a servant? It is because it has been thought more important that information should be given freely, than that a man should be protected from what under other circumstances would be an actionable wrong. Why is a man at liberty to set up a business which he knows will ruin his neighbor? It is because the public good is supposed to be best subserved by free competition. Obviously such judgments of relative importance may vary in different times and places. . . .

I think that the judges themselves have failed adequately to recognize their duty of weighing considerations of social advantage. The duty is inevitable, and the result of the often proclaimed judicial aversion to deal with such considerations is simply to leave the very ground and foundation of judgments inarticulate, and often unconscious, as I have said. When socialism first began to be talked about, the comfortable classes of the community were a good deal frightened. I suspect that this fear has influenced judicial action both here and in England, yet it is certain that it is not a conscious factor in the decisions to which I refer. I think that something similar has led people who no longer hope to control the legislatures to look to the courts as expounders of the Constitutions, and that in some courts new principles have been discovered outside the bodies of those instruments, which may be generalized into acceptance of the economic doctrines which prevailed about fifty years ago, and a wholesale prohibition of what a tribunal of lawyers does not think about right. I cannot but believe that if the training of lawyers led them habitually to consider more definitely and explicitly the social advantage on which the rule they lay down must be justified, they sometimes would hesitate where now they are confident, and see that really they were taking sides upon debatable and often burning questions.

So much for the fallacy of logical form. Now let us consider the present condition of the law as a subject for study, and the ideal toward which it tends. We still are far from the point of view which I desire to see reached. No one has reached it or can reach it as yet. We are only at the beginning of a philosophical reaction, and of a reconsideration of the worth of doctrines which for the most part still are taken for granted without any deliberate, conscious, and systematic questioning of their grounds. The development of our law has gone on for nearly a thousand years, like the development of a plant, each generation taking the inevitable next step, mind, like matter, simply obeying a law of spontaneous growth. It is perfectly natural and right that it should have been so. Imitation is a necessity of human nature, as has been illustrated by a remarkable French writer, M. Tarde, in an admirable book, "Les Lois de l'Imitation." Most of the things we do, we do for no better reason than that our fathers have done them or that our neighbors do them, and the same is true of a larger part than we suspect of what we think. The reason is a good one, because our short life gives us no time for a better, but it is not the best. It does not follow, because we all are compelled to take on faith at second hand most of the rules on which we base our action and our thought, that each of us may not try to set some corner of his world in the order of reason, or that all of us collectively should not aspire to carry reason as far as it will go throughout the whole domain. In regard to the law, it is true, no doubt, that an evolutionist will hesitate to affirm universal validity for his social ideals, or for the principles which he thinks should be embodied in legislation. He is content if he can prove them best for here and now. He may be ready to admit that he knows nothing about an absolute best in the cosmos, and even that he knows next to nothing about a permanent best for men. Still it is true that a body of law is more rational and more civilized when every rule it contains is referred articulately and definitely to an end which it subserves, and when the grounds for desiring that end are stated or are ready to be stated in words. . . .

. . . The rational study of law is still to a large extent a study of history. History must be a part of the study, because without it we cannot know the precise scope of rules which it is our business to know. It is a part of the rational study, because it is the first step toward an enlightened scepticism, that is, toward a deliberate reconsideration of the worth of those rules. When you get the dragon out of his cave on to the plain and in the daylight, you can count his teeth and claws, and see just what is his strength. But to get him out is only the first step. The next is either to kill him, or to tame him and make him a useful animal. For the rational study of the law the black-letter man may be the man of the present, but the man of the future is the man of statistics and the master of economics. It is revolting to have no better reason for a rule of law than that so it was laid down in the time of Henry IV. It is still more revolting if the grounds upon which it was laid down have vanished long since, and the rule simply persists from blind imitation of the past. I am thinking of the technical rule as to trespass *ab initio*, as it is called, which I attempted to explain in a recent Massachusetts case. . . .

Far more fundamental questions still await a better answer than that we do as our fathers have done. What have we better than a blind guess to show that the criminal law in its present form does more good than harm? I do not stop to refer to the effect which it has had in degrading prisoners and in plunging them further into crime, or to the question whether fine and imprisonment do not fall more heavily on a criminal's wife and children than on himself. I have in mind more far-reaching questions. Does punishment deter? Do we deal with criminals on proper principles? A modern school of Continental criminalists plumes itself on the formula, first suggested, it is said, by Gall, that we must consider the criminal rather than the crime. The formula does not carry us very far, but the inquiries which have been started look toward an answer of my questions based on science for the first time. If the typical criminal is a degenerate, bound to swindle or to murder by as deep seated an organic necessity as that which makes the rattlesnake bite, it is idle to talk of deterring him by the classical method of imprisonment. He must be got rid of; he cannot be improved, or frightened out of his structural reaction. If, on the other hand, crime, like normal human conduct, is mainly a matter of imitation, punishment fairly may be expected to help to keep it out of fashion. The study of criminals has been thought by some well known men of science to sustain the former hypothesis. The statistics of the relative increase of crime in crowded places like large cities, where example has the greatest chance to work, and in less populated parts, where the contagion spreads more slowly, have been used with great force in favor of the latter view. But there is weighty authority for the belief that, however this may be, "not the nature of the crime, but the dangerousness of the criminal, constitutes the only reasonable legal criterion to guide the inevitable social reaction against the criminal.". . .

I trust that no one will understand me to be speaking with disrespect of the law, because I criticise it so freely. I venerate the law, and especially our system of law, as one of the vastest products of the human mind. No one knows better than I do the countless number of great intellects that have spent themselves in making some addition or improvement, the greatest of which is trifling when compared with the mighty whole. It has the final title to respect that it exists, that it is not a Hegelian dream, but a part of the lives of men. But one may criticise even what one reveres. Law is the business to which my life is devoted, and I should show less than devotion if I did not do what in me lies to improve it, and, when I perceive what seems to me the ideal of its future, if I hesitated to point it out and to press toward it with all my heart. . . .

. . . I look forward to a time when the part played by history in the explanation of dogma shall be very small, and instead of ingenious research we shall spend our energy on a study of the ends sought to be attained and the reasons for desiring them. As a step toward that ideal it seems to me that every lawyer ought to seek an understanding of economics. The present divorce between the schools of political economy and law seems to me an evidence of how much progress in philosophical study still remains to be made. In the present state of political economy, indeed, we come again upon history on a larger scale, but there we are called on to consider and weigh the ends of legislation, the means of attaining them, and the cost. We learn that for everything we have to give up something else, and we are taught to set the advantage we gain against the other advantage we lose, and to know what we are doing when we elect.

There is another study which sometimes is undervalued by the practical minded, for which I wish to say a good word, although I think a good deal of pretty poor stuff goes under that name. I mean the study of what is called jurisprudence. Jurisprudence, as I look at it, is simply law in its most generalized part. Every effort to reduce a case to a rule is an effort of jurisprudence, although the name as used in English is confined to the broadest rules and most fundamental conceptions. One mark of a great lawyer is that he sees the application of the broadest rules. There is a story of a Vermont justice of the peace before whom a suit was brought by one farmer against another for breaking a churn. The justice took time to consider, and then said that he had looked through the statutes and could find nothing about churns, and gave judgment for the defendant. The same state of mind is shown in all our common digests and text-books. Applications of rudimentary rules of contract or tort are tucked away under the head of Railroads or Telegraphs or go to swell treatises on historical subdivisions, such as Shipping or Equity, or are gathered under an arbitrary title which is thought likely to appeal to the practical mind, such as Mercantile Law. If a man goes into law it pays to be a master of it, and to be a master of it means to look straight through all the dramatic incidents and to discern the true basis for prophecy. Therefore, it is well to have an accurate notion of what you mean by law, by a right, by a duty, by malice, intent, and negligence, by ownership, by possession, and so forth. . . .

I have been speaking about the study of the law, and I have said next to nothing of what commonly is talked about in that connection,—text-books and the case system, and all the machinery with which a student comes most immediately in contact. Nor shall I say anything about them. Theory is my subject, not practical details. The modes of teaching have been improved since my time, no doubt, but ability and industry will master the raw material with any mode. Theory is the most important part of the dogma of the law, as the architect is the most important man who takes part in the building of a house. The most important improvements of the last twenty-five years are improvements in theory. It is not to be feared as unpractical, for, to the competent, it simply means going to the bottom of the subject. For the incompetent, it sometimes is true, as has been said, that an interest in general ideas means an absence of particular knowledge. I remember in army days reading of a youth who, being examined for the lowest grade and being asked a question about squadron drill, answered that he never had considered the evolutions of less than ten thousand men. But the weak and foolish must be left to their folly. The danger is that the able and practical minded should look with indifference or distrust upon ideas the connection of which with their business is remote. I heard a story, the other day, of a man who had a valet to whom he paid high wages, subject to deduction for faults. One of his deductions was, "For lack of imagination, five dollars." The lack is not confined to valets. The object of ambition, power, generally presents itself nowadays in the form of money alone. Money is the most immediate form, and is a proper object of desire. "The fortune," said Rachel, "is the measure of the intelligence." That is a good text to waken people out of a fool's paradise. But, as Hegel says, "It is in the end not the appetite, but the opinion, which has to be satisfied." To an imagination of any scope the most far-reaching form of power is not money, it is the command of ideas. If you want great examples read Mr. Leslie Stephen's "History of English Thought in the Eighteenth Century," and see how a hundred years after his death the abstract speculation of Descartes had become a practical force controlling the conduct of men. Read the works of the great German jurists, and see how much more the world is governed to-day by Kant than by Bonaparte. We cannot all be Descartes or Kant, but we all want happiness. And happiness, I am sure from having known many successful men, cannot be won simply by being counsel for great corporations and having an income of fifty thousand dollars. An intellect great enough to win the prize needs other food beside success. The remoter and more general aspects of the law are those which give it universal interest. It is through them that you not only become a great master in your calling, but connect your subject with the universe and catch an echo of the infinite, a glimpse of its unfathomable process, a hint of the universal law.

The abuses of reason attacked by Holmes in "The Path" certainly did not disappear the next day. Indeed one of Holmes's concerns, how to keep logic on a suitably taut leash without incapacitating it for proper uses, remains a perennial problem for legal philosophy. What is clear, however, is that a remarkable change in the temper of legal reasoning took place during the first half of this century. No doubt Holmes had his share in bringing this change about. But it is equally certain that it would to some extent have occurred without him. During the same period in Germany and France, for example, a similar reaction was taking place against methods of legal thinking characteristic of the last half of the nineteenth century—methods that on the Continent as well as in this country had become abstract, dogmatic, and Lebensfremd.

Aside from its contribution to a general change in the atmosphere of legal scholarship, Holmes's thought had a quite traceable and significant influence on a movement during the 1920's and '30's that came to be known as American Legal Realism. The participants in this movement, it need hardly be said, were not realists in the Platonic sense; their self-image was that of tough-minded empiricists with little use for abstractions and universals. Holmes took no personal part in this movement and in fact tended to view it with a considerable detachment. No doubt he did not find to his liking what might be called its style. One can hardly imagine his subscribing to the Realist definition of law as "the behavior patterns of judges and other state officials," though this definition merely converted into the clichés of the day his own conception of law as a prophecy of what courts will do in fact.

Perhaps the most infelicitous turn of thought in "The Path" is to be found in Holmes's discussion of legal rights and duties. He accused legal theorists of putting the cart before the horse when they regarded rights and duties as giving rise to consequences—when they said, for example, that the defendant in a particular case had violated a duty and therefore ought to pay damages. According to Holmes, "a legal duty so called is nothing but a prediction that if a man does or omits certain things he will be made to suffer in this or that way by judgment of the court;—and so of a legal right."

Now it is quite true that a bad man—or at least the rather special kind of bad man postulated by Holmes—is not interested in being told about his duties. He simply wants to know how likely he is to be hit by the ax of state power if he follows a particular course of action. On the other hand, he is interested in predicting judicial decisions; this is, indeed, the whole point of his appearance in Holmes's analysis. But if the concept of duty plays no part in the reasoning of judges, it is hard to see how it can serve as a tool of prediction. If the man who enters a contract merely subjects himself to the alternative of performing or of paying damages, it is hard to see why the word "duty" is more appropriate for one branch of this alternative than for the other, or, from the bad man's point of view, why there is any reason to use it at all. In other words, instead of startling his audience with a novel and paradoxical definition of the word "duty," Holmes would have done better simply to have said that from a certain point of view toward the law the term becomes irrelevant.

Unfortunately the confusion Holmes introduced proved contagious. For example, Arthur L. Corbin and Walter Wheeler Cook, following the lead of Wesley Newcomb Hohfeld, became interested in clarifying the meaning of such terms as "duty," "right," "privilege," and "power." They criticized the courts for using these terms in confused and improper ways. In doing so they plainly violated Holmes's injunction not to put the cart before the horse; they were treating duties as giving rise to consequences, as playing a significant role in legal reasoning. On the other hand, they found the predictive theory too attractive to be abandoned; so we find Corbin writing (in the Yale Law Journal, XXIX, 163–64):

> When we state that some particular legal relation [such as a duty] exists we are impliedly asserting the existence of certain facts, and we are expressing our present mental concept of the societal consequences that will normally follow in the future. A statement that a legal relation exists between A and B is a prediction as to what society, acting through its courts or executive agents, will do or not do for one and against the other.

Yet if the term "duty" merely expresses a prediction of the probable future course of judicial decisions, whether they are well reasoned or not, it is hard to see how Corbin can criticize courts for using the term improperly, for he certainly doesn't mean that they are incorrectly predicting today what they are going to do tomorrow. With a proper harness you can put the horse either behind or in front of the cart; the one thing certain is that you can't put him in both places at once. Yet this is precisely what Corbin and Cook—no doubt out of their reverence for Holmes—tried to do.

Curiously, this confusion could have been avoided if heed had been given to words written by Holmes himself in 1872, a quarter of a century before "The Path." These words plainly refute his whole argument that duty expresses merely vulnerability to a sanction, rather than a reason for imposing a sanction:

> The notion of duty involves something more than a tax on a certain line of conduct. A protective tariff on iron does not create a duty not to bring it into the country. The word imports the existence of an absolute wish on the part of the power imposing it to bring about a certain course of conduct, and to prevent the contrary. A legal duty cannot be said to exist if the law intends to allow the person supposed to be subject to it an option at a certain price.

What impulse it was that led Holmes to desert the unexciting wisdom of this passage for the sparkling paradoxes of "The Path" must remain a mystery, though in seeking some clue to it we may recall William James's remark about the friend of his youth: "Wendell amuses me by being composed of at least two and a half different people rolled into one, and the way he keeps them together in one tight skin, without quarrelling any more than they do, is remarkable."

Surveying "The Path" from the perspective of the present, we can safely conclude that the Holmesian influence on American Legal Realism and the Hohfeldian analysis has now run its full course and made its final contribution, whether negative or affirmative.

John Dewey
My Pedagogic Creed
1897

EDITED BY LAWRENCE A. CREMIN

It was in the spring of 1896 that Ossian H. Lang, editor of the School Journal, first conceived the idea of running a series of "pedagogic creeds" by eminent American educators. Lang, a serious student of the theory and history of education, had long been concerned with what struck him as a pervasive aimlessness among American teachers. "There is something radically and fatally wrong with a teacher who has no educational creed," he once observed. "Education is a responsible and complicated work, which must be carefully planned from beginning to end. There must be a definite aim and a clear understanding of the ways and means of reaching it. In other words, the educator must have in his mind some fixed principles of action."

How might teachers come by such fixed principles? Lang thought the writings of the ancients were certainly a prime source, as were the insights of contemporary Europeans, such as Pestalozzi, Herbart, and Froebel. Yet something more was needed. Americans had committed themselves to universal public education, one of the most novel and radical experiments in history. If the commitment was to mean anything, American teachers would need to work out a whole new set of principles, thoroughly consistent with the values and demands of their own civilization. And in working out such principles, there was no better place to begin than the wisdom of their own leaders.

Lang's series of "pedagogic creeds" was explicitly designed to make that wisdom readily available, and his list of invited authors was appropriately star-studded. It included William T. Harris, the universally esteemed United States Commissioner of Education; Francis W. Parker, the redoubtable principal of the Cook County (Illinois) Normal School; Burke A. Hinsdale, the eminent professor of pedagogy at the University of Michigan; and a young psychologist named John Dewey, who had been brought to the University of Chicago in 1894 to head the combined departments of philosophy, psychology, and education.

We know that Lang's letters of invitation went out during the spring of 1896; and we know that Dewey's particular contribution appeared in the School Journal for January 16, 1897, as the ninth in the series. Since the various "creeds" seem to have appeared in order of receipt, Dewey probably prepared his statement sometime during the autumn of 1896. That, incidentally, would place the writing squarely within the formative period of the Laboratory School of the University of Chicago, which Dr. and Mrs. Dewey founded in 1896 for the express purpose of testing in practice the very sort of proposition Dewey enunciated in the "creed."

ARTICLE I. WHAT EDUCATION IS.

I BELIEVE that all education proceeds by the participation of the individual in the social consciousness of the race. This process begins unconsciously almost at birth, and is continually shaping the individual's powers, saturating his consciousness, forming his habits, training his ideas, and arousing his feelings and emotions. Through this unconscious education the individaul gradually comes to share in the intellectual and moral resources which humanity has succeeded in getting together. He becomes an inheritor of the funded capital of civilization. The most formal and technical education in the world cannot safely depart from this general process. It can only organize it; or differentiate it in some particular direction.

I believe that the only true education comes through the stimulation of the child's powers by the demands of the social situations in which he finds himself. Through these demands he is stimulated to act as a member of a unity, to emerge from his original narrowness of action and

The text is reprinted as it originally appeared in the *School Journal*, LIV (January 16, 1897), 77–80.

feeling and to conceive of himself from the standpoint of the welfare of the group to which he belongs. Through the responses which others make to his own activities he comes to know what these mean in social terms. The value which they have is reflected back into them. For instance, through the response which is made to the child's instinctive babblings the child comes to know what those babblings mean; they are transformed into articulate language and thus the child is introduced into the consolidated wealth of ideas and emotions which are now summed up in language.

I believe that this educational process has two sides—one psychological and one sociological; and that neither can be subordinated to the other or neglected without evil results following. Of these two sides, the psychological is the basis. The child's own instincts and powers furnish the material and give the starting point for all education. Save as the efforts of the educator connect with some activity which the child is carrying on of his own initiative independent of the educator, education becomes reduced to a pressure from without. It may, indeed, give certain external results but cannot truly be called educative. Without insight into the psychological structure and activities of the individual, the educative process will, therefore, be haphazard and arbitrary. If it chances to coincide with the child's activity it will get a leverage; if it does not, it will result in friction, or disintegration, or arrest of the child nature.

I believe that knowledge of social conditions, of the present state of civilization, is necessary in order properly to interpret the child's powers. The child has his own instincts and tendencies, but we do not know what these mean until we can translate them into their social equivalents. We must be able to carry them back into a social past and see them as the inheritance of previous race activities. We must also be able to project them into the future to see what their outcome and end will be. In the illustration just used, it is the ability to see in the child's babblings the promise and potency of a future social intercourse and conversation which enables one to deal in the proper way with that instinct.

I believe that the psychological and social sides are organically related and that education cannot be regarded as a compromise between the two, or a superimposition of one upon the other. We are told that the psychological definition of education is barren and formal—that it gives us only the idea of a development of all the mental powers without giving us any idea of the use to which these powers are put. On the other hand, it is urged that the social definition of education, as getting adjusted to civilization, makes of it a forced and external process, and results in subordinating the freedom of the individual to a preconceived social and political status.

I believe each of these objections is true when urged against one side isolated from the other. In order to know what a power really is we must know what its end, use, or function is; and this we cannot know save as we conceive of the individual as active in social relationships. But, on the other hand, the only possible adjustment which we can give to the child under existing conditions, is that which arises through putting him in complete possession of all his powers. With the advent of democracy and modern industrial conditions, it is impossible to foretell definitely just what civilization will be twenty years from now. Hence it is impossible to prepare the child for any precise set of conditions. To prepare him for the future life means to give him command of himself; it means so to train him that he will have the full and ready use of all his capacities; that his eye and ear and hand may be tools ready to command, that his judgment may be capable of grasping the conditions under which it has to work, and the executive forces be trained to act economically and efficiently. It is impossible to reach this sort of adjustment save as constant regard is had to the individual's own powers, tastes, and interests—say, that is, as education is continually converted into psychological terms.

In sum, I believe that the individual who is to be educated is a social individual and that society is an organic union of individuals. If we eliminate the social factor from the child we are left only with an abstraction; if we eliminate the individual factor from society, we are left only with an inert and lifeless mass. Education, therefore, must begin with a psychological insight into the child's capacities, interests, and habits. It must be controlled at every point by reference to these same considerations. These powers, interests, and habits must be continually interpreted—we must know what they mean. They must be translated into terms of their social equivalents—into terms of what they are capable of in the way of social service.

ARTICLE II. WHAT THE SCHOOL IS.

I believe that the school is primarily a social institution. Education being a social process, the school is simply that form of community life in which all those agencies are concentrated that will be most effective in bringing the child to share in the inherited resources of the race, and to use his own powers for social ends.

I believe that education, therefore, is a process of living and not a preparation for future living.

I believe that the school must represent present life—life as real and vital to the child as that which he carries on in the home, in the neighborhood, or on the play-ground.

I believe that education which does not occur through forms of life, or that are worth living for their own sake, is always a poor substitute for the genuine reality and tends to cramp and to deaden.

I believe that the school, as an institution, should simplify existing social life; should reduce it, as it were, to an embryonic form. Existing life is so complex that the child cannot be brought into contact with it without either confusion or distraction; he is either overwhelmed by the multiplicity of activities which are going on, so that he loses his own power of orderly reaction, or he is so stimulated by these various activities that his powers are prematurely called into play and he becomes either unduly specialized or else disintegrated.

I believe that, as such simplified social life, the school life should grow gradually out of the home life; that it should take up and continue the activities with which the child is already familiar in the home.

I believe that it should exhibit these activities to the child, and reproduce them in such ways that the child will gradually learn the meaning of them, and be capable of playing his own part in relation to them.

I believe that this is a psychological necessity, because it is the only way of securing continuity in the child's growth, the only way of giving a back-ground of past experience to the new ideas given in school.

I believe it is also a social necessity because the home is the form of social life in which the child has been nurtured and in connection with which he has had his moral training. It is the business of the school to deepen and extend his sense of the values bound up in his home life.

I believe that much of present education fails because it neglects this fundamental principle of the school as a form of community life. It conceives the school as a place where certain information is to be given, where certain lessons are to be learned, or where certain habits are to be formed. The value of these is conceived as lying largely in the remote future; the child must do these things for the sake of something else he is to do; they are mere preparation. As a result they do not become a part of the life experience of the child and so are not truly educative.

I believe that the moral education centers about this conception of the school as a mode of social life, that the best and deepest moral training is precisely that which one gets through having to enter into proper relations with others in a unity of work and thought. The present educational systems, so far as they destroy or neglect this unity, render it difficult or impossible to get any genuine, regular moral training.

I believe that the child should be stimulated and controlled in his work through the life of the community.

I believe that under existing conditions far too much of the stimulus and control proceeds from the teacher, because of neglect of the idea of the school as a form of social life.

I believe that the teacher's place and work in the school is to be interpreted from this same basis. The teacher is not in the school to impose certain ideas or to form certain habits in the child, but is there as a member of the community to select the influences which shall affect the child and to assist him in properly responding to these influences.

I believe that the discipline of the school should proceed from the life of the school as a whole and not directly from the teacher.

I believe that the teacher's business is simply to determine on the basis of larger experience and riper wisdom, how the discipline of life shall come to the child.

I believe that all questions of the grading of the child and his promotion should be determined by reference to the same standard. Examinations are of use only so far as they test the child's fitness for social life and reveal the place in which he can be of the most service and where he can receive the most help.

ARTICLE III. THE SUBJECT-MATTER OF EDUCATION.

I believe that the social life of the child is the basis of concentration, or correlation, in all his training or growth. The social life gives the unconscious unity and the background of all his efforts and of all his attainments.

I believe that the subject-matter of the school curriculum should mark a gradual differentiation out of the primitive unconscious unity of social life.

I believe that we violate the child's nature and render difficult the best ethical results, by introducing the child too abruptly to a number of

613

special studies, of reading, writing, geography, etc., out of relation to this social life.

I believe, therefore, that the true center of correlation on the school subjects is not science, nor literature, nor history, nor geography, but the child's own social activities.

I believe that education cannot be unified in the study of science, or so called nature study, because apart from human activity, nature itself is not a unity; nature in itself is a number of diverse objects in space and time, and to attempt to make it the center of work by itself, is to introduce a principle of radiation rather than one of concentration.

I believe that literature is the reflex expression and interpretation of social experience; that hence it must follow upon and not precede such experience. It, therefore, cannot be made the basis, although it may be made the summary of unification.

I believe once more that history is of educative value in so far as it presents phases of social life and growth. It must be controlled by reference to social life. When taken simply as history it is thrown into the distant past and becomes dead and inert. Taken as the record of man's social life and progress it becomes full of meaning. I believe, however, that it cannot be so taken excepting as the child is also introduced directly into social life.

I believe accordingly that the primary basis of education is in the child's powers at work along the same general constructive lines as those which have brought civilization into being.

I believe that the only way to make the child conscious of his social heritage is to enable him to perform those fundamental types of activity which make civilization what it is.

I believe, therefore, in the so-called expressive or constructive activities as the center of correlation.

I believe that this gives the standard for the place of cooking, sewing, manual training, etc., in the school.

I believe that they are not special studies which are to be introduced over and above a lot of others in the way of relaxation or relief, or as additional accomplishments. I believe rather that they represent, as types, fundamental forms of social activity; and that it is possible and desirable that the child's introduction into the more formal subjects of the curriculum be through the medium of these activities.

I believe that the study of science is educational in so far as it brings out the materials and processes which make social life what it is.

I believe that one of the greatest difficulties in the present teaching of science is that the material is presented in purely objective form, or is treated as a new peculiar kind of experience which the child can add to that which he has already had. In reality, science is of value because it gives the ability to interpret and control the experience already had. It should be introduced, not as so much new subject-matter, but as showing the factors already involved in previous experience and as furnishing tools by which that experience can be more easily and effectively regulated.

I believe that at present we lose much of the value of literature and language studies because of our elimination of the social element. Language is almost always treated in the books of pedagogy simply as the expression of thought. It is true that language is a logical instrument, but it is fundamentally and primarily a social instrument. Language is the device for communication; it is the tool through which one individual comes to share the ideas and feelings of others. When treated simply as a way of getting individual information, or as a means of showing off what one has learned, it loses its social motive and end.

I believe that there is, therefore, no succession of studies in the ideal school curriculum. If education is life, all life has, from the outset, a scientific aspect; an aspect of art and culture and an aspect of communication. It cannot, therefore, be true that the proper studies for one grade are mere reading and writing, and that at a later grade, reading, or literature, or science, may be introduced. The progress is not in the succession of studies but in the development of new attitudes towards, and new interests in, experience.

I believe finally, that education must be conceived as a continuing reconstruction of experience; that the process and the goal of education are one and the same thing.

I believe that to set up any end outside of education, as furnishing its goal and standard, is to deprive the educational process of much of its meaning and tends to make us rely upon false and external stimuli in dealing with the child.

ARTICLE IV. THE NATURE OF METHOD.

I believe that the question of method is ultimately reducible to the question of the order of development of the child's powers and interests. The law for presenting and treating material is the law implicit within the child's own nature. Because this is so I believe the following statements are of supreme importance as determining the spirit in which education is carried on:

1. I believe that the active side precedes the passive in the development of the child nature; that expression comes before conscious impression; that the muscular development precedes the sensory; that movements come before conscious sensations; I believe that consciousness is essentially motor or impulsive; that conscious states tend to project themselves in action.

I believe that the neglect of this principle is the cause of a large part of the waste of time and strength in school work. The child is thrown into a passive, receptive or absorbing attitude. The conditions are such that he is not permitted to follow the law of his nature; the result is friction and waste.

I believe that ideas (intellectual and rational processes) also result from action and devolve for the sake of the better control of action. What we term reason is primarily the law of orderly or effective action. To attempt to develop the reasoning powers, the powers of judgment, without reference to the selection and arrangement of means in action, is the fundamental fallacy in our present methods of dealing with this matter. As a result we present the child with arbitrary symbols. Symbols are a necessity in mental development, but they have their place as tools for economizing effort; presented by themselves they are a mass of meaningless and arbitrary ideas imposed from without.

2. I believe that the image is the great instrument of instruction. What a child gets out of any subject presented to him is simply the images which he himself forms with regard to it.

I believe that if nine tenths of the energy at present directed towards making the child learn certain things, were spent in seeing to it that the child was forming proper images, the work of instruction would be indefinitely facilitated.

I believe that much of the time and attention now given to the preparation and presentation of lessons might be more wisely and profitably expended in training the child's power of imagery and in seeing to it that he was continually forming definite, vivid, and growing images of the various subjects with which he comes in contact in his experience.

3. I believe that interests are the signs and symptoms of growing power. I believe that they represent dawning capacities. Accordingly the constant and careful observation of interests is of the utmost importance for the educator.

I believe that these interests are to be observed as showing the state of development which the child has reached.

I believe that they prophesy the stage upon which he is about to enter.

I believe that only through the continual and sympathetic observation of childhood's interests can the adult enter into the child's life and see what it is ready for, and upon what material it could work most readily and fruitfully.

I believe that these interests are neither to be humored nor repressed. To repress interest is to substitute the adult for the child, and so to weaken intellectual curiosity and alertness, to suppress initiative, and to deaden interest. To humor the interests is to substitute the transient for the permanent. The interest is always the sign of some power below; the important thing is to discover this power. To humor the interest is to fail to penetrate below the surface and its sure result is to substitute caprice and whim for genuine interest.

4. I believe that the emotions are the reflex of actions.

I believe that to endeavor to stimulate or arouse the emotions apart from their corresponding activities, is to introduce an unhealthy and morbid state of mind.

I believe that if we can only secure right habits of action and thought, with reference to the good, the true, and the beautiful, the emotions will for the most part take care of themselves.

I believe that next to deadness and dullness, formalism and routine, our education is threatened with no greater evil than sentimentalism.

I believe that this sentimentalism is the necessary result of the attempt to divorce feeling from action.

ARTICLE V. THE SCHOOL AND SOCIAL PROGRESS.

I believe that education is the fundamental method of social progress and reform.

I believe that all reforms which rest simply upon the enactment of law, or the threatening of certain penalties, or upon changes in mechanical or outward arrangements, are transitory and futile.

I believe that education is a regulation of the process of coming to share in the social consciousness; and that the adjustment of individual activity on the basis of this social consciousness is the only sure method of social reconstruction.

I believe that this conception has due regard for both the individualistic and socialistic ideals. It is duly individual because it recognizes the formation of a certain character as the only genuine basis of right living. It is socialistic because it recognizes that this right character is not to be formed by merely individual precept, example, or exhortation, but rather by the influence of a certain form of institutional or community life upon the individual, and that the social organism through the school, as its organ, may determine ethical results.

I believe that in the ideal school we have the reconciliation of the individualistic and the institutional ideals.

I believe that the community's duty to education is, therefore, its paramount moral duty. By law and punishment, by social agitation and discussion, society can regulate and form itself in a more or less haphazard and chance way. But through education society can formulate its own purposes, can organize its own means and resources, and thus shape itself with definiteness and economy in the direction in which it wishes to move.

I believe that when society once recognizes the possibilities in this direction, and the obligations which these possibilities impose, it is impossible to conceive of the resources of time, attention, and money which will be put at the disposal of the educator.

I believe it is the business of every one interested in education to insist upon the school as the primary and most effective interest of social progress and reform in order that society may be awakened to realize what the school stands for, and aroused to the necessity of endowing the educator with sufficient equipment properly to perform his task.

I believe that education thus conceived marks the most perfect and intimate union of science and art conceivable in human experience.

I believe that the art of thus giving shape to human powers and adapting them to social service, is the supreme art; one calling into its service the best of artists; that no insight, sympathy, tact, executive power is too great for such service.

I believe that with the growth of psychological service, giving added insight into individual structure and laws of growth; and with growth of social science, adding to our knowledge of the right organization of individuals, all scientific resources can be utilized for the purposes of education.

I believe that when science and art thus join hands the most commanding motive for human action will be reached; the most genuine springs of human conduct aroused and the best service that human nature is capable of guaranteed.

I believe, finally, that the teacher is engaged, not simply in the training of individuals, but in the formation of the proper social life.

I believe that every teacher should realize the dignity of his calling; that he is a social servant set apart for the maintenance of proper social order and the securing of the right social growth.

I believe that in this way the teacher always is the prophet of the true God and the usherer in of the true kingdom of God.

University of Chicago.   JOHN DEWEY

There is a story that soon after Dewey had drafted his "pedagogic creed," he read it to the faculty of the Cook County Normal School, which had been a leading center of educational reform ever since Colonel Francis W. Parker had assumed the principalship in 1883. Parker, whom Dewey once referred to as the "father of progressive education," was one of those artist-teachers whose zeal for educational improvement is always better expressed in practice than in theory. The story goes that when Dewey finished his reading, Parker jumped to his feet and exclaimed: "This educational theory I have never been able to state satisfactorily. This is what I have been struggling all my life to put into action."

Apparently, Dewey served a whole generation of reformist educators in similar fashion. He was truly one of Emerson's "representative men," those rare individuals who can articulate clearly and fully what their contemporaries feel only vaguely and partially. In brief, Dewey was able to synthesize the many and varied impulses that went to make up the progressive-education movement into a single comprehensive view of education. This view appeared for the first time in the "pedagogic creed." It was elaborated substantially in Dewey's 1899 lecture series, The School and Society. And it received its fullest—and now classic—statement in what Dewey himself believed to be his most comprehensive philosophical work, Democracy and Education (1916).

That Dewey's "creed" would somehow stand apart from the others in Lang's series was early apparent. In the School Journal for March 20, 1897, John S. Clark, Director of Prang Normal Art Classes in Boston, wrote his contribution to the series simply as a commentary on Dewey's statement, contending that it was the most sound, sensible, and suggestive contribution to the literature of education since Herbert Spencer's essays. In 1898, when Lang republished the whole series in book form, Dewey's "creed" was no longer ninth in order, as it had been originally, but first, and it was followed by Clark's. Moreover, Lang's recognition was only the beginning. The "creed" was translated into Italian in 1913, into German in 1925, into French and Spanish in 1931, and into Polish in 1933. Next to The School and Society, it has probably given Dewey his largest audience abroad.

In the United States, the document was first republished in pamphlet form in 1897 (along with an essay by Dewey's colleague, Albion W. Small), and then again in 1910. In 1929 the Progressive Education Association reissued it in recognition of Dewey's seventieth birthday. More significant, perhaps, the National Education Association also republished the "creed" that year in its Journal, observing that Dewey's text now belonged in the "professional Bible" of every teacher. The comments accompanying the "creed" on that occasion tell us much about the place it had come to occupy in the liturgy of American pedagogy. The editor of the NEA Journal called it "the emancipation proclamation of childhood." The school superintendent of Sioux City, Iowa, referred to it as "the genesis of public school education." And his counterpart in Ithaca, New York, was moved to rank Dewey as one of the world's four greatest educational reformers, noting that he "strove successfully to free children from formalism in education." By 1929 the fervor of Dewey's propositions, and their effectiveness in synthesizing the educational-reform currents of the Progressive era, had made his "creed" a document of general inspiration, in which teachers of virtually every persuasion could find something of value.

Reform movements have a way of running their course, and the years after 1945 saw a rapid decline in the vitality and influence of progressive education. Throughout the United States, there were charges that progressive theory had hardened into clichés, that progressive practice had ossified into a new traditionalism. Dewey himself, in a 1952 essay that was destined to be one of his last, expressed dismay over what had become of the progressive cause. And yet even in these circumstances his "creed" remained pertinent, as relevant for the critics of progressive education as it had once been for the partisans. In 1961, when Jerome Bruner of Harvard, one of the leading theorists of the post-progressive era, sought to clarify his own pedagogical position vis-à-vis that of the progressives, he titled his essay "After John Dewey, What?" and he began with the ringing phrases of the 1897 "creed," still the most succinct and powerful statement of the revolution through which American education had so recently passed.

Albert J. Beveridge
The March of the Flag
1898

EDITED BY ERNEST R. MAY

"The March of the Flag" was a speech delivered in Tomlinson's Hall, Indianapolis, on September 16, 1898, by Albert Jeremiah Beveridge. Then twenty days short of his thirty-sixth birthday, Beveridge was a lawyer, an active campaigner for the Republican Party, and an orator already famed outside his own state of Indiana. In April, 1898, shortly after the United States declared war on Spain, he had spoken at a banquet of the Middlesex Club in Boston. Although Admiral Dewey had not yet won his victory at Manila Bay and most Americans did not even know that Spain had a colony in the Far East, Beveridge called at that time for conquest of the Philippine Islands. By the date of his Tomlinson's Hall address, the war with Spain was over and an American army occupied Manila. It was not clear whether or not the McKinley Administration intended to keep the Islands. The armistice terms left the question to be decided during negotiations for a peace treaty, and those negotiations were in progress in Paris. Leading Democrats, including former President Cleveland and William Jennings Bryan, had come out in opposition to holding the Philippines as a colony. Beveridge wanted the Republican Administration to annex the islands and the Republican Party to adopt a frankly imperialist policy. His speech was designed to prod McKinley, to provide his party with battlecries for the approaching state and congressional campaigns, and, not incidentally, to further his own prospects for election to the United States Senate if the Republicans should win the

*Indiana legislature. Short, slim, handsome, immaculately dressed, looking
even younger than his years, Beveridge spoke from a memorized text,
making few gestures but using the full range of a practiced and
penetrating voice.*

IT IS a noble land that God has given us; a land that can feed and
clothe the world; a land whose coastlines would inclose half the
countries of Europe; a land set like a sentinel between the two
imperial oceans of the globe, a greater England with a nobler destiny.

It is a mighty people that He has planted on this soil; a people sprung
from the most masterful blood of history; a people perpetually revital-
ized by the virile, man-producing working-folk of all the earth; a people
imperial by virtue of their power, by right of their institutions, by
authority of their Heaven-directed purposes—the propagandists and not
the misers of liberty.

It is a glorious history our God has bestowed upon His chosen people;
a history heroic with faith in our mission and our future; a history of
statesmen who flung the boundaries of the Republic out into unexplored
lands and savage wilderness; a history of soldiers who carried the flag
across blazing deserts and through the ranks of hostile mountains, even
to the gates of sunset; a history of a multiplying people who overran a
continent in half a century; a history of prophets who saw the
consequences of evils inherited from the past and of martyrs who died to
save us from them; a history divinely logical, in the process of whose
tremendous reasoning we find ourselves to-day.

Therefore, in this campaign, the question is larger than a party
question. It is an American question. It is a world question. Shall the
American people continue their march toward the commercial supremacy of the world? Shall free institutions broaden their blessed reign as
the children of liberty wax in strength, until the empire of our principles
is established over the hearts of all mankind?

Have we no mission to perform, no duty to discharge to our fellow-

---

The speech was first published in the *Indianapolis Journal* for September 17,
1898. With minor revisions it appeared in pamphlet form immediately afterward.
This text, following exactly that of the pamphlet, was incorporated by Beveridge in
a collection of essays and orations, *The Meaning of the Times* (Indianapolis: The
Bobbs-Merrill Company, 1908), pp. 47–57.

man? Has God endowed us with gifts beyond our deserts and marked us
as the people of His peculiar favor, merely to rot in our own selfishness,
as men and nations must, who take cowardice for their companion and
self for their deity—as China has, as India has, as Egypt has?

Shall we be as the man who had one talent and hid it, or as he who
had ten talents and used them until they grew to riches? And shall we
reap the reward that waits on our discharge of our high duty; shall we
occupy new markets for what our farmers raise, our factories make, our
merchants sell—aye, and, please God, new markets for what our ships
shall carry?

Hawaii is ours; Porto Rico is to be ours; at the prayer of her people
Cuba finally will be ours; in the islands of the East, even to the gates of
Asia, coaling stations are to be ours at the very least; the flag of a liberal
government is to float over the Philippines, and may it be the banner
that Taylor unfurled in Texas and Fremont carried to the coast.

The Opposition tells us that we ought not to govern a people without
their consent. I answer, The rule of liberty that all just government
derives its authority from the consent of the governed, applies only to
those who are capable of self-government. We govern the Indians
without their consent, we govern our territories without their consent,
we govern our children without their consent. How do they know that
our government would be without their consent? Would not the people
of the Philippines prefer the just, humane, civilizing government of this
Republic to the savage, bloody rule of pillage and extortion from which
we have rescued them?

And, regardless of this formula of words made only for enlightened,
self-governing people, do we owe no duty to the world? Shall we turn
these peoples back to the reeking hands from which we have taken them?
Shall we abandon them, with Germany, England, Japan, hungering for
them? Shall we save them from those nations, to give them a self-rule of
tragedy?

They ask us how we shall govern these new possessions. I answer: Out
of local conditions and the necessities of the case methods of government will grow. If England can govern foreign lands, so can America. If
Germany can govern foreign lands, so can America. If they can supervise
protectorates, so can America. Why is it more difficult to administer
Hawaii than New Mexico or California? Both had a savage and an alien
population; both were more remote from the seat of government when
they came under our dominion than the Philippines are to-day.

Will you say by your vote that American ability to govern has decayed; that a century's experience in self-rule has failed of a result? Will you affirm by your vote that you are an infidel to American power and practical sense? Or will you say that ours is the blood of government; ours the heart of dominion; ours the brain and genius of administration? Will you remember that we do but what our fathers did —we but pitch the tents of liberty farther westward, farther southward —we only continue the march of the flag?

The march of the flag! In 1789 the flag of the Republic waved over 4,000,000 souls in thirteen states, and their savage territory which stretched to the Mississippi, to Canada, to the Floridas. The timid minds of that day said that no new territory was needed, and, for the hour, they were right. But Jefferson, through whose intellect the centuries marched; Jefferson, who dreamed of Cuba as an American state; Jefferson, the first Imperialist of the Republic—Jefferson acquired that imperial territory which swept from the Mississippi to the mountains, from Texas to the British possessions, and the march of the flag began!

The infidels to the gospel of liberty raved, but the flag swept on! The title to that noble land out of which Oregon, Washington, Idaho and Montana have been carved was uncertain; Jefferson, strict constructionist of constitutional power though he was, obeyed the Anglo-Saxon impulse within him, whose watchword then and whose watchword throughout the world to-day is, "Forward!": another empire was added to the Republic, and the march of the flag went on!

Those who deny the power of free institutions to expand urged every argument, and more, that we hear, to-day; but the people's judgment approved the command of their blood, and the march of the flag went on!

A screen of land from New Orleans to Florida shut us from the Gulf, and over this and the Everglade Peninsula waved the saffron flag of Spain; Andrew Jackson seized both, the American people stood at his back, and, under Monroe, the Floridas came under the dominion of the Republic, and the march of the flag went on! The Cassandras prophesied every prophecy of despair we hear, to-day, but the march of the flag went on!

Then Texas responded to the bugle calls of liberty, and the march of the flag went on! And, at last, we waged war with Mexico, and the flag swept over the southwest, over peerless California, past the Gate of Gold to Oregon on the north, and from ocean to ocean its folds of glory blazed.

And, now, obeying the same voice that Jefferson heard and obeyed, that Jackson heard and obeyed, that Monroe heard and obeyed, that Seward heard and obeyed, that Grant heard and obeyed, that Harrison heard and obeyed, our President to-day plants the flag over the islands of the seas, outposts of commerce, citadels of national security, and the march of the flag goes on!

Distance and oceans are no arguments. The fact that all the territory our fathers bought and seized is contiguous, is no argument. In 1819 Florida was farther from New York than Porto Rico is from Chicago to-day; Texas, farther from Washington in 1845 than Hawaii is from Boston in 1898; California, more inaccessible in 1847 than the Philippines are now. Gibraltar is farther from London than Havana is from Washington; Melbourne is farther from Liverpool than Manila is from San Francisco.

The ocean does not separate us from lands of our duty and desire— the oceans join us, rivers never to be dredged, canals never to be repaired. Steam joins us; electricity joins us—the very elements are in league with our destiny. Cuba not contiguous! Porto Rico not contiguous! Hawaii and the Philippines not contiguous! The oceans make them contiguous. And our navy will make them contiguous.

But the Opposition is right—there is a difference. We did not need the western Mississippi Valley when we acquired it, nor Florida, nor Texas, nor California, nor the royal provinces of the far northwest. We had no emigrants to people this imperial wilderness, no money to develop it, even no highways to cover it. No trade awaited us in its savage fastnesses. Our productions were not greater than our trade. There was not one reason for the land-lust of our statesmen from Jefferson to Grant, other than the prophet and the Saxon within them. But, to-day, we are raising more than we can consume, making more than we can use. Therefore we must find new markets for our produce.

And so, while we did not need the territory taken during the past century at the time it was acquired, we do need what we have taken in 1898, and we need it now. The resources and the commerce of these immensely rich dominions will be increased as much as American energy is greater than Spanish sloth. In Cuba, alone, there are 15,000,000 acres of forest unacquainted with the ax, exhaustless mines of iron, priceless deposits of manganese, millions of dollars' worth of which we must buy, to-day, from the Black Sea districts. There are millions of acres yet unexplored.

The resources of Porto Rico have only been trifled with. The riches of the Philippines have hardly been touched by the finger-tips of modern methods. And they produce what we consume, and consume what we produce—the very predestination of reciprocity—a reciprocity "not made with hands, eternal in the heavens." They sell hemp, sugar, cocoanuts, fruits of the tropics, timber of price like mahogany; they buy flour, clothing, tools, implements, machinery and all that we can raise and make. Their trade will be ours in time. Do you indorse that policy with your vote?

Cuba is as large as Pennsylvania, and is the richest spot on the globe. Hawaii is as large as New Jersey; Porto Rico half as large as Hawaii; the Philippines larger than all New England, New York, New Jersey and Delaware combined. Together they are larger than the British Isles, larger than France, larger than Germany, larger than Japan.

If any man tells you that trade depends on cheapness and not on government influence, ask him why England does not abandon South Africa, Egypt, India. Why does France seize South China, Germany the vast region whose port is Kaouchou?

Our trade with Porto Rico, Hawaii and the Philippines must be as free as between the states of the Union, because they are American territory, while every other nation on earth must pay our tariff before they can compete with us. Until Cuba shall ask for annexation, our trade with her will, at the very least, be like the preferential trade of Canada with England. That, and the excellence of our goods and products; that, and the convenience of traffic; that, and the kinship of interests and destiny, will give the monopoly of these markets to the American people.

The commercial supremacy of the Republic means that this Nation is to be the sovereign factor in the peace of the world. For the conflicts of the future are to be conflicts of trade—struggles for markets—commercial wars for existence. And the golden rule of peace is impregnability of position and invincibility of preparedness. So, we see England, the greatest strategist of history, plant her flag and her cannon on Gibraltar, at Quebec, in the Bermudas, at Vancouver, everywhere.

So Hawaii furnishes us a naval base in the heart of the Pacific; the Ladrones another, a voyage further on; Manila another, at the gates of

Asia—Asia, to the trade of whose hundreds of millions American merchants, manufacturers, farmers, have as good right as those of Germany or France or Russia or England; Asia, whose commerce with the United Kingdom alone amounts to hundreds of millions of dollars every year; Asia, to whom Germany looks to take her surplus products; Asia, whose doors must not be shut against American trade. Within five decades the bulk of Oriental commerce will be ours.

No wonder that, in the shadows of coming events so great, free-silver is already a memory. The current of history has swept past that episode. Men understand, to-day, that the greatest commerce of the world must be conducted with the steadiest standard of value and most convenient medium of exchange human ingenuity can devise. Time, that unerring reasoner, has settled the silver question. The American people are tired of talking about money—they want to make it. Why should the farmer get a half-measure dollar of money any more than he should give a half-measure bushel of grain?

Why should not the proposition for the free coinage of silver be as dead as the proposition of irredeemable paper money? It is the same proposition in a different form. If the Government stamp can make a piece of silver, which you can buy for 45 cents, pass for 100 cents, the Government stamp can make a piece of pewter, worth one cent, pass for 100 cents, and a piece of paper, worth a fraction of a cent, pass for 100 cents. Free-silver is the principle of fiat money applied to metal. If you favor fiat silver, you necessarily favor fiat paper.

If the Government can make money with a stamp, why does the Government borrow money? If the Government can create value out of nothing, why not abolish all taxation?

And if it is not the stamp of the Government that raises the value, but the demand which free coinage creates, why has the value of silver gone down at a time when more silver was bought and coined by the Government than ever before? Again, if the people want more silver, why do they refuse what we already have? And if free silver makes money more plentiful, how will *you* get any of it? Will the silver-mine owner give it to you? Will he loan it to you? Will the Government give or loan it to you? Where do you or I come in on this free-silver proposition?

The American people want this money question settled for ever. They want a uniform currency, a convenient currency, a currency that grows as business grows, a currency based on science and not on chance.

And now, on the threshold of our new and great career, is the time permanently to adjust our system of finance. The American people have the mightiest commerce of the world to conduct. They can not halt to unsettle their money system every time some ardent imagination sees a vision and dreams a dream. Think of Great Britain becoming the commercial monarch of the world with her financial system periodically assailed! Think of Holland or Germany or France bearing their burdens, and, yet, sending their flag to every sea, with their money at the mercy of politicians-out-of-an-issue. Let us settle the whole financial system on principles so sound that no agitation can shake it. And then, like men and not like children, let us on to our tasks, our mission and our destiny.

There are so many real things to be done—canals to be dug, railways to be laid, forests to be felled, cities to be builded, fields to be tilled, markets to be won, ships to be launched, peoples to be saved, civilization to be proclaimed and the flag of liberty flung to the eager air of every sea. Is this an hour to waste upon triflers with nature's laws? Is this a season to give our destiny over to word-mongers and prosperity-wreckers? No! It is an hour to remember our duty to our homes. It is a moment to realize the opportunities fate has opened to us. And so it is an hour for us to stand by the Government.

Wonderfully has God guided us. Yonder at Bunker Hill and York-town His providence was above us. At New Orleans and on ensanguined seas His hand sustained us. Abraham Lincoln was His minister and His was the altar of freedom the Nation's soldiers set up on a hundred battle-fields. His power directed Dewey in the East and delivered the Spanish fleet into our hands, as He delivered the elder Armada into the hands of our English sires two centuries ago. The American people can not use a dishonest medium of exchange; it is ours to set the world its example of right and honor. We can not fly from our world duties; it is ours to execute the purpose of a fate that has driven us to be greater than our small intentions. We can not retreat from any soil where Providence has unfurled our banner; it is ours to save that soil for liberty and civilization.

Beveridge's speech had immediate impact. Some 300,000 copies of it were distributed in pamphlet form during the campaigns then in progress for seats in Congress and the state legislature. Since McKinley reached

his decision in favor of Philippine annexation at about the time when the speech was delivered, it seems unlikely that Beveridge's words affected the President. But there were many Republican triumphs in areas where Beveridge's speech had circulated. Beveridge's personal ambition was fulfilled, for in January, 1899, the Indiana legislature elected him to the United States Senate. Although he did not take his seat until after the Senate debate on the peace treaty, his voice was heard in Indiana and other states repeating the themes of the "March of the Flag" address. His election and his oratory may have had some effect on the close vote by which the Senate approved the treaty and the annexation of the Philippines.

But, whatever its immediate consequences, the "March of the Flag" address was to have more importance later. Imperialism drew the attention of powerful theoretical minds. In 1902 the English economist J. A. Hobson published Imperialism: A Study. In 1916 Lenin brought out in Zürich Imperialism: The Highest Stage of Capitalism, a commentary on Hobson. Although neither Hobson nor Lenin mentioned Beveridge, their disciples in America soon saw how his words could be used to support Hobson's thesis that imperialism flowed from industrial overproduction or to buttress Lenin's subtler, more complex argument that imperialism came at "the monopoly stage of capitalism." Taken together, the "March of the Flag" speech and Beveridge's earlier Middlesex Club oration urging conquest of the Philippines became key texts in the interpretation of American imperialism. In The Idea of National Interest (1934), The Open Door at Home (1935), and other works, Charles A. Beard relied heavily on Beveridge's words in advancing an economic interpretation of the expansionism of the 1890's. The two speeches were also to be cited in Soviet and Chinese works on the United States written during the Cold War (among them, the books of A. A. Fursenko, S. B. Gorelik, and Sun Ho-gan). Writers contesting the Sino-Soviet point of view also went to Beveridge, making different exegeses of his language. Julius W. Pratt in Expansionists of 1898 (1936) emphasized Beveridge's predestinarianism. Returning again and again to "The March of the Flag" and the Middlesex Club speech, Albert K. Weinberg in Manifest Destiny (1935) pointed out in them a variety of strands of rationalization for expansionism—the ideas of geographical predestination, God-given title, divine mission, duty, paramount interest, political affinity, and self-defense. Beveridge's words, meant to affect a single partisan campaign, lived on to be read, even in remote parts of the world, as keys to the explanation of his country's motives, behavior, and character.

John Wanamaker
On the Department Store
1900

EDITED BY MALCOLM P. MCNAIR

The application of large sums of capital to the business of retailing came relatively late in the Industrial Revolution. Indeed, most of this development in the United States occurred after the Civil War, lasting into the twentieth century. At first this retail manifestation of capitalism took predominantly the form of the department store, offering a wide range of consumer merchandise under one roof. It is true that even before the Civil War Alexander Stewart in New York City had shown that it was practical to conduct a retail dry-goods business on a large scale, but he limited himself to dry goods and did not organize departmentally. Furthermore, like many other retail merchants of the time, he was also engaged in the wholesale business.

No single person can be said to have invented the department store. The idea, both in Europe and in the United States, developed independently, as merchants, principally with backgrounds in dry goods or men's clothing, sometimes as wholesalers, sometimes as retailers, sought ways of bringing very large numbers of customers to their stores. Nevertheless, one man, John Wanamaker, was mainly responsible for developing and promoting the idea of the department store; and in the last two decades of the nineteenth century his establishment in Philadelphia became the largest department store in the United States and probably in the world.

John Wanamaker was a man with a great flair for publicity and a gift for writing distinctive advertising. He was also a strongly religious person, active in Presbyterian church and Sunday school work, a crusader who exemplified the best of the Protestant ethic. Referring to John Wanamaker, the late Professor N. S. B. Gras of the Harvard Business School often remarked to his business history class that Calvinism was a religion of enthusiasm, fervor, and hustling, and that anyone with a Presbyterian training was likely to have a religious background favorable to capitalism. Wanamaker had established a men's clothing store, Oak Hall, before he was twenty-five years old, following this a few years later with another store, Chestnut Street, for the carriage trade. In his mid-thirties he began revolving in his mind the idea of a "new kind of store" by means of which he might make his business one of the nation's largest retailing enterprises. In late 1874 or early 1875, he had the opportunity to buy from the Pennsylvania Railroad its old freight depot at Thirteenth and Market Streets; the building had become obsolete because of the plan to build a new city hall immediately to the west. Although the structure was much larger than required for his immediate needs, and although it was a considerable distance west of what was then the retailing hub of the city, John Wanamaker could not resist buying the old freight depot.

The first new use of this building was to house a series of revival meetings held by Dwight L. Moody and Ira D. Sankey, who had sought to rent the premises only to find that John Wanamaker held the option. Wanamaker's reaction on hearing of their wishes was characteristic. "The new store can wait a few months for its opening; the Lord's business first." And he promptly came home from Europe to help organize the revival meetings.

At this time Wanamaker was also playing a major part in promoting the Centennial Exposition of 1876, and he saw the opportunity to tie in his new acquisition with this important celebration. After the end of the Moody and Sankey meetings he remodeled the old freight depot; and, still sticking to the men's and boys' clothing business, he opened a huge store there May 6, 1876—essentially an expanded version of his existing retail businesses, Oak Hall and Chestnut Street. During the Centennial Exposition large crowds visited this store; and as the celebration drew to a close, Wanamaker began to cast about for some concept of a retail business with inherent attractions of its own that would continue to bring in crowds. He drew on the ideas that had been accumulating in his mind for several years, particularly those suggested by his study of the large dry-goods stores of Paris during his European trip in 1875. In early

1877, after extensive remodeling, the new store was ready to open. For a week a double-column advertisement in all the Philadelphia papers announced "The Inauguration of the Dry Goods Business at the Grand Depot will take place March 12, from 9 to 6 o'clock." Then on the Saturday preceding the opening the announcement read in part:

NEXT MONDAY THE GRAND INAUGURATION OF THE
DRY GOODS BUSINESS AT THE GRAND DEPOT,
JOHN WANAMAKER, THIRTEENTH STREET
AND NEW CITY HALL

TO THE LADIES.   TO THE LADIES.

In introducing the Dry Goods business as the principal feature at the Grand Depot for merchandise (Thirteenth Street and new City Hall), it seems proper to say that the growth of the city and the accommodation of the public seemed to call for such a central and extensive point for shopping.

John Wanamaker in his advertising repeatedly emphasized the basic policies of the new business. It was not, however, until a number of years later, after the enterprise had overcome early vicissitudes which called forth all the courage and resourcefulness of the founder, that Wanamaker, at the annual meeting of the American Academy of Political and Social Science in Philadelphia in 1900, comprehensively summed up the guiding policies of his "new kind of store-keeping" in an address entitled "The Evolution of Mercantile Business."

MY TOPIC is one car of the long train made up by the general subject of the afternoon—"Combination of Capital as a Factor of Industrial Progress." This annual congress forms a kind of sounding-board for live questions for the entire country, and because of this I wish to contribute what I can to the general stock of information.

About half of Wanamaker's speech on "The Evolution of Mercantile Business" is given here. It is quoted as it originally appeared in *Corporations and Public Welfare: Addresses at the Fourth Annual Meeting of the American Academy of Political and Social Science, April 19–20, 1900. Supplement to the Annals of the American Academy of Political and Social Science* (Philadelphia: American Academy of Political and Social Science, May, 1900), pp. 123–34.

Evolution is that series of steps through which anything has passed in acquiring its present characteristics. The term "mercantile" covers everything relating to trade and commerce. . . .

As late as forty years ago, or before the war, the transaction of business in producing and distributing merchandise required many agencies: the manufacturer, importer, commission men, bankers, jobbers, commercial travelers, and retailers.

Until twenty years ago trade rules limited the sales of manufacturers to commission men, and those of commission houses to jobbers, so that the only market door open to retailers was the jobbers, whose goods were loaded, when they reached the retailer, with three or four unavoidable profits incident to passing the various fixed stages toward the consumer.

The conditions governing the placing of goods in the retailer's hands were not only heavily weighted with expense, but, in the main, the retail merchant was badly handicapped as a rule by

(a) Small capital, commonly borrowed by long credit for merchandise.
(b) Necessity of selling upon credit.
(c) Necessity for larger percentage of profit.
(d) Impossibility of utilizing to advantage store and people all seasons of the year.
(e) Non-accumulation of capital.

The consequence was, according to accepted statistics, that but four out of every hundred merchants succeeded in business. Getting a mere living forty years ago was generally secured in part by the occupancy of a part of the store premises as a residence. Naturally, an undercurrent of discontent with these conditions manifested itself, protesting against two or more prices for the same article, meagre assortments of goods, high prices and the custom that probably grew out of one rate to cash buyers and a different rate to buyers upon credit.

The Centennial Exposition of 1876 was, in my judgment, the moving cause of a departure toward general business by single ownership. The rising tide of popular desire to assemble under one roof articles used in every home and with freedom to purchase was a constant suggestion in 1876, not alone because of its convenience, but because to some degree it would form a permanent and useful exhibition. This idea culminated in the formation of a Permanent Exhibition Company, which succeeded the Centennial. Being located in Fairmount Park and not in a business centre, and without skilled management, the scheme was abandoned in a short time.

Up to 1877, so far as now known, no extensive, well-systemized mercantile retail establishment upon a large scale existed in the United States. The nearest approach was the A. T. Stewart store in New York, which limited itself to dry goods of the higher class, until the death of Mr. A. T. Stewart, when it took on lower classes of goods, and a wider, but still limited scope.

That Centennial Exhibition in 1876 at Philadelphia, the principal manufacturing centre of the country, the first great exhibition in America, opened a new vision to the people of the United States. It was the cornerstone upon which manufacturers everywhere rebuilt their businesses to new fabrics, new fashions and more courageous undertakings by reason of the lessons taught them from the exhibits of the nations of the world. The continuing outgrowth of that exhibition has revolutionized the methods of almost every class of mercantile business in the United States.

The tendency of the age toward simplification of business systems and to remove unnecessary duplication of expenses, awakened throughout the United States a keen study of means to bring about a closer alliance with the producer and consumer. Almost simultaneously in a number of cities, long-established stores gradually enlarged and new stores sprang up to group at one point masses of merchandise in more or less variety. The movement everywhere arrested attention and provoked discussion because of the approval and practical support of the people at large. . . .

Though there probably was never a time in any city that there were not bankruptcies of merchants and vacant stores, yet after the opening of the large stores, it everywhere became common with storekeepers and renters to charge all the causes of disaster to the large stores, then and now commonly called department stores, and an unsuccessful effort was made to decry them as monopolies. . . .

I respectfully submit that the evolution in mercantile business during the last quarter of a century has been wrought not by combinations of capital, corporations or trusts, but by the natural growth of individual mercantile enterprises born of new conditions out of the experience, mistakes and losses of old-time trading; that the underlying basis of the new order of business and its principal claim for favor is that it distributes to the consumer in substance or cash compounded earnings hitherto wasted unnecessarily on middlemen; that thus far the enlarged retailing has practically superseded agents, commission houses, importers and large and small jobbers, thereby saving rentals, salaries and various expenses of handling; that the establishing of direct relations with mills and makers proves to be not only desirable for the saving of such costs as are dispensed with, but because less risks are incurred in preparing products and finding quick markets, thereby favoring lower prices; that the people must be taken into the equation when considering the right of certain businesses to a title of life, as they are responsible for the new conditions, highly value and heartily support them.

It is an old axiom that the water of a stream cannot rise beyond its level. Neither can any business rise or thrive except at the will of the people who are served by it.

I contend that the department store development would not be here but for its service to society; that it has done a public service in retiring middlemen; that its organization neither denies rights to others nor claims privileges of state franchises, or favoritism of national tariff laws; that if there is any suffering from it it is by the pressure of competition, and not from the pressure of monopoly; that so long as competition is not suppressed by law, monopolies cannot exist in storekeeping, and that the one quarter of the globe that cannot be captured by trusts is most assuredly that of the mercantile trading world.

I hold that the evolution in trade was inevitable, because it was waterlogged by old customs that overtaxed purchasers; that there was at work for a long time a resistless force moving towards the highest good of humanity; that the profit therefrom to individuals who have risked their own capital, as any man may still do if he chooses, has been insignificant, compared to the people benefited both by the cheapening of the comforts of life and by the improved condition of persons employed. . . .

I believe the new American system of storekeeping is the most powerful factor yet discovered to compel minimum prices. Perhaps some one will ask what relation reduced prices of merchandise have upon labor. It is a noticeable fact that lowered prices stimulate consumption and require additional labor in producing, transporting and distributing. The care of such large stocks, amounting in one single store upon an average at all times to between four and five millions of dollars, and the preparation of and handling from reserves to forward stocks, require large corps of men. Under old conditions of storekeeping a man and his wife or daughter did all the work between daylight and midnight. The new systems make shorter hours of duty and thus the number of employes is increased, while many entirely new avenues of employment for women are opened, as typewriters, stenographers, cashiers, check-clerks, inspectors, wrappers, mailing clerks and the like. The division of labor creates many places for talented and high-priced men, whose salaries range alongside of presidents of banks and trust companies and similar important positions. It is universally admitted that the sanitary conditions that surround the employes of the large stores are better than in the old-time smaller stores and that employes are considerably better paid. . . .

Public service is the sole basic condition of retail business growth. To give the best merchandise at the least cost is the modern retailer's ambition. He cannot control costs of production, but he can modify costs of distribution and his own profits. His principle is the minimum of profit for the creation of the maximum of business. The keen rivalry of retail trading is inimical to a combination between different and competing firms and companies. . . .

The evolution in business which I have endeavored to discuss has not sought nor has it the power to limit production or stifle competition or raise prices. On the contrary, its chief objectors are those who claim that it makes prices too low. It affects articles of supply of every home and of so many thousands of kinds and ever changing character that no other restriction can obtain than the natural demand. The fact that it deals with distribution and affords intelligent and economic treatment of merchandise increases employment.

It has demonstrated advantages to the public hitherto not common, if at all possible, to former systems. In increasing values of real estate, wherever large businesses are located, smaller stores crowd around them, in some instances changing the values of an entire neighborhood. Statistics prove that it does not anywhere crowd out competent and useful merchants. It saves a multiplication of agencies to the benefit of the consumer in reduced prices. . . .

In after years John Wanamaker, describing the inception of his "new kind of store," said, "The fact was that business in Philadelphia had gone along in the same ancient way so long that innovation was almost a duty." The innovation by which he reinvigorated retail competition was based on a combination of policies:

A large variety of merchandise offered to the shopper under one roof through a departmental form of organization.

Low competitive prices made possible by large volume and direct dealing with manufacturing suppliers.

Assumption of full responsibility to the consumer for quality and values, with one price to all comers and a guarantee of "money back if not satisfied."

Vigorous and distinctive large-scale advertising.

Not all these concepts were original, but the combination and publicizing of them and their widespread imitation created a greater impact on retailing than perhaps any previous development in American business. As always, innovation was stoutly opposed. John Wanamaker was ridiculed, abused, threatened, and plotted against; and the new business narrowly escaped failure on more than one occasion. But, as always in the history of American marketing, when the customers embraced the innovation its long-run success was assured. Merchants in other cities who had been thinking along the same lines were encouraged, and imitators rapidly appeared. By the turn of the century the acceptance of the department store was unquestioned, and institutions such as Macy's, Gimbel's, Marshall Field, and Jordan Marsh were well established. At that time Wanamaker had the largest retail business in Philadelphia, and also in New York, where he had acquired the former A. T. Stewart store.

With his searching mind and lively imagination, John Wanamaker continued to pioneer throughout his life; and over the years his business has been credited, perhaps not always accurately, with a long series of "firsts," comprising such diverse innovations as customer restaurants, store lighting by electricity, a continuing educational program for store employees, August and February furniture sales events, summer vacations with pay, use of pneumatic tubes as cash carriers, Christmas bonuses, and the installation of Marconi wireless stations. That age did not lessen John Wanamaker's capacity for imaginative leadership is shown by his inauguration, in May, 1920 (only a little more than two years before his death), of the famous 20-per-cent store-wide price reduction in both the Philadelphia and New York stores which signalized the end of the great price inflation following World War I.

Wanamaker's vigorous assertion that large-scale operations in retailing would enhance the social effectiveness of competition and in no way conduce to monopoly has been amply verified. So long as retail distribution remained predominantly in the hands of small neighborhood shopkeepers, competition at the retail level was ineffective. Small specialty shops enjoyed their neighborhood monopolies, and competition existed only at the manufacturing level. The advent of large-scale retail operations, first the department store and later mail-order, chain-store, and other types, changed all this. These innovations broke down small-scale monopolies by drawing trade from much wider areas; they competed vigorously not only with the older trade channels but also among themselves; and eventually they added a whole new dimension to competition by raising retail enterprise to such stature and economic importance that it could exercise countervailing power in bargaining with manufacturers, and even in assuming such functions as brand ownership and merchandise development. It was a significant and exciting chapter in American business that John Wanamaker started to write in 1877, and the chapter is not yet closed.

In the eastern seaboard cities in the 1870's the time was undoubtedly ripe for mercantile innovation. For roughly the next fifty years the conditions of urban growth continued to be highly favorable to large downtown department stores. Public transportation systems—street cars, elevated lines, subways, and commuter rail service—all radiated from the downtown centers, where the department stores were located, like the spokes of a wheel; and as they extended their radius and increased their speed they brought larger and larger consumer markets into the retail trading areas of the department stores. At the same time, the growth of newspaper circulation went hand in hand with the increase in department-store advertising, each reinforcing the other and carrying the merchandise message to a larger and larger community. Thus the period of wide acceptance and great growth of the original department-store type of business in the United States extended well into the 1920's, almost coinciding, in fact, with John Wanamaker's business lifetime. Subsequently, far-reaching social, economic, and technological changes were to create greatly different patterns of living and transportation, setting the stage for fresh developments in department-store retailing.

The first major challenge to the department store in its mature phase began to appear just before World War II and grew rapidly in the immediate postwar years. This development stemmed from the "suburban revolution," with its substantially changed patterns of living and transportation. As consumers moved farther away from central business districts and found it increasingly difficult to use their preferred form of transportation (the private automobile) to reach downtown locations in large and medium-size cities, stores had to go where their customers were. And department stores, with their heavy investment in downtown structures housing enormous varieties and quantities of merchandise under one roof, found themselves dangerously inflexible. They were handicapped for making the transition to suburbia, in comparison with the multistore organizations, such as the variety chains and the general merchandise chains (Sears had perceived the trend long before anyone else). Nevertheless, the department stores rallied their forces and met this challenge. They opened suburban branches, drawing in many instances half their volume from these stores. In fact, the department stores themselves played a large part in one of the most important new retail developments of the mid-century—the planned regional shopping center. The full transition is not yet completed. The obverse side of the coin is the problem that has arisen of renovating downtown, and here department stores are still seeking to find a solution that is right for them as well as for the other business and civic interests of the metropolitan complex. But by transforming themselves successfully into multistore organizations, the department stores have clearly met the major challenge growing out of the suburban revolution.

Following closely on the suburban revolution, indeed in some ways a part of it, has come another marked innovation in retailing, the discount department store, utilizing supermarket self-service methods for non-food lines (and frequently offering food as well on a low-price basis). This kind of store, by its rapid growth in the late 1950's and early 1960's, has posed a challenge alike to department stores, to general merchandise and variety chains, and to conventional food supermarket chains. How the department store is meeting this challenge cannot yet be fully appraised. But evidence points to such policies as greater flexibility in serving a more sharply segmented market, with increased emphasis on the service image for some segments and on cost-reducing innovations for other segments. In the meantime all the important retail marketing institutions are beginning to think about the potential challenges from the innovations that are growing out of the current new retailing revolution, namely, the technological revolution in data processing, inventory logistics, and materials handling. Thus as of the mid-1960's the department store is still a retail marketing institution of great vitality.

It is pleasant to note that the Wanamaker business itself continues to exemplify this vitality of the department store as an institution. Although a substantial number of other department-store organizations, many of them operating on a national basis, have surpassed it in total sales volume, John Wanamaker Philadelphia with its five area branches, built or being built, is still the largest department store in that city; and it is managed wholly for the Wanamaker family interest by a Board of Trustees headed by John R. Wanamaker, the great-grandson of the founder. Not without effect has been the injunction inscribed in the capstone of the new store building in 1910:

LET THOSE WHO FOLLOW ME
CONTINUE TO BUILD
WITH THE PLUMB OF HONOR
THE LEVEL OF TRUTH
AND THE SQUARE OF INTEGRITY
EDUCATION, COURTESY
AND MUTUALITY

Jacob A. Riis
Introduction to "The Battle with the Slum"
1902

EDITED BY RICHARD C. WADE

Jacob A. Riis's How the Other Half Lives appeared in 1890. The book not only added a familiar phrase to American speech, but also introduced a new issue and a new author to a national audience. If the phrase "the other half" quickly became a synonym for the poor, so too the problem of the slum soon insinuated itself into every discussion of social questions, and Jacob Riis emerged as a popular spokesman for the conscience of the community on housing reform. It was "a curiously popular book," Riis could write with surprise more than a decade after its publication.

There was nothing contrived about the issue Riis raised. Residential congestion in American cities at the end of the nineteenth century was greater than anywhere else in the world. New York presented the problem in its starkest form. In the Tenth Ward the population density reached 1,000 per acre and over 300,000 people per square mile. No other city matched these figures, but everywhere American metropolises were faced with unparalleled housing pressures. Old commercial buildings were transformed into dwelling space; single-family homes were converted into crowded apartments; new tenements were designed to accommodate the flood of newcomers. With the resultant congestion came disease, crime, want, and deprivation as well as a large harvest of stunted opportunity for youth and abandoned hope for adults.

And Riis knew these conditions well. Coming to New York City as a

641

young immigrant from Denmark, he had difficulty in finding his footing in America. Unemployed for weeks at a time, he had gone hungry and even resorted to police lodging houses for shelter and sleep. In 1877, however, he became a newspaper reporter and began a career which would give him a national reputation. For twenty-two years his beat included the "foul core of New York's slums," where such notorious spots as Bandit's Roost, Bottle Alley, Kerosene Row, and Thieves' Alley became as much a part of his life as his own comfortable neighborhood in Richmond Hills.

Riis was not the first person to discover the slums; by 1890 others had already marshaled the grim statistics and pointed to the mounting danger. Riis's contribution lay in the human dimension he gave to the problem. "I had but a vague idea of these horrors," James Russell Lowell wrote, "before you brought them so feelingly home to me." Riis rejected the more scientific and "sociological" approach because it would "reduce men and women and children to mere items" and "classify and sub-classify" them until they were dry. "One throb of the human heart," he concluded, "is worth a whole book" of theory.

Riis disliked the label of "reformer," yet he found himself an increasingly important part of a campaign to improve the dreadful conditions he had described. Civic organizations, political groups, and even some public agencies mounted a determined attack on the slum. It was an uneven war, with as many failures as victories. In 1902 he wrote The Battle with the Slum as a report on the first ten years of the struggle. It should be viewed, in Riis's words, as a "sequel" to How the Other Half Lives, because it "tells how far we have come and how." The volume contained detailed accounts of particular engagements, especially the replacement of some of the most infected buildings with Mulberry Bend Park. But in the Introduction, Riis put the problem of the slum in its broadest context and viewed it less as a mere matter of housing and more as a measure of the standard of civilization.

THE SLUM is as old as civilization. Civilization implies a race to get ahead. In a race there are usually some who for one cause or another cannot keep up, or are thrust out from among their fellows. They fall behind, and when they have been left far in the rear they lose hope and ambition, and give up. Thenceforward, if left to their own resources, they are the victims, not the masters, of their environment; and it is a bad master. They drag one another always farther down. The bad environment becomes the heredity of the next generation. Then, given the crowd, you have the slum ready-made.

The battle with the slum began the day civilization recognized in it her enemy. It was a losing fight until conscience joined forces with fear and self-interest against it. When common sense and the golden rule obtain among men as a rule of practice, it will be over. The two have not always been classed together, but here they are plainly seen to belong together. Justice to the individual is accepted in theory as the only safe groundwork of the commonwealth. When it is practised in dealing with the slum, there will shortly be no slum. We need not wait for the millennium, to get rid of it. We can do it now. All that is required is that it shall not be left to itself. That is justice to it and to us, since its grievous ailment is that it cannot help itself. When a man is drowning, the thing to do is to pull him out of the water; afterward there will be time for talking it over. We got at it the other way in dealing with our social problems. The wise men had their day, and they decided to let bad enough alone; that it was unsafe to interfere with "causes that operate sociologically," as one survivor of these unfittest put it to me. It was a piece of scientific humbug that cost the age which listened to it dear. "Causes that operate sociologically" are the opportunity of the political and every other kind of scamp who trades upon the depravity and helplessness of the slum, and the refuge of the pessimist who is useless in the fight against them. We have not done yet paying the bills he ran up for us. Some time since we turned to, to pull the drowning man out, and it was time. A little while longer, and we should hardly have escaped being dragged down with him.

The slum complaint had been chronic in all ages, but the great changes which the nineteenth century saw, the new industry, political freedom, brought on an acute attack which put that very freedom in jeopardy. Too many of us had supposed that, built as our common-

Riis's Introduction, entitled "What the Fight Is About," is taken from *The Battle with the Slum* (New York: The Macmillan Company, 1902), pp. 1–8.

wealth was on universal suffrage, it would be proof against the complaints that harassed older states; but in fact it turned out that there was extra hazard in that. Having solemnly resolved that all men are created equal and have certain inalienable rights, among them life, liberty, and the pursuit of happiness, we shut our eyes and waited for the formula to work. It was as if a man with a cold should take the doctor's prescription to bed with him, expecting it to cure him. The formula was all right, but merely repeating it worked no cure. When, after a hundred years, we opened our eyes, it was upon sixty cents a day as the living wage of the working-woman in our cities; upon "knee pants" at forty cents a dozen for the making; upon the Potter's Field taking tithe of our city life, ten per cent each year for the trench, truly the Lost Tenth of the slum. Our country had grown great and rich; through our ports was poured food for the millions of Europe. But in the back streets multitudes huddled in ignorance and want. The foreign oppressor had been vanquished, the fetters stricken from the black man at home; but his white brother, in his bitter plight, sent up a cry of distress that had in it a distinct note of menace. Political freedom we had won; but the problem of helpless poverty, grown vast with the added offscourings of the Old World, mocked us, unsolved. Liberty at sixty cents a day set presently its stamp upon the government of our cities, and it became the scandal and the peril of our political system.

So the battle began. Three times since the war that absorbed the nation's energies and attention had the slum confronted us in New York with its challenge. In the darkest days of the great struggle it was the treacherous mob; [1] later on, the threat of the cholera, which found swine foraging in the streets as the only scavengers, and a swarming host, but little above the hog in its appetites and in the quality of the shelter afforded it, peopling the back alleys. Still later, the mob, caught looting the city's treasury with its idol, the thief Tweed, at its head, drunk with power and plunder, had insolently defied the outraged community to do its worst. There were meetings and protests. The rascals were turned out for a season; the arch-chief died in jail. I see him now, going through the gloomy portals of the Tombs, whither, as a newspaper reporter, I had gone with him, his stubborn head held high as ever. I asked myself more than once, at the time when the vile prison was torn down, whether the comic clamor to have the ugly old gates preserved and set up in Central

---

[1] The draft riots of 1863.

Park had anything to do with the memory of the "martyred" thief, or whether it was in joyful celebration of the fact that others had escaped. His name is even now one to conjure with in the Sixth Ward. He never "squealed," and he was "so good to the poor"—evidence that the slum is not laid by the heels by merely destroying Five Points and the Mulberry Bend. There are other fights to be fought in that war, other victories to be won, and it is slow work. It was nearly ten years after the Great Robbery before decency got a good upper grip. That was when the civic conscience awoke in 1879.

And after all that, the Lexow disclosures of inconceivable rottenness of a Tammany police; the woe unto you! of Christian priests calling vainly upon the chief of the city "to save its children from a living hell," and the contemptuous reply on the witness-stand of the head of the party of organized robbery, at the door of which it was all laid, that he was "in politics, working for his own pocket all the time, same as you and everybody else!"

Slow work, yes! but be it ever so slow, the battle has got to be fought, and fought out. For it is one thing or the other: either we wipe out the slum, or it wipes out us. Let there be no mistake about this. It cannot be shirked. Shirking means surrender, and surrender means the end of government by the people.

If any one believes this to be needless alarm, let him think a moment. Government by the people must ever rest upon the people's ability to govern themselves, upon their intelligence and public spirit. The slum stands for ignorance, want, unfitness, for mob-rule in the day of wrath. This at one end. At the other, hard-heartedness, indifference, self-seeking, greed. It is human nature. We are brothers whether we own it or not, and when the brotherhood is denied in Mulberry Street we shall look vainly for the virtue of good citizenship on Fifth Avenue. When the slum flourishes unchallenged in the cities, their wharves may, indeed, be busy, their treasure-houses filled—wealth and want go so together,—but patriotism among their people is dead.

As long ago as the very beginning of our republic, its founders saw that the cities were danger-spots in their plan. In them was the peril of democratic government. At that time, scarce one in twenty-five of the people in the United States lived in a city. Now it is one in three. And to the selfishness of the trader has been added the threat of the slum. Ask yourself then how long before it would make an end of us, if let alone.

Put it this way: you cannot let men live like pigs when you need their

645

votes as freemen; it is not safe.[1] You cannot rob a child of its childhood, of its home, its play, its freedom from toil and care, and expect to appeal to the grown-up voter's manhood. The children are our to-morrow, and as we mould them to-day so will they deal with us then. Therefore that is not safe. Unsafest of all is any thing or deed that strikes at the home, for from the people's home proceeds citizen virtue, and nowhere else does it live. The slum is the enemy of the home. Because of it the chief city of our land came long ago to be called "The Homeless City." When this people comes to be truly called a nation without homes there will no longer be any nation.

Hence, I say, in the battle with the slum we win or we perish. There is no middle way. We shall win, for we are not letting things be the way our fathers did. But it will be a running fight, and it is not going to be won in two years, or in ten, or in twenty. For all that, we must keep on fighting, content if in our time we avert the punishment that waits upon the third and the fourth generation of those who forget the brother-hood. As a man does in dealing with his brother so it is the way of God that his children shall reap, that through toil and tears we may make out the lesson which sums up all the commandments and alone can make the earth fit for the kingdom that is to come.

In his Introduction, Riis transformed housing reform into a general attack on the broad range of problems which increasingly afflict an urban society. Practical experience had convinced him that the slum was merely a symptom of a deeper environmental malaise. Moreover, the nation's future was irretrievably cast with the city; every year the exodus from the farms indicated that the twentieth century would be shaped by the metropolis. If the slums were permitted to enlarge and fester, the new age would produce a sorry climax to the historic hopes and ideals of the Republic.

The clue to a better future was to be found in the young generation.

---

[1] "The experiment has been long tried on a large scale, with a dreadful success, affording the demonstration that if, from early infancy, you allow human beings to *live* like brutes, you can degrade them down to their level, leaving them scarcely more intellect, and no feelings and affections proper to human hearts."—*Report on the Health of British Towns.*

Children were the special victims of the slums. "The boy who flings mud and stones," he wrote, "is entering his protest in his own way against the purblind policy that gave him jails for schools and the gutter for a playground; that gave him dummies for laws and the tenement for a home." Better housing thus became the major instrument in breaking the vicious cycle of poverty, inadequate education, and limited opportunity. "The home, the family are the rallying points of civilization," he contended. "The greatness of a city is to be measured, not by its balance sheets of exports and imports, not by its fleet of merchantmen, or by its miles of paved streets, nor even by its colleges, its art museums, its schools of learning, but by its homes."

The method of civic improvement was political action. From the free ballot, wisely used, would flow new tenement legislation, better schools, new playgrounds, and attractive neighborhoods. This faith led Riis, as well as later urban reformers, into continual conflict with local city bosses and political machines. To the reformer the central battleground for civic improvement was the political arena, and the great object was the control of City Hall. Riis could conveniently use Tammany as a symbol of the evil forces which prevented needed changes, but it was simply a New York expression of the enemy which frustrated decent people in every city.

Despite the apparent odds in this contest against the slums and its allies—entrenched economic interests and exasperating public apathy—Riis was optimistic about the future. He never doubted that men of good will would eventually conquer the tenement, eliminate substandard housing, and create a better metropolis. The more sophisticated might consider this faith naive, and the Annals of the American Academy of Political and Social Science might observe slightingly that "with his usual hopefulness," Riis "is still looking forward to better things in the future," yet later events were to vindicate his uncomplicated optimism.

The slums, of course, endured, but not to the extent or with the virulence of fifty or seventy-five years ago. In the 1960's the air would be filled with complaints about spreading blight, the decay of old neighborhoods, and the sickness of the ghetto. In historical perspective, however, the situation had vastly changed. Each year since World War II the proportion of substandard housing had declined. Federal, state, and local programs had wiped out many of the worst buildings, and a general prosperity made it possible for the children of former slum dwellers to move into better neighborhoods. The "other half" had been reduced to

647

less than a fifth. To be sure, too many, especially Negroes, still languished in congestion and deprivation, but the mayors of cities like New York, Chicago, and Atlanta were for the first time predicting the elimination of slums in the foreseeable future. When this generation declared war on poverty, it owed more than it knew to those like Jacob Riis who had established a beachhead against the enemy more than half a century before.

Lincoln Steffens
The Shame of the Cities
1902–1904

EDITED BY ARTHUR MANN

The Shame of the Cities, published as a book in 1904 after first appearing as a series of articles in McClure's Magazine from October, 1902, to November, 1903, is a muckraking classic directed against municipal corruption during the Progressive Era. Yet its genesis was wholly unrelated to muckraking, urban politics, or progressivism. Lincoln Steffens stumbled into his subject by wandering, and he arrived at his purpose through afterthought.

The wandering resulted from a conversation at McClure's on a December day in 1901. Steffens had been the managing editor of that popular monthly for three months, and his publisher, S. S. McClure, was telling him that he did not know how to manage a magazine. When Steffens asked how he was to learn, McClure advised him to get out of the office, board a train, and travel. "Meet people, find out what's on, and write yourself." The thirty-five-year-old journalist left for the Midwest, visiting a dozen cities or so by May 18, 1902, when he wrote to his father from Detroit: "My business is to find subjects and writers, to educate myself in the way the world is wagging, so as to bring the magazine up to date."

This odyssey of an editor in search of his craft led by chance to St. Louis, the subject of the first article of the series that grew into The Shame of the Cities. Yet the future dean of muckraking failed, at first, to recognize that he had happened on his vocation. When the circuit (district) attorney of that corrupt river town revealed to Steffens a tale of bribery, Steffens commissioned a St. Louis reporter, Claude H. Wetmore, to write the article for McClure's, and then returned to his New York City desk. "I was not yet a muckraker," he later wrote.

Then came the afterthought. Steffens compared what he had just learned about the Butler machine with what he already knew about Tammany Hall. Were "the extraordinary conditions of St. Louis and New York," he asked himself, "the ordinary conditions of city government in the United States?" Not yet certain that bribery was "a revolutionary process . . . going on in all our cities," he inserted the idea as a hypothesis in Wetmore's manuscript, which he entitled "Tweed Days in St. Louis" and co-signed in order to take responsibility for adding lurid details the Missouri newsman had been afraid to include.

By the time the public read the article in the October, 1902, issue of McClure's, Steffens was back on the road, seeking proof for his hypothesis from bosses, reformers, crooks, cops, and businessmen; and installment followed installment, without the collaboration of local Wetmores, on the shame or near-shame or shamelessness of Minneapolis, again of St. Louis, of Pittsburgh, Philadelphia, Chicago, and New York. But Steffens was more than a reporter of graft; his exposés were aimed toward igniting a civic revival that would redeem democracy from dishonest politicians before corruption destroyed the American experiment in representative government. The series' last article, which follows immediately, expressed his purpose with particular force.

JUST about the time this article will appear, Greater New York will be holding a local election on what has come to be a national question—good government. . . . We can grasp firmly the essential issues involved and then watch with equanimity the returns for the answer, plain yes or no, which New York will give to the only questions that concern us all: *

The article, entitled "New York: Good Government to the Test," appeared first in *McClure's Magazine*, XXII (November, 1903), 84–92. It is reprinted here from *The Shame of the Cities* (New York: McClure, Phillips and Company, 1904), pp. 279–94, 302–3. The one footnote was part of the original text.

* Tammany tried to introduce national issues, but failed, and "good government" was practically the only question raised.

Do we Americans really want good government? Do we know it when we see it? Are we capable of that sustained good citizenship which alone can make democracy a success? Or, to save our pride, one other: Is the New York way the right road to permanent reform?

For New York has good government, or, to be more precise, it has a good administration. It is not a question there of turning the rascals out and putting the honest men into their places. The honest men are in, and this election is to decide whether they are to be kept in, which is a very different matter. Any people is capable of rising in wrath to overthrow bad rulers. Philadelphia has done that in its day. New York has done it several times. With fresh and present outrages to avenge, particular villains to punish, and the mob sense of common anger to excite, it is an emotional gratification to go out with the crowd and "smash something." This is nothing but revolt, and even monarchies have uprisings to the credit of their subjects. But revolt is not reform, and one revolutionary administration is not good government. That we free Americans are capable of such assertions of our sovereign power, we have proven; our lynchers are demonstrating it every day. That we can go forth singly also, and, without passion, with nothing but mild approval and dull duty to impel us, vote intelligently to sustain a fairly good municipal government, remains to be shown. And that is what New York has the chance to show; New York, the leading exponent of the great American anti-bad government movement for good government.

According to this, the standard course of municipal reform, the politicians are permitted to organize a party on national lines, take over the government, corrupt and deceive the people, and run things for the private profit of the boss and his ring, till the corruption becomes rampant and a scandal. Then the reformers combine the opposition: the corrupt and unsatisfied minority, the disgruntled groups of the majority, the reform organizations; they nominate a mixed ticket, headed by a "good business man" for mayor, make a "hot campaign" against the government with "Stop, thief!" for the cry, and make a "clean sweep." Usually, this effects only the disciplining of the reckless grafters and the improvement of the graft system of corrupt government. The good mayor turns out to be weak or foolish or "not so good." The politicians "come it over him," as they did over the business mayors who followed the "Gas Ring" revolt in Philadelphia, or the people become disgusted as they did with Mayor Strong, who was carried into office by the anti-

Tammany rebellion in New York after the Lexow exposures. Philadelphia gave up after its disappointment, and that is what most cities do.
The repeated failures of revolutionary reform to accomplish more than
the strengthening of the machine have so discredited this method that
wide-awake reformers in several cities—Pittsburg, Cincinnati, Cleveland, Detroit, Minneapolis, and others—are following the lead of
Chicago.

The Chicago plan does not depend for success upon any one man or
any one year's work, nor upon excitement or any sort of bad government.
The reformers there have no ward organizations, no machine at all; their
appeal is solely to the intelligence of the voter and their power rests
upon that. This is democratic and political, not bourgeois and business
reform, and it is interesting to note that whereas reformers elsewhere are
forever seeking to concentrate all the powers in the mayor, those of
Chicago talk of stripping the mayor to a figurehead and giving his
powers to the aldermen who directly represent the people, and who
change year by year.

The Chicago way is but one way, however, and a new one, and it must
be remembered that this plan has not yet produced a good administration. New York has that. Chicago, after seven years' steady work, has
a body of aldermen honest enough and competent to defend the city's
interests against boodle capital, but that is about all; it has a wretched
administration. New York has stuck to the old way. Provincial and self-
centered, it hardly knows there is any other. Chicago laughs and other
cities wonder, but never mind, New York, by persistence, has at last
achieved a good administration. Will the New Yorkers continue it?
That is the question. What Chicago has, it has secure. Its independent
citizenship is trained to vote every time and to vote for uninteresting,
good aldermen. New York has an independent vote of 100,000, a
decisive minority, but the voters have been taught to vote only once in a
long while, only when excited by picturesque leadership and sensational
exposures, only *against*. New York has been so far an anti-bad government, anti-Tammany, not a good-government town. Can it vote,
without Tammany in to incite it, for a good mayor? I think this election,
which will answer this question, should decide other cities how to go
about reform.

The administration of Mayor Seth Low may not have been perfect,
not in the best European sense: not expert, not co-ordinated, certainly
not wise. Nevertheless, for an American city, it has been not only honest,

but able, undeniably one of the best in the whole country. Some of the departments have been dishonest; others have been so inefficient that they made the whole administration ridiculous. But what of that? Corruption also is clumsy and makes absurd mistakes when it is new and untrained. The "oaths" and ceremonies and much of the boodling of the St. Louis ring seemed laughable to my corrupt friends in Philadelphia and Tammany Hall, and New York's own Tweed régime was "no joke," only because it was so general, and so expensive—to New York. It took time to perfect the "Philadelphia plan" of misgovernment, and it took time to educate Croker and develop his Tammany Hall. It will take time to evolve masters of the (in America) unstudied art of municipal government—time and demand. So far there has been no market for municipal experts in this country. All we are clamoring for to-day in our meek, weak-hearted way, is that mean, rudimentary virtue miscalled "common honesty." Do we really want it? Certainly Mayor Low is pecuniarily honest. He is more; he is conscientious and experienced and personally efficient. Bred to business, he rose above it, adding to the training he acquired in the conduct of an international commercial house, two terms as mayor of Brooklyn, and to that again a very effective administration, as president, of the business of Columbia University. He began his mayoralty with a study of the affairs of New York; he has said himself that he devoted eight months to its finances: and he mastered this department and is admitted to be the master in detail of every department which has engaged his attention. In other words, Mr. Low has learned the business of New York; he is just about competent now to become the mayor of a great city. Is there a demand for Mr. Low?

No. When I made my inquiries—before the lying had begun—the Fusion leaders of the anti-Tammany forces, who nominated Mr. Low, said they might renominate him. "Who else was there?" they asked. And they thought he "might" be re-elected. The alternative was Richard Croker or Charles F. Murphy, his man, for no matter who Tammany's candidate for mayor was, if Tammany won, Tammany's boss would rule. The personal issue was plain enough. Yet was there no assurance for Mr. Low.

Why? There are many forms of the answer given, but they nearly all reduce themselves to one—the man's personality. It is not very engaging. Mr. Low has many respectable qualities, but these never are amiable. "Did you ever see his smile?" said a politician who was trying to account for his instinctive dislike for the mayor. I had; there is no laughter back of it, no humor, and no sense thereof. The appealing human element is lacking all through. His good abilities are self-sufficient; his dignity is smug; his courtesy seems not kind; his self-reliance is called obstinacy because, though he listens, he seems not to care; though he understands, he shows no sympathy, and when he decides, his reasoning is private. His most useful virtues—probity, intelligence, and conscientiousness—in action are often an irritation; they are so contented. Mr. Low is the bourgeois reformer type. Even where he compromises he gets no credit, his concessions make the impression of surrenders. A politician can say "no" and make a friend, where Mr. Low will lose one by saying "yes." Cold and impersonal, he cools even his heads of departments. Loyal public service they give, because his taste is for men who would do their duty for their own sake, not for his, and that excellent service the city has had. But members of Mr. Low's administration helped me to characterize him; they could not help it. Mr. Low's is not a lovable character.

But what of that? Why should his colleagues love him? Why should anybody like him? Why should he seek to charm, win affection, and make friends? He was elected to attend to the business of his office and to appoint subordinates who should attend to the business of their offices, not to make "political strength" and win elections. William Travers Jerome, the picturesque District Attorney, whose sincerity and intellectual honesty made sure the election of Mr. Low two years ago, detests him as a bourgeois, but the mayoralty is held in New York to be a bourgeois office. Mr. Low is the ideal product of the New York theory that municipal government is business, not politics, and that a business man who would manage the city as he would a business corporation, would solve for us all our troubles. Chicago reformers think we have got to solve our own problems; that government is political business; that men brought up in politics and experienced in public office will make the best administrators. They have refused to turn from their politician mayor, Carter H. Harrison, for the most ideal business candidate, and I have heard them say that when Chicago was ripe for a better mayor they would prefer a candidate chosen from among their well-tried aldermen. Again, I say, however, that this is only one way, and New York has another, and this other is the standard American way.

But again I say, also, that the New York way is on trial, for New York has what the whole country has been looking for in all municipal crises —the non-political ruler. Mr. Low's very faults, which I have emphasized for the purpose, emphasize the point. They make it impossible for him to be a politician even if he should wish to be. As for his selfishness, his lack of tact, his coldness—these are of no consequence. He has done his duty all the better for them. Admit that he is uninteresting; what does that matter? He has served the city. Will the city not vote for him because it does not like the way he smiles? Absurd as it sounds, that is what all I have heard against Low amounts to. But to reduce the situation to a further absurdity, let us eliminate altogether the personality of Mr. Low. Let us suppose he has no smile, no courtesy, no dignity, no efficiency, no personality at all; suppose he were an It and had not given New York a good administration, but had only honestly tried. What then?

Tammany Hall? That is the alternative. The Tammany politicians see it just as clear as that, and they are not in the habit of deceiving themselves. They say "it is a Tammany year," "Tammany's turn." They say it and they believe it. They study the people, and they know it is all a matter of citizenship; they admit that they cannot win unless a goodly part of the independent vote goes to them; and still they say they can beat Mr. Low or any other man the anti-Tammany forces may nominate. So we are safe in eliminating Mr. Low and reducing the issue to plain Tammany.

Tammany is bad government; not inefficient, but dishonest; not a party, not a delusion and a snare, hardly known by its party name— Democracy; having little standing in the national councils of the party and caring little for influence outside of the city. Tammany is Tammany, the embodiment of corruption. All the world knows and all the world may know what it is and what it is after. For hypocrisy is not a Tammany vice. Tammany is for Tammany, and the Tammany men say so. Other rings proclaim lies and make pretensions; other rogues talk about the tariff and imperialism. Tammany is honestly dishonest. Time and time again, in private and in public, the leaders, big and little, have said they are out for themselves and their own; not for the public, but for "me and my friends"; not for New York, but for Tammany. Richard Croker said under oath once that he worked for his own pockets all the time, and Tom Grady, the Tammany orator, has brought his crowds to their feet cheering sentiments as primitive, stated with candor as brutal.

The man from Mars would say that such an organization, so self-confessed, could not be very dangerous to an intelligent people. Foreigners marvel at it and at us, and even Americans—Pennsylvanians, for example—cannot understand why we New Yorkers regard Tammany as so formidable. I think I can explain it. Tammany is corruption with consent; it is bad government founded on the suffrages of the people. The Philadelphia machine is more powerful. It rules Philadelphia by fraud and force and does not require the votes of the people. The Philadelphians do not vote for their machine; their machine votes for them. Tammany used to stuff the ballot boxes and intimidate voters; to-day there is practically none of that. Tammany rules, when it rules, by right of the votes of the people of New York.

Tammany corruption is democratic corruption. That of the Philadelphia ring is rooted in special interests. Tammany, too, is allied with "vested interests"—but Tammany labors under disadvantages not known in Philadelphia. The Philadelphia ring is of the same party that rules the State and the nation, and the local ring forms a living chain with the State and national rings. Tammany is a purely local concern. With a majority only in old New York, it has not only to buy what it wants from the Republican majority in the State, but must trade to get the whole city. Big business everywhere is the chief source of political corruption, and it is one source in New York; but most of the big businesses represented in New York have no plants there. Offices there are, and head offices, of many trusts and railways, for example, but that is all. There are but two railway terminals in the city, and but three railways use them. These have to do more with Albany than New York. So with Wall Street. Philadelphia's stock exchange deals largely in Pennsylvania securities, New York's in those of the whole United States. There is a small Wall Street group that specializes in local corporations, and they are active and give Tammany a Wall Street connection, but the biggest and the majority of our financial leaders, bribers though they may be in other cities and even in New York State, are independent of Tammany Hall, and can be honest citizens at home. From this class, indeed, New York can, and often does, draw some of its reformers. Not so Philadelphia. That bourgeois opposition which has persisted for thirty years in the fight against Tammany corruption was squelched in Philadelphia after its first great uprising. Matt Quay, through the banks, railways, and other business interests, was able to reach it. A large part of his power is negative; there is no opposition. Tammany's power is positive. Tammany cannot reach all the largest interests and its hold is upon the people.

Tammany's democratic corruption rests upon the corruption of the people, the plain people, and there lies its great significance; its grafting system is one in which more individuals share than any I have studied. The people themselves get very little; they come cheap, but they are interested. Divided into districts, the organization subdivides them into precincts or neighborhoods, and their sovereign power, in the form of votes, is bought up by kindness and petty privileges. They are forced to a surrender, when necessary, by intimidation, but the leader and his captains have their hold because they take care of their own. They speak pleasant words, smile friendly smiles, notice the baby, give picnics up the River or the Sound, or a slap on the back; find jobs, most of them at the city's expense, but they have also news-stands, peddling privileges, railroad and other business places to dispense; they permit violations of the law, and, if a man has broken the law without permission, see him through the court. Though a blow in the face is as readily given as a shake of the hand, Tammany kindness is real kindness, and will go far, remember long, and take infinite trouble for a friend.

The power that is gathered up thus cheaply, like garbage, in the districts is concentrated in the district leader, who in turn passes it on through a general committee to the boss. This is a form of living government, extra-legal, but very actual, and, though the beginnings of it are purely democratic, it develops at each stage into an autocracy. In Philadelphia the boss appoints a district leader and gives him power. Tammany has done that in two or three notable instances, but never without causing a bitter fight which lasts often for years. In Philadelphia the State boss designates the city boss. In New York, Croker has failed signally to maintain vice-bosses whom he appointed. The boss of Tammany Hall is a growth, and just as Croker grew, so has Charles F. Murphy grown up to Croker's place. Again, whereas in Philadelphia the boss and his ring handle and keep almost all of the graft, leaving little to the district leaders, in New York the district leaders share handsomely in the spoils. . . .

Tammany leaders are usually the natural leaders of the people in these districts, and they are originally good-natured, kindly men. No one has a more sincere liking than I for some of those common but generous fellows; their charity is real, at first. But they sell out their own people. They do give them coal and help them in their private troubles, but, as they grow rich and powerful, the kindness goes out of the charity and they not only collect at their saloons or in rents—cash for their "good-

657

ness"; they not only ruin fathers and sons and cause the troubles they relieve; they sacrifice the children in the schools; let the Health Department neglect the tenements, and, worst of all, plant vice in the neighborhood and in the homes of the poor.

This is not only bad; it is bad politics; it has defeated Tammany. Woe to New York when Tammany learns better. Honest fools talk of the reform of Tammany Hall. It is an old hope, this, and twice it has been disappointed, but it is not vain. That is the real danger ahead. The reform of a corrupt ring means, as I have said before, the reform of its system of grafting and a wise consideration of certain features of good government. Croker turned his "best chief of police," William S. Devery, out of Tammany Hall, and, slow and old as he was, Croker learned what clean streets were from Colonel Waring, and gave them. Now there is a new boss, a young man, Charles F. Murphy, and unknown to New Yorkers. He looks dense, but he acts with force, decision, and skill. The new mayor will be his man. He may divide with Croker and leave to the "old man" all his accustomed graft, but Charlie Murphy will rule Tammany and, if Tammany is elected, New York also. . . .

As a New Yorker, I fear Murphy will prove sagacious enough to do just that: stop the scandal, put all the graft in the hands of a few tried and true men, and give the city what it would call good government. Murphy says he will nominate for mayor a man so "good" that his goodness will astonish New York. I don't fear a bad Tammany mayor; I dread the election of a good one. For I have been to Philadelphia.

The Shame of the Cities was an immediate success and helped to prepare the ground for a new era in popular journalism. Steffens' second installment, on Minneapolis, appeared in the same issue that carried Ida Tarbell's "History of the Standard Oil" and Ray Stannard Baker's "The Right to Work." S. S. McClure explained: "We did not plan it so; it is a coincidence that this number contains three arraignments of American character such as should make every one of us stop and think." The coincidence was so well received that arraignments became McClure's trademark, and Steffens was soon writing to his father that circulation

had increased by 55 per cent. Other magazines followed suit; by 1904 muckraking was a movement.

Previously a successful enough young reporter (on the Evening Post) and newspaper editor (of the Commercial Advertiser) whose audience had been limited to New York City, Steffens became a braintruster to reformers—from E. A. Filene's Boston to Rudolph Spreckels' San Francisco. In 1906 he turned down an offer from William Randolph Hearst, the most flamboyant muckraker of the age, to edit a new journal at a salary of $20,000 a year, plus a half share in the net profits. Steffens started his own American Magazine that year. His first book (four others were to follow by 1913) had made his reputation. Deriving immense personal satisfaction from his triumph, he confided to his father: "Why not the praise? I won it without a sacrifice, without one single compromise."

That self-estimate was fair. The Shame of the Cities was carefully researched, honestly indignant, and relatively free of the sentimental claptrap that Steffens would later compose about the paradox of good bad bosses. And if he was wrong to suppose that bribery was the norm for "all" American cities, he was right to think that it was a national problem. No other writer before, not even the celebrated Lord Bryce, made the American people so conscious of that fact.

Yet the movements that stemmed from that consciousness were only temporarily successful. Corrupt rulers were thrown out of office, but they came back, and the cycle of exposé and reform had to begin again. Why, after the public was alerted, did crooked government return? In a letter to President Theodore Roosevelt in 1908, Steffens located the cause of corruption in the need of businesses for special privileges from government, but not until his Autobiography, published in 1931, did he carry this idea to what he then thought was its inevitable conclusion about the uselessness of American liberalism.

And it is here that we touch on the Marxist misuse of The Shame of the Cities, for which Steffens himself was to blame.

Writing under the influence of the Russian Revolution and convinced that the Depression had doomed American capitalism, the former muckraker retold his experiences as a municipal reformer during the Progressive Era and concluded that it had been futile to try to patch up the System. The only solution was to take away the means of production and exchange from private ownership. Just how many readers agreed with this message is unknown, but for "those of us who were well on our way to Communism when the Autobiography appeared," Granville Hicks has written, "the book . . . showed that there was a strictly American path to Communist conclusions. . . ." Although Steffens did not join the Communist Party, he openly blessed it and, what is equally important, used his immense prestige to denounce liberal reform. Had he not tried it, led it, sustained it, and failed at it?

According to Hicks, Steffens had always been an absolutist, his pragmatic stance notwithstanding. The Autobiography strongly supports this interpretation, but the Letters, published in 1938, suggest the presence of an open, inquiring, flexible mind to about the time of World War I. Yet, whatever the final verdict will be about Steffens' quest for certitude, it is clear that the Autobiography read uses into The Shame of the Cities that were not there in 1904.

The Steffens who acclaimed Lenin as "the greatest of liberals" was not the same Steffens who had expressed qualified admiration for Mayor Seth Low. Where the later ideologue insisted that all roads must lead to Moscow, the earlier reporter had perceived that what worked in Chicago was not necessarily the way to improve New York. Every city has its own history, its own causes for graft, its own resources for progressive change. Before he succumbed to the metaphysics of inevitability and the mysticism of utopianism, Steffens' high moral purpose had assumed a respect for evidence, an appreciation for diversity, and an understanding that freedom means choice. The Shame of the Cities belongs to our usable past because it reminds us, in plain yet passionate language, that the struggle for good government is varied and unending. And that one must be prepared for disappointments.

Oliver Wendell Holmes, Jr.
Two Dissenting Opinions
1904, 1919

EDITED BY PAUL A. FREUND

LOCHNER v. NEW YORK

As part of a comprehensive law regulating the conditions of labor in
bakeries, the New York legislature in 1897 made it a misdemeanor to
allow any bakery employee to work more than ten hours a day or sixty
hours a week. Lochner, a proprietor of a bakery in Utica, was convicted
under the law for permitting an employee to work in excess of the weekly
limit. The highest court of the state upheld the conviction by a four-to-
three decision, and an appeal was taken to the Supreme Court of the
United States. On April 17, 1905, that Court reversed the conviction,
dividing five to four.

The central issue was whether the law violated the due-process clause
of the Fourteenth Amendment of the United States Constitution: "nor
shall any state deprive any person of life, liberty or property without due
process of law." For the majority of the Supreme Court, Mr. Justice
Peckham asserted that a legal limitation on hours of labor of able-bodied
men in industries not peculiarly unhealthful was an arbitrary deprivation
of the employer's and the employees' liberty of contract. Such restrictions, he said, were "mere meddlesome interferences with the rights of
the individual." A dissenting opinion of Mr. Justice Harlan, joined by
two associates, drew upon studies showing the actual conditions con-
fronting workers in bakeshops, and the bearing of excessive hours upon
the health of workers. The dissenting opinion of Mr. Justice Holmes,

661

here printed, spoke for himself alone. Eschewing alike the abstractions of the majority regarding liberty of contract, and the empirical data garnered by the other dissenters, he pitched his position characteristically on philosophic ground: the responsibility of the judge called on to apply the vague terms of an enduring constitution to novel social legislation with which as a private individual he may have no sympathy.

I REGRET sincerely that I am unable to agree with the judgment in this case, and that I think it my duty to express my dissent. This case is decided upon an economic theory which a large part of the country does not entertain. If it were a question whether I agreed with that theory, I should desire to study it further and long before making up my mind. But I do not conceive that to be my duty, because I strongly believe that my agreement or disagreement has nothing to do with the right of a majority to embody their opinions in law. It is settled by various decisions of this court that state constitutions and state laws may regulate life in many ways which we as legislators might think as injudicious or if you like as tyrannical as this, and which equally with this interfere with the liberty to contract. Sunday laws and usury laws are ancient examples. A more modern one is the prohibition of lotteries. The liberty of the citizen to do as he likes so long as he does not interfere with the liberty of others to do the same, which has been a shibboleth for some well-known writers, is interfered with by school laws, by the Post Office, by every state or municipal institution which takes his money for purposes thought desirable, whether he likes it or not. The Fourteenth Amendment does not enact Mr. Herbert Spencer's Social Statics. The other day we sustained the Massachusetts vaccination law. *Jacobson v. Massachusetts*, 197 U.S. 11. United States and state statutes and decisions cutting down the liberty to contract by way of combination are familiar to this court. *Northern Securities Co. v. United States*, 193 U.S. 197. Two years ago we upheld the prohibition of sales of stock on margins or for future delivery in the constitution of California. *Otis v. Parker*, 187 U.S. 606. The decision sustaining an eight hour law for miners is still recent. *Holden v. Hardy*, 169 U.S. 366. Some of these laws embody convictions or prejudices which judges are likely to

---

The opinion is reprinted here from 198 U.S. 74 (1904).

share. Some may not. But a constitution is not intended to embody a particular economic theory, whether of paternalism and the organic relation of the citizen to the State or of laissez faire. It is made for people of fundamentally differing views, and the accident of our finding certain opinions natural and familiar or novel and even shocking ought not to conclude our judgment upon the question whether statutes embodying them conflict with the Constitution of the United States.

General propositions do not decide concrete cases. The decision will depend on a judgment or intuition more subtle than any articulate major premise. But I think that the proposition just stated, if it is accepted, will carry us far toward the end. Every opinion tends to become a law. I think that the word liberty in the Fourteenth Amendment is perverted when it is held to prevent the natural outcome of a dominant opinion, unless it can be said that a rational and fair man necessarily would admit that the statute proposed would infringe fundamental principles as they have been understood by the traditions of our people and our law. It does not need research to show that no such sweeping condemnation can be passed upon the statute before us. A reasonable man might think it a proper measure on the score of health. Men whom I certainly could not pronounce unreasonable would uphold it as a first instalment of a general regulation of the hours of work. Whether in the latter aspect it would be open to the charge of inequality I think it unnecessary to discuss.

In an address delivered in 1913, nine years after the Lochner dissent, Justice Holmes described the issue with a candor reserved for extrajudicial utterances: "When twenty years ago a vague terror went over the earth and the word socialism began to be heard, I thought and still think that fear was translated into doctrines that had no proper place in the Constitution or the common law. . . . We too need education in the obvious—to learn to transcend our own convictions and to leave room for much that we hold dear to be done away with short of revolution by the orderly change of law."

But the tide was beginning to recede. The Lochner decision itself was probably the high-water mark of judicial vetoes of social legislation by judges indoctrinated with a laissez faire philosophy. In the precise field of that decision, the setting of maximum hours of labor, the Court in 1917 sustained an Oregon ten-hour law as a valid health measure. The Lochner case was not even mentioned in the Court's opinion; as Holmes was to say later, it was given a deserved repose. Indeed the Oregon law was more sweeping than the earlier New York act, since it applied to all forms of manufacturing establishments. Thus, as Holmes had foreseen in his dissenting opinion, the ten-hour day for bakers was the "first instalment of a general regulation of the hours of work."

As legislative controls came to permeate more and more deeply the American economic structure, the special quality of Holmes's opinion became increasingly significant. The older view of the so-called constitutional police powers of the state—that they were to be exercised for the public health, safety, or morals—was hardly adequate for the more pervasive and sophisticated forms of modern social legislation. Hours-of-labor laws themselves moved a long way from the ten-hour day at which the Court had balked. A thirty-hour week, with provision for overtime rates of pay, can scarcely find its justification as a protection against fatigue; it must be dealt with as a measure to spread employment or increase actual wages. And so, by taking broad constitutional ground, by calling on judges to transcend the limitations of their private outlook, Holmes laid the basis for judicial toleration of economic legislation more novel and sophisticated than that which, primitive as it was, a majority of his own colleagues in 1904 had frustrated.

Holmes's constitutional philosophy was carried on and strengthened by his later colleagues Hughes, Brandeis, and Stone, and his successor, Cardozo. Not until after his death was a majority of the Court mustered, in 1937, to sustain a minimum-wage law. But thereafter Herbert Spencer's social statics ceased to place constitutional obstacles in the Supreme Court to economic regulation, whether of hours, wages, prices, competitive practices, or even the aesthetics of zoning. The debate over state intervention centers, as Holmes insisted it should, on issues of public policy rather than constitutional law. Indeed the question is sometimes raised whether the Court has gone too far in its abstention; whether, that is, some kinds of economic regulation, like restrictions on access to certain occupations, touch so centrally the development of human personality that they should be reviewed more critically by the Court under the rubric of liberty in the Fourteenth Amendment.

☆

ABRAMS v. UNITED STATES

The wartime Espionage Act of 1917, as amended in 1918, made it a felony punishable by imprisonment up to twenty years to urge the curtailment of production of any things necessary to the prosecution of the war, with intent to hinder its prosecution. Abrams and four associates were indicted for conspiracy to violate this Act; they were accused of having printed and disseminated leaflets assailing in vehement terms the dispatch of American forces to Russia in 1918, and of having urged workers to strike rather than produce arms to be used against the Soviet people. The defendants were young Russian immigrants employed in a hat factory in New York City. Their trial was presided over by Judge Clayton of Alabama, sitting by special assignment in New York. Upon a finding of guilty by the jury, they were sentenced to the maximum term of twenty years. Their case was appealed to the United States Supreme Court and was decided there on November 10, 1919. By a vote of seven to two the convictions were affirmed. Mr. Justice Holmes was joined in his dissenting opinion by Mr. Justice Brandeis.

The opening part (not printed here) of Holmes's dissenting opinion is concerned with the question whether the leaflets could in fact be said to violate the terms of the statute in view of the equivocal intention of the defendants. They were heartily opposed to Germany and German militarism; their animus was directed at a military expedition which in their view (and in the view of some competent military critics and historians) did not contribute to the successful prosecution of the war against Germany, but instead was a threat to the revolutionary struggle going on within Russia. From his analysis of the issue of specific intent required by the law, Holmes proceeded to the larger question of the constitutional guarantee of freedom of speech. Here he advances the test of "clear and present danger" in order to mark the line between permissible speech and criminal incitement; in this case, he argued, the circumstances were short of any clear and imminent danger of actual obstruction of the conduct of the war, and hence the defendants were constitutionally immune from liability for their words.

In correspondence with Holmes following the decision, Sir Frederick Pollock remarked that the defendants' conduct, if punished at all in England, would have met with a sentence of perhaps three months' imprisonment. The severity of the sentence, however, was not a matter over which the Supreme Court of the United States could exercise a reviewing authority. In fact, the sentences of the defendants were commuted by the President late in 1921, on condition that they be deported to Russia.

IT SEEMS to me that this statute must be taken to use its words in a strict and accurate sense. They would be absurd in any other. A patriot might think that we were wasting money on aeroplanes, or making more cannon of a certain kind than we needed, and might advocate curtailment with success, yet even if it turned out that the curtailment hindered and was thought by other minds to have been obviously likely to hinder the United States in the prosecution of the war, no one would hold such conduct a crime. I admit that my illustration does not answer all that might be said but it is enough to show what I think and to let me pass to a more important aspect of the case. I refer to the First Amendment to the Constitution that Congress shall make no law abridging the freedom of speech.

I never have seen any reason to doubt that the questions of law that alone were before this Court in the cases of *Schenck, Frohwerk* and *Debs*, 249 U.S. 47, 204, 211, were rightly decided. I do not doubt for a moment that by the same reasoning that would justify punishing persuasion to murder, the United States constitutionally may punish speech that produces or is intended to produce a clear and imminent danger that it will bring about forthwith certain substantive evils that the United States constitutionally may seek to prevent. The power undoubtedly is greater in time of war than in time of peace because war opens dangers that do not exist at other times.

But as against dangers peculiar to war, as against others, the principle of the right to free speech is always the same. It is only the present danger of immediate evil or an intent to bring it about that warrants Congress in setting a limit to the expression of opinion where private rights are not concerned. Congress certainly cannot forbid all effort to change the mind of the country. Now nobody can suppose that the surreptitious publishing of a silly leaflet by an unknown man, without more, would present any immediate danger that its opinions would hinder the success of the government arms or have any appreciable tendency to do so. Publishing those opinions for the very purpose of

The opinion is reprinted here from 250 U.S. 627 (1919).

obstructing however, might indicate a greater danger and at any rate would have the quality of an attempt. So I assume that the second leaflet if published for the purposes alleged in the fourth count might be punishable. But it seems pretty clear to me that nothing less than that would bring these papers within the scope of this law. An actual intent in the sense that I have explained is necessary to constitute an attempt, where a further act of the same individual is required to complete the substantive crime, for reasons given in *Swift & Co. v. United States*, 196 U.S. 375, 396. It is necessary where the success of the attempt depends upon others because if that intent is not present the actor's aim may be accomplished without bringing about the evils sought to be checked. An intent to prevent interference with the revolution in Russia might have been satisfied without any hindrance to carrying on the war in which we were engaged.

I do not see how anyone can find the intent required by the statute in any of the defendants' words. The second leaflet is the only one that affords even a foundation for the charge, and there, without invoking the hatred of German militarism expressed in the former one, it is evident from the beginning to the end that the only object of the paper is to help Russia and stop American intervention there against the popular government—not to impede the United States in the war that it was carrying on. To say that two phrases taken literally might import a suggestion of conduct that would have interference with the war as an indirect and probably undesired effect seems to me by no means enough to show an attempt to produce that effect.

I return for a moment to the third count. That charges an intent to provoke resistance to the United States in its war with Germany. Taking the clause in the statute that deals with that in connection with the other elaborate provisions of the act, I think that resistance to the United States means some forcible act of opposition to some proceeding of the United States in pursuance of the war. I think the intent must be the specific intent that I have described and for the reasons that I have given I think that no such intent was proved or existed in fact. I also think that there is no hint at resistance to the United States as I construe the phrase.

In this case sentences of twenty years imprisonment have been imposed for the publishing of two leaflets that I believe the defendants had as much right to publish as the Government has to publish the Constitution of the United States now vainly invoked by them. Even if I am technically wrong and enough can be squeezed from these poor and puny anonymities to turn the color of legal litmus paper; I will add, even if what I think the necessary intent were shown; the most nominal punishment seems to me all that possibly could be inflicted, unless the defendants are to be made to suffer not for what the indictment alleges but for the creed that they avow—a creed that I believe to be the creed of ignorance and immaturity when honestly held, as I see no reason to doubt that it was held here, but which, although made the subject of examination at the trial, no one has a right even to consider in dealing with the charges before the Court.

Persecution for the expression of opinions seems to me perfectly logical. If you have no doubt of your premises or your power and want a certain result with all your heart you naturally express your wishes in law and sweep away all opposition. To allow opposition by speech seems to indicate that you think the speech impotent, as when a man says that he has squared the circle, or that you do not care whole-heartedly for the result, or that you doubt either your power or your premises. But when men have realized that time has upset many fighting faiths, they may come to believe even more than they believe the very foundations of their own conduct that the ultimate good desired is better reached by free trade in ideas—that the best test of truth is the power of the thought to get itself accepted in the competition of the market, and that truth is the only ground upon which their wishes safely can be carried out. That at any rate is the theory of our Constitution. It is an experiment, as all life is an experiment. Every year if not every day we have to wager our salvation upon some prophecy based upon imperfect knowledge. While that experiment is part of our system I think that we should be eternally vigilant against attempts to check the expression of opinions that we loathe and believe to be fraught with death, unless they so imminently threaten immediate interference with the lawful and pressing purposes of the law that an immediate check is required to save the country. I wholly disagree with the argument of the Government that the First Amendment left the common law as to seditious libel in force. History seems to me against the notion. I had conceived that the United States through many years had shown its repentance for the Sedition Act of 1798, by repaying fines that it imposed. Only the emergency that makes it immediately dangerous to leave the correction of evil counsels to time warrants making any exception to the sweeping command, "Congress shall make no law . . . abridging the freedom of

668

speech." Of course I am speaking only of expressions of opinion and exhortations, which were all that were uttered here, but I regret that I cannot put into more impressive words my belief that in their conviction upon this indictment the defendants were deprived of their rights under the Constitution of the United States.

The problem which Justice Holmes faced in the Abrams case is near the center of the theory of democracy: when, if ever, is a state justified in suppressing the speech of nonconformity; in Milton's words, what are the utterances that "no law can possibly permit, that intends not to unlaw itself"? As a student of the common law Holmes drew on an analogy from the law of crimes: the line between mere preparation to commit an offense, which is left unpunished by the law, and an attempt to do so which is sufficiently close to fruition to constitute a social danger recognized by the law.

As a criterion in constitutional law for marking the bounds of speech that must be immune under the First Amendment, the doctrine of "clear and present danger" has had a significant role, though it has been subjected to some refinements and qualifications. In the field of seditious speech, where it had its origin, it proved most decisive in the case of Herndon v. Lowry, decided in 1937, where the Supreme Court reversed the conviction of a Negro Communist in Georgia who was in possession of a booklet urging a Negro insurrection and Negro rule in an interstate domain in the South. In other cases the ambiguities of the doctrine produced certain modifications. Must the evil which is threatened in consequence of the speech be that which the speaker has meant to produce? It has been reasonably clear that no such identity is required; speech intended to produce a revolution may lose its immunity if it presents a clear and present danger of inciting a riot. But suppose the unlawful consequence which is imminent is relatively trivial, like trespass to land, and the speech itself is on a great public theme. In such a balance, Mr. Justice Brandeis suggested that, despite the clear and present danger of unlawful acts, the speech would retain its immunity, for the evil to be avoided must be relatively serious in relation to the significance of the speech. Thus the test, in the hands of a sensitive judge, is far from a mechanical one.

669

In the contemporary world the converse problem has proved still more troublesome—a danger to the state of utmost seriousness, but not an imminent one. The prosecution of officers of the Communist Party under the Smith Act of 1940 elicited a qualification of the doctrine moving in the opposite direction from Justice Brandeis. Judge Learned Hand in the Federal Court of Appeals, and Chief Justice Vinson for a majority of the Supreme Court, formulated the doctrine as permitting punishment where the gravity of the danger, discounted by its improbability, represented, in the judgment of the legislature and of the Court, a threat calling for intervention by the law. More recent decisions have placed limits on the law not so much through the application of a modified "clear and present danger" test as through an interpretation of the statutory term "advocacy" to require something like a call to action and not simply an abstract or philosophic effort at persuasion.

The question remains open how far the "clear and present danger" test is appropriate for speech not in the area of sedition. If the rationale of the doctrine is that the free play of ideas must be permitted so long as there is time to meet them with counter-speech, the doctrine has limited relevance to speech which by its nature is not part of the forum of ideas. Thus problems of obscenity and of newspaper comment on pending trials can be distinguished in that the evils apprehended are not of a kind which can be counteracted by offsetting speech. In these kinds of cases the Supreme Court has divided on the pertinence of the "clear and present danger" doctrine.

A further aspect of Holmes's dissenting opinion deserves to be noticed. In this case he formulated a standard of judicial review of legislation quite different from that in his dissenting opinion in the Lochner case. There the legislative judgment was to prevail unless patently arbitrary; here the legislative judgment must satisfy a stricter standard. Taken together, the two opinions pose implicitly the problem of what has been called a double standard in judicial review of legislation; or, as it has sometimes been put, whether the basic freedoms of speech, press, and assembly have a "preferred position" among constitutionally protected interests. While explanations have differed, there has been general agreement on the Supreme Court that the two approaches to judicial review are not rationally inconsistent. Perhaps the most articulate reconciliation holds that, while the legislative judgment is normally to be given every presumptive support, a law which by interfering with speech or press or assembly fetters the political process itself should be viewed more critically just because the respect normally owing to the legislative product presupposes a properly functioning political process.

The final theme of Holmes's opinion is a pervasive skepticism (tempered for him by a puritanic sense of duty and a romantic faith in action —the soldier's faith, he called it). How far does his argument for freedom of speech depend on his skeptical view of truth? That view has brought condemnation of Holmes by a number of natural-law philosophers. But other orthodox theologians have in effect come to Holmes's position by another path: absolute truth can be apprehended by man in only a fragmentary, historically distorted form, and hence it behooves us not to suppress, in our historical predicament, even the most radical questionings.

William L. Riordon
Plunkitt of Tammany Hall
1905

EDITED BY JOHN P. ROCHE

George Washington Plunkitt was at the turn of this century what students of American politics sometimes call a "second-level political entrepreneur," an erudite term for a ward boss and inside man at City Hall. It was Plunkitt's good fortune to meet William L. Riordon, a political reporter for the New York Evening Post who was impressed by the old rascal and began taking notes of their conversations. At regular intervals Riordon would call on Plunkitt at his "office"—Graziano's shoeshine parlor in the New York County Court House—and stimulate the Tammany sage to deliver his thoughts on events of the day. The result was a "Series of Very Plain Talks on Very Practical Politics" which Riordon published in the Post and later the same year, 1905, published as a book under the title Plunkitt of Tammany Hall.

In his introduction, Riordon gave the following summary of Plunkitt's career:

He was born, as he proudly tells, in Central Park—that is, in the territory now included in the park. He began life as a driver of a cart, then became a butcher's boy, and later went into the butcher business for himself. . . . He was in the [New York State] Assembly soon after he cast his first vote and has held office most of the time for forty years. [At one point in his career he] drew three salaries at once—a record unexampled in New York politics.

Needless to say, Plunkitt was an Irish-American stalwart and an important cog in the Irish political machine which dominated Manhattan, with occasional intervals of Anglo-Saxon Protestant reform, for almost a century. Elsewhere in his discourses Plunkitt expresses his frank view of the reformers. In a curious anticipation of Max Weber's thesis on the interconnection between Protestantism and capitalism, Plunkitt argued that the reformers were miserly thieves who had no sense of community obligation and puritanically refused to share the loot.

There have been suggestions that Riordon may have improved a little on his original, but Plunkitt never complained. Like a Boston politician who was quoted by a newspaperman in most felicitous fashion to the suspicious astonishment of his intimates, Plunkitt could well have observed, "If I didn't say it, by God I should have." And Socrates, of course, owes his good press to Plato. Yet even if Plunkitt of Tammany Hall was a triumph of art over life, the views expressed were in substance clearly authentic—as was the "Tribute" penned by Tammany's austere boss, "Mister" Murphy, at the beginning of the book:

> Senator Plunkitt is a straight organization man. He believes in party government; he does not indulge in cant and hypocrisy and he is never afraid to say exactly what he thinks. He is a believer in thorough political organization and all-the-year-around work, and he holds to the doctrine that, in making appointments to office, party workers should be preferred if they are fitted to perform the duties of the office. Plunkitt is one of the veteran leaders of the organization; he has always been faithful and reliable, and he has performed valuable services for Tammany Hall.
>
> CHARLES F. MURPHY

HONEST GRAFT AND DISHONEST GRAFT

EVERYBODY is talkin' these days about Tammany men growin' rich on graft, but nobody thinks of drawin' the distinction between honest graft and dishonest graft. There's all the difference in the world between the two. Yes, many of our men have grown rich in politics. I have myself. I've made a big fortune out of the game, and I'm gettin' richer every day, but I've not gone in for dishonest graft—blackmailin' gamblers, saloonkeepers, disorderly people, etc.—and neither has any of the men who have made big fortunes in politics.

The first three chapters of the book are reprinted from *Plunkitt of Tammany Hall*, edited by William L. Riordon (New York: McClure, Phillips and Company, 1905).

There's an honest graft, and I'm an example of how it works. I might sum up the whole thing by sayin': "I seen my opportunities and I took 'em."

Just let me explain by examples. My party's in power in the city, and it's goin' to undertake a lot of public improvements. Well, I'm tipped off, say, that they're going to lay out a new park at a certain place.

I see my opportunity and I take it. I go to that place and I buy up all the land I can in the neighborhood. Then the board of this or that makes its plan public, and there is a rush to get my land, which nobody cared particular for before.

Ain't it perfectly honest to charge a good price and make a profit on my investment and foresight? Of course, it is. Well, that's honest graft.

Or supposin' it's a new bridge they're goin' to build. I get tipped off and I buy as much property as I can that has to be taken for approaches. I sell at my own price later on and drop some more money in the bank.

Wouldn't you? It's just like lookin' ahead in Wall Street or in the coffee or cotton market. It's honest graft, and I'm lookin' for it every day in the year. I will tell you frankly that I've got a good lot of it, too.

I'll tell you of one case. They were goin' to fix up a big park, no matter where. I got on to it, and went lookin' about for land in that neighborhood.

I could get nothin' at a bargain but a big piece of swamp, but I took it fast enough and held on to it. What turned out was just what I counted on. They couldn't make the park complete without Plunkitt's swamp, and they had to pay a good price for it. Anything dishonest in that?

Up in the watershed I made some money, too. I bought up several bits of land there some years ago and made a pretty good guess that they would be bought up for water purposes later by the city.

Somehow, I always guessed about right, and shouldn't I enjoy the profit of my foresight? It was rather amusin' when the condemnation commissioners came along and found piece after piece of the land in the name of George Plunkitt of the Fifteenth Assembly District, New York City. They wondered how I knew just what to buy. The answer is—I seen my opportunity and I took it. I haven't confined myself to land; anything that pays is in my line.

For instance, the city is repavin' a street and has several hundred thousand old granite blocks to sell. I am on hand to buy, and I know just what they are worth.

How? Never mind that. I had a sort of monopoly of this business for a while, but once a newspaper tried to do me. It got some outside men to come over from Brooklyn and New Jersey to bid against me.

Was I done? Not much. I went to each of the men and said: "How many of these 250,000 stones do you want?" One said 20,000, and another wanted 15,000, and other wanted 10,000. I said: "All right, let me bid for the lot, and I'll give each of you all you want for nothin'."

They agreed, of course. Then the auctioneer yelled: "How much am I bid for these 250,000 fine pavin' stones?"

"Two dollars and fifty cents," says I.

"Two dollars and fifty cents!" screamed the auctioneer. "Oh, that's a joke! Give me a real bid."

He found the bid was real enough. My rivals stood silent. I got the lot for $2.50 and gave them their share. That's how the attempt to do Plunkitt ended, and that's how all such attempts end.

I've told you how I got rich by honest graft. Now, let me tell you that most politicians who are accused of robbin' the city get rich the same way.

They didn't steal a dollar from the city treasury. They just seen their opportunities and took them. That is why, when a reform administration comes in and spends a half million dollars in tryin' to find the public robberies they talked about in the campaign, they don't find them.

The books are always all right. The money in the city treasury is all right. Everything is all right. All they can show is that the Tammany heads of departments looked after their friends, within the law, and gave them what opportunities they could to make honest graft. Now, let me tell you that's never goin' to hurt Tammany with the people. Every good man looks after his friends, and any man who doesn't isn't likely to be popular. If I have a good thing to hand out in private life, I give it to a friend. Why shouldn't I do the same in public life?

Another kind of honest graft. Tammany has raised a good many salaries. There was an awful howl by the reformers, but don't you know that Tammany gains ten votes for every one it lost by salary raisin'?

The Wall Street banker thinks it shameful to raise a department clerk's salary from $1500 to $1800 a year, but every man who draws a salary himself says: "That's all right. I wish it was me." And he feels very much like votin' the Tammany ticket on election day, just out of sympathy.

Tammany was beat in 1901 because the people were deceived into believin' that it worked dishonest graft. They didn't draw a distinction between dishonest and honest graft, but they saw that some Tammany men grew rich, and supposed they had been robbin' the city treasury or levyin' blackmail on disorderly houses, or workin' in with the gamblers and lawbreakers.

As a matter of policy, if nothing else, why should the Tammany leaders go into such dirty business, when there is so much honest graft lyin' around when they are in power? Did you ever consider that?

Now, in conclusion, I want to say that I don't own a dishonest dollar. If my worst enemy was given the job of writin' my epitaph when I'm gone, he couldn't do more than write:

"George W. Plunkitt. He Seen His Opportunities, and He Took 'Em."

HOW TO BECOME A STATESMAN

There's thousands of young men in this city who will go to the polls for the first time next November. Among them will be many who have watched the careers of successful men in politics, and who are longin' to make names and fortunes for themselves at the same game. It is to these youths that I want to give advice. First, let me say that I am in a position to give what the courts call expert testimony on the subject. I don't think you can easily find a better example than I am of success in politics. After forty years' experience at the game I am—well, I'm George Washington Plunkitt. Everybody knows what figure I cut in the greatest organization on earth, and if you hear people say that I've laid away a million or so since I was a butcher's boy in Washington Market, don't come to me for an indignant denial. I'm pretty comfortable, thank you.

Now, havin' qualified as an expert, as the lawyers say, I am goin' to give advice free to the young men who are goin' to cast their first votes, and who are lookin' forward to political glory and lots of cash. Some young men think they can learn how to be successful in politics from books, and they cram their heads with all sorts of college rot. They couldn't make a bigger mistake. Now, understand me, I ain't sayin' nothin' against colleges. I guess they'll have to exist as long as there's bookworms, and I suppose they do some good in a certain way, but they don't count in politics. In fact, a young man who has gone through the college course is handicapped at the outset. He may succeed in politics, but the chances are 100 to 1 against him.

Another mistake: some young men think that the best way to prepare for the political game is to practice speakin' and becomin' orators. That's all wrong. We've got some orators in Tammany Hall, but they're chiefly ornamental. You never heard of Charlie Murphy delivering a speech, did you? Or Richard Croker, or John Kelly, or any other man who has been a real power in the organization? Look at the thirty-six district leaders of Tammany Hall today. How many of them travel on their tongues? Maybe one or two, and they don't count when business is doin' at Tammany Hall. The men who rule have practiced keepin' their tongues still, not exercisin' them. So you want to drop the orator idea unless you mean to go into politics just to perform the skyrocket act.

Now, I've told you what not to do; I guess I can explain best what to do to succeed in politics by tellin' you what I did. After goin' through the apprenticeship of the business while I was a boy by workin' around the district headquarters and hustlin' about the polls on election day, I set out when I cast my first vote to win fame and money in New York City politics. Did I offer my services to the district leader as a stump-speaker? Not much. The woods are always full of speakers. Did I get up a book on municipal government and show it to the leader? I wasn't such a fool. What I did was to get some marketable goods before goin' to the leaders. What do I mean by marketable goods? Let me tell you: I had a cousin, a young man who didn't take any particular interest in politics. I went to him and said: "Tommy, I'm goin' to be a politician, and I want to get a followin'; can I count on you?" He said: "Sure, George." That's how I started in business. I got a marketable commodity—one vote. Then I went to the district leader and told him I could command two votes on election day, Tommy's and my own. He smiled on me and told me to go ahead. If I had offered him a speech or a bookful of learnin', he would have said, "Oh, forget it!"

That was beginnin' business in a small way, wasn't it? But that is the only way to become a real lastin' statesman. I soon branched out. Two young men in the flat next to mine were school friends. I went to them, just as I went to Tommy, and they agreed to stand by me. Then I had a followin' of three voters and I began to get a bit chesty. Whenever I dropped into district headquarters, everybody shook hands with me, and the leader one day honored me by lightin' a match for my cigar. And so it went on like a snowball rollin' down a hill. I worked the flat-house that I lived in from the basement to the top floor, and I got about a dozen young men to follow me. Then I tackled the next house and so on down the block and around the corner. Before long I had sixty men back of me, and formed the George Washington Plunkitt Association.

What did the district leader say then when I called at headquarters? I didn't have to call at headquarters. He came after me and said: "George, what do you want? If you don't see what you want, ask for it. Wouldn't you like to have a job or two in the departments for your friends?" I said: "I'll think it over; I haven't yet decided what the George Washington Plunkitt Association will do in the next campaign." You ought to have seen how I was courted and petted then by the leaders of the rival organizations. I had marketable goods and there was bids for them from all sides, and I was a risin' man in politics. As time went on, and my association grew, I thought I would like to go to the Assembly. I just had to hint at what I wanted, and three different organizations offered me the nomination. Afterwards, I went to the Board of Aldermen, then to the State Senate, then became leader of the district, and so on up and up till I became a statesman.

That is the way and the only way to make a lastin' success in politics. If you are goin' to cast your first vote next November and want to go into politics, do as I did. Get a followin', if it's only one man, and then go to the district leader and say: "I want to join the organization. I've got one man who'll follow me through thick and thin." The leader won't laugh at your one-man followin'. He'll shake your hand warmly, offer to propose you for membership in his club, take you down to the corner for a drink and ask you to call again. But go to him and say: "I took first prize at college in Aristotle; I can recite all Shakespeare forwards and backwards; there ain't nothin' in science that ain't as familiar to me as blockades on the elevated roads and I'm the real thing in the way of silver-tongued orators." What will he answer? He'll probably say: "I guess you are not to blame for your misfortunes, but we have no use for you here."

THE CURSE OF CIVIL SERVICE REFORM

The civil service law is the biggest fraud of the age. It is the curse of the nation. There can't be no real patriotism while it lasts. How are you goin' to interest our young men in their country if you have no offices to give them when they work for their party? Just look at things in this city today. There are ten thousand good offices, but we can't get at more than a few hundred of them. How are we goin' to provide for the thousands of men who worked for the Tammany ticket? It can't be done. These men were full of patriotism a short time ago. They expected to be servin' their city, but when we tell them that we can't place them, do you think their patriotism is goin' to last? Not much. They say: "What's the use of workin' for your country anyhow? There's nothin' in the game." And what can they do? I don't know, but I'll tell you what I do know. I know more than one young man in past years who worked for the ticket and was just overflowin' with patriotism, but when he was knocked out by the civil service humbug he got to hate his country and became an Anarchist.

This ain't no exaggeration. I have good reason for sayin' that most of the Anarchists in this city today are men who ran up against civil service examinations. Isn't it enough to make a man sour on his country when he wants to serve it and won't be allowed unless he answers a lot of fool questions about the number of cubic inches of water in the Atlantic and the quality of sand in the Sahara desert? There was once a bright young man in my district who tackled one of these examinations. The next I heard of him he had settled down in Herr Most's saloon smokin' and drinkin' beer and talkin' socialism all day. Before that time he had never drank anything but whisky. I knew what was comin' when a young Irishman drops whisky and takes to beer and long pipes in a German saloon. That young man is today one of the wildest Anarchists in town. And just to think! He might be a patriot but for that cussed civil service.

Say, did you hear about that Civil Service Reform Association kickin' because the tax commissioners want to put their fifty-five deputies on the exempt list, and fire the outfit left to them by Low? That's civil service for you. Just think! Fifty-five Republicans and mugwumps holdin' $3000 and $4000 and $5000 jobs in the tax department when 1555 good Tammany men are ready and willin' to take their places! It's an outrage! What did the people mean when they voted for Tammany? What is representative government, anyhow? Is it all a fake that this is a government of the people, by the people and for the people? If it isn't a fake, then why isn't the people's voice obeyed and Tammany men put in all the offices?

When the people elected Tammany, they knew just what they were doin'. We didn't put up any false pretenses. We didn't go in for humbug civil service and all that rot. We stood as we have always stood, for rewardin' the men that won the victory. They call that the spoils system. All right; Tammany is for the spoils system, and when we go in we fire every anti-Tammany man from office that can be fired under the law. It's an elastic sort of law and you can bet it will be stretched to the limit. Of course the Republican State Civil Service Board will stand in the way of our local Civil Service Commission all it can; but say!— suppose we carry the State sometime, won't we fire the upstate Board all right? Or we'll make it work in harmony with the local board, and that means that Tammany will get everything in sight. I know that the civil service humbug is stuck into the constitution, too, but, as Tim Campbell said: "What's the constitution among friends?"

Say, the people's voice is smothered by the cursed civil service law; it is the root of all evil in our government. You hear of this thing or that thing goin' wrong in the nation, the State or the city. Look down beneath the surface and you can trace everything wrong to civil service. I have studied the subject and I know. The civil service humbug is underminin' our institutions and if a halt ain't called soon this great republic will tumble down like a Park Avenue house when they were buildin' the subway, and on its ruins will rise another Russian government.

This is an awful serious proposition. Free silver and the tariff and imperialism and the Panama Canal are triflin' issues when compared to it. We could worry along without any of these things, but civil service is sappin' the foundation of the whole shootin' match. Let me argue it out for you. I ain't up on sillygisms, but I can give you some arguments that nobody can answer.

First, this great and glorious country was built up by political parties; second, parties can't hold together if their workers don't get the offices when they win; third, if the parties go to pieces, the government they built up must go to pieces, too; fourth, then there'll be h——— to pay.

Could anything be clearer than that? Say, honest now; can you answer that argument? Of course you won't deny that the government was built up by the great parties. That's history, and you can't go back of the returns. As to my second proposition, you can't deny that either. When parties can't get offices, they'll bust. They ain't far from the bustin' point now, with all this civil service business keepin' most of the good things from them. How are you goin' to keep up patriotism if this thing goes on? You can't do it. Let me tell you that patriotism has been dying out fast for the last twenty years. Before then when a party won, its workers got everything in sight. That was somethin' to make a man patriotic. Now, when a party wins and its men come forward and ask for their rewards, the reply is, "Nothin' doin', unless you can answer a list of questions about Egyptian mummies and how many years it will take for a bird to wear out a mass of iron as big as the earth by steppin' on it once in a century?"

I have studied politics and men for forty-five years, and I see how things are driftin'. Sad indeed is the change that has come over the young men, even in my district, where I try to keep up the fire of patriotism by gettin' a lot of jobs for my constituents, whether Tammany is in or out. The boys and men don't get excited any more when they see a United States flag or hear "The Star-Spangled Banner." They don't care no more for firecrackers on the Fourth of July. And why should they? What is there in it for them? They know that no matter how hard they work for their country in a campaign, the jobs will go to fellows who can tell about the mummies and the bird steppin' on the iron. Are you surprised then that the young men of the country are beginnin' to look coldly on the flag and don't care to put up a nickel for firecrackers?

Say, let me tell of one case. After the battle of San Juan Hill, the Americans found a dead man with a light complexion, red hair and blue eyes. They could see he wasn't a Spaniard, although he had on a Spanish uniform. Several officers looked him over, and then a private of the Seventy-first Regiment saw him and yelled, "Good Lord, that's Flaherty." That man grew up in my district, and he was once the most patriotic American boy on the West Side. He couldn't see a flag without yellin' himself hoarse.

Now, how did he come to be lying dead with a Spanish uniform on? I found out all about it, and I'll vouch for the story. Well, in the municipal campaign of 1897, that young man, chockful of patriotism, worked day and night for the Tammany ticket. Tammany won, and the young man determined to devote his life to the service of the city. He picked out a place that would suit him, and sent in his application to the head of department. He got a reply that he must take a civil service examination to get the place. He didn't know what these examinations were, so he went, all lighthearted, to the Civil Service Board. He read the questions about the mummies, the bird on the iron, and all the other

681

fool questions—and he left that office an enemy of the country that he had loved so well. The mummies and the bird blasted his patriotism. He went to Cuba, enlisted in the Spanish army at the breakin' out of the war, and died fightin' his country.

That is but one victim of the infamous civil service. If that young man had not run up against the civil examination, but had been allowed to serve his country as he wished, he would be in a good office today, drawin' a good salary. Ah, how many young men have had their patriotism blasted in the same way!

Now, what is goin' to happen when civil service crushes out patriotism? Only one thing can happen: the republic will go to pieces. Then a czar or a sultan will turn up, which brings me to the fourthly of my argument —that is, there will be h——— to pay. And that ain't no lie.

These selections may seem quaint, and, of course, they do have an archaic flavor at a time when an Irish-American Harvard graduate has recently occupied the White House and the old Irish ghettos have long since vanished from the big cities. However, a serious student of the history of American politics can learn a good deal from Plunkitt's random, and seemingly immoral, observations.

In New York, or Boston, or Chicago, or any other big immigrant center a century, or even a half-century, ago, the choice was not between Good Government and Bad Government, but rather between two varieties of corruption. The upstate, Protestant farmers in New York (or the downstate rurals in Illinois) were no less corrupt in their political machinations than the city organizations. Indeed, in our day authorities are generally agreed that the greatest source of political corruption in the United States is county government. But city corruption was highly visible; it was in a sense philanthropic corruption: while some got more than others, nobody was left to starve. A corrupt rural machine controlling the State House would operate in a different fashion. Factory safety laws, health laws, franchises would be manipulated for the benefit of a few, but starvation among the slum dwellers could be viewed with equanimity: if those immigrants don't like it here, let them go back where they came from. A contemporary manifestation of this philosophy occurred in 1963 when the Illinois state legislature, dominated by downstate Republicans, cut off relief for the unemployed (overwhelmingly Negroes) in Chicago. In Massachusetts, dominated by lineal descendants of Plunkitt, this would be inconceivable; a Boston politician who would engage in a "sweetheart deal," or put three generations of his family on the public payroll, without blinking an eye would be horrified by the immorality of letting voters starve. Even, as Plunkitt emphasizes, if they are Republicans.

From the 1880's, when urbanization began to accelerate at a fantastic rate, to the 1930's (and later in some states, notably Pennsylvania) the big cities lived in a state of political siege. Gerrymandering cut down their representation in the state legislatures and in Congress, and often state constitutions made it impossible for the cities ever to achieve real self-government. Alfred E. Smith once observed that the New York state legislature was Republican by constitutional enactment: no more than 40 per cent of the state senate could come from any two adjoining counties, a provision whose purpose becomes clear when one looks at a map of New York City and its five counties. Other states had their own gimmicks; it is symbolic that in only a few instances are state capitols located in major population centers.

In political terms, the warfare between the states and the cities was a battle between the so-called reform movements and the city machines. The city reform movements were, in other words, the urban task-forces of the rural armies. Characteristically these reform movements were led by upper-class urban Protestants, and, while they contained a large number of genuinely dedicated reformers, their major objective was to restore the urban areas to the feudal jurisdiction of the state organizations. The reformers were especially interested in civil service. Theoretically they hoped to improve the public service by eliminating political appointments—and dismissals—and by establishing instead a tradition of "merit." In fact, as opposed to theory, civil service has been used as a weapon by groups in power to protect their appointees from the opposition. Let us take the national case: in 1895 there were 54,222 officials of the national government holding "protected" jobs; that is, under the Pendleton Act of 1884 these positions were exempted from patronage and their occupants could not be dismissed on political grounds by a new administration. In 1896, the figure suddenly jumped to 87,044, and the innocent observer may conclude that the spirit of reform was carrying all before it. Nothing could be further from the truth. What happened was that the Democrats lost the election of 1896 and hastily blanketed in their faithful officeholders; i.e., Congress enacted a statute which widened civil service coverage and protected those currently holding the jobs. In fact, in 1896 only 5,086 individuals were appointed to office under the competitive merit system.

The Hatch Acts of 1939 and 1940 must be understood in this same framework. In essence, this legislation prohibited federal officeholders, and state officeholders whose salaries were drawn from federal funds, from engaging in partisan political activities. It was hailed by what Plunkitt would have called the "goo-goos" (the good government militants) as a noble act of disinterested public policy; in reality it was designed by shrewd congressmen to frustrate any attempts by President Franklin D. Roosevelt to build a national political party with government workers as his cadres. Southern Democratic legislators were particularly concerned lest Roosevelt use the W.P.A. and other work-relief programs as the basis for political machines that might compete with their own "court-house rings"; their solution was to sterilize politically all federal employees while, of course, maintaining the patronage system at full throttle on the state and local level where their strength was rooted.

In the context Plunkitt was examining, civil service was the weapon of the rural, educated Protestants against the urban, badly educated Catholic immigrants. In the common-sense view of the Irish, Italian, or Polish proletarian there was no legitimate connection between ability to answer questions on an examination and ability to dig up streets, run street cars, or serve in the police or fire department. James Michael Curley, Boston's engaging addition to the line-up of Irish-American bosses, first became beloved among his constituents for his willingness to take civil service examinations in their behalf, and in their name. He was jailed for it, but that did little to tarnish his reputation; since time immemorial, it has been no crime among the oppressed to swindle the oppressors.

In short, George Washington Plunkitt provides sharp insights into a real "class struggle" which, though it did not proceed in Marxist terms, had all the elements of confrontation between an old élite and a new, including a fair amount of violence. Immigrant America confronted Jeffersonian America across an abyss which reached the proportions of a chasm in the 1920's, particularly in the presidential election of 1928. In that contest Al Smith, a Tammany product, a Catholic, and "sopping wet" (not a big drinker—he was not—but a militant opponent of

Prohibition), went down in defeat before a wave of scurrility and bigotry. Then, almost before anyone realized it, the real crisis was over: a new generation, faced by a different set of problems such as Depression and War, simply abandoned the old battlefield. In certain ways, then, Plunkitt of Tammany Hall must be understood as a battle monument.

William James
Pragmatism
1907

EDITED BY SIDNEY HOOK

William James's Pragmatism is indisputably the most important book in American philosophy. It is important not so much because of its profundity as because of its popular influence. At home and especially abroad it is accepted as representative of a distinctively American philosophy, and is considered a work that articulates with candor and dash those elements and attitudes in the American experience which transformed the pioneers of a trackless waste into the masters of a supremely powerful technological civilization.

Pragmatism was published in May, 1907. It contains the substance of James's popular lectures delivered in 1906 at the Lowell Institute in Boston and in 1907 at Columbia University. Long before the publication of the book, James had begun developing its central ideas in other lectures and articles. He expressed the pragmatic theory of meaning as early as 1878 and the pragmatic theory of truth a few years later. But in Pragmatism James sought to bring together and to give systematic expression to some of the central notions of his philosophic thought. His pragmatic theory of meaning held that the meaning of an idea is clarified by explicating its consequences in experience; according to his pragmatic theory of truth, the truth of an idea depends upon whether its consequences lead to useful results or work satisfactorily in helping to solve the problem at issue. In addition, James also briefly discussed, with a vivid imagery unsurpassed in the writings of any other philosopher, his conceptions of God, man, and experience. There is no doubt that James in writing Pragmatism felt at the top of his form. Of the delivery and reception of the lectures at Columbia University, he wrote that they were "certainly the high tide of my existence, so far as energizing and being 'recognized' were concerned."

Nonetheless, despite, or because of, James's ability to command attention—he was incapable of writing a dull line even on abstruse themes—he spent the rest of the few years left him after the publication of Pragmatism in amplifying his positions, replying to critics, repudiating misconceptions, and pleading that his words not be read with near-sighted literalness. But the price of imprecision on matters of moment is excited misunderstanding. Even those who sympathized with James's philosophic intent had difficulty in accepting his formulations as an adequate analysis of meaning and truth.

James dedicated his Pragmatism to John Stuart Mill. Because of this dedication, as well as the subtitle of the work—"A New Name for Some Old Ways of Thinking"—and the brilliant drumfire James kept up against intellectualism and traditional rationalism, many critics failed to grasp the extent to which he had abandoned the positions of British empiricism from Locke to Mill. In his Principles of Psychology, James had already given the coup de grâce to the theory of association and to the belief that the mind is passive in knowing. Pragmatism eloquently reinforces James's central conception that the mind is active in knowing and that the truth is not a matter of origins or agreement with an antecedently existing reality but depends upon the future outcome of the changes we set up in acting upon our ideas. James's empiricism was nothing short of a revolutionary reconstruction of the entire tradition of previous empiricism. By emphasizing the active, prospective character of attention and interest in human thinking, James brought the theory of knowledge into line with the deliverances of biology and psychology. Although James inveighed against vicious intellectualism and otiose rationalism, he did so on the ground that they had a false conception of the actual role of reason and intelligence in human experience and not on the ground that they had no value. On the contrary. Intelligence for him had a creative function even though it could not create its own conditions. To believe that the world is rational through and through or in and of itself is as absurd, according to James, as the belief that intelligence is an ineffectual spectator limited to idle commentary on

687

events. The function of thought is to make human decisions, actions, and institutions as reasonable as possible. James was not an existentialist.

This strand of James's thought is apparent in his attempt to assimilate pragmatism to the methods and logic of modern science, with its recognition of the indispensability of hypotheses, which are conceived not as summaries of past experience but as plans or experiments for acting on the world in order to win new insights into, and power over, the future. James pointed to Dewey as the heir and continuator of pragmatism so conceived, whose origins go back to the early writings of Charles Peirce—to whom James made overgenerous acknowledgment.

There was another interest in behalf of which James sought to use pragmatism—religion. Like Faust, James could have said, "Ach! zwei Seelen wohnen in meinem Brust." He was not only a tough-minded scientist seeking clarity and new truth, but a tender-minded literary and religious man in quest of salvation. He sought to vindicate on rational grounds the right to believe in what, with a reasonable interpretation of the logic and ethics of scientific inquiry, one could not legitimately believe in save on faith. This dichotomy is the basic source of the difficulties in his work and must be recognized even by those who are sympathetic to one or another of his specific philosophical doctrines.

THE PRAGMATIC method is primarily a method of settling metaphysical disputes that otherwise might be interminable. Is the world one or many?—fated or free?—material or spiritual?—here are notions either of which may or may not hold good of the world; and disputes over such notions are unending. The pragmatic method in such cases is to try to interpret each notion by tracing its respective practical consequences. What difference would it practically make to any one if this notion rather than that notion were true? If no practical difference whatever can be traced, then the alternatives mean practically the same thing, and all dispute is idle. Whenever a dispute is serious, we ought to be able to show some practical difference that must follow from one side or the other's being right.

The passages given here come from the original edition of *Pragmatism* (New York: Longmans, Green and Company, 1907). They comprise about one-sixth of the whole and are taken from Lectures II, VI, and VIII.

A glance at the history of the idea will show you still better what pragmatism means. The term is derived from the same Greek word πράγμα, meaning action, from which our words 'practice' and 'practical' come. It was first introduced into philosophy by Mr. Charles Peirce in 1878. In an article entitled 'How to Make Our Ideas Clear', in the 'Popular Science Monthly' for January of that year, Mr. Peirce, after pointing out that our beliefs are really rules for action, said that, to develop a thought's meaning, we need only determine what conduct it is fitted to produce: that conduct is for us its sole significance. And the tangible fact at the root of all our thought-distinctions, however subtle, is that there is no one of them so fine as to consist in anything but a possible difference of practice. To attain perfect clearness in our thoughts of an object, then, we need only consider what conceivable effects of a practical kind the object may involve—what sensations we are to expect from it, and what reactions we must prepare. Our conception of these effects, whether immediate or remote, is then for us the whole of our conception of the object, so far as that conception has positive significance at all. . . .

To take in the importance of Peirce's principle, one must get accustomed to applying it to concrete cases. I found a few years ago that Ostwald, the illustrious Leipzig chemist, had been making perfectly distinct use of the principle of pragmatism in his lectures on the philosophy of science, though he had not called it by that name.

"All realities influence our practice," he wrote me, "and that influence is their meaning for us. I am accustomed to put questions to my classes in this way: In what respects would the world be different if this alternative or that were true? If I can find nothing that would become different, then the alternative has no sense."

That is, the rival views mean practically the same thing, and meaning, other than practical, there is for us none. Ostwald in a published lecture gives this example of what he means. Chemists have long wrangled over the inner constitution of certain bodies called 'tautomerous'. Their properties seemed equally consistent with the notion that an instable hydrogen atom oscillates inside of them, or that they are instable mixtures of two bodies. Controversy raged, but was never decided. "It would never have begun," says Ostwald, "if the combatants had asked themselves what particular experimental fact could have been made different by one or the other view being correct. For it would then have appeared that no difference of fact could possibly ensue; and the quarrel was as unreal as if, theorizing in primitive times about the raising of dough by yeast, one party should have invoked a 'brownie,' while another insisted on an 'elf' as the true cause of the phenomonon."

It is astonishing to see how many philosophical disputes collapse into insignificance the moment you subject them to this simple test of tracing a concrete consequence. There can *be* no difference anywhere that doesn't *make* a difference elsewhere—no difference in abstract truth that doesn't express itself in a difference in concrete fact and in conduct consequent upon that fact, imposed on somebody, somehow, somewhere, and somewhen. The whole function of philosophy ought to be to find out what definite difference it will make to you and me, at definite instants of our life, if this world-formula or that world-formula be the true one. . . .

Pragmatism represents a perfectly familiar attitude in philosophy, the empiricist attitude, but it represents it, as it seems to me, both in a more radical and in a less objectionable form than it has ever yet assumed. A pragmatist turns his back resolutely and once for all upon a lot of inveterate habits dear to professional philosophers. He turns away from abstraction and insufficiency, from verbal solutions, from bad *a priori* reasons, from fixed principles, closed systems, and pretended absolutes and origins. He turns towards concreteness and adequacy, towards facts, towards action and towards power. That means the empiricist temper regnant and the rationalist temper sincerely given up. It means the open air and possibilities of nature, as against dogma, artificiality, and the pretence of finality in truth.

At the same time it does not stand for any special results. It is a method only. But the general triumph of that method would mean an enormous change in what I called in my last lecture the 'temperament' of philosophy. Teachers of the ultra-rationalistic type would be frozen out, much as the courtier type is frozen out in republics, as the ultramontane type of priest is frozen out in protestant lands. Science and metaphysics would come much nearer together, would in fact work absolutely hand in hand.

Metaphysics has usually followed a very primitive kind of quest. You know how men have always hankered after unlawful magic, and you know what a great part in magic *words* have always played. If you have his name, or the formula of incantation that binds him, you can control the spirit, genie, afrite, or whatever the power may be. Solomon knew the names of all the spirits, and having their names, he held them subject to his will. So the universe has always appeared to the natural mind as a kind of enigma, of which the key must be sought in the shape of some illuminating or power-bringing word or name. That word names the universe's *principle*, and to possess it is after a fashion to possess the universe itself. 'God,' 'Matter,' 'Reason,' 'the Absolute,' 'Energy,' are so many solving names. You can rest when you have them. You are at the end of your metaphysical quest.

But if you follow the pragmatic method, you cannot look on any such word as closing your quest. You must bring out of each word its practical cash-value, set it at work within the stream of your experience. It appears less as a solution, then, than as a program for more work, and more particularly as an indication of the ways in which existing realities may be *changed*.

Theories thus become instruments, not answers to enigmas, in which we can rest. We don't lie back upon them, we move forward, and, on occasion, make nature over again by their aid. Pragmatism unstiffens all our theories, limbers them up and sets each one at work. Being nothing essentially new, it harmonizes with many ancient philosophic tendencies. It agrees with nominalism for instance, in always appealing to particulars; with utilitarianism in emphasizing practical aspects; with positivism in its disdain for verbal solutions, useless questions and metaphysical abstractions. . . .

No particular results then, so far, but only an attitude of orientation, is what the pragmatic method means. *The attitude of looking away from first things, principles, 'categories,' supposed necessities; and of looking towards last things, fruits, consequences, facts.* . . .

. . . The word pragmatism has come to be used in a still wider sense, as meaning also a certain *theory of truth*. . . .

One of the most successfully cultivated branches of philosophy in our time is what is called inductive logic, the study of the conditions under which our sciences have evolved. Writers on this subject have begun to show a singular unanimity as to what the laws of nature and elements of fact mean, when formulated by mathematicians, physicists and chemists. When the first mathematical, logical and natural uniformities, the first *laws*, were discovered, men were so carried away by the clearness, beauty and simplification that resulted, that they believed themselves to have deciphered authentically the eternal thoughts of the Almighty. His mind also thundered and reverberated in syllogisms. He also thought in conic sections, squares and roots and ratios, and geometrized like Euclid.

He made Kepler's laws for the planets to follow; he made velocity increase proportionally to the time in falling bodies; he made the law of sines for light to obey when refracted; he established the classes, orders, families and genera of the plants and animals, and fixed the distances between them. He thought the archetypes of all things, and devised their variations; and when we rediscover any one of these his wondrous institutions, we seize his mind in its very literal intention.

But as the sciences have developed farther, the notion has gained ground that most, perhaps all, of our laws are only approximations. The laws themselves, moreover, have grown so numerous that there is no counting them; and so many rival formulations are proposed in all the branches of science that investigators have become accustomed to the notion that no theory is absolutely a transcript of reality, but that any one of them may from some point of view be useful. Their great use is to summarize old facts and to lead to new ones. They are only a man-made language, a conceptual short-hand as some one calls them, in which we write our reports of nature; and languages, as is well known, tolerate much choice of expression and many dialects.

Thus human arbitrariness has driven divine necessity from scientific logic. If I mention the names of Sigwart, Mach, Ostwald, Pearson, Milhaud, Poincaré, Duhem, Ruyssen, those of you who are students will easily identify the tendency I speak of, and will think of additional names.

Riding now on the front of this wave of scientific logic Messrs. Schiller and Dewey appear with their pragmatic account of what truth everywhere signifies. Everywhere, these teachers say, 'truth' in our ideas and beliefs means the same thing that it means in science. It means, they say, nothing but this, *that ideas (which themselves are but parts of our experience) become true just in so far as they help us to get into satisfactory relation with other parts of our experience*, to summarize them and get about among them by conceptual short-cuts instead of following the interminable succession of particular phenomena. Any idea upon which we can ride, so to speak; any idea that will carry us prosperously from any one part of our experience to any other part, linking things satisfactorily, working securely, simplifying, saving labor; is true for just so much, true in so far forth, true *instrumentally*. This is the 'instrumental' view of truth taught so successfully at Chicago, the view that truth in our ideas means their power to 'work,' promulgated so brilliantly at Oxford. . . .

The observable process which Schiller and Dewey particularly singled out for generalization is the familiar one by which any individual settles into *new opinions*. The process here is always the same. The individual has a stock of old opinions already, but he meets a new experience that puts them to a strain. Somebody contradicts them; or in a reflective moment he discovers that they contradict each other; or he hears of facts with which they are incompatible; or desires arise in him which they cease to satisfy. The result is an inward trouble to which his mind till then had been a stranger, and from which he seeks to escape by modifying his previous mass of opinions. He saves as much of it as he can, for in this matter of belief we are all extreme conservatives. So he tries to change first this opinion, and then that (for they resist change very variously), until at last some new idea comes up which he can graft upon the ancient stock with a minimum of disturbance of the latter, some idea that mediates between the stock and the new experience and runs them into one another most felicitously and expediently. . . .

. . . A new opinion counts as 'true' just in proportion as it gratifies the individual's desire to assimilate the novel in his experience to his beliefs in stock. It must both lean on old truth and grasp new fact; and its success (as I said a moment ago) in doing this, is a matter for the individual's appreciation. When old truth grows, then, by new truth's addition, it is for subjective reasons. We are in the process and obey the reasons. That new idea is truest which performs most felicitously its function of satisfying our double urgency. It makes itself true, gets itself classed as true, by the way it works; grafting itself then upon the ancient body of truth, which thus grows much as a tree grows by the activity of a new layer of cambium. . . .

The trail of the human serpent is thus over everything. Truth independent; truth that we *find* merely; truth no longer malleable to human need; truth incorrigible, in a word; such truth exists indeed superabundantly—or is supposed to exist by rationalistically minded thinkers; but then it means only the dead heart of the living tree, and its being there means only that truth also has its paleontology, and its 'prescription,' and may grow stiff with years of veteran service and petrified in men's regard by sheer antiquity. But how plastic even the oldest truths nevertheless really are has been vividly shown in our day by the transformation of logical and mathematical ideas, a transformation which seems even to be invading physics. The ancient formulas are reinterpreted as special expressions of much wider principles, principles that our ancestors never got a glimpse of in their present shape and formulation. . . .

. . . Pragmatism is uncomfortable away from facts. Rationalism is comfortable only in the presence of abstractions. This pragmatist talk about truths in the plural, about their utility and satisfactoriness, about the success with which they 'work,' etc., suggests to the typical intellectualist mind a sort of coarse lame second-rate makeshift article of truth. Such truths are not real truths. Such tests are merely subjective. As against this, objective truth must be something non-utilitarian, haughty, refined, remote, august, exalted. It must be an absolute correspondence of our thoughts with an equally absolute reality. It must be what we *ought* to think unconditionally. The conditioned ways in which we *do* think are so much irrelevance and matter for psychology. Down with psychology, up with logic, in all this question!

See the exquisite contrast of the types of mind! The pragmatist clings to facts and concreteness, observes truth at its work in particular cases, and generalizes. Truth, for him, becomes a class-name for all sorts of definite working-values in experience. For the rationalist it remains a pure abstraction, to the bare name of which we must defer. When the pragmatist undertakes to show in detail just *why* we must defer, the rationalist is unable to recognize the concretes from which his own abstraction is taken. He accuses us of denying truth; whereas we have only sought to trace exactly why people follow it and always ought to follow it. Your typically ultra-abstractionist fairly shudders at concreteness; other things equal, he positively prefers the pale and spectral. If the two universes were offered, he would always choose the skinny outline rather than the rich thicket of reality. It is so much purer, clearer, nobler. . . .

Men who are strongly of the fact-loving temperament, you may remember me to have said, are liable to be kept at a distance by the small sympathy with facts which that philosophy from the present-day fashion of idealism offers them. It is far too intellectualistic. Old fashioned theism was bad enough, with its notion of God as an exalted monarch, made up of a lot of unintelligible or preposterous 'attributes'; but, so long as it held strongly by the argument from design, it kept some touch with concrete realities. Since, however, darwinism has once for all displaced design from the minds of the 'scientific,' theism has lost that foothold; and some kind of an immanent or pantheistic deity working *in* things rather than above them is, if any, the kind recommended to our contemporary imagination. Aspirants to a philosophic religion turn, as a rule, more hopefully nowadays towards idealistic pantheism than towards the older dualistic theism, in spite of the fact that the latter still counts able defenders. . . .

. . . The brand of pantheism offered is hard for them to assimilate if they are lovers of facts, or empirically minded. . . .

Now pragmatism, devoted though she be to facts, has no such materialistic bias as ordinary empiricism labors under. Moreover, she has no objection whatever to the realizing of abstractions, so long as you get about among particulars with their aid and they actually carry you somewhere. Interested in no conclusions but those which our minds and our experiences work out together, she has no *a priori* prejudices against theology. *If theological ideas prove to have a value for concrete life, they will be true, for pragmatism, in the sense of being good for so much. For how much more they are true, will depend entirely on their relations to the other truths that also have to be acknowledged.* . . .

I am well aware how odd it must seem to some of you to hear me say that an idea is 'true' so long as to believe it is profitable to our lives. That it is *good*, for as much as it profits, you will gladly admit. If what we do by its aid is good, you will allow the idea itself to be good in so far forth, for we are the better for possessing it. But is it not a strange misuse of the word 'truth,' you will say, to call ideas also 'true' for this reason? . . .

. . . Let me now say only this, that truth is one *species of good*, and not, as is usually supposed, a category distinct from good, and co-ordinate with it. *The true is the name of whatever proves itself to be good in the way of belief, and good, too, for definite, assignable reasons.* Surely you must admit this, that if there were *no* good for life in true ideas, or if the knowledge of them were positively disadvantageous and false ideas the only useful ones, then the current notion that truth is divine and precious, and its pursuit a duty, could never have grown up or become a dogma. In a world like that, our duty would be to *shun* truth, rather. But in this world, just as certain foods are not only agreeable to our taste, but good for our teeth, our stomach, and our tissues; so certain ideas are not only agreeable to think about, or agreeable as supporting other ideas that we are fond of, but they are also helpful in life's practical struggles. If there be any life that it is really better we should lead, and if there be any idea which, if believed in, would help us to lead that life, then it would be really *better for us* to believe in that idea, *unless, indeed, belief in it incidentally clashed with other greater vital benefits.*

'What would be better for us to believe'! This sounds very like a definition of truth. It comes very near to saying 'what we *ought* to believe': and in *that* definition none of you would find any oddity. Ought we ever not to believe what it is *better for us* to believe? And can we then keep the notion of what is better for us, and what is true for us, permanently apart?

Pragmatism says no, and I fully agree with her. Probably you also agree, so far as the abstract statement goes, but with a suspicion that if we practically did believe everything that made for good in our own personal lives, we should be found indulging all kinds of fancies about this world's affairs, and all kinds of sentimental superstitions about a world hereafter. Your suspicion here is undoubtedly well founded, and it is evident that something happens when you pass from the abstract to the concrete that complicates the situation.

I said just now that what is better for us to believe is true *unless the belief incidentally clashes with some other vital benefit.* Now in real life what vital benefits is any particular belief of ours most liable to clash with? What indeed except the vital benefits yielded by *other beliefs* when these prove incompatible with the first ones? In other words, the greatest enemy of any one of our truths may be the rest of our truths. Truths have once for all this desperate instinct of self-preservation and of desire to extinguish whatever contradicts them. My belief in the Absolute, based on the good it does me, must run the gauntlet of all my other beliefs. Grant that it may be true in giving me a moral holiday. Nevertheless, as I conceive it,—and let me speak now confidentially, as it were, and merely in my own private person,—it clashes with other truths of mine whose benefits I hate to give up on its account. It happens to be associated with a kind of logic of which I am the enemy, I find that it entangles me in metaphysical paradoxes that are inacceptable, etc. But as I have enough trouble in life already without adding the trouble of carrying these intellectual inconsistencies, I personally just give up the Absolute. I just *take* my moral holidays; or else as a professional philosopher, I try to justify them by some other principle. . . .

. . . Rationalism sticks to logic and the empyrean. Empiricism sticks to the external senses. Pragmatism is willing to take anything, to follow either logic or the senses and to count the humblest and most personal experiences. She will count mystical experiences if they have practical consequences. She will take a God who lives in the very dirt of private fact—if that should seem a likely place to find him.

Her only test of probable truth is what works best in the way of leading us, what fits every part of life best and combines with the collectivity of experience's demands, nothing being omitted. If theological ideas should do this, if the notion of God, in particular, should prove to do it, how could pragmatism possibly deny God's existence? She could see no meaning in treating as 'not true' a notion that was pragmatically so successful. What other kind of truth could there be, for her, than all this agreement with concrete reality? . . .

I fully expect to see the pragmatist view of truth run through the classic stages of a theory's career. First, you know, a new theory is attacked as absurd; then it is admitted to be true, but obvious and insignificant; finally it is seen to be so important that its adversaries claim that they themselves discovered it. Our doctrine of truth is at present in the first of these three stages, with symptoms of the second stage having begun in certain quarters. I wish that this lecture might help it beyond the first stage in the eyes of many of you.

Truth, as any dictionary will tell you, is a property of certain of our ideas. It means their 'agreement,' as falsity means their disagreement, with 'reality.' Pragmatists and intellectualists both accept this definition as a matter of course. They begin to quarrel only after the question is raised as to what may precisely be meant by the term 'agreement,' and what by the term 'reality,' when reality is taken as something for our ideas to agree with.

In answering these questions the pragmatists are more analytic and painstaking, the intellectualists more offhand and irreflective. The popular notion is that a true idea must copy its reality. Like other popular views, this one follows the analogy of the most usual experience. Our true ideas of sensible things do indeed copy them. Shut your eyes and think of yonder clock on the wall, and you get just such a true picture or copy of its dial. But your idea of its 'works' (unless you are a clockmaker) is much less of a copy, yet it passes muster, for it in no way clashes with the reality. Even though it should shrink to the mere word 'works,' that word still serves you truly; and when you speak of the 'time-keeping function' of the clock, or of its spring's 'elasticity,' it is hard to see exactly what your ideas can copy.

You perceive that there is a problem here. Where our ideas cannot

697

copy definitely their object, what does agreement with that object mean? Some idealists seem to say that they are true whenever they are what God meant that we ought to think about that object. Others hold the copy-view all through, and speak as if our ideas possessed truth just in proportion as they approach to being copies of the Absolute's eternal way of thinking. . . .

These views, you see, invite pragmatistic discussion. But the great assumption of the intellectualists is that truth means essentially an inert static relation. When you've got your true idea of anything, there's an end of the matter. You're in possession; you *know*; you have fulfilled your thinking destiny. You are where you ought to be mentally; you have obeyed your categorical imperative; and nothing more need follow on that climax of your rational destiny. Epistemologically you are in stable equilibrium.

Pragmatism, on the other hand, asks its usual question. "Grant an idea or belief to be true," it says, "what concrete difference will its being true make in any one's actual life? How will the truth be realized? What experiences will be different from those which would obtain if the belief were false? What, in short, is the truth's cash-value in experiential terms?"

The moment pragmatism asks this question, it sees the answer: *True ideas are those that we can assimilate, validate, corroborate and verify.* That is the practical difference it makes to us to have true ideas; that, therefore, is the meaning of truth, for it is all that truth is known-as.

This thesis is what I have to defend. The truth of an idea is not a stagnant property inherent in it. Truth *happens* to an idea. It *becomes* true, is *made* true by events. Its verity *is* in fact an event, a process: the process namely of its verifying itself, its veri-*fication*. Its validity is the process of its valid-*ation*.

But what do the words verification and validation themselves pragmatically mean? They again signify certain practical consequences of the verified and validated idea. It is hard to find any one phrase that characterizes these consequences better than the ordinary agreement-formula—just such consequences being what we have in mind whenever we say that our ideas 'agree' with reality. They lead us, namely, through the acts and other ideas which they instigate, into or up to, or towards, other parts of experience with which we feel all the while—such feeling being among our potentialities—that the original ideas remain in agreement. The connexions and transitions come to us from point to point as being progressive, harmonious, satisfactory. This function of agreeable leading is what we mean by an idea's verification. . . .

Let me begin by reminding you of the fact that the possession of true thought means everywhere the possession of invaluable instruments of action; and that our duty to gain truth, so far from being a blank command from out of the blue, or a 'stunt' self-imposed by our intellect, can account for itself by excellent practical reasons. The importance to human life of having true beliefs about matters of fact is a thing too notorious. We live in a world of realities that can be infinitely useful or infinitely harmful. Ideas that tell us which of them to expect count as the true ideas in all this primary sphere of verification, and the pursuit of such ideas is a primary human duty. The possession of truth, so far from being here an end in itself, is only a preliminary means towards other vital satisfactions. If I am lost in the woods and starved, and find what looks like a cow-path, it is of the utmost importance that I should think of a human habitation at the end of it, for if I do so and follow it, I save myself. The true thought is useful here because the house which is its object is useful. The practical value of true ideas is thus primarily derived from the practical importance of their objects to us. Their objects are, indeed, not important at all times. I may on another occasion have no use for the house; and then my idea of it, however verifiable, will be practically irrelevant, and had better remain latent. Yet since almost any object may some day become temporarily important, the advantage of having a general stock of *extra* truths, of ideas that shall be true of merely possible situations, is obvious. We store such extra truths away in our memories, and with the overflow we fill our books of reference. Whenever such an extra truth becomes practically relevant to one of our emergencies, it passes from cold-storage to do work in the world and our belief in it grows active. You can say of it then either that 'it is useful because it is true' or that 'it is true because it is useful.' Both these phrases mean exactly the same thing, namely that here is an idea that gets fulfilled and can be verified. True is the name for whatever idea starts the verification-process, useful is the name for its completed function in experience. True ideas would never have been singled out as such, would never have acquired a class-name, least of all a name suggesting value, unless they had been useful from the outset in this way.

From this simple cue pragmatism gets her general notion of truth as something essentially bound up with the way in which one moment in our experience may lead us towards other moments which it will be worth while to have been led to. Primarily, and on the common-sense level, the truth of a state of mind means this function of *a leading that is worth while*. When a moment in our experience, of any kind whatever, inspires us with a thought that is true, that means that sooner or later we dip by that thought's guidance into the particulars of experience again and make advantageous connexion with them. This is a vague enough statement, but I beg you to retain it, for it is essential. . . .

Realities mean, then, either concrete facts, or abstract kinds of things and relations perceived intuitively between them. They furthermore and thirdly mean, as things that new ideas of ours must no less take account of, the whole body of other truths already in our possession. But what now does 'agreement' with such threefold realities mean?—to use again the definition that is current.

Here it is that pragmatism and intellectualism begin to part company. Primarily, no doubt, to agree means to copy, but we say that the mere word 'clock' would do instead of a mental picture of its works, and that of many realities our ideas can only be symbols and not copies. 'Past times,' 'power,' 'spontaneity,'—how can our mind copy such realities?

To 'agree' in the widest sense with a reality *can only mean to be guided either straight up to it or into its surroundings, or to be put into such working touch with it as to handle either it or something connected with it better than if we disagreed.* Better either intellectually or practically! And often agreement will only mean the negative fact that nothing contradictory from the quarter of that reality comes to interfere with the way in which our ideas guide us elsewhere. To copy a reality is, indeed, one very important way of agreeing with it, but it is far from being essential. The essential thing is the process of being guided. Any idea that helps us to *deal*, whether practically or intellectually, with either the reality or its belongings, that doesn't entangle our progress in frustrations, that *fits*, in fact and adapts our life to the reality's whole setting, will agree sufficiently to meet the requirement. It will hold true of that reality.

Thus, *names* are just as 'true' or 'false' as definite mental pictures are. They set up similar verification-processes, and lead to fully equivalent practical results.

All human thinking gets discursified; we exchange ideas; we lend and borrow verifications, get them from one another by means of social intercourse. All truth thus gets verbally built out, stored up, and made available for every one. Hence, we must talk consistently just as we must *think* consistently: for both in talk and thought we deal with kinds. Names are arbitrary, but once understood they must be kept to. We mustn't now call Abel 'Cain' or Cain 'Abel.' If we do, we ungear ourselves from the whole book of Genesis, and from all its connexions with the universe of speech and fact down to the present time. We throw ourselves out of whatever truth that entire system of speech and fact may embody.

The overwhelming majority of our true ideas admit of no direct or face-to-face verification—those of past history, for example, as of Cain and Abel. The stream of time can be remounted only verbally, or verified indirectly by the present prolongations or effects of what the past harbored. Yet if they agree with these verbalities and effects, we can know that our ideas of the past are true. *As true as past time itself was,* so true was Julius Caesar, so true were antediluvian monsters, all in their proper dates and settings. That past time itself was, is guaranteed by its coherence with everything that's present. True as the present *is,* the past *was* also.

Agreement thus turns out to be essentially an affair of leading— leading that is useful because it is into quarters that contain objects that are important. True ideas lead us into useful verbal and conceptual quarters as well as directly up to useful sensible termini. They lead to consistency, stability and flowing human intercourse. They lead away from eccentricity and isolation, from foiled and barren thinking. The untrammelled flowing of the leading-process, its general freedom from clash and contraction, passes for its indirect verification; but all roads lead to Rome, and in the end and eventually, all true processes must lead to the face of directly verifying sensible experiences *somewhere,* which somebody's ideas have copied.

Such is the large loose way in which the pragmatist interprets the word agreement. He treats it altogether practically. He lets it cover any process of conduction from a present idea to a future terminus, provided only it run prosperously. It is only thus that 'scientific' ideas, flying as they do beyond common sense, can be said to agree with their realities. It is, as I have already said, *as if* reality were made of ether, atoms or electrons, but we mustn't think so literally. The term 'energy' doesn't even pretend to stand for anything 'objective.' It is only a way of measuring the surface of phenomena so as to string their changes on a simple formula.

Yet in the choice of these man-made formulas we can not be capricious with impunity any more than we can be capricious on the common-sense practical level. We must find a theory that will *work*; and that means something extremely difficult; for our theory must mediate between all previous truths and certain new experiences. It must derange common sense and previous belief as little as possible, and it must lead to some sensible terminus or other that can be verified exactly. To 'work' means both these things; and the squeeze is so tight that there is little loose play for any hypothesis. Our theories are wedged and controlled as nothing else is. Yet sometimes alternative theoretic formulas are equally compatible with all the truths we know, and then we choose between them for subjective reasons. We choose the kind of theory to which we are already partial; we follow 'elegance' or 'economy.' Clerk-Maxwell somewhere says it would be 'poor scientific taste' to choose the more complicated of two equally well-evidenced conceptions; and you will all agree with him. Truth in science is what gives us the maximum possible sum of satisfactions, taste included, but consistency both with previous truth and with novel fact is always the most imperious claimant. . . .

. . . 'The true,' to put it very briefly, is only the expedient in the way of our thinking, just as 'the right' is only the expedient in the way of our behaving.' Expedient in almost any fashion; and expedient in the long run and on the whole of course; for what meets expediently all the experience in sight won't necessarily meet all farther experiences equally satisfactorily. Experience, as we know, has ways of *boiling over*, and making us correct our present formulas.

The 'absolutely' true, meaning what no farther experience will ever alter, is that ideal vanishing-point towards which we imagine that all our temporary truths will some day converge. It runs on all fours with the perfectly wise man, and with the absolutely complete experience; and, if these ideals are ever realized, they will all be realized together. Meanwhile we have to live to-day by what truth we can get to-day, and be ready to-morrow to call it falsehood. Ptolemaic astronomy, euclidean space, aristotelian logic, scholastic metaphysics, were expedient for centuries, but human experience has boiled over those limits, and we now call these things only relatively true, or true within those borders of experience. 'Absolutely' they are false; for we know that those limits were casual, and might have been transcended by past theorists just as they are by present thinkers.

When new experiences lead to retrospective judgments, using the past tense, what these judgments utter *was* true, even tho no past thinker had been led there. We live forwards, a Danish thinker has said, but we understand backwards. The present sheds a backward light on the world's previous processes. They may have been truth-processes for the actors in them. They are not so for one who knows the later revelations of the story.

This regulative notion of a potential better truth to be established later, possibly to be established some day absolutely, and having powers of retroactive legislation, turns its face, like all pragmatist notions, towards concreteness of fact, and towards the future. Like the half-truths, the absolute truth will have to be *made*, made as a relation incidental to the growth of a mass of verification-experience, to which the half-true ideas are all along contributing their quota.

I have already insisted on the fact that truth is made largely out of previous truths. Men's beliefs at any time are so much experience *funded*. But the beliefs are themselves parts of the sum total of the world's experience, and become matter, therefore, for the next day's funding operations. So far as reality means experienceable reality, both it and the truths men gain about it are everlastingly in process of mutation —mutation towards a definite goal, it may be—but still mutation.

Mathematicians can solve problems with two variables. On the Newtonian theory, for instance, acceleration varies with distance, but distance also varies with acceleration. In the realm of truth-processes facts come independently and determine our beliefs provisionally. But these beliefs make us act, and as fast as they do so, they bring into sight or into existence new facts which re-determine the beliefs accordingly. So the whole coil and ball of truth, as it rolls up, is the product of a double influence. Truths emerge from facts; but they dip forward into facts again and add to them; which facts again create or reveal new truth (the word is indifferent) and so on indefinitely. The 'facts' themselves meanwhile are not *true*. They simply *are*. Truth is the function of the beliefs that start and terminate among them.

The case is like a snowball's growth, due as it is to the distribution of the snow on the one hand, and to the successive pushes of the boys on the other, with these factors co-determining each other incessantly. . . .

I fear that my previous lectures, confined as they have been to human and humanistic aspects, may have left the impression on many of you that pragmatism means methodically to leave the superhuman out. I have shown small respect indeed for the Absolute, and I have until this moment spoken of no other superhuman hypothesis but that. But I trust that you see sufficiently that the Absolute has nothing but its superhumanness in common with the theistic God. On pragmatistic principles, if the hypothesis of God works satisfactorily in the widest sense of the word, it is true. Now whatever its residual difficulties may be, experience shows that it certainly does work, and that the problem is to build it out and determine it so that it will combine satisfactorily with all the other working truths. I can not start upon a whole theology at the end of this last lecture; but when I tell you that I have written a book on men's religious experience, which on the whole has been regarded as making for the reality of God, you will perhaps exempt my own pragmatism from the charge of being an atheistic system. I firmly disbelieve, myself, that our human experience is the highest form of experience extant in the universe. I believe rather that we stand in much the same relation to the whole of the universe as our canine and feline pets do to the whole of human life. They inhabit our drawing-rooms and libraries. They take part in scenes of whose significance they have no inkling. They are merely tangent to curves of history the beginning and ends and forms of which pass wholly beyond their ken. So we are tangent to the wider life of things. But, just as many of the dog's and cat's ideals coincide with our ideals, and the dogs and cats have daily living proof of the fact, so we may well believe, on the proofs that religious experience affords, that higher powers exist and are at work to save the world on ideal lines similar to our own.

You see that pragmatism can be called religious, if you allow that religion can be pluralistic or merely melioristic in type. But whether you will finally put up with that type of religion or not is a question that only you yourself can decide. Pragmatism has to postpone dogmatic answer, for we do not yet know certainly which type of religion is going to work best in the long run. The various overbeliefs of men, their several faith-ventures, are in fact what are needed to bring the evidence in. You will probably make your own ventures severally. If radically tough, the hurly-burly of the sensible facts of nature will be enough for you, and you will need no religion at all. If radically tender, you will take up with the more monistic form of religion: the pluralistic form, with its reliance on possibilities that are not necessities, will not seem to afford you security enough.

☆

If success be measured by the interest aroused in the general public, the intensity of the intellectual excitement generated, and the number of criticisms and refutations published, then no book in the history of American philosophy, possibly in the history of American thought, has been as successful as William James's Pragmatism. It seemed as if the author's jubilant anticipation in a letter to his brother, Henry James, that his book would be "rated 'epoch-making' . . . something quite like the protestant reformation" was about to be realized. But if success be measured by the influence the book had on professional philosophers on both sides of the Atlantic, by its fruitfulness in clarifying philosophical issues and establishing a consensus of agreement among philosophers, it was a profound failure. With few exceptions, the American and European philosophers rejected its central contentions. Even John Dewey, in reviewing the book, felt that some of James's formulations contributed to further misunderstanding of what pragmatism meant by "practical." Whatever intellectual influence James's pragmatism had in law, religion, and psychology,—and its indirect effects were considerable —in philosophy James established no school and won no following. To this day he remains a towering figure, still more alive than most living philosophers, appealing to readers in virtue of his insights, his personality, and his attitude of open-mindedness. He remains influential insofar as some of the specific doctrines he espoused are concerned—his pluralism, temporalism, and radical empiricism—but unconvincing with respect to the particular pragmatic doctrines he treasured most.

Two generic reasons account for James's failure to make of pragmatism a plausible philosophical doctrine. The first is the impression his colorful rhetoric gives that he denies the possibility of objective truth, "that by saying whatever you find it pleasant to say and calling it truth you fulfil every pragmatistic requirement." These are the words which James puts in the mouths of his prospective critics and he denounces in advance such an interpretation of pragmatism as "an impudent slander." Nonetheless, the expressions James uses to describe his theory of truth are a perennial source of this misunderstanding. His statement, "On pragmatistic principles, if the hypothesis of God works satisfactorily in the widest sense of the word, it is true," has often been read as justifying the attribution of "truth" to beliefs which are useful, pleasant, convenient, or expedient, despite the fact that it is perfectly comprehensible to speak of a useful or pleasant, a convenient or expedient—indeed, of a satisfactory —falsehood.

The second reason is more technical and more important. The pragmatic theory of meaning is an oversimplification of highly complex linguistic phenomena. Although James's pragmatic theory contributed substantially to further exploration of the meaning of meaning, it did not make the necessary explicit distinctions among various senses or types of meaning recognized in human discourse, even when we restrict ourselves, as James did, to meanings of statements of which truth or falsity can be predicated.

There are at least three senses of meaning involved in James's pragmatic theory of meaning. The first sense is derived from the fact that expressions are used for purposes of communication on the basis of a certain familiarity long before we seek to specify their consequences in experience. For example, "Diamonds are harder than lead" and "Women are more merciful than men" have an intelligible sense in the funded traditions of ordinary discourse independent of the experimental or practical consequences which their assertion implies. Otherwise we would be unable to indicate which set of experimental consequences follows from which assertion.

The second sense of meaning is the one which James is most interested in. It is closest to the verifiability theory of meaning subsequently developed by logical empiricists and operationalists. This is the sense in which James maintains that every intelligible statement which purports to give knowledge about human affairs must in principle lead to some possible set of concrete observations, that every cognitive distinction must make some experimental or practical difference, and that if the sets of consequences implied by the assertion of two different expressions are indistinguishable from each other, then their intellectual meaning is the same. A great many technical difficulties arise in the quest for a precise formulation of the criteria of meaningfulness, but it would not be unjust to say that, according to James, unless we can indicate the kind of evidence which would tend to confirm or disconfirm an assertion about any state of affairs, the assertion would not have cognitive significance.

There is a third sense of meaning in James which he himself does not distinguish from the second. A statement is meaningful if belief in it has some bearing on human conduct. Here the consequences are not the actual or possible observations following from an experimental or controlled procedure that tests the statement, but are consequences of the psychological act of belief in the statement. This introduces an altogether different order of considerations. A statement may be false or even self-contradictory in the second sense above, but belief in it may have consequences which, even if confirmed, have no relevance whatsoever to the truth, falsity, or meaningfulness of the statement. For example, "Santa Claus exists" is a false statement which no set of consequences of belief in his existence, regardless of their beneficial or useful or convenient character, can in any way affect. This confusion between the second and third senses of meaning contributed to the interpretation of James's theory of pragmatism as a method by which the emotional demands of our nature received gratification at the sacrifice of intellectual responsibility. The statement "Santa Claus exists" may be false, and the statement "Belief in the existence of Santa Claus is beneficial to children" may be true. The truth of this latter statement does not itself depend upon the consequences of belief in it.

When pruned of inconsistencies and dissociated from the needs of religious apologetics, the pragmatic theory of meaning and truth has left a permanent bequest to schools of philosophical thought which take science and scientific methods as paradigms of human knowledge and of the most reliable ways of winning new truths. The pragmatic theory of meaning seeks to clarify expressions of discourse by examining carefully the contexts in which they are used, and the range of their applications, positive and negative. The pragmatic theory of truth tends to identify the meaning of truth with the criteria of evidence which warrants assertion. It denies that ideas are images and that true ideas are maps of an antecedent reality. If the truth of a statement is defined independently of the criteria of evidence, it would follow that we could never be warranted in asserting the truth of any statement of fact. The very growth of scientific knowledge justifies the pragmatic conception of truth in its refusal to define truth about matters of fact in absolute terms.

Theodore Roosevelt
The New Nationalism
1910

EDITED BY ELTING E. MORISON

Theodore Roosevelt, on his way home from all the exciting times in Africa, arrived in London in May, 1910, to represent his country at the funeral of Edward VII. Elihu Root, setting out for a vacation on the Continent, broke the trip to visit his old friend, who was staying at Dorchester House. There on May 30 the two discussed at length the fortunes of the Republican Party as they had developed since the close of Roosevelt's second term as President, and while he had been off on his long safari. At the end Roosevelt, as his visitor recalled, gave his word to stay out of "things political" on his return to the United States. Such indeed seems to have been his intention for, a few days earlier, he had written to President Taft that he was taking pains to keep his mind open and his mouth shut.

The intention expressed, it soon appeared, was easier to keep on the far side of the water than on home ground. Roosevelt arrived in New York on June 18, 1910, to an ecstatic welcome from his fascinated countrymen. In the days that followed, men concerned with the developing fortunes of the Republican Party made their way out to Sagamore Hill to talk with the great man. One of the matters they talked about most often was Governor Charles Evans Hughes's decision to call a special session of the New York legislature to consider a measure whereby candidates for certain state offices would be nominated by direct primaries. The governor's action pleased progressive members of the party, but roused

708

the antagonism of the new party boss in the state, William Barnes, Jr. This difference between governor and boss had produced a cleavage within the Republican Party in the state at the moment Roosevelt arrived home. He was put under pressure by both sides to make a public declaration of his position. For a few days he resisted these importunities, mindful perhaps of his words with Root. Then he went off to the Harvard Commencement exercises on June 29, where he met both Henry Cabot Lodge and Governor Hughes. While the former whispered words of caution, the latter spoke convincingly for action. Persuaded by the appeal for his help, Roosevelt at noon announced his support of the direct-primary legislation.

Thus Theodore Roosevelt became mixed up again in "things political." There have been various explanations. He was ambitious and his ambitions were played upon by schemers like the Pinchots, who saw in him a source of further power for themselves. He was annoyed by the ineptitudes of his successor, William Howard Taft, and therefore annoyed with himself for picking Taft to succeed him. He was at fifty-two a healthy, high-spirited man seeking once again a legitimate outlet for his frustrated energies in the only task in the country that fitted his ample powers. He was moved by his sense of loyalty to certain public officials who had supported him—Bass of New Hampshire, Garfield of Ohio, Osborn of Missouri, Hadley of Michigan, Stimson of New York, and to all those others less renowned who had shared the burden and the heat of an earlier day with him.

Doubtless he was moved in subtle ways by all these influences—mean and noble, conscious and unconscious—as most men have been. But he was moved too by another concern. Once, near the turn of the century, he had said to a friend that there was in a society that rested upon industry the constant danger of barbarism. Unhappily prominent in American life, he went on, was "the spirit of the Birmingham School, the spirit of the banker, the broker, the mere manufacturer, the mere merchant." Such a spirit, he came early in his Presidency to believe, if left ungoverned would in time destroy even the society that held out the last best hopes of earth. Therefore, he had said, "It behooves us to look ahead and plan out the right kind of civilization as that which we intend to develop from these wonderful new conditions of vast industrial growth."

In the years from 1901 to 1909 Roosevelt as President had given life to these sentiments. From a hundred platforms, at a thousand whistle stops, he had given the society an objective by defining in striking words the nature of what he believed was the right kind of civilization, and by a score of bold and skillful actions he had demonstrated it was possible to create out of an industrial society a satisfying environment. He had used his authority to set safe limits on the power of the corporation, to conserve the natural resources of the country, to produce a more equitable distribution of goods, services, and opportunities among the citizens. Upon leaving office in 1909 he looked to the Republican Party as the instrument to continue his efforts.

And so when he returned to this country in 1910, an election year, it was in the nature of things political for him, as he told Henry Cabot Lodge, "to try to help the Republican Party at the polls this fall." By so doing he would perform "the greatest service I can render to Taft, the service which beyond all others will tend to secure his renomination and to make that renomination of use" by ensuring Taft's re-election in 1912.

Here was the problem confronted by Roosevelt in 1910. The conflict that had brought Roosevelt back into politics, the struggle between the enlightened Governor Hughes and the party boss Barnes in New York, was a conflict that extended in fact within the Republican Party throughout the country. Broadly speaking, what divided the members was a difference of opinion about the proper role of the central government. The liberal spirits—the insurgents or progressives as they were called—believed that the state should play a large part in the ordering of affairs within the economy; the conservative spirits—the Old Guard—were inclined to leave well enough alone. Roosevelt was one of the liberal spirits—a man with a specific program that added up to what he called doing good to the nation and a man who believed the central government was under obligation to take action to do this good. So in 1910 he wanted to help the party win and he wanted to make it take what he thought of as "the proper position." On July 23, 1910, he started out on a speaking tour that began in New York and wound through the Middle West to Colorado. In many states and places he gave specifically his support to Republican candidates simply because they were Republicans. Then in other places, where the nature of the occasion seemed to take matters beyond the mere search for votes, he cut loose with his own ideas. By this means he hoped both to elect Republicans and to define advanced positions from which, after election, the party could not retreat.

The best opportunity to speak his full mind occurred on August 31 at Osawatomie, Kansas. Roosevelt there took part in a celebration dedicating the ancient field where John Brown in 1856 entered our history. The place was appropriate for a striking statement. It was here that Roosevelt first fully defined what he called "The New Nationalism," a phrase which became one of the great passwords of American politics.

WE COME here to-day to commemorate one of the epoch-making events of the long struggle for the rights of man—the long struggle for the uplift of humanity. Our country—this great Republic—means nothing unless it means the triumph of a real democracy, the triumph of popular government, and, in the long run, of an economic system under which each man shall be guaranteed the opportunity to show the best that there is in him. That is why the history of America is now the central feature of the history of the world; for the world has set its face hopefully toward our democracy; and, O my fellow citizens, each one of you carries on your shoulders not only the burden of doing well for the sake of your own country, but the burden of doing well and of seeing that this nation does well for the sake of mankind.

There have been two great crises in our country's history: first, when it was formed, and then, again, when it was perpetuated; and, in the second of these great crises—in the time of stress and strain which culminated in the Civil War, on the outcome of which depended the justification of what had been done earlier, you men of the Grand Army, you men who fought through the Civil War, not only did you justify your generation, not only did you render life worth living for our generation, but you justified the wisdom of Washington and Washington's colleagues. If this Republic had been founded by them only to be split asunder into fragments when the strain came, then the judgment of the world would have been that Washington's work was not worth doing. It was you who crowned Washington's work, as you carried to achievement the high purpose of Abraham Lincoln.

The speech is reprinted here from the National Edition of *The Works of Theodore Roosevelt*, edited by Hermann Hagedorn (20 vols.; New York: Charles Scribner's Sons, 1926), XVII, 5–22.

Now, with this second period of our history the name of John Brown will be forever associated; and Kansas was the theatre upon which the first act of the second of our great national life dramas was played. It was the result of the struggle in Kansas which determined that our country should be in deed as well as in name devoted to both union and freedom; that the great experiment of democratic government on a national scale should succeed and not fail. In name we had the Declaration of Independence in 1776; but we gave the lie by our acts to the words of the Declaration of Independence until 1865; and words count for nothing except in so far as they represent acts. This is true everywhere; but, O my friends, it should be truest of all in political life. A broken promise is bad enough in private life. It is worse in the field of politics. No man is worth his salt in public life who makes on the stump a pledge which he does not keep after election; and, if he makes such a pledge and does not keep it, hunt him out of public life. I care for the great deeds of the past chiefly as spurs to drive us onward in the present. I speak of the men of the past partly that they may be honored by our praise of them, but more that they may serve as examples for the future.

It was a heroic struggle; and, as is inevitable with all such struggles, it had also a dark and terrible side. Very much was done of good, and much also of evil; and, as was inevitable in such a period of revolution, often the same man did both good and evil. For our great good fortune as a nation, we, the people of the United States as a whole, can now afford to forget the evil, or, at least, to remember it without bitterness, and to fix our eyes with pride only on the good that was accomplished. Even in ordinary times there are very few of us who do not see the problems of life as through a glass, darkly; and when the glass is clouded by the murk of furious popular passion, the vision of the best and the bravest is dimmed. Looking back, we are all of us now able to do justice to the valor and the disinterestedness and the love of the right, as to each it was given to see the right, shown both by the men of the North and the men of the South in that contest which was finally decided by the attitude of the West. We can admire the heroic valor, the sincerity, the self-devotion shown alike by the men who wore the blue and the men who wore the gray; and our sadness that such men should have had to fight one another is tempered by the glad knowledge that ever hereafter their descendants shall be found fighting side by side, struggling in peace as well as in war for the uplift of their common country, all alike resolute to raise to the highest pitch of honor and usefulness the nation to which they all belong. As for the veterans of the Grand Army of the Republic, they deserve honor and recognition such as is paid to no other citizens of the Republic; for to them the republic owes its all; for to them it owes its very existence. It is because of what you and your comrades did in the dark years that we of to-day walk, each of us, head erect, and proud that we belong, not to one of a dozen little squabbling contemptible commonwealths, but to the mightiest nation upon which the sun shines.

I do not speak of this struggle of the past merely from the historic standpoint. Our interest is primarily in the application to-day of the lessons taught by the contest of half a century ago. It is of little use for us to pay lip-loyalty to the mighty men of the past unless we sincerely endeavor to apply to the problems of the present precisely the qualities which in other crises enabled the men of that day to meet those crises. It is half melancholy and half amusing to see the way in which well-meaning people gather to do honor to the men who, in company with John Brown, and under the lead of Abraham Lincoln, faced and solved the great problems of the nineteenth century, while, at the same time, these same good people nervously shrink from, or frantically denounce, those who are trying to meet the problems of the twentieth century in the spirit which was accountable for the successful solution of the problems of Lincoln's time.

Of that generation of men to whom we owe so much, the man to whom we owe most is, of course, Lincoln. Part of our debt to him is because he forecast our present struggle and saw the way out. He said:

"I hold that while man exists it is his duty to improve not only his own condition, but to assist in ameliorating mankind."

And again:

"Labor is prior to, and independent of, capital. Capital is only the fruit of labor, and could never have existed if labor had not first existed. Labor is the superior of capital, and deserves much the higher consideration."

If that remark was original with me, I should be even more strongly denounced as a Communist agitator than I shall be anyhow. It is Lincoln's. I am only quoting it; and that is one side; that is the side the capitalist should hear. Now, let the working man hear his side.

"Capital has its rights, which are as worthy of protection as any other rights. . . . Nor should this lead to a war upon the owners of property.

Property is the fruit of labor; . . . property is desirable; is a positive good in the world."

And then comes a thoroughly Lincolnlike sentence:

"Let not him who is houseless pull down the house of another, but let him work diligently and build one for himself, thus by example assuring that his own shall be safe from violence when built."

It seems to me that, in these words, Lincoln took substantially the attitude that we ought to take; he showed the proper sense of proportion in his relative estimates of capital and labor, of human rights and property rights. Above all, in this speech, as in many others, he taught a lesson in wise kindliness and charity; an indispensable lesson to us of to-day. But this wise kindliness and charity never weakened his arm or numbed his heart. We cannot afford weakly to blind ourselves to the actual conflict which faces us to-day. The issue is joined, and we must fight or fail.

In every wise struggle for human betterment one of the main objects, and often the only object, has been to achieve in large measure equality of opportunity. In the struggle for this great end, nations rise from barbarism to civilization, and through it people press forward from one stage of enlightenment to the next. One of the chief factors in progress is the destruction of special privilege. The essence of any struggle for healthy liberty has always been, and must always be, to take from some one man or class of men the right to enjoy power, or wealth, or position, or immunity, which has not been earned by service to his or their fellows. That is what you fought for in the Civil War, and that is what we strive for now.

At many stages in the advance of humanity, this conflict between the men who possess more than they have earned and the men who have earned more than they possess is the central condition of progress. In our day it appears as the struggle of freemen to gain and hold the right of self-government as against the special interests, who twist the methods of free government into machinery for defeating the popular will. At every stage, and under all circumstances, the essence of the struggle is to equalize opportunity, destroy privilege, and give to the life and citizenship of every individual the highest possible value both to himself and to the commonwealth. That is nothing new. All I ask in civil life is what you fought for in the Civil War. I ask that civil life be carried on according to the spirit in which the army was carried on. You never get perfect justice, but the effort in handling the army was to bring to the front the men who could do the job. Nobody grudged promotion to Grant, or Sherman, or Thomas, or Sheridan, because they earned it. The only complaint was when a man got promotion which he did not earn.

Practical equality of opportunity for all citizens, when we achieve it, will have two great results. First, every man will have a fair chance to make of himself all that in him lies; to reach the highest point to which his capacities, unassisted by special privilege of his own and unhampered by the special privilege of others, can carry him, and to get for himself and his family substantially what he has earned. Second, equality of opportunity means that the commonwealth will get from every citizen the highest service of which he is capable. No man who carries the burden of the special privileges of another can give to the commonwealth that service to which it is fairly entitled.

I stand for the square deal. But when I say that I am for the square deal, I mean not merely that I stand for fair play under the present rules of the game, but that I stand for having those rules changed so as to work for a more substantial equality of opportunity and of reward for equally good service. One word of warning, which, I think, is hardly necessary in Kansas. When I say I want a square deal for the poor man, I do not mean that I want a square deal for the man who remains poor because he has not got the energy to work for himself. If a man who has had a chance will not make good, then he has got to quit. And you men of the Grand Army, you want justice for the brave man who fought, and punishment for the coward who shirked his work. Is not that so?

Now, this means that our government, National and State, must be freed from the sinister influence or control of special interests. Exactly as the special interests of cotton and slavery threatened our political integrity before the Civil War, so now the great special business interests too often control and corrupt the men and methods of government for their own profit. We must drive the special interests out of politics. That is one of our tasks to-day. Every special interest is entitled to justice— full, fair, and complete—and, now, mind you, if there were any attempt by mob-violence to plunder and work harm to the special interest, whatever it may be, that I most dislike, and the wealthy man, whomsoever he may be, for whom I have the greatest contempt, I would fight for him, and you would if you were worth your salt. He should have justice. For every special interest is entitled to justice, but not one is entitled to a vote in Congress, to a voice on the bench, or to representation in any public office. The Constitution guarantees protection to property, and we must make that promise good. But it does not give the right of suffrage to any corporation.

The true friend of property, the true conservative, is he who insists that property shall be the servant and not the master of the commonwealth; who insists that the creature of man's making shall be the servant and not the master of the man who made it. The citizens of the United States must effectively control the mighty commercial forces which they have themselves called into being.

There can be no effective control of corporations while their political activity remains. To put an end to it will be neither a short nor an easy task, but it can be done.

We must have complete and effective publicity of corporate affairs, so that the people may know beyond peradventure whether the corporations obey the law and whether their management entitles them to the confidence of the public. It is necessary that laws should be passed to prohibit the use of corporate funds directly or indirectly for political purposes; it is still more necessary that such laws should be thoroughly enforced. Corporate expenditures for political purposes, and especially such expenditures by public-service corporations, have supplied one of the principal sources of corruption in our political affairs.

It has become entirely clear that we must have government supervision of the capitalization, not only of public-service corporations, including, particularly, railways, but of all corporations doing an interstate business. I do not wish to see the nation forced into the ownership of the railways if it can possibly be avoided, and the only alternative is thoroughgoing and effective regulation, which shall be based on a full knowledge of all the facts, including a physical valuation of property. This physical valuation is not needed, or, at least, is very rarely needed, for fixing rates; but it is needed as the basis of honest capitalization.

We have come to recognize that franchises should never be granted except for a limited time, and never without proper provision for compensation to the public. It is my personal belief that the same kind and degree of control and supervision which should be exercised over public-service corporations should be extended also to combinations which control necessaries of life, such as meat, oil, and coal, or which deal in them on an important scale. I have no doubt that the ordinary man who has control of them is much like ourselves. I have no doubt he would like to do well, but I want to have enough supervision to help him realize that desire to do well.

I believe that the officers, and, especially, the directors, of corporations should be held personally responsible when any corporation breaks the law.

Combinations in industry are the result of an imperative economic law which cannot be repealed by political legislation. The effort at prohibiting all combination has substantially failed. The way out lies, not in attempting to prevent such combinations, but in completely controlling them in the interest of the public welfare. For that purpose the Federal Bureau of Corporations is an agency of first importance. Its powers, and, therefore, its efficiency, as well as that of the Interstate Commerce Commission, should be largely increased. We have a right to expect from the Bureau of Corporations and from the Interstate Commerce Commission a very high grade of public service. We should be as sure of the proper conduct of the interstate railways and the proper management of interstate business as we are now sure of the conduct and management of the national banks, and we should have as effective supervision in one case as in the other. The Hepburn Act, and the amendment to the act in the shape in which it finally passed Congress at the last session, represent a long step in advance, and we must go yet further.

There is a wide-spread belief among our people that, under the methods of making tariffs which have hitherto obtained, the special interests are too influential. Probably this is true of both the big special interests and the little special interests. These methods have put a premium on selfishness, and, naturally, the selfish big interests have gotten more than their smaller, though equally selfish, brothers. The duty of Congress is to provide a method by which the interest of the whole people shall be all that receives consideration. To this end there must be an expert tariff commission, wholly removed from the possibility of political pressure or of improper business influence. Such a commission can find the real difference between cost of production, which is mainly the difference of labor cost here and abroad. As fast as its recommendations are made, I believe in revising one schedule at a time. A general revision of the tariff almost inevitably leads to logrolling and the subordination of the general public interest to local and special interests.

The absence of effective State, and, especially, national, restraint upon unfair money-getting has tended to create a small class of enormously wealthy and economically powerful men, whose chief object is to hold

717

and increase their power. The prime need is to change the conditions which enable these men to accumulate power which it is not for the general welfare that they should hold or exercise. We grudge no man a fortune which represents his own power and sagacity, when exercised with entire regard to the welfare of his fellows. Again, comrades over there, take the lesson from your own experience. Not only did you not grudge, but you gloried in the promotion of the great generals who gained their promotion by leading the army to victory. So it is with us. We grudge no man a fortune in civil life if it is honorably obtained and well used. It is not even enough that it should have been gained without doing damage to the community. We should permit it to be gained only so long as the gaining represents benefit to the community. This, I know, implies a policy of a far more active governmental interference with social and economic conditions in this country than we have yet had, but I think we have got to face the fact that such an increase in governmental control is now necessary.

No man should receive a dollar unless that dollar has been fairly earned. Every dollar received should represent a dollar's worth of service rendered—not gambling in stocks, but service rendered. The really big fortune, the swollen fortune, by the mere fact of its size acquires qualities which differentiate it in kind as well as in degree from what is possessed by men of relatively small means. Therefore, I believe in a graduated income tax on big fortunes, and in another tax which is far more easily collected and far more effective—a graduated inheritance tax on big fortunes, properly safeguarded against evasion and increasing rapidly in amount with the size of the estate.

The people of the United States suffer from periodical financial panics to a degree substantially unknown among the other nations which approach us in financial strength. There is no reason why we should suffer what they escape. It is of profound importance that our financial system should be promptly investigated, and so thoroughly and effectively revised as to make it certain that hereafter our currency will no longer fail at critical times to meet our needs.

It is hardly necessary for me to repeat that I believe in an efficient army and a navy large enough to secure for us abroad that respect which is the surest guaranty of peace. A word of special warning to my fellow citizens who are as progressive as I hope I am. I want them to keep up their interest in our internal affairs; and I want them also continually to remember Uncle Sam's interests abroad. Justice and fair dealing among nations rest upon principles identical with those which control justice and fair dealing among the individuals of which nations are composed, with the vital exception that each nation must do its own part in international police work. If you get into trouble here, you can call for the police; but if Uncle Sam gets into trouble, he has got to be his own policeman, and I want to see him strong enough to encourage the peaceful aspirations of other peoples in connection with us. I believe in national friendships and heartiest good-will to all nations; but national friendships, like those between men, must be founded on respect as well as on liking, on forbearance as well as upon trust. I should be heartily ashamed of any American who did not try to make the American Government act as justly toward the other nations in international relations as he himself would act toward any individual in private relations. I should be heartily ashamed to see us wrong a weaker power, and I should hang my head forever if we tamely suffered wrong from a stronger power.

Of conservation I shall speak more at length elsewhere. Conservation means development as much as it does protection. I recognize the right and duty of this generation to develop and use the natural resources of our land; but I do not recognize the right to waste them, or to rob, by wasteful use, the generations that come after us. I ask nothing of the nation except that it so behave as each farmer here behaves with reference to his own children. That farmer is a poor creature who skins the land and leaves it worthless to his children. The farmer is a good farmer who, having enabled the land to support himself and to provide for the education of his children, leaves it to them a little better than he found it himself. I believe the same thing of a nation.

Moreover, I believe that the natural resources must be used for the benefit of all our people, and not monopolized for the benefit of the few, and here again is another case in which I am accused of taking a revolutionary attitude. People forget now that one hundred years ago there were public men of good character who advocated the nation selling its public lands in great quantities, so that the nation could get the most money out of it, and giving it to the men who could cultivate it for their own uses. We took the proper democratic ground that the land should be granted in small sections to the men who were actually to till it and live on it. Now, with the water-power, with the forests, with the mines, we are brought face to face with the fact that there are many people who will go with us in conserving the resources only if they are to be allowed to exploit them for their benefit. That is one of the fundamental reasons why the special interests should be driven out of politics. Of all the questions which can come before this nation, short of the actual preservation of its existence in a great war, there is none which compares in importance with the great central task of leaving this land even a better land for our descendants than it is for us, and training them into a better race to inhabit the land and pass it on. Conservation is a great moral issue, for it involves the patriotic duty of insuring the safety and continuance of the nation. Let me add that the health and vitality of our people are at least as well worth conserving as their forests, waters, lands, and minerals, and in this great work the national government must bear a most important part.

I have spoken elsewhere also of the great task which lies before the farmers of the country to get for themselves and their wives and children not only the benefits of better farming, but also those of better business methods and better conditions of life on the farm. The burden of this great task will fall, as it should, mainly upon the great organizations of the farmers themselves. I am glad it will, for I believe they are all well able to handle it. In particular, there are strong reasons why the Departments of Agriculture of the various States, the United States Department of Agriculture, and the agricultural colleges and experiment stations should extend their work to cover all phases of farm life, instead of limiting themselves, as they have far too often limited themselves in the past, solely to the question of the production of crops. And now a special word to the farmer. I want to see him make the farm as fine a farm as it can be made; and let him remember to see that the improvement goes on indoors as well as out; let him remember that the farmer's wife should have her share of thought and attention just as much as the farmer himself.

Nothing is more true than that excess of every kind is followed by reaction; a fact which should be pondered by reformer and reactionary alike. We are face to face with new conceptions of the relations of property to human welfare, chiefly because certain advocates of the rights of property as against the rights of men have been pushing their claims too far. The man who wrongly holds that every human right is secondary to his profit must now give way to the advocate of human welfare, who rightly maintains that every man holds his property subject to the general right of the community to regulate its use to whatever degree the public welfare may require it.

But I think we may go still further. The right to regulate the use of wealth in the public interest is universally admitted. Let us admit also the right to regulate the terms and conditions of labor, which is the chief element of wealth, directly in the interest of the common good. The fundamental thing to do for every man is to give him a chance to reach a place in which he will make the greatest possible contribution to the public welfare. Understand what I say there. Give him a chance, not push him up if he will not be pushed. Help any man who stumbles; if he lies down, it is a poor job to try to carry him; but if he is a worthy man, try your best to see that he gets a chance to show the worth that is in him. No man can be a good citizen unless he has a wage more than sufficient to cover the bare cost of living, and hours of labor short enough so that after his day's work is done he will have time and energy to bear his share in the management of the community, to help in carrying the general load. We keep countless men from being good citizens by the conditions of life with which we surround them. We need comprehensive workmen's compensation acts, both State and national laws to regulate child labor and work for women, and, especially we need in our common schools not merely education in book-learning, but also practical training for daily life and work. We need to enforce better sanitary conditions for our workers and to extend the use of safety appliances for our workers in industry and commerce, both within and between the States. Also, friends, in the interest of the working man himself we need to set our faces like flint against mob-violence just as against corporate greed; against violence and injustice and lawlessness by wage-workers just as much as against lawless cunning and greed and selfish arrogance of employers. If I could ask but one thing of my fellow countrymen, my request would be that, whenever they go in for reform, they remember the two sides, and that they always exact justice from one side as much as from the other. I have small use for the public servant who can always see and denounce the corruption of the capitalist, but who cannot persuade himself, especially before election, to say a word about lawless mob-violence. And I have equally small use for the man, be he a judge on the bench, or editor of a great paper, or wealthy and influential private citizen, who can see clearly enough and denounce the lawlessness of mob-violence, but whose eyes are closed so that he is blind when the question is one of corruption in business on a gigantic scale. Also remember what I said about excess in reformer and reactionary alike. If the reactionary man, who thinks of nothing but the rights of property, could have his way, he would bring about a revolution; and one of my chief fears in connection with progress comes because I do not want to see our people, for lack of proper leadership, compelled to follow men whose intentions are excellent, but whose eyes are a little too wild to make it really safe to trust them. Here in Kansas there is one paper which habitually denounces me as the tool of Wall Street, and at the same time frantically repudiates the statement that I am a Socialist on the ground that that is an unwarranted slander of the Socialists.

National efficiency has many factors. It is a necessary result of the principle of conservation widely applied. In the end it will determine our failure or sucess as a nation. National efficiency has to do, not only with natural resources and with men, but it is equally concerned with institutions. The State must be made efficient for the work which concerns only the people of the State; and the nation for that which concerns all the people. There must remain no neutral ground to serve as a refuge for lawbreakers, and especially for lawbreakers of great wealth, who can hire the vulpine legal cunning which will teach them how to avoid both jurisdictions. It is a misfortune when the national legislature fails to do its duty in providing a national remedy, so that the only national activity is the purely negative activity of the judiciary in forbidding the State to exercise power in the premises.

I do not ask for overcentralization; but I do ask that we work in a spirit of broad and far-reaching nationalism when we work for what concerns our people as a whole. We are all Americans. Our common interests are as broad as the continent. I speak to you here in Kansas exactly as I would speak in New York or Georgia, for the most vital problems are those which affect us all alike. The National Government belongs to the whole American people, and where the whole American people are interested, that interest can be guarded effectively only by the National Government. The betterment which we seek must be accomplished, I believe, mainly through the National Government.

The American people are right in demanding that New Nationalism, without which we cannot hope to deal with new problems. The New Nationalism puts the national need before sectional or personal advantage. It is impatient of the utter confusion that results from local legislatures attempting to treat national issues as local issues. It is still more impatient of the impotence which springs from overdivision of governmental powers, the impotence which makes it possible for local selfishness or for legal cunning, hired by wealthy special interests, to bring national activities to a deadlock. This New Nationalism regards the executive power as the steward of the public welfare. It demands of the judiciary that it shall be interested primarily in human welfare rather than in property, just as it demands that the representative body shall represent all the people rather than any one class or section of the people.

I believe in shaping the ends of government to protect property as well as human welfare. Normally, and in the long run, the ends are the same; but whenever the alternative must be faced, I am for men and not for property, as you were in the Civil War. I am far from underestimating the importance of dividends; but I rank dividends below human character. Again, I do not have any sympathy with the reformer who says he does not care for dividends. Of course, economic welfare is necessary, for a man must pull his own weight and be able to support his family. I know well that the reformers must not bring upon the people economic ruin, or the reforms themselves will go down in the ruin. But we must be ready to face temporary disaster, whether or not brought on by those who will war against us to the knife. Those who oppose all reform will do well to remember that ruin in its worst form is inevitable if our national life brings us nothing better than swollen fortunes for the few and the triumph in both politics and business of a sordid and selfish materialism.

If our political institutions were perfect, they would absolutely prevent the political domination of money in any part of our affairs. We need to make our political representatives more quickly and sensitively responsive to the people whose servants they are. More direct action by the people in their own affairs under proper safeguards is vitally necessary. The direct primary is a step in this direction, if it is associated with a corrupt-practices act effective to prevent the advantage of the man willing recklessly and unscrupulously to spend money over his more honest competitor. It is particularly important that all moneys received or expended for campaign purposes should be publicly accounted for, not only after election, but before election as well. Political action must be made simpler, easier, and freer from confusion for every citizen. I believe that the prompt removal of unfaithful or incompetent public servants should be made easy and sure in whatever way experience shall show to be most expedient in any given class of cases.

One of the fundamental necessities in a representative government such as ours is to make certain that the men to whom the people delegate their power shall serve the people by whom they are elected, and not the special interests. I believe that every national officer, elected or appointed, should be forbidden to perform any service or receive any compensation, directly or indirectly, from interstate corporations; and a similar provision could not fail to be useful within the States.

The object of government is the welfare of the people. The material progress and prosperity of a nation are desirable chiefly so far as they lead to the moral and material welfare of all good citizens. Just in proportion as the average man and woman are honest, capable of sound judgment and high ideals, active in public affairs—but, first of all, sound in their home life, and the father and mother of healthy children whom they bring up well—just so far, and no farther, we may count our civilization a success. We must have—I believe we have already—a genuine and permanent moral awakening, without which no wisdom of legislation or administration really means anything; and, on the other hand, we must try to secure the social and economic legislation without which any improvement due to purely moral agitation is necessarily evanescent. Let me again illustrate by a reference to the Grand Army. You could not have won simply as a disorderly and disorganized mob. You needed generals; you needed careful administration of the most advanced type; and a good commissary—the cracker line. You well remember that success was necessary in many different lines in order to bring about general success. You had to have the administration at Washington good, just as you had to have the administration in the field; and you had to have the work of the generals good. You could not have triumphed without that administration and leadership; but it would all have been worthless if the average soldier had not had the right stuff in him. He had to have the right stuff in him, or you could not get it out of him. In the last analysis, therefore, vitally necessary though it was to have the right kind of organization and the right kind of generalship, it was even more vitally necessary that the average soldier should have the fighting edge, the right character. So it is in our civil life. No matter now honest and decent we are in our private lives, if we do not have the right kind of law and the right kind of administration of the law, we cannot go forward as a nation. That is imperative; but it must be an addition to, and not a substitution for, the qualities that make us good citizens. In the last analysis, the most important elements in any man's career must be the sum of those qualities which, in the aggregate, we speak of as character. If he has not got it, then no law that the wit of man can devise, no administration of the law by the boldest and strongest executive, will avail to help him. We must have the right kind of character—character that makes a man, first of all, a good man in the home, a good father, a good husband—that makes a man a good neighbor. You must have that, and, then, in addition, you must have the kind of law and the kind of administration of the law which will give to those qualities in the private citizen the best possible chance for development. The prime problem of our nation is to get the right type of good citizenship, and, to get it, we must have progress, and our public men must be genuinely progressive.

Much that Roosevelt said of "the new nationalism" he had said—one way and another, in one place or another—before. Indeed Elihu Root remarked that "the only real objection I see to it is calling it 'new.'" Still, the speaker did succeed in defining his political philosophy in such a way that he seemed to many citizens not only in advance of his party but also in advance of his time. Especially, he suggested that the rights of human beings were on the whole superior to property rights. He tried to make this suggestion more palatable to the more laggard members in his following by supporting it with a quotation from Lincoln, but this device simply mortified one group in his party even more. In fact, the ideas presented throughout the speech disturbed the Old Guard as much as they excited the progressives in the party. In a sense, from Roosevelt's speech, it can be made to appear, flowed great consequences to the Republican Party. In 1910 in New York an election was lost and a division was created between the good man who was President of the United States and the man who had been his great predecessor in office. In 1911 confusion and disorder mounted in the Grand Old Party. Finally, in 1912, came the decisive defeat of all the forces of the divided party.

On September 2, 1920, Elihu Root was again in the city of London. Walking along Park Lane that afternoon, he came to Dorchester House. Before that impressive old structure he paused, looked up, and said to his companion, "It is there that I had an interesting interview with Roosevelt. And if he had done as he promised me—kept out of things political—we would have been spared much of our past trouble." It is possible, indeed it is probable, that in the somber mood of his own personal recollections, Root overstated the case. The troubles visited upon his party could not all have been produced simply because Theodore Roosevelt changed his mind. But still, Root was an acute observer, and no doubt some of the troubles were the product of Theodore Roosevelt's decision to return to things political.

For this reason the speech is important in our history. But there are other reasons for reading it. For instance, those who search for irony as the primary substance in history will be pleased to know that Warren Gamaliel Harding took the "Osawatomie speech [as] the platform on which he stood" in 1920. And those who search for continuity as the source of meaning in history will be reassured to note in this speech many if not most of the ideas and attitudes that Theodore Roosevelt's cousin, Franklin, thought up as novelties a quarter of a century later.

Walter Rauschenbusch
Prayers of the Social Awakening
1910

EDITED BY WINTHROP S. HUDSON

Walter Rauschenbusch has been called "the real founder of social Christianity" in the United States and "its most brilliant and generally satisfying exponent." He gained his social passion as a young man when he was pastor of a small Baptist church near the tough "Hell's Kitchen" section of New York City. There at first hand he became acquainted with the ills suffered by the families of immigrant workingmen. Later he became professor of church history in the Rochester Theological Seminary, and in 1907 the publication of his Christianity and the Social Crisis, won him national fame and centered attention upon him as a major voice of the Christian church. Other books by him dealing with the same theme followed—Christianizing the Social Order (1912), Dare We Be Christians? (1914), The Social Principles of Jesus (1916), and A Theology for the Social Gospel (1917). His "favorite book," however, was a small volume published in 1910 under the title For God and the People: Prayers of the Social Awakening.

Rauschenbusch had become convinced that the new social movement within the churches would never be deeply rooted until it found expression in the prayers of the people. The traditional prayers of the church lacked social feeling. They were too individualistic in concern, too general in scope, too antique in language; and they seldom voiced either the needs or the aspirations of modern man. In the seminary chapel and at conferences and other public gatherings, Rauschenbusch sought to rectify this deficiency by fashioning "models" which would be suggestive to others. He also composed prayers for specific vocational groups. One of these prayers was published as the frontispiece in each issue of the American Magazine in 1910. The publication of these created something of a sensation, and before the year was out the little volume known in subsequent editions as Prayers of the Social Awakening had been rushed through the press in order to satisfy a widespread popular demand. In addition to an introductory exposition of the social meaning of the Lord's Prayer, there were prayers for morning, noon, and night; prayers for specific groups and classes (workingmen and employers, doctors and nurses, newspapermen and teachers, artists and musicians, lawyers and judges, legislators and public officials, immigrants and the unemployed); prayers of wrath; and prayers for the progress of humanity. Later editions of the book contained seven additional prayers and "A Social Litany."

PREFACE

THE NEW social purpose, which has laid its masterful grasp on modern life and thought, is enlarging and transforming our whole conception of the meaning of Christianity. The Bible and all past history speak a new and living language. The life of men about us stands out with an open-air color and vividness which it never had in the dusky solemnity of the older theological views about humanity. All the older tasks of church life have taken on a new significance, and vastly larger tasks are emerging as from the mists of a new morning.

Many ideas that used to seem fundamental and satisfying seem strangely narrow and trivial in this greater world of God. Some of the old religious appeals have utterly lost their power over us. But there are others, unknown to our fathers, which kindle religious passions of wonderful intensity and purity. The wrongs and sufferings of the people and the vision of a righteous and brotherly social life awaken an almost painful compassion and longing, and these feelings are more essentially Christian than most of the fears and desires of religion in the past. Social Christianity is adding to the variety of religious experience, and is

---

The prayers reprinted here comprise about one-fifth of the total which appeared in *For God and the People: Prayers of the Social Awakening* (Boston: The Pilgrim Press, 1910).

creating a new type of Christian man who bears a striking family likeness to Jesus of Galilee.

The new religious emotions ought to find conscious and social expression. But the Church, which has brought down so rich an equipment from the past for the culture of individual religion, is poverty-stricken in the face of this new need. The ordinary church hymnal rarely contains more than two or three hymns in which the triumphant chords of the social hope are struck. Our liturgies and devotional manuals offer very little that is fit to enrich and purify the social thoughts and feelings.

Even men who have absorbed the social ideals are apt to move within the traditional round in public prayer. The language of prayer always clings to the antique for the sake of dignity, and plain reference to modern facts and contrivances jars the ear. So we are inclined to follow the broad avenues beaten by the feet of many generations when we approach God. We need to blaze new paths to God for the feet of modern men.

I offer this little book as an attempt in that direction. . . . I realize keenly the limitations which are inevitable when one mind is to furnish a vehicle for the most intimate spiritual thoughts of others. But whenever a great movement stirs the deeper passions of men, a common soul is born, and all who feel the throb of the new age have such unity of thought and aim and feeling, that the utterance of one man may in a measure be the voice of all. . . .

WALTER RAUSCHENBUSCH

Rochester, N.Y.

INTRODUCTORY: THE SOCIAL MEANING OF THE LORD'S PRAYER

The Lord's Prayer is recognized as the purest expression of the mind of Jesus. It crystallizes his thoughts. It conveys the atmosphere of his childlike trust in the Father. It gives proof of the transparent clearness and peace of his soul.

It first took shape against the wordy flattery with which men tried to wheedle their gods. He demanded simplicity and sincerity in all expressions of religion, and offered this as an example of the straightforwardness with which men might deal with their Father. . . .

The Lord's Prayer is so familiar to us that few have stopped to understand it. The general tragedy of misunderstanding which has followed Jesus throughout the centuries has frustrated the purpose of his model prayer also. He gave it to stop vain repetitions, and it has been turned into a contrivance for incessant repetition. . . .

The Lord's Prayer is part of the heritage of social Christianity which has been appropriated by men who have had little sympathy with its social spirit. It belongs to the equipment of the soldiers of the kingdom of God. I wish to claim it here as the great charter of all social prayers.

When he bade us say, "Our Father," Jesus spoke from that consciousness of human solidarity which was a matter of course in all his thinking. He compels us to clasp hands in spirit with all our brothers and thus to approach the Father together. This rules out all selfish isolation in religion. Before God no man stands alone. Before the All-seeing he is surrounded by the spiritual throng of all to whom he stands related near and far, all whom he loves or hates, whom he serves or oppresses, whom he wrongs or saves. We are one with our fellow-men in all our needs. We are one in our sin and our salvation. To recognize that oneness is the first step toward praying the Lord's Prayer aright. That recognition is also the foundation of social Christianity.

The three petitions with which the prayer begins express the great desire which was fundamental in the heart and mind of Jesus: "Hallowed be thy name. Thy kingdom come. Thy will be done, as in heaven, so on earth." Together they express his yearning faith in the possibility of a reign of God on earth in which his name shall be hallowed and his will be done. They look forward to the ultimate perfection of the common life of humanity on this earth, and pray for the divine revolution which is to bring that about. . . .

With that understanding we can say that the remaining petitions deal with personal needs.

Among these the prayer for the daily bread takes first place. Jesus was never as "spiritual" as some of his later followers. He never forgot or belittled the elemental need of men for bread. The fundamental place which he gives to this petition is a recognition of the economic basis of life.

But he lets us pray only for the bread that is needful, and for that only when it becomes needful. The conception of what is needful will expand as human life develops. But this prayer can never be used to cover luxuries that debilitate, nor accumulations of property that can never be used but are sure to curse the soul of the holder with the diverse diseases of mammonism.

In this petition, too, Jesus compels us to stand together. We have to ask in common for our daily bread. We sit at the common table in God's great house, and the supply of each depends on the security of all. The more society is socialized, the clearer does that fact become, and the more just and humane its organization becomes, the more will that recognition be at the bottom of all our institutions. As we stand thus in common, looking up to God for our bread, every one of us ought to feel the sin and shame of it if he habitually takes more than his fair share and leaves others hungry that he may surfeit. It is inhuman, irreligious, and indecent.

The remaining petitions deal with the spiritual needs. Looking backward, we see that our lives have been full of sin and failure, and we realize the need of forgiveness. Looking forward, we tremble at the temptations that await us and pray for deliverance from evil.

In these prayers for the inner life, where the soul seems to confront God alone, we should expect to find only individualistic religion. But even here the social note sounds clearly.

This prayer will not permit us to ask for God's forgiveness without making us affirm that we have forgiven our brothers and are on a basis of brotherly love with all men: "Forgive us our debts, as we also have forgiven our debtors." We shall have to be socially right if we want to be religiously right. Jesus will not suffer us to be pious toward God and merciless toward men.

In the prayer, "Lead us not into temptation," we feel the human trembling of fear. Experience has taught us our frailty. Every man can see certain contingencies just a step ahead of him and knows that his moral capacity for resistance would collapse hopelessly if he were placed in these situations. Therefore Jesus gives voice to our inarticulate plea to God not to bring us into such situations. . . . No church can interpret this petition intelligently which closes its mind to the debasing or invigorating influence of the spiritual environment furnished by society. No man can utter this petition without conscious or unconscious hypocrisy who is helping to create the temptations in which others are sure to fall.

The words "Deliver us from the evil one" have in them the ring of battle. They bring to mind the incessant grapple between God and the permanent and malignant powers of evil in humanity. To the men of the first century that meant Satan and his host of evil spirits who ruled in the oppressive, extortionate, and idolatrous powers of Rome. Today the original spirit of that prayer will probably be best understood by those who are pitted against the terrible powers of organized covetousness and institutionalized oppression.

Thus the Lord's Prayer is the great prayer of social Christianity. It is charged with what we call "social consciousness." It assumes the social solidarity of men as a matter of course. It recognizes the social basis of all moral and religious life even in the most intimate personal relations to God. . . . Its dominating thought is the moral and religious transformation of mankind in all its social relations. It was left us by Jesus, the great initiator of the Christian revolution; and it is the rightful property of those who follow his banner in the conquest of the world.

∙ ∙ ∙

PRAYERS FOR THE PROGRESS OF HUMANITY

FOR THE KINGDOM OF GOD

O Christ, thou hast bidden us to pray for the coming of thy Father's kingdom, in which his righteousness shall be done on earth. We have treasured thy words, but we have forgotten their meaning, and thy great hope has grown dim in thy Church. We bless thee for the inspired souls of all ages who saw afar the shining city of God, and by faith left the profit of the present to follow their vision. We rejoice that today the hope of these lonely hearts is becoming the clear faith of millions. Help us, O Lord, in the courage of faith to seize what has now come so near, that the glad day of God may dawn at last. As we have mastered Nature that we might gain wealth, help us now to master the social relations of mankind that we may gain justice and a world of brothers. For what shall it profit our nation if it gain numbers and riches, and lose the sense of the living God and the joy of human brotherhood?

Make us determined to live by truth and not by lies, to found our common life on the eternal foundations of righteousness and love, and no longer to prop the tottering house of wrong by legalized cruelty and force. Help us to make the welfare of all the supreme law of our land, that so our commonwealth may be built strong and secure on the love of all its citizens. Cast down the throne of Mammon who ever grinds the life of men, and set up thy throne, O Christ, for thou didst die that men might live. Show thy erring children at last the way from the City of Destruction to the City of Love, and fulfil the longings of the prophets of humanity. Our Master, once more we make thy faith our prayer: "Thy kingdom come! Thy will be done on earth!"

FOR THOSE WHO COME AFTER US

O God, we pray thee for those who come after us, for our children, and the children of our friends, and for all the young lives that are marching up from the gates of birth, pure and eager, with the morning sunshine on their faces. We remember with a pang that these will live in the world we are making for them. We are wasting the resources of the earth in our headlong greed, and they will suffer want. We are building sunless houses and joyless cities for our profit, and they must dwell therein. We are making the burden heavy and the pace of work pitiless, and they will fall wan and sobbing by the wayside. We are poisoning the air of our land by our lies and our uncleanness, and they will breathe it.

O God, thou knowest how we have cried out in agony when the sins of our fathers have been visited upon us, and how we have struggled vainly against the inexorable fate that coursed in our blood or bound us in a prison-house of life. Save us from maiming the innocent ones who come after us by the added cruelty of our sins. Help us to break the ancient force of evil by a holy and steadfast will and to endow our children with a purer blood and nobler thoughts. Grant us grace to leave the earth fairer than we found it; to build upon it cities of God in which the cry of needless pain shall cease; and to put the yoke of Christ upon our business life that it may serve and not destroy. Lift the veil of the future and show us the generation to come as it will be if blighted by our guilt, that our lust may be cooled and we may walk in the fear of the Eternal. Grant us a vision of the far-off years as they may be if redeemed by the sons of God, that we may take heart and do battle for thy children and ours.

ON THE HARM WE HAVE DONE

Our Father, we look back on the years that are gone and shame and sorrow come upon us, for the harm we have done to others rises up in our memory to accuse us. Some we have seared with the fire of our lust, and some we have scorched by the heat of our anger. In some we helped to quench the glow of young ideals by our selfish pride and craft, and in some we have nipped the opening bloom of faith by the frost of our unbelief.

We might have followed thy blessed footsteps, O Christ, binding up the bruised hearts of our brothers and guiding the wayward passions of the young to firmer manhood. Instead, there are poor hearts now broken and darkened because they encountered us on the way, and some perhaps remember us only as the beginning of their misery or sin.

O God, we know that all our prayers can never bring back the past, and no tears can wash out the red marks with which we have scarred some life that stands before our memory with accusing eyes. Grant that at least a humble and pure life may grow out of our late contrition, that in the brief days still left to us we may comfort and heal where we have scorned and crushed. Change us by the power of thy saving grace from sources of evil into forces for good, that with all our strength we may fight the wrongs we have aided, and aid the right we have clogged. Grant us this boon, that for every harm we have done, we may do some brave act of salvation, and that for every soul that has stumbled or fallen through us, we may bring to thee some other weak or despairing one, whose strength has been renewed by our love, that so the face of thy Christ may smile upon us and the light within us may shine undimmed.

. . .

FOR A SHARE IN THE WORK OF REDEMPTION

O God, thou great Redeemer of mankind, our hearts are tender in the thought of thee, for in all the afflictions of our race thou hast been afflicted, and in the sufferings of thy people it was thy body that was crucified. Thou hast been wounded by our transgressions and bruised by our iniquities, and all our sins are laid at last on thee. Amid the groaning of creation we behold thy spirit in travail till the sons of God shall be born in freedom and holiness.

We pray thee, O Lord, for the graces of a pure and holy life that we may no longer add to the dark weight of the world's sin that is laid upon thee, but may share with thee in thy redemptive work. As we have thirsted with evil passions to the destruction of men, do thou fill us now with hunger and thirst for justice that we may bear glad tidings to the poor and set at liberty all who are in the prison-house of want and sin. Lay thy Spirit upon us and inspire us with a passion of Christlike love that we may join our lives to the weak and oppressed and may strengthen their cause by bearing their sorrows. And if the evil that is threatened turns to smite us and if we must learn the dark malignity of sinful power, comfort us by the thought that thus we are bearing in our body the marks of Jesus, and that only those who share in his free sacrifice shall feel the plenitude of thy life. Help us in patience to carry forward the eternal cross of Christ, counting it joy if we, too, are sown as grains of wheat in the furrows of the world, for only by the agony of the righteous comes redemption.

FOR THE CHURCH

O God, we pray for thy Church, which is set today amid the perplexities of a changing order, and face to face with a great new task. We remember with love the nurture she gave to our spiritual life in its infancy, the tasks she set for our growing strength, the influence of the devoted hearts she gathers, the steadfast power for good she has exerted. When we compare her with all other human institutions, we rejoice, for there is none like her. But when we judge her by the mind of her Master, we bow in pity and contrition. Oh, baptize her afresh in the life-giving spirit of Jesus! Grant her a new birth, though it be with the travail of repentance and humiliation. Bestow upon her a more imperious responsiveness to duty, a swifter compassion with suffering, and an utter loyalty to the will of God. Put upon her lips the ancient gospel of her Lord. Help her to proclaim boldly the coming of the kingdom of God and the doom of all that resist it. Fill her with the prophets' scorn of tyranny, and with a Christlike tenderness for the heavy-laden and down-trodden. Give her faith to espouse the cause of the people, and in their hands that grope after freedom and light to recognize the bleeding hands of the Christ. Bid her cease from seeking her own life, lest she lose it. Make her valiant to give up her life to humanity, that like her crucified Lord she may mount by the path of the cross to a higher glory.

FOR OUR CITY

O God, we pray thee for this, the city of our love and pride. We rejoice in her spacious beauty and her busy ways of commerce, in her

735

stores and factories where hand joins hand in toil, and in her blessed homes where heart joins heart for rest and love.

Help us to make our city the mighty common workshop of our people, where every one will find his place and task, in daily achievement building up his own life to resolute manhood, keen to do his best with hand and mind. Help us to make our city the greater home of our people, where all may live their lives in comfort, unafraid, loving their loves in peace and rounding out their years in strength.

Bind our citizens, not by the bond of money and of profit alone, but by the glow of neighborly good will, by the thrill of common joys, and the pride of common possessions. As we set the greater aims for the future of our city, may we ever remember that her true wealth and greatness consist, not in the abundance of the things we possess, but in the justice of her institutions and the brotherhood of her children. Make her rich in her sons and daughters and famous through the lofty passions that inspire them.

We thank thee for the patriot men and women of the past whose generous devotion to the common good has been the making of our city. Grant that our own generation may build worthily on the foundation they have laid. If in the past there have been some who have sold the city's good for private gain, staining her honor by their cunning and greed, fill us, we beseech thee, with the righteous anger of true sons that we may purge out the shame lest it taint the future years.

Grant us a vision of our city, fair as she might be: a city of justice, where none shall prey on others; a city of plenty, where vice and poverty shall cease to fester; a city of brotherhood, where all success shall be founded on service, and honor shall be given to nobleness alone; a city of peace, where order shall not rest on force, but on the love of all for the city, the great mother of the common life and weal. Hear thou, O Lord, the silent prayer of all our hearts as we each pledge our time and strength and thought to speed the day of her coming beauty and righteousness.

The immediate response to Rauschenbusch's little manual of devotion was astonishing. Letters flooded in from everywhere. The prayers were reprinted in the Baltimore Sun and other newspapers. Individual prayers

were printed on wall cards to be hung in offices and homes. The Child Labor Commission printed 13,000 copies of the prayer "For Children Who Work." The labor press featured the prayers "For Workingmen" and "For Women Who Toil." The prayer "For All True Lovers" was incorporated into marriage services. Other prayers were printed in books of public worship, in hymnals as aids to worship, and in manuals for private devotion. And the book itself continued to live—a French translation being published in 1914, an English edition in 1927, a German translation in 1928, and a Japanese translation in 1932.

A curious reversal, however, has taken place in the years since 1910. Rauschenbusch sought to fashion prayers that were pointed and specific, and those that were most pointed and specific won the greatest immediate response and were most widely used at the time the book was published. With changing social conditions many of these became dated and "antique." It is the more general prayers that have endured and have found their place in the living liturgy of the American churches, where they continue to provide luminous language for the expression of the needs and aspirations of worshippers.

Frederick W. Taylor
On Scientific Management
1912

EDITED BY DANIEL BELL

Frederick W. Taylor was born in Germantown, Pennsylvania, on March 20, 1856, of parents who on both sides traced descent from English colonial families. His father, a lawyer, was a Quaker. His mother, a fervent abolitionist, was a Puritan. It was the mother's character and will that prevailed in Taylor's upbringing and personality. He received his early education at home from her. Then, at his father's insistence, he spent two years in school in France and Germany, and another year and a half traveling on the Continent, an experience of which he remarked later, characteristically, "all of which I disapprove for a young boy." At sixteen, Fred Taylor entered Philips Exeter Academy to prepare for Harvard Law School, but he broke down from overwork, his eyesight impaired, and though he graduated two years later, he abandoned the idea of a career in law. Since his doctor had prescribed manual labor, Taylor went into a machine shop, owned by a friend of the family, to learn the trade of pattern-maker and machinist. In 1878, after four years of apprenticeship, he took a job as a common laborer at the Midvale Steel Company, where he soon became a foreman. He obtained a degree in mechanical engineering from the Stevens Institute of Technology by studying at night, and at age twenty-eight, six years after he had begun work at the Midvale plant, he was made chief engineer there. In engineering he found his métier.

In Frederick W. Taylor, character and work were fused in one. He

738

always looked back, with admiration, to the "very severe Exeter discipline" as "perhaps the very best experience of my early life." He did not drink or smoke, or use such stimulants as tea or coffee—not on moral grounds, but as the result, his biographer Frank Copley remarks, "of a truly scientific analysis of ways to conserve one's forces." He split his world into its minutest parts. When he walked, he counted his steps to learn the most efficient stride. Playing croquet, he plotted carefully the angles of his strokes. Sports, which he loved (in 1881, with C. M. Clark, he won the U.S. doubles championship in tennis), took possession of him with the same terribly earnest spirit of his work, and became equally exhausting. Nervous, high-strung, he was a victim all his life of insomnia and nightmares, and, fearing somehow to lie on his back, he could sleep in peace only when bolstered upright in a bed or in a chair for the night. He never loafed, and he hated to see anyone else do so. It was this compulsive character that Taylor stamped onto a civilization.

Taylor proved himself, among other things, a talented inventor. He designed the largest successful steam hammer ever built in the United States. Later, with a colleague, he devised a process of tempering tool steel which allowed for high-speed methods of cutting metals, a process that was eventually used in machine shops all over the world. Altogether, he secured over a hundred patents in his lifetime.

But his fame came from the career, which he began in 1903, as a consulting engineer. His business card read: "Systematizing Shop Management and Manufacturing Costs a Specialty." Taylor was a consulting engineer in the vocational sense for only a brief period, however. For him, "scientific management," as he called the new system he had begun to develop, became an evangelical creed. Gathering a number of disciples about him, he began to spread the gospel, first through publishing (in 1903) his book Shop Management, then by training younger men to install his system into industry. Other men, such as Frank Gilbreth, took up the cause by systematizing motion study. Harrington Emerson popularized the title "efficiency engineer," with a plan of bonuses and incentives in work. By 1910, the movement had become almost a fad and hundreds of persons proclaimed themselves efficiency engineers, promising to install the Taylor system in half the two to four years' time Taylor said was necessary for the scientific study of a job, and for the "mental revolution" management and workers would have to undergo before they could accept his principles.

The rapid spread of "Taylorism" resulted, in part, from the eagerness of many firms to "speed up" work and to "sweat" labor. A strong reaction against scientific management developed within the labor movement. In 1912, Congress voted to set up a special House Committee, under Congressman William B. Wilson, a former official of the Miners Union (soon to become the first Secretary of Labor), "to investigate the Taylor and other systems of shop management." Before this Committee, Taylor made a cogent and eloquent defense of his ideas and methods.

The Chairman. In developing and collating the different parts of this system and in introducing it in different establishments, by what name have you designated it?

Mr. Taylor. The first general designation was a "piece-rate system," because the prominent feature—the feature which at that time interested me most—was a new and radically different type of piecework than anything introduced before. I afterwards pointed out, however, that piecework was really one of the comparatively unimportant elements of our system of management. The next paper written by me on the subject was called "Shop Management," and in that paper the task idea—the idea of setting a measured standard of work for each man to do each day—was the most prominent feature, and for some time after this, the system was called the "task system." The word "task," however, had a severe sound and did not at all adequately represent the sentiment of the system; it sounded as though you were treating men severely, whereas the whole idea underlying our system is justice and not severity. So it was recognized that this designation was not the proper one, but at the time no better name appeared. Finally, the name was agreed upon which I think is correct and which does represent the system better than any other name yet suggested, namely, "scientific management.". . .

The selections reprinted here first appeared, with one brief exception, in *Hearings Before the Special Committee of the House of Representatives to Investigate the Taylor and Other Systems of Shop Management Under the Authority of House Resolution 90* (1912), III, 1377–1508. The exception is the seventh paragraph of the present text, beginning "At the works of the Bethlehem Steel Company"; this originally appeared in Taylor's Book *The Principles of Scientific Management* (New York: Harper and Brothers, 1911), p. 39.

DANIEL BELL

I ordinarily begin with a description of the pig-iron handler. For some
reason, I don't know exactly why, this illustration has been talked about
a great deal, so much, in fact, that some people seem to think that the
whole of scientific management consists in handling pig iron. The only
reason that I ever gave this illustration, however, was that pig-iron
handling is the simplest kind of human effort; I know of nothing that is
quite so simple as handling pig-iron. A man simply stoops down and
with his hands picks up a piece of iron, and then walks a short distance
and drops it on the ground. Now, it doesn't look as if there was very
much room for the development of a science; it doesn't seem as if there
was much room here for the scientific selection of the man nor for his
progressive training, nor for cooperation between the two sides; but, I
can say, without the slightest hesitation, that the science of handling
pig-iron is so great that the man who is fit to handle pig-iron as his daily
work cannot possibly understand that science; the man who is physically
able to handle pig-iron and is sufficiently phlegmatic and stupid to
choose this for his occupation is rarely able to comprehend the science of
handling pig-iron; and this inability of the man who is fit to do the work
to understand the science of doing his work becomes more and more
evident as the work becomes more complicated, all the way up the scale.
I assert, without the slightest hesitation, that the high class mechanic
has a far smaller chance of ever thoroughly understanding the science of
his work than the pig-iron handler has of understanding the science of
his work, and I am going to try and prove to your satisfaction,
gentlemen, that the law is almost universal—not entirely so, but nearly
so—that the man who is fit to work at any particular trade is unable to
understand the science of that trade without the kindly help and
cooperation of men of a totally different type of education, men whose
education is not necessarily higher but a different type from his
own. . . .

Under the old system you would call in a first-rate shoveler and say,
"See here, Pat, how much ought you to take on at one shovel load?"
And if a couple of fellows agreed, you would say that's about the right
load and let it go at that. But under scientific management absolutely
every element in the work of every man in your establishment, sooner or
later, becomes the subject of exact, precise, scientific investigation and
knowledge to replace the old, "I believe so," and "I guess so." Every
motion, every small fact becomes the subject of careful, scientific
investigation. . . .

Now, gentlemen, I know you will laugh when I talk again about the science of shoveling. I dare say some of you have done some shoveling. Whether you have or not, I am going to try to show you something about the science of shoveling, and if any of you have done much shoveling, you will understand that there is a good deal of science about it. . . .

There is a good deal of refractory stuff to shovel around a steel works; take ore, or ordinary bituminous coal, for instance. It takes a good deal of effort to force the shovel down into either of these materials from the top of the pile, as you have to when you are unloading a car. There is one right way of forcing the shovel into materials of this sort, and many wrong ways. Now, the way to shovel refractory stuff is to press the forearm hard against the upper part of the right leg just below the thigh, like this (indicating), take the end of the shovel in your right hand and when you push the shovel into the pile, instead of using the muscular effort of your arms, which is tiresome, throw the weight of your body on the shovel like this (indicating); that pushes your shovel in the pile with hardly any exertion and without tiring the arms in the least. Nine out of ten workmen who try to push a shovel in a pile of that sort will use the strength of their arms, which involves more than twice the necessary exertion. Any of you men who don't know this fact just try it. This is one illustration of what I mean when I speak of the science of shoveling, and there are many similar elements of this science. . . .

[At the works of the Bethlehem Steel Company, for example . . . Instead of allowing each shoveler to select and own his own shovel, it became necessary to provide some 8 to 10 different kinds of shovels, etc., each one appropriate to handling a given type of material; not only so as to enable the men to handle an average load of 21 pounds, [i.e., the ideal weight for least fatigue and greatest productivity] but also to adapt the shovel to several other requirements which became perfectly evident when this work is studied as a science. A large shovel tool room was built, in which were stored not only shovels but carefully designed and standardized labor implements of all kinds such as picks, crowbars, etc. This made it possible to issue to each workman a shovel which would hold a load of 21 pounds of whatever class of material they were to handle: a small shovel for ore, say, or a large one for ashes. Iron ore is one of the heavy materials which are handled in a works of this kind, and rice coal, owing to the fact that it is so slippery on the shovel, is one of the lightest materials. And it was found on studying the rule-of-thumb plan at the Bethlehelm Steel Company, where each shoveler owned his own shovel, that he would frequently go from shoveling ore, with a load of about 30 pounds per shovel, to handling rice coal, with a load on the same shovel of less than 4 pounds. In one case he was so overloaded that it was impossible for him to do a full day's work, and in the other case he was so ridiculously underloaded that it was manifestly impossible to even approximate a day's work. . . .]

. . . Under the old method the work of 50 or 60 men was weighed up together; the work done by a whole gang was measured together. But under scientific management we are dealing with individual man and not with gangs of men. And in order to study and develop each man you must measure accurately each man's work. At first we were told that this would be impossible. The former managers of this work told me, "You cannot possibly measure up the work of each individual laborer in this yard; you might be able to do it in a small yard, but our work is of such an intricate nature that it is impossible to do it here. . . .

At the end of some three and a half years we had the opportunity of proving whether or not scientific management did pay in its application to yard labor. When we went to the Bethlehelm Steel Co. we found from 400 to 600 men at work in that yard, and when we got through, 140 men were doing the work of the 400 to 600, and these men handled several million tons of material a year.

. . . Under the old system the cost of handling a ton of materials had been running between 7 and 8 cents. . . . Now, after paying all the clerical work which was necessary under the new system for the time study and the teachers, for building and running the labor office and the implement room, for constructing a telephone system for moving men about the yard, for a great variety of duties not performed under the old system, after paying for all these things incident to the development of the science of shoveling and managing the men the new way, and including the wages of the workmen, the cost of handling a ton of material was brought down from between 7 and 8 cents to between 3 and 4 cents. . . . That is what the company got out of it; while the men who were on the labor gang received an average of sixty per cent more wages than their brothers got or could get anywhere around that part of the country. And none of them were overworked, for it is no part of scientific management ever to overwork any man . . . because it is one of the first requirements of scientific management that no man shall ever

743

be given a job which he cannot do and thrive under through a long term of years. . . .

The illustration of shoveling . . . which I have given you has thus far been purposely confined to the more elementary types of work, so that a very strong doubt must still remain as to whether this kind of coopera-tion is desirable in the case of more intelligent mechanics, that is, in the case of men who are more capable of generalization, and who would therefore be more likely, of their own volition, to choose the more scientific and better methods. The following illustration will be given for the purpose of demonstrating the fact that in the higher classes of work the scientific laws which are developed are so intricate that the high-priced mechanic needs—even more than the cheap laborer—the cooper-ation of men better educated than himself in finding the laws, and then in selecting, developing, and training him to work in accordance with these laws. This illustration should make perfectly clear my original proposition that in practically all of the mechanic arts the science which underlies each workman's act is so great and amounts to so much that the workman who is best suited to actually doing the work is incapable, either through lack of education or through insufficient mental capacity, of understanding this science. . . .

A number of years ago, a company employing in one of their departments about 300 men, which had been manufacturing the same machine for 10 to 15 years, sent for my friend Mr. Barth to report as to whether any gain could be made in their work through the introduction of scientific management. . . .

The machine selected by the superintendent fairly represented the work of the shop. It had been run for 10 or 12 years by a first-class mechanic, who was more than equal in his ability to the average workmen in the establishment. . . . A careful record was therefore made, in the presence of both parties, of the time actually taken in finishing each of the parts which this man worked upon. The total time required by the old-fashioned skilled lathe hand to finish each piece, as well as the exact speeds and feeds which he took, were noted, and a record was kept of the time which he took in setting the work in the machine and in removing it. . . .

By means of . . . four quite elaborate slide rules which have been made especially for the purpose of determining the all-round capacity of metal cutting machines, Mr. Barth made a careful analysis of every element of this machine in its relation to the work in hand. Its pulling power at various speeds, its feeding capacity, and its proper speeds were determined by means of the slide rules, and changes were then made in the countershaft and driving pulleys so as to run the lathe at its proper speed. Tools made of high-speed steel and of the proper shapes were properly dressed, treated, and ground. . . . Mr. Barth then made a large special slide rule, by means of which the exact speeds and feeds were indicated at which each kind of work could be done in the shortest possible time in this particular lathe. . . .

. . . the scientifically equipped man, Mr. Barth, who had never before seen these particular jobs, and who had never worked on this machine, [was able] to do work from two and one-half to nine times as fast as it had been done before by a good mechanic who had spent his whole time for some 10 to 12 years in doing this very work upon this particular machine. In a word, this was possible because the art of cutting metals involves a true science of no small magnitude, a science, in fact, so intricate that it is impossible for any machinist who is suited to running a lathe year in and year out either to understand it or to work according to its laws without the help of men who have made this their specialty. . . .

. . . In the early eighties, about the time that I started to make the investigations above referred to to determine the proper movements to be made by machinists in putting their work into and removing it from machines and time required to do this work, I also obtained permission of Mr. William Sellers, the president of the Midvale Steel Co., to make a series of experiments to determine what angles and shapes of tools were the best for cutting steel, and also to try to determine the proper cutting speed for steel. At the time that these experiments were started it was my belief that they would not last longer than six months. . . .

Experiments in this field were carried on, with occasional interruptions, through a period of about 26 years, in the course of which 10 different experimental machines were especially fitted up to do this work. Between 30,000 and 50,000 experiments were carefully recorded, and many other experiments were made of which no record was kept. In studying these laws more than 800,000 pounds of steel and iron was cut up into chips with the experimental tools. . . .

All of these experiments were made to enable us to answer correctly the two questions which face every machinist each time that he does a piece of work in a metal-cutting machine, such as a lathe, planer, drill press or milling machine. The two questions are:

In order to do the work in the quickest time, at what cutting speed shall I run my machine? and what feed shall I use?

These questions sound so simple that they would appear to call for merely the trained judgment of any good mechanic. In fact, however, after working 26 years, it has been found that the answer in every case involves the solution of an intricate mathematical problem, in which the effect of 12 independent variables must be determined. . . .

It may seem preposterous to many people that it should have required a period of 26 years to investigate the effect of these 12 variables upon the cutting speed of metals. To those, however, who have had personal experience as experimenters it will be appreciated that the great difficulty of the problem lies in the fact that it contains so many variable elements. And, in fact, the great length of time consumed in making each single experiment was caused by the difficulty of holding 11 variables constant and uniform throughout the experiment, while the effect of the twelfth variable was being investigated. Holding the 11 variables constant was far more difficult than the investigation of the twelfth element. . . .

I want to clear the deck, sweep away a good deal of rubbish first by pointing out what scientific management is not.

Scientific management is not any efficiency device, not a device of any kind for securing efficiency; nor is it any bunch or group of efficiency devices. It is not a new system of figuring costs; it is not a new scheme of paying men; it is not a piecework system; it is not a bonus system; it is not a premium system; it is no scheme for paying men; it is not holding a stop watch on a man and writing things down about him; it is not time study; it is not motion study nor an analysis of the movements of men; it is not the printing and ruling and unloading of a ton or two of blanks on a set of men and saying, "Here's your system; go use it." It is not divided foremanship or functional foremanship; it is not any of the devices which the average man calls to mind when scientific management is spoken of. The average man thinks of one or more of these things when he hears the words "scientific management" mentioned, but scientific management is not any of these devices. I am not sneering at cost-keeping systems, at time study, at functional foremanship, nor at any new and improved scheme of paying men, nor at any efficiency devices, if they are really devices that make for efficiency. I believe in them; but what I am emphasizing is that these devices in whole or in part are not scientific management; they are useful adjuncts to scientific management, so are they also useful adjuncts of other systems of management.

In its essence, scientific management involves a complete mental revolution on the part of the workingman engaged in any particular establishment or industry—a complete mental revolution on the part of these men as to their duties toward their work, toward their employers. And it involves the equally complete mental revolution on the part of those on the management's side—the foreman, the superintendent, the owner of the business, the board of directors—a complete mental revolution on their part as to their duties toward their fellow workers in the management, toward their workmen, and toward all of their daily problems. And without this complete mental revolution on both sides scientific management does not exist. . . .

The great revolution that takes place in the mental attitudes of the two parties under scientific management is that both sides take their eyes off the division of the surplus as the all important matter, and together turn their attention toward increasing the size of the surplus until this surplus becomes so large that it is unnecessary to quarrel over how it shall be divided. . . .

. . . This, gentlemen, is the beginning of the great mental revolution which constitutes the first step toward scientific management. It is along this line of complete change in the mental attitude of both sides; of the substitution of peace for war; the substitution of hearty brotherly cooperation for contention and strife; of both pulling hard in the same direction instead of pulling apart; of replacing suspicious watchfulness with mutual confidence; of becoming friends instead of enemies; it is along this line, I say, that scientific management must be developed.

. . . There is, however, one more change in viewpoint which is absolutely essential to the existence of scientific management. Both sides must recognize as essential the substitution of exact scientific investigation and knowledge for the old individual judgment or opinion, either of the workingmen or the boss, in all matters relating to the work done in the establishment. And this applies both as to the methods to be employed in doing the work and the time in which each job should be done.

Scientific management cannot be said to exist, then, in any establishment until after this change has taken place in the mental attitude of both the management and the men, both as to their duty to cooperate in producing the largest possible surplus and as to the necessity for substituting exact scientific knowledge for opinions or the old rule-of-thumb or individual knowledge.

These are two absolutely essential elements of scientific management.

Taylor's genius consisted in the simple introduction of the idea of measurement in work. Traditional management, operating by rule of thumb, intuition, or experience, had little exact knowledge of the time a job should take, the tools best adapted to a task, or the pace at which a man should work. Taylor's innovations, based on painstaking study rather than on any new technique or technology, consisted of applying the experimental method to the analysis of work: of breaking down each job into its simplest components, varying each component systematically (in one instance, it took twenty-six years to work out a problem with twelve variables), and arriving at a mathematical formula which would specify the "one best way" in which the job should be done. Out of Taylor's work came time and motion study, the incentive and bonus system, differential rates of pay based on distinctive skill classification, the standardization of tools and equipment, and, most important, the removal of all planning and scheduling from the work floor into a new function, directed by a figure new in the history of work, the industrial engineer.

To many people today, Taylorism represents the dehumanization of work: the breakdown of tasks into their simplest components treats men as "objects," as appendages to machines; the primary emphasis on productivity ignores the question of the human satisfactions of the man on the job. Yet, in a way, this view is paradoxical, for when Taylorism first appeared, it was hailed as "progressive" and "advanced," and indeed, many of Taylor's disciples, such as Morris L. Cooke and Henry Gantt, played distinguished political roles as liberals. One has to appreciate the historical setting to understand the subtle change in the nature of these evaluations and the resolution of the paradox.

Scientific management had actually begun to emerge in the 1880's as a response to a fundamental alteration in the character of production, namely, the introduction of the mechanical engineer as the key figure in the new movement of mechanization. It was this development which led Thorstein Veblen some time later to talk of an inherent cleavage

748

between "business" (represented by the financier looking only at the balance sheet) and "industry" (symbolized by the engineer who focused his attention on production). Veblen saw in the engineer, "the General Staff of the Industrial System," the agency of radical change in society. And he saw in the machine the basis of new rationalistic modes of thought. Could there be a metaphysical dispute, he asked, about the amount of stress a bridge could take? On the contrary, he felt, there had to be a factual answer.

The engineer, and his new methods, were indeed forcing a change in the old-fashioned practices of management. When Taylor, for example, on assuming office as president of the American Society of Mechanical Engineers in 1906, circulated a questionnaire asking companies how many of them sponsored research, the characteristic response was: "Why do I need research? Don't I know my own business?" The magic word for Taylor was "science." Science was for him inherently progressive. And to his disciples, scientific management was "the extension to industrial organization of the 'positive' movement in current thought." The positive movement, or positivism, the philosophical system elaborated by Auguste Comte, saw society as passing in a social evolution through defined stages in which the scientific had finally begun to replace the earlier—and inadequate—theological and metaphysical stages of the human mind.

For Taylor himself, rationality had become a religion, and his chief purpose in developing the system of scientific management, as his biographer, Frank Copley, puts it, was "to find a remedy for the labor problem that had grown up . . . in consequence of the development of large-scale production." As a rationalist, Taylor saw no inherent conflict of interest between management and worker (as, in effect, Comte had seen none fifty years before). In his social physics, once work was scientifically plotted, there could be no dispute about how hard a man should work or how much he should receive for his labor. All such matters could be settled by impersonal, impartial judgment. One man who appreciated Taylor was V. I. Lenin; in an article in Pravda in 1918, Lenin urged "the study and teaching of the Taylor system and its systematic trial and adoption."

In a personal sense, the source of Taylor's zeal and drive was the Puritan inheritance from his mother, which, despite a current tendency to read that thought as a narrowness of spirit, represented for Taylor an independence of judgment, a discipline of mind, and a search for rational proofs. But this drive, harnessed as it was to mechanics, became an abstract rationality, the rationality of things, of functional adjustments of means, and not the questioning of ends. And here one sees the resolution of the paradox. For what American industry took from Taylor—and his stamp is everywhere—was the techniques: the stop watch, the job classifications, the functional principle of organization; but in this drive for the rationalization of work, the spirit of inquiry and the moral dimension which had infused the original Puritanism had ebbed away.

Calvin Coolidge
Have Faith in Massachusetts

1914

EDITED BY WALTER MUIR WHITEHILL

Calvin Coolidge, son of a storekeeper in Plymouth Notch, Vermont, was born on Independence Day, 1872. After graduation from Amherst College in 1895, he settled in Northampton, Massachusetts, where he studied and practiced law. Almost immediately after admission to the bar, Coolidge began to climb the local and state political ladder as a member of the Republican Party. In 1898 he was elected to the Northampton city council; the following year he became city solicitor. In 1906 he was elected to the Massachusetts House of Representatives, where he served two terms. In 1910 and 1911 he was mayor of Northampton. For the next two years he was again in Boston as a state senator.

In February and March, 1912, during his first term, Coolidge was chairman of a conciliation committee of three senators and five representatives that succeeded in settling the Lawrence strike. Although party custom normally dictated retirement from the senate at the end of a second term, Coolidge again sought re-election in 1913 because of a possibility of succeeding to the presidency of the senate. In both attempts he was successful. This is the speech that he gave on January 7, 1914, to the state senate of Massachusetts on being elected its president. It was, in William Allen White's words, "the crowning plea of scholarly conservatism in a day of reaction." Of the background of this laconic address, Coolidge wrote in his Autobiography in 1929:

751

It appeared to me in January, 1914, that a spirit of radicalism prevailed which unless checked was likely to prove very destructive. It had been encouraged by the opposition and by a large faction of my own party.

It consisted of the claim in general that in some way the government was to be blamed because everybody was not prosperous, because it was necessary to work for a living, and because our written constitution, the legislatures, and the courts protected the rights of private owners especially in relation to large aggregations of property.

The previous session had been overwhelmed with a record number of bills introduced, many of them in an attempt to help the employee by impairing the property of the employer. Though anxious to improve the condition of our wage earners, I believed this doctrine would soon destroy business and deprive them of a livelihood. What was needed was a restoration of confidence in our institutions and in each other, on which economic progress might rest.

In taking the chair as President of the Senate I therefore made a short address, which I had carefully prepared, appealing to the conservative spirit of the people. I argued that the government could not relieve us from toil, that large concerns are necessary for the progress in which capital and labor all have a common interest, and I defended representative government and the integrity of the courts. The address has since been known as "Have Faith in Massachusetts." Many people in the Commonwealth had been waiting for such a word, and the effect was beyond my expectation. Confusion of thought began to disappear, and unsound legislative proposals to diminish.

Or, as William Allen White described it: "Moses smote the water and the sea gave way."

I THANK you—with gratitude for the high honor given, with appreciation for the solemn obligations assumed—I thank you.

This Commonwealth is one. We are all members of one body. The welfare of the weakest and the welfare of the most powerful are inseparably bound together. Industry cannot flourish if labor languish. Transportation cannot prosper if manufactures decline. The general welfare cannot be provided for in any one act, but it is well to remember that the benefit of one is the benefit of all, and the neglect of one is the

The speech is reprinted from *Have Faith in Massachusetts: A Collection of Speeches and Messages*, by Calvin Coolidge (2d ed.; Boston: Houghton Mifflin Company, 1919), pp. 3–9.

neglect of all. The suspension of one man's dividends is the suspension of another man's pay envelope.

Men do not make laws. They do but discover them. Laws must be justified by something more than the will of the majority. They must rest on the eternal foundation of righteousness. That state is most fortunate in its form of government which has the aptest instruments for the discovery of laws. The latest, most modern, and nearest perfect system that statesmanship has devised is representative government. Its weakness is the weakness of us imperfect human beings who administer it. Its strength is that even such administration secures to the people more blessings than any other system ever produced. No nation has discarded it and retained liberty. Representative government must be preserved.

Courts are established, not to determine the popularity of a cause, but to adjudicate and enforce rights. No litigant should be required to submit his case to the hazard and expense of a political campaign. No judge should be required to seek or receive political rewards. The courts of Massachusetts are known and honored wherever men love justice. Let their glory suffer no diminution at our hands. The electorate and judiciary cannot combine. A hearing means a hearing. When the trial of causes goes outside the court-room, Anglo-Saxon constitutional government ends.

The people cannot look to legislation generally for success. Industry, thrift, character, are not conferred by act or resolve. Government cannot relieve from toil. It can provide no substitute for the rewards of service. It can, of course, care for the defective and recognize distinguished merit. The normal must care for themselves. Self-government means self-support.

Man is born into the universe with a personality that is his own. He has a right that is founded upon the constitution of the universe to have property that is his own. Ultimately, property rights and personal rights are the same thing. The one cannot be preserved if the other be violated. Each man is entitled to his rights and the rewards of his service be they never so large or never so small.

History reveals no civilized people among whom there were not a highly educated class, and large aggregations of wealth, represented usually by the clergy and the nobility. Inspiration has always come from above. Diffusion of learning has come down from the university to the common school—the kindergarten is last. No one would now expect to aid the common school by abolishing higher education.

It may be that the diffusion of wealth works in an analogous way. As the little red schoolhouse is builded in the college, it may be that the fostering and protection of large aggregations of wealth are the only foundation on which to build the prosperity of the whole people. Large profits mean large pay rolls. But profits must be the result of service performed. In no land are there so many and such large aggregations of wealth as here; in no land do they perform larger service; in no land will the work of a day bring so large a reward in material and spiritual welfare.

Have faith in Massachusetts. In some unimportant detail some other States may surpass her, but in the general results, there is no place on earth where the people secure, in a larger measure, the blessings of organized government, and nowhere can those functions more properly be termed self-government.

Do the day's work. If it be to protect the rights of the weak, whoever objects, do it. If it be to help a powerful corporation better to serve the people, whatever the opposition, do that. Expect to be called a stand-patter, but don't be a stand-patter. Expect to be called a demagogue, but don't be a demagogue. Don't hesitate to be as revolutionary as science. Don't hesitate to be as reactionary as the multiplication table. Don't expect to build up the weak by pulling down the strong. Don't hurry to legislate. Give administration a chance to catch up with legislation.

We need a broader, firmer, deeper faith in the people—a faith that men desire to do right, that the Commonwealth is founded upon a righteousness which will endure, a reconstructed faith that the final approval of the people is given not to demagogues, slavishly pandering to their selfishness, merchandising with the clamor of the hour, but to statesmen, ministering to their welfare, representing their deep, silent, abiding convictions.

Statutes must appeal to more than material welfare. Wages won't satisfy, be they never so large. Nor houses; nor lands; nor coupons, though they fall thick as the leaves of autumn. Man has a spiritual nature. Touch it, and it must respond as the magnet responds to the pole. To that, not to selfishness, let the laws of the Commonwealth appeal. Recognize the immortal worth and dignity of man. Let the laws of Massachusetts proclaim to her humblest citizen, performing the most menial task, the recognition of his manhood, the recognition that all

754

men are peers, the humblest with the most exalted, the recognition that all work is glorified. Such is the path to equality before the law. Such is the foundation of liberty under the law. Such is the sublime revelation of man's relation to man—Democracy.

The speech was like the man, a simple Vermont performance—"hard granite," as Mark Sullivan characterized all of Coolidge's public remarks. Coolidge clearly wrote it. It exemplifies the "adequate brevity" that President Meiklejohn praised in conferring an Amherst LL.D. upon him in 1919. This speech so enchanted conservatives who wished to preserve the existing order that it brought Coolidge support from unexpected quarters. Early in 1915 Coolidge's Amherst classmate, Dwight W. Morrow, called him to the attention of Frank Waterman Stearns, Amherst '78, a Boston dry-goods merchant. A few weeks later Stearns arranged a complimentary dinner for Coolidge with representative Amherst graduates to be present; as a preliminary for this he distributed a hundred reprints of the speech. Stearns soon became convinced that Coolidge was, politically, destined for a limitless future, and backed his conviction with warm friendship and generous support.

With the blessing of the Republican Party and with Stearns's steady assistance, Coolidge was elected lieutenant governor in 1915 and governor of Massachusetts three years later. In 1919, during Coolidge's second term as governor, with the thought of letting him speak for himself, Stearns instigated the publication by Houghton Mifflin Company of a volume of selections from Coolidge's addresses, originally to be called Bay State Orations. The final title, Have Faith in Massachusetts, was taken from the present 1914 address to the state senate by Roger L. Scaife, then an editor for Houghton Mifflin. While the galley proof was being read, the Boston Police Strike occurred, and several of Coolidge's messages concerning it were hastily added, among them the telegram of September 14, 1919, to Samuel Gompers containing the sentence, "There is no right to strike against the public safety by anybody, anywhere, any time." Although less than 8,000 copies of the book sold during the next twenty years, by Mr. Stearns's indefatigable efforts more than 65,000 were distributed to libraries, newspapers, and any individuals anywhere who might be helpful to Coolidge within the Republican

Party. Stearns was unsuccessful in obtaining the Republican presidential nomination for Coolidge at Chicago in 1920, but the second place on the ticket became Coolidge's in considerable part through the image created by Have Faith in Massachusetts. William Allen White noted that, as delegates and alternates to the Republican National Convention were chosen in all parts of the country, they were each sent a copy of Have Faith in Massachusetts, accompanied by a pleasant note from Frank Stearns calling their attention to the author, "who might possibly interest them later on." On the death of Harding in 1923, Coolidge became the thirtieth President of the United States. His six years in the White House might never have occurred without the 1914 address to the Massachusetts senate.

Opinions of the speech, as of its author, differ markedly. As early as 1916, Stearns reported that Theodore N. Vail, president of the American Telephone and Telegraph Company, had read it four or five times and had stated, "That is the greatest speech ever made by an American." Harold J. Laski, who regarded Coolidge as "dull, illiterate, stupid, and obstinate," "a third-rate, ungenerous person with a low mean cunning that is contemptible," wrote Mr. Justice Holmes on August 7, 1923, in support of this view: "Look at his volume of speeches and you will have no further illusions." But Holmes, just after the 1924 election that returned Coolidge to the White House in his own right, countered to Laski: "If I had had a vote I should have voted for Coolidge. . . . I think your judgment of Coolidge is prejudiced—and while I don't expect anything very astonishing from him I don't want anything very astonishing." Neither did a majority of the American voters in that year. The conservative sentiments and laconic Vermont phrases of this speech so moved thousands and thousands of his fellow men that, in Walter Lippmann's words of 1926, "At a time when Puritanism as a way of life is at its lowest ebb among the people, the people are delighted with a Puritan as their national symbol." To all except his devout admirers, who were many, Coolidge seemed colorless, passive, inactive, and somnolent. On his death in 1933 H. L. Mencken concluded an obituary entitled "The Darling of the Gods" with the sentence: "He had no ideas, and he was not a nuisance." The second phrase is incontrovertible; the first is not strictly true, for the ideas that he had were succinctly expressed in this speech. But to Laski they were the ideas of "a natural churchwarden in a rural parish who has by accident strayed into great affairs." Is not this speech one of the major causes of the accident?

Louis D. Brandeis
The Curse of Bigness
1915

EDITED BY ALPHEUS THOMAS MASON

The McNamara brothers were on trial. Despairing of helping the workingman by peaceful means, these desperate union officials had dynamited the antilabor Los Angeles Times, killing twenty people. Shortly after two o'clock on December 1, 1911, Clarence Darrow, attorney for the defendants, nodded to a colleague who rose to announce: "May it please the Court, our clients wish to change their plea from not guilty to guilty." It was a dark day for organized labor; the use of violence shocked America's sensibilities. The long-run benefits, however, redounded to the good of all, leading to the creation of the United States Commission on Industrial Relations.

What is wrong in our society, Lincoln Steffens asked, when men feel that the only way to improve working conditions is to destroy lives and property? Paul U. Kellogg, editor of the Survey, set out to find the answer, addressing Steffens' query to prominent persons in various fields, including the Boston lawyer Louis D. Brandeis. The replies were published in the magazine's issue of December 30, 1911, along with a petition to President William Howard Taft, urging the creation of a Federal Commission on Industrial Relations. Brandeis' name was among the signatories. On February 2, 1912, the President sent a message to Congress, calling for a "searching inquiry into the subject of industrial relations." The Commission was authorized August 23, but Taft's nominations for membership were never confirmed. Appointments to the Commission fell to his successor, Woodrow Wilson.

Brandeis, who had been seriously considered for Cabinet posts in the new administration, was Wilson's first choice for the chairmanship of the Commission. "There is no one in the United States," the President wrote in making the offer, "who could preside over and direct such an inquiry so well as you could." After conferring with the President, Brandeis declined. But he was still available as a willing and eloquent witness.

A stickler for facts with a rare gift for forging them into effective instruments of social action, Brandeis had already explored the roots of industrial unrest. "Is there not a causal connection," he asked in his letter to the Survey, "between the development of these huge, indomitable trusts and the horrible crimes now under investigation? . . . Is it not irony to speak of equality of opportunity in a country cursed with bigness?" Broad experience had developed in Brandeis a profound sense of urgency. He had fought corporate waste and aggrandizement in New England transportation and in Boston's public utilities. He had waged a bitter war against the abuses of wage earners' insurance. For New York's strife-torn garment industry, he had invented the preferential union shop. Drawing on this vast experience, he prepared for Harper's Weekly a series of ten articles, a massive arsenal of facts and figures indicting "Our Financial Oligarchy"; the articles were later published as a book under the title Other People's Money. The eighth essay of the series bore the searing title with which Brandeis' name is closely linked—"The Curse of Bigness."

The ill effects of bigness weighed heavily on both men and things. "By their by-products," he had told the Senate Committee on Interstate Commerce in 1911, "shall ye know the trusts." Study them "through the spectacles of peoples' rights and peoples' interests. . . . When you do that you will realize the extraordinary perils to our institutions which attend the trusts. . . . " Aside from whether a corporation has exceeded the power of "greatest economic efficiency or not, it may be too large to be tolerated among the people who desire to be free."

Brandeis' habit of mind was, as he said, "to move from one problem to another giving to each, while it is before me, my undivided study." "I have my opinions," he told an interviewer, "but I am not doctrinaire." Since Brandeis was a man of action, his method did not lend itself to abstraction or to the isolated utterance of a single document. His views on "the curse of bigness"—the dominant theme in his social philosophy —are effectively voiced in the statements made before the United States

758

Commission on Industrial Relations. No stranger to committee hearing rooms, Brandeis appeared on April 16, 1914. Recalled on January 23, 1915, he gave the testimony that appears here.

CHAIRMAN FRANK P. WALSH. Do . . . financial directors, in your opinion, Mr. Brandeis, have sufficient knowledge of industrial conditions and social conditions to qualify them to direct labor policies involving hundreds of thousands of men?

MR. BRANDEIS. I should think most of them did not; but what is perhaps more important or fully as important is the fact that neither these same men nor anybody else can properly deal with these problems without a far more intimate knowledge of the facts than it is possible for men to get who undertake to have a voice in so many different businesses. They are prevented from obtaining an understanding not so much because of their point of view or motive, but because of human limitations. These men have endeavored to cover far more ground than it is possible for men to cover properly and without an intimate knowledge of the facts they can not possibly deal with the problems involved.

CHAIRMAN WALSH. Does the fact that many large corporations with thousands of stockholders, among whom are large numbers of employees, in anyway whatever affect the policy of large corporations?

MR. BRANDEIS. I do not believe that the holding of stock by employees —what is practically almost an insignificant participation, considering their percentage to the whole body of stockholders in large corporations —improves the condition of labor in those corporations. I think its effect is rather the opposite. . . .

My observation leads me to believe that while there are many contributing causes to unrest, that there is one cause which is fundamental. That is the necessary conflict—the contrast between our political liberty and our industrial absolutism. We are as free politically, perhaps, as free as it is possible for us to be. Every male has his voice and vote; and the law has endeavored to enable, and has succeeded practically, in

The text is excerpted from "Testimony before the U.S. Commission on Industrial Relations, January 23, 1915," *Senate Documents*, 64th Cong. 1st sess., 1915–1916, XXVI, *Commission on Industrial Relations Report and Testimony*, VIII, 7658–76, *passim*.

enabling him to exercise his political franchise without fear. He therefore has his part; and certainly can secure an adequate part in the Government of the country in all of its political relations; that is, in all relations which are determined directly by legislation or governmental administration.

On the other hand, in dealing with industrial problems the position of the ordinary worker is exactly the reverse. The individual employee has no effective voice or vote. And the main objection, as I see it, to the very large corporation is, that it makes possible—and in many cases makes inevitable—the exercise of industrial absolutism. It is not merely the case of the individual worker against employer which, even if he is a reasonably sized employer, presents a serious situation calling for the interposition of a union to protect the individual. But we have the situation of an employer so potent, so well-organized, with such concentrated forces and with such extraordinary powers of reserve and the ability to endure against strikes and other efforts of a union, that the relatively loosely organized masses of even strong unions are unable to cope with the situation. We are dealing here with a question, not of motive, but of condition. Now, the large corporation and the managers of the powerful corporation are probably in large part actuated by motives just the same as an employer of a tenth of their size. Neither of them, as a rule, wishes to have his liberty abridged; but the smaller concern usually comes to the conclusion that it is necessary that it should be, where an important union must be dealt with. But when a great financial power has developed—when there exists these powerful organizations, which can successfully summon forces from all parts of the country, which can afford to use tremendous amounts of money in any conflict to carry out what they deem to be their business principle, and can also afford to suffer large losses—you have necessarily a condition of inequality between the two contending forces. Such contests, though undertaken with the best motives and with strong conviction on the part of the corporate managers that they are seeking what is for the best interests not only of the company but of the community, lead to absolutism. The result, in the cases of these large corporations, may be to develop a benevolent absolutism, but it is an absolutism all the same; and it is that which makes the great corporation so dangerous. There develops within the State a state so powerful that the ordinary social and industrial forces existing are insufficient to cope with it.

I noted, Mr. Chairman, that the question you put to me concerning the employees of these large corporations related to their physical condition. Their mental condition is certainly equally important. Unrest, to my mind, never can be removed—and fortunately never can be removed—by mere improvement of the physical and material condition of the workingman. If it were possible we should run great risk of improving their material condition and reducing their manhood. We must bear in mind all the time that however much we may desire material improvement and must desire it for the comfort of the individual, that the United States is a democracy, and that we must have, above all things, men. It is the development of manhood to which any industrial and social system should be directed. We Americans are committed not only to social justice in the sense of avoiding things which bring suffering and harm, like unjust distribution of wealth; but we are committed primarily to democracy. The social justice for which we are striving is an incident of our democracy, not the main end. It is rather the result of democracy—perhaps its finest expression—but it rests upon democracy, which implies the rule by the people. And therefore the end for which we must strive is the attainment of rule by the people, and that involves industrial democracy as well as political democracy. That means that the problem of a trade should be no longer the problems of the employer alone. The problems of his business, and it is not the employer's business alone, are the problems of all in it. The union can not shift upon the employer the responsibility for conditions, nor can the employer insist upon determining, according to his will, the conditions which shall exist. The problems which exist are the problems of the trade; they are the problems of employer and employee. Profit sharing, however liberal, can not meet the situation. That would mean merely dividing the profits of business. Such a division may do harm or it might do good, dependent on how it is applied.

There must be a division not only of profits, but a division also of responsibilities. The employees must have the opportunity of participating in the decisions as to what shall be their condition and how the business shall be run. They must learn also in sharing that responsibility that they must bear the suffering arising from grave mistakes, just as the employer must. But the right to assist in making the decisions, the right of making their own mistakes, if mistakes there must be, is a privilege which should not be denied to labor. We must insist upon labor sharing the responsibilities for the result of the business.

Now, to a certain extent we are gradually getting it—in smaller businesses. The grave objection to the large business is that, almost inevitably, the form of organization, the absentee stockholdings, and its remote directorship prevent participation, ordinarily, of the employees in such management. The executive officials become stewards in charge of the details of the operation of the business, they alone coming into direct relation with labor. Thus we lose that necessary cooperation which naturally flows from contact between employers and employees— and which the American aspirations for democracy demand. It is in the resultant absolutism that you will find the fundamental cause of prevailing unrest; no matter what is done with the superstructure, no matter how it may be improved in one way or the other, unless we eradicate that fundamental difficulty, unrest will not only continue, but, in my opinion, will grow worse.

CHAIRMAN WALSH. From your observation, Mr. Brandeis, what would you say is the responsibility of these so-called absentee owners of industries for conditions, wages, and other conditions existing in the corporations in which they are financially interested? . . .

MR. BRANDEIS. . . . The obligation of a director must be held to be absolute. Of course, I said a little while ago that one of the grave objections to this situation with large corporations was the directors did not know what was going on, and they could not therefore pass an intelligent judgment on these questions of the relations between employer and employee, because they did not have the facts.

Nobody can form a judgment that is worth having without a fairly detailed and intimate knowledge of the facts, and the circumstances of these gentlemen, largely bankers of importance, with a multitude of different associations and occupations—the fact that these men can not know the facts is conclusive to my mind against a system by which the same men are directors in many different companies. I doubt whether anybody who is himself engaged in any important business has time to be a director in more than one large corporation. If he seeks to know about the affairs of that one corporation as much as he should know, not only in the interest of the stockholders, but in the interest of the community, he will have a field for study that will certainly occupy all the time that he has.

CHAIRMAN WALSH. Have you observed, Mr. Brandeis, in the development of these large corporations, the percentage of stock which might give control, or in practical everyday life does give control. . . .

MR. BRANDEIS. . . . These corporations are not controlled through a majority of the stock; they are controlled very largely by position. And that is an almost inevitable result of the wide distribution of stock.

From the standpoint of the community, the welfare of the community and the welfare of the workers in the company, what is called a democratization in the ownership through the distribution of stock is positively harmful. Such a wide distribution of the stock dissipates altogether the responsibility of stockholders, particularly of those with 5 shares, 10 shares, 15 shares, or 50 shares. They recognize that they have no influence in a corporation of hundreds of millions of dollars capital. Consequently they consider it immaterial whatever they do, or omit to do, the net result is that it becomes almost impossible to dislodge the men who are in control, unless there should be such a scandal in the corporation as to make it clearly necessary for the people on the outside to combine for self-protection. Probably even that necessity would not be sufficient to ensure a new management. That comes rarely except when those in control withdraw because they have been found guilty of reprehensible practices resulting in financial failure.

The wide distribution of stock, instead of being a blessing, constitutes, to my mind, one of the gravest dangers to the community. It is absentee landlordism of the worst kind. It is more dangerous, far more dangerous than the absentee landlordism from which Ireland suffered. There, at all events, control was centered in a few individuals. By the distribution of nominal control among ten thousand or a hundred thousand stockholders, there is developed a sense of absolute irresponsibility on the part of the person who holds that stock. The few men that are in position continue absolute control without any responsibility except to their stockholders of continuing and possibly increasing the dividends.

Now, that responsibility, while proper enough in a way, may lead to action directly contrary to the public interest.

CHAIRMAN WALSH. For the purpose of illustration, take a corporation such as the Steel Corporation and explain what you mean by the democratization of industry. . . .

MR. BRANDEIS. I think the difficulty of applying it to that corporation, I mean a corporation as large as that and as powerful as that, is this: The unit is so large that it is almost inconceivable that the men in control can be made to realize the necessity of yielding a part of their power to the employee.

Now, when they resist a particular labor policy, for instance, the unionization of shops, and they do resist it violently, most of the officials do so in absolute good faith, convinced that they are doing what they ought to do. They have in mind the excesses of labor unions and their obligations to stockholders to protect the property; and having those things in mind and exaggerating, no doubt, the dangers of the situation, they conclude that they can not properly submit to so-called union demands. They are apt to believe that it is "un-American" to do so—and declare it to be contrary to our conceptions of liberty and the rest. And they believe they are generally sincere in their statements.

The possession of almost absolute power makes them believe this. It is exactly the same condition that presents itself often in the political world.

No doubt the Emperor of Russia means just as well toward each of his subjects as most rulers of a constitutional government or the executives of a Republic. But he is subject to a state of mind that he cannot overcome. The fact that he possesses the power and that he is the final judge of what is right or wrong prevents his seeing clearly and doing that which is necessary to give real liberty and freedom.

It is almost inconceivable to my mind that a corporation with powers so concentrated as the Steel Corporation could get to a point where it would be willing to treat with the employees on equal terms. And unless they treat on equal terms then there is no such thing as democratization. The treatment on equal terms with them involves not merely the making of a contract; it must develop into a continuing relation. The making of a contract with a union is a long step. It is collective bargaining—a great advance. But it is only the first step. In order that collective bargaining should result in industrial democracy it must go further and create practically an industrial government—a relation between employer and employee where the problems as they arise from day to day, or from month to month, or from year to year, may come up for consideration and solution as they come up in our political government.

In that way conditions are created best adapted to securing proper consideration of any question arising. The representative of each party is heard—and strives to advance the interest he represents. It is the conflict of these opposing forces which produces the contract ultimately. But to adequately solve the trade problems there must be some machinery which will deal with these problems as they arise from day to day. You must create something akin to a government of the trade before you reach a real approach to democratization. . . .

CHAIRMAN WALSH. Past experience indicates that large corporations can be trusted to bring about these reforms themselves?

MR. BRANDEIS. I think all of our human experience shows that no one with absolute power can be trusted to give it up even in part. That has been the experience with political absolutism; it must prove the same with industrial absolutism. Industrial democracy will not come by gift. It has got to be won by those who desire it. And if the situation is such that a voluntary organization like a labor union is powerless to bring about the democratization of a business, I think we have in this fact some proof that the employing organization is larger than is consistent with the public interest. I mean by larger, is more powerful, has a financial influence too great to be useful to the State; and the State must in some way come to the aid of the workingmen if democratization is to be secured.

CHAIRMAN WALSH. Are the workmen employed by large corporations in a position to work out their own salvation by trade-union organization to-day?

MR. BRANDEIS. I think our experience, taking the steel trade as an example, has certainly shown that they are not. And this is true also of many other lines of business. Even in case of corporations very much smaller than the Steel Corporation, the unions have found it impossible to maintain their position against the highly centralized, well-managed, highly financed company. Such corporations as a means of overcoming union influence and democratization frequently grant their employees more in wages and comforts than the union standard demands. But "man can not live by bread alone." Men must have industrial liberty as well as good wages.

CHAIRMAN WALSH. Do you believe that the existing State and Federal legislation is adequately and properly drawn to provide against abuses in industry, so far as the employees are concerned?

MR. BRANDEIS. I have grave doubt as to how much can be accomplished by legislation, unless it be to set a limit upon the size of corporate units. I believe in dealing with this labor problem, as in dealing with the problem of credit, we must meet this question.

CHAIRMAN WALSH. Of what?

MR. BRANDEIS. Size. And in dealing with the problem of industrial democracy there underlies all of the difficulties the question of the concentration of power. This factor so important in connection with the subject of credit and in connection with the subject of trusts and monopolies is no less important in treating the labor problem. As long as there is such concentration of power no effort of the workingmen to secure democratization will be effective. The statement that size is not a crime is entirely correct when you speak of it from the point of motive. But size may become such a danger in its results to the community that the community may have to set limits. A large part of our protective legislation consists of prohibiting things which we find are dangerous, according to common experience. Concentration of power has been shown to be dangerous in a democracy, even though that power may be used beneficently. For instance, on our public highways we put a limit on the size of an autotruck, no matter how well it is run. It may have the most skillful and considerate driver, but its mere size may make it something which the community can not tolerate, in view of the other uses of the highway and the danger inherent in its occupation to so large an extent by a single vehicle. . . .

COMMISSIONER JOHN B. LENNON. Now, to apply it to the work that the unions have done for physical betterment, increase of wages and limitation of the hours and the elimination of children like in the coal industry.

MR. BRANDEIS. Oh, I think those are all positive gains, unqualified gains.

COMMISSIONER LENNON. Gains for manhood?

MR. BRANDEIS. They are all gains for manhood; and we recognize that manhood is what we are striving for in America. We are striving for democracy; we are striving for the development of men. It is absolutely essential in order that men may develop that they be properly fed and properly housed, and that they have proper opportunities of education and recreation. We can not reach our goal without those things. But we may have all those things and have a nation of slaves. . . .

COMMISSIONER HARRIS WEINSTOCK. . . . Now, as an economic student do you believe there is such a thing as overproduction, or is it because of underconsumption?

MR. BRANDEIS. I think it is underconsumption, or maladjustment in distribution. I think it is entirely true that at a given time you may have produced an amount that the market can not take. You may disarrange conditions or produce an article which the market does not want. But we have not the power to produce more than there is a potential desire to consume.

COMMISSIONER WEINSTOCK. In other words, so long as there are hungry mouths and naked bodies in the world there can not be overproduction?

MR. BRANDEIS. Not only hungry mouths and naked bodies, but there are many other things that people want.

COMMISSIONER WEINSTOCK. Well, then, if we are laboring under a condition of underconsumption rather than of overproduction, is it or is it not wise to minimize production?

MR. BRANDEIS. I believe it is one of the greatest economic errors to put any limitation upon production. If we took all the property there is in the country to-day and distributed it equally among the people of the country, we should not improve conditions materially. The only way in which we can bring that improvement in the condition of the workers . . . is to make not only the worker but all the people produce more so that there will be more to divide. . . .

And I have felt in connection with scientific management, with the introduction of that method of producing more, that we ought to make up for the opportunity we lost when we changed from hand labor to machine labor. I think it is perfectly clear that when that change was made the employer got more than he ought to have got; and labor did not get its share, because labor was not organized. Now, when labor is to a very considerable extent organized, labor ought to insist upon scientific management. It has a just cause of complaint if a business is not well managed. Then, when the proceeds of good management are secured, labor ought to insist upon getting its share; and, as I have said, I think its share ought to be large, because of the reason that when machines were introduced labor did not get its share.

COMMISSIONER WEINSTOCK. . . . will you be good enough to point out, Mr. Brandeis, what you have observed to be the mistakes of employers in dealing with labor. . . .

MR. BRANDEIS. I think the main mistake that the employers have made has been a failure to acquire understanding of the conditions and facts concerning labor. There has been ignorance in this respect on the part of employers—ignorance due in large part to lack of imagination. Employers have not been able to think themselves into the labor position. They do not understand labor and many successful business men have never recognized that labor presents the most important problem in the business. . . .

The other cause of employers' difficulties is a failure to think clearly. The employers' refusal to deal with a union is ordinarily due to erroneous reasoning or false sentiment. The man who refuses to deal with the union acts ordinarily from a good motive. He is impressed with "union dictation." He is apt to think "this is my business and the

American has the right of liberty of contract." He honestly believes that he is standing up for a high principle and is willing often to run the risk of having his business ruined rather than abandon that principle. They have not thought out clearly enough that liberty means exercising one's rights consistently with a like exercise of rights by other people; that liberty is distinguished from license in that it is subject to certain restrictions, and that no one can expect to secure liberty in the sense in which we recognize it in America without having his rights curtailed in those respects in which it is necessary to limit them in the general public interest. The failure of many employers to recognize these simple truths is a potent reason why employers have not been willing to deal with unions. . . .

COMMISSIONER WEINSTOCK. On the other hand, Mr. Brandeis, what are the mistakes of organized labor, as you see them? . . .

MR. BRANDEIS. . . . Now, what the employer needs most is to have proper representatives of labor understand the problems of his business; how serious they are, how great is the chance of losing money, how relatively small is the chance of making large profits, and how great is the percentage of failures. Put a competent representative of labor on your board of directors; make him grapple with the problems whether to do or not to do a specific thing, and undertake to balance the advantages and disadvantages presented, and he will get a realizing sense of how difficult it is to operate a business successfully and what the dangers are of the destruction of the capital in the business. . . .

COMMISSIONER JAMES O'CONNELL. You believe that all things, except possibly the question of wages, . . . should be regulated by law?

MR. BRANDEIS. No; I think the question of what we should regulate by law is purely a question to be determined by experience. We should not regulate anything by law except where an evil exists which the existing forces of unionism or otherwise, labor, are unable to deal with it. You can not lay down any better rule than this, that it is desirable that people should be left with the powers of free contract between one another except so far as experience shows that the existing forces will prevent contracts fair in their results. The provisions made for the protection of women and children or for sanitary conditions and safety of all wage earners are justified, so far and only so far as experience shows that without them we shall suffer evils. We ought to go as far as, from time to time, it may be necessary to protect the community from those evils, but no further. . . .

768

COMMISSIONER O'CONNELL. Has the single individual as a wage worker or wealth producer in our town any opportunity or chance, as an individual, to protect and take care of himself and get right and justice as a wage worker? . . .

MR. BRANDEIS. . . . As an industry develops into a larger unit, the chances of the individual being able to protect himself diminishes. Self-protection is possible only where real freedom of contract exists. The only freedom the individual worker has is to leave and go to another employer. But if that is the only alternative and the other employer is equally as large, then the worker passes from pillar to post, and he has no protection at all. But where the situation is that the workman has some other alternative or where the employer needs the workman as much as the workman needs the employer, he may get protection, even without being a member of a union. But such cases are growing constantly less. . . .

COMMISSIONER AUSTIN B. GARRETSON. . . . It has been testified to before this commission that control—financial control—of industrial and transportation interests can be traced to certain well-defined banking groups. . . . If you feel free to tell us from your experience and information I would be glad to know whether you think such control can be traced?

MR. BRANDEIS. I believe it perfectly clear that it can be traced. . . . Those who deny control are using that word "control" in a very restricted sense. They mean that these particular individuals have not definitely said, "This thing shall be done and that thing shall not be done." But, as a matter of fact, control is exercised and exercised to an extraordinary degree by the existence of a great power whom people believe and usually have reason to believe, would be pleased or displeased with the adoption or rejection of a given course. Great power controls without issuing orders.

No specific legislation came out of the Commission's hearings and reports, yet Brandeis' contributions have endured. His dissenting opinion of 1932 in Liggett v. Lee reads like a page from his testimony before the Commission on Industrial Relations. By that time "able and discerning scholars" were aware of the economic and social results of removing all limitations on the size of business corporations. The evil consequences

were then recognized as "so fundamental and far-reaching as to lead these scholars to compare the evolving corporate system with the feudal system; and to lead other men of insight and experience to assert that this master institution of civilized life is converting us to the rule of a plutocracy."

Certain of Brandeis' ideas were translated into Franklin D. Roosevelt's New Deal. Others have been challenged as obsolete; still others seem radical fifty years later. The combiners continued to combine; interlocking directorates flourished. Congressional investigations during the early 1930's revealed Samuel Insull serving on more than eighty boards, Richard B. Mellon on nearly fifty, and Percy A. Rockefeller on sixty-eight. The collapse of 1929 confirmed Brandeis' forecast. Gains came largely through government action. The war Brandeis declared on the "money trust" in 1913 was finally won with the passage of the Banking Act of 1933, requiring national and member banks to divest themselves of their securities affiliates. A year later, legislation struck at such "combiners" as the House of Morgan, against which Brandeis had battled two decades earlier. The Securities Act of 1933 fulfilled his demand for publicity. "The mere substitution of knowledge for ignorance," he had said, "of publicity for secrecy will go far toward preventing monopoly." The Public Utility Holding Company Act of 1935 was a direct assault on bigness, requiring the elimination of the upper layers in the holding-company structures, and conferring extensive regulatory power upon the Securities Exchange Commission. All this was a source of gratification. "There is evidence that the difficulties of bigness are being realized in government matters," the Justice wrote Norman Hapgood, October 31, 1934. The curb had set in on a wide front. He noted "decentralization of plants by big concerns as a step—; and federal legislation going a little way is imminent."

Though certain of the measures enacted were welcome, no frontal attack was made on the major curse—industrial and financial bigness. Aggravating his concern was the evidence he saw on all sides of the dreaded curse spreading to government itself. Repelled by the encouragement of bigness implicit in the National Industrial Recovery Act (1933), Brandeis singled out the Court's unanimous decision outlawing the Blue Eagle—Black Monday, New Dealers called it—as "the most important day in the history of the Court and the most beneficent." "Tell the President we're not going to let this government centralize everything," he warned Tommy Corcoran. Big government was no solution. "Many men are all wool," he said, "but none is more than a yard wide."

Echoes of Brandeis' forebodings are still heard. Joined in 1948 by three colleagues, Justice William O. Douglas deplored "the power of a handful of men over our economy." "Industrial power," Douglas pleaded, "should be decentralized. It should be scattered into many hands so that the fortunes of the people will not be dependent on the whim or caprice, the political prejudices, the emotional stability of a few self-appointed men." That same year, Theodore K. Quinn, formerly vice president of General Electric, sounded a familiar, humanistic note. "Monster organizations," Quinn declared, were "creating an increasingly dependent society where only masses count, genuine individual freedom languished and individual opportunity and expression are strangled."

In certain quarters, bigness is now considered inevitable. "Bigness is with us and the technicians tell us it is necessary," Adolf A. Berle, Jr., comments. Contending that in big business "we have a social institution that promotes the human freedom and individualism," David Lilienthal cautions against the "curse of smallness." But the continuing vitality of Brandeis' thought does not depend on whether or not bigness is efficient or predestined. Material gains may obscure the prime consideration—man himself. "We must have, above all things, men. It is the development of manhood to which every industrial system should be directed."

Though Brandeis' ideas on industrial self-government are still far from realized, certain recent developments, here and abroad, incorporate his basic thought—that division of responsibility for management must go hand in hand with the division of profits. Some contracts now provide for joint company-union committees to deal with the troublesome issues growing out of automation, including distribution of its benefits; others offer continuous negotiation as a safeguard against breakdowns at contract time. In Germany and Yugoslavia, workers participate in the actual management of business. Unconscionable tie-ups in basic industries underscore the growing need for a fresh approach.

Over fifty years have elapsed since Brandeis appeared before the U.S. Commission on Industrial Relations. The ideas he then expressed transcend time and circumstance.

Woodrow Wilson
"Fourteen Points" Address
1918

EDITED BY ARTHUR S. LINK

Colonel Edward M. House, intimate adviser of President Woodrow Wilson, arrived at the White House at nine o'clock on the evening of Friday, January 4, 1918. House ate dinner hurriedly; then he and Wilson went to the President's study to discuss a matter that seemed too important to permit further delay. It was the preparation of a statement of American objectives in the war against Germany. Wilson had been tempted several times during 1917 to make a definitive avowal, particularly after the moderate Socialist government of Russia and the German Reichstag had issued calls for a peace based on the principles of no annexations and no indemnities. Wilson had been deterred from speaking out only by warnings from advisers at home and Allied governments abroad that dissensions among the Allies would ensue and that the strategic situation did not augur well, from the Allied point of view, for peace discussions.

Wilson believed by the beginning of 1918 that he did not dare to wait any longer. The Bolsheviks (radical Socialists) had seized control of the Russian government on November 7, 1917, and appealed to the Allies to seek an armistice with Germany upon the basis of no annexations and no indemnities. When the Allies refused, the Bolsheviks concluded an armistice with Germany on December 5 and then appealed to the workers of the Western belligerents to overthrow their capitalistic and allegedly imperialistic governments. At the same time they published Russia's secret treaties with the Western Allies to prove their claim that both sides were fighting for spoils and plunder. This move stirred much discussion in labor and liberal circles in the United States and western Europe; and Wilson concluded that some definitive answer to the Bolsheviks had to be made.

Wilson and House discussed the proposed statement in general terms during the late evening of January 4. Their guide was a long report on the general diplomatic situation and war objectives prepared by the "inquiry," a group of experts assembled by House at Wilson's request in September, 1917. The two men met again in the President's study on the following morning, January 5, and discussed the various points that Wilson should make in his address. Wilson typed them on three sheets of note paper on his own portable Hammond typewriter, and House numbered them, grouping the general points first, the specific points next. Wilson accepted House's arrangement, except to place the general point concerning the League of Nations last for emphasis.

Wilson began to draft his speech in shorthand and then to transcribe it on his typewriter soon after House left his study on Saturday afternoon. He had finished a first draft by late Sunday afternoon, January 6, and read it to House then. The colonel returned to the White House for a final conference on Monday afternoon. Wilson made only one important change at this meeting. It was to say that Alsace-Lorraine "should" be returned to France. He also went over the points again, deciding when to use "must" and when to use "should" in defining their urgency. Then he read the text to Secretary of State Robert Lansing, making a few verbal changes at Lansing's suggestion. Wilson gave the text of his typewritten copy, by now much altered, to Charles L. Swem, his private secretary, for copying. Since there was not time for the Government Printing Office to print a reading copy, Wilson may have used the typewritten copy when he delivered the address to a joint session of Congress on the morning of January 8, 1918.

ONCE MORE, as repeatedly before, the spokesmen of the Central Empires have indicated their desire to discuss the objects of the war and the possible bases of a general peace. Parleys have been in progress at Brest-Litovsk between representatives of the Central

---

The text of Wilson's address given here is that of the original typewritten copy. The President handed this copy to his daughter, Mrs. Francis B. Sayre, as they were walking out of the chamber of the House of Representatives after he had delivered the speech; the copy is now in the Woodrow Wilson papers at the Library of Congress.

Powers to which the attention of all the belligerents has been invited for the purpose of ascertaining whether it may be possible to extend these parleys into a general conference with regard to terms of peace and settlement. The Russian representatives presented not only a perfectly definite statement of the principles upon which they would be willing to conclude peace but also an equally definite programme of the concrete application of these principles. The representatives of the Central Powers, on their part, presented an outline of settlement which, if much less definite, seemed susceptible of liberal interpretation until their specific programme of practical terms was added. That programme proposed no concessions at all either to the sovereignty of Russia or to the preferences of the populations with whose fortunes it dealt, but meant, in a word, that the Central Empires were to keep every foot of territory their armed forces had occupied,—every province, every city, every point of vantage,—as a permanent addition to their territories and their power. It is a reasonable conjecture that the general principles of settlement which they at first suggested originated with the more liberal statesmen of Germany and Austria, the men who have begun to feel the force of their own peoples' thought and purpose, while the concrete terms of actual settlement came from the military leaders who have no thought but to keep what they have got. The negotiations have been broken off. The Russian representatives were sincere and in earnest. They cannot entertain such proposals of conquest and domination.

The whole incident is full of significance. It is also full of perplexity. With whom are the Russian representatives dealing? For whom are the representatives of the Central Empires speaking? Are they speaking for the majorities of their respective parliaments or for the minority parties, that military and imperialistic minority which has so far dominated their whole policy and controlled the affairs of Turkey and of the Balkan states which have felt obliged to become their associates in this war? The Russian representatives have insisted, very justly, very wisely, and in the true spirit of modern democracy, that the conferences they have been holding with the Teutonic and Turkish statesmen should be held within open, not closed, doors, and all the world has been audience, as was desired. To whom have we been listening, then? To those who speak the spirit and intention of the Resolutions of the German Reichstag of the ninth of July last, the spirit and intention of the liberal leaders and parties of Germany, or to those who resist and defy that spirit and intention and insist upon conquest and subjugation? Or are we listening, in fact, to both, unreconciled and in open and hopeless contradiction? These are very serious and pregnant questions. Upon the answer to them depends the peace of the world.

But, whatever the results of the parleys at Brest-Litovsk, whatever the confusions of counsel and of purpose in the utterances of the spokesmen of the Central Empires, they have again attempted to acquaint the world with their objects in the war and have again challenged their adversaries to say what their objects are and what sort of settlement they would deem just and satisfactory. There is no good reason why that challenge should not be responded to, and responded to with the utmost candor. We did not wait for it. Not once, but again and again, we have laid our whole thought and purpose before the world, not in general terms only, but each time with sufficient definition to make it clear what sort of definitive terms of settlement must necessarily spring out of them. Within the last week Mr. Lloyd George has spoken with admirable candor and in admirable spirit for the people and Government of Great Britain. There is no confusion of counsel among the adversaries of the Central Powers, no uncertainty of principle, no vagueness of detail. The only secrecy of counsel, the only lack of fearless frankness, the only failure to make definite statement of the objects of the war, lies with Germany and her Allies. The issues of life and death hang upon these definitions. No statesman who has the least conception of his responsibility ought for a moment to permit himself to continue this tragical and appalling outpouring of blood and treasure unless he is sure beyond a peradventure that the objects of the vital sacrifice are part and parcel of the very life of Society and that the people for whom he speaks think them right and imperative as he does.

There is, moreover, a voice calling for these definitions of principle and of purpose which is, it seems to me, more thrilling and more compelling than any of the many moving voices with which the troubled air of the world is filled. It is the voice of the Russian people. They are prostrate and all but helpless, it would seem, before the grim power of Germany, which has hitherto known no relenting and no pity. Their power, apparently, is shattered. And yet their soul is not subservient. They will not yield either in principle or in action. Their conception of what is right, of what it is humane and honorable for them to accept, has been stated with a frankness, a largeness of view, a generosity of spirit, and a universal human sympathy which must challenge the admiration of every friend of mankind; and they have refused to

775

compound their ideals or desert others that they themselves may be safe. They call to us to say what it is that we desire, in what, if in anything, our purpose and our spirit differ from theirs; and I believe that the people of the United States would wish me to respond, with utter simplicity and frankness. Whether their present leaders believe it or not, it is our heartfelt desire and hope that some way may be opened whereby we may be privileged to assist the people of Russia to attain their utmost hope of liberty and ordered peace.

It will be our wish and purpose that the processes of peace, when they are begun, shall be absolutely open and that they shall involve and permit henceforth no secret understandings of any kind. The day of conquest and aggrandizement is gone by; so is also the day of secret covenants entered into in the interest of particular governments and likely at some unlooked-for moment to upset the peace of the world. It is this happy fact, now clear to the view of every public man whose thoughts do not still linger in an age that is dead and gone, which makes it possible for every nation whose purposes are consistent with justice and the peace of the world to avow now or at any other time the objects it has in view.

We entered this war because violations of right had occurred which touched us to the quick and made the life of our own people impossible unless they were corrected and the world secured once for all against their recurrence. What we demand in this war, therefore, is nothing peculiar to ourselves. It is that the world be made fit and safe to live in; and particularly that it be made safe for every peace-loving nation which, like our own, wishes to live its own life, determine its own institutions, be assured of justice and fair dealing by the other peoples of the world as against force and selfish aggression. All the peoples of the world are in effect partners in this interest, and for our own part we see very clearly that unless justice be done to others it will not be done to us. The programme of the world's peace, therefore, is our programme; and that programme, the only possible programme, as we see it, is this:

I. Open covenants of peace, openly arrived at, after which there shall be no private international understandings of any kind but diplomacy shall proceed always frankly and in the public view.

II. Absolute freedom of navigation upon the seas, outside territorial waters, alike in peace and in war, except as the seas may be closed in whole or in part by international action for the enforcement of international covenants.

III. The removal, so far as possible, of all economic barriers and the establishment of an equality of trade conditions among all the nations consenting to the peace and associating themselves for its maintenance.

IV. Adequate guarantees given and taken that national armaments will be reduced to the lowest point consistent with domestic safety.

V. A free, open-minded, and absolutely impartial adjustment of all colonial claims, based upon a strict observance of the principle that in determining all such questions of sovereignty the interests of the populations concerned must have equal weight with the equitable claims of the government whose title is to be determined.

VI. The evacuation of all Russian territory and such a settlement of all questions affecting Russia as will secure the best and freest cooperation of the other nations of the world in obtaining for her an unhampered and unembarrassed opportunity for the independent determination of her own political development and national policy and assure her of a sincere welcome into the society of free nations under institutions of her own choosing; and, more than a welcome, assistance also of every kind that she may need and may herself desire. The treatment accorded Russia by her sister nations in the months to come will be the acid test of their good will, of their comprehension of her needs as distinguished from their own interests, and of their intelligent and unselfish sympathy.

VII. Belgium, the whole world will agree, must be evacuated and restored, without any attempt to limit the sovereignty which she enjoys in common with all other free nations. No other single act will serve as this will serve to restore confidence among the nations in the laws which they have themselves set and determined for the government of their relations with one another. Without this healing act the whole structure and validity of international law is forever impaired.

VIII. All French territory should be freed and the invaded portions restored, and the wrong done to France by Prussia in 1871 in the matter of Alsace-Lorraine, which has unsettled the peace of the world for nearly fifty years, should be righted, in order that peace may once more be made secure in the interest of all.

IX. A readjustment of the frontiers of Italy should be effected along clearly recognizable lines of nationality.

X. The peoples of Austria-Hungary, whose place among the nations we wish to see safeguarded and assured, should be accorded the freest opportunity of autonomous development.

XI. Rumania, Serbia, and Montenegro should be evacuated; occupied

777

territories restored; Serbia accorded free and secure access to the sea; and the relations of the several Balkan states to one another determined by friendly counsel along historically established lines of allegiance and nationality; and international guarantees of the political and economic independence and territorial integrity of the several Balkan states should be entered into.

XII. The Turkish portions of the present Ottoman Empire should be assured a secure sovereignty, but the other nationalities which are now under Turkish rule should be assured an undoubted security of life and an absolutely unmolested opportunity of autonomous development, and the Dardanelles should be permanently opened as a free passage to the ships and commerce of all nations under international guarantees.

XIII. An independent Polish state should be erected which should include the territories inhabited by indisputably Polish populations, which should be assured a free and secure access to the sea, and whose political and economic independence and territorial integrity should be guaranteed by international covenant.

XIV. A general association of nations must be formed under specific covenants for the purpose of affording mutual guarantees of political independence and territorial integrity to great and small states alike.

In regard to these essential rectifications of wrong and assertions of right we feel ourselves to be intimate partners of all the governments and peoples associated together against the Imperialists. We cannot be separated in interest or divided in purpose. We stand together until the end.

For such arrangements and covenants we are willing to fight and to continue to fight until they are achieved; but only because we wish the right to prevail and desire a just and stable peace such as can be secured only by removing the chief provocations to war, which this programme does remove. We have no jealousy of German greatness, and there is nothing in this program that impairs it. We grudge her no achievement or distinction of learning or of pacific enterprise such as have made her record very bright and very enviable. We do not wish to injure her or to block in any way her legitimate influence or power. We do not wish to fight her either with arms or with hostile arrangements of trade if she is willing to associate herself with us and the other peace-loving nations of the world in covenants of justice and law and fair dealing. We wish her only to accept a place of equality among the peoples of the world,—the new world in which we now live,—instead of a place of mastery.

Neither do we presume to suggest to her any alteration or modification of her institutions. But it is necessary, we must frankly say, and necessary as a preliminary to any intelligent dealings with her on our part, that we should know whom her spokesmen speak for when they speak to us, whether for the Reichstag majority or for the military party and the men whose creed is imperial domination.

We have spoken now, surely, in terms too concrete to admit of any further doubt or question. An evident principle runs through the whole programme I have outlined. It is the principle of justice to all peoples and nationalities, and their right to live on equal terms of liberty and safety with one another, whether they be strong or weak. Unless this principle be made its foundation no part of the structure of international justice can stand. The people of the United States could act upon no other principle; and to the vindication of this principle they are ready to devote their lives, their honor, and everything that they possess. The moral climax of this the culminating and final war for human liberty has come, and they are ready to put their own strength, their own highest purpose, their own integrity and devotion to the test.

The "Fourteen Points" Address at once became the single great manifesto of World War I. It was Western democracy's answer in its first full-dress debate with international communism. It raised a standard to which men of good will in all nations, Germany included, could rally. This was true, first, because of Wilson's striking success in synthesizing what might be called the liberal peace program. Not a single one of the Fourteen Points was original. All of them had been proposed and discussed by various groups of idealists and pacifists in all leading belligerent countries. But Wilson did more than recapitulate the liberal peace program. He also succeeded in assimilating many of the announced German peace objectives. Restoration of Belgium, freedom of the seas, destruction of barriers to trade, and establishment of an independent Poland were all as much German objectives as they were Allied objectives.

Wilson, in fact, hoped that the Fourteen Points Address would lead to conversations with the German and Austrian governments concerning the conclusion of peace. The Austrian Foreign Minister replied responsively on January 24, but the German Chancellor was evasive in a speech delivered on the same day. Then the Germans gave their answer by imposing a Carthaginian peace on Russia on March 3 and by beginning a great offensive to win the war on the western front two weeks later. There was but one response the American people could make, Wilson said on April 6: "Force, Force to the utmost, Force without stint or limit, the righteous and triumphant Force which shall make Right the law of the world, and cast every selfish dominion down in the dust."

The Fourteen Points Address did not sink out of sight even while the fighting in France reached a crescendo. It became the single most important weapon in the American and Allied propaganda campaign to undermine German morale. Hundreds of thousands of copies were dropped by airplanes over German cities and lines. Opinions differ only as to the degree of its effectiveness; no authority doubts that it helped to shorten the war.

The Fourteen Points Address enjoys the unique distinction of being the only speech that served as the documentary basis for the ending of a great war and conclusion of a general settlement. The German government, frightened by an Allied and American counteroffensive that seemed destined to thrust into Germany, appealed on October 3, 1918, for an armistice looking toward a peace treaty based on the Fourteen Points and Wilson's subsequent elaborations of war aims. The Pre-Armistice Agreement of November 11, which ended World War I, specifically recognized the Fourteen Points and other Wilsonian pronouncements as the standard for peacemaking, subject to reservations on freedom of the seas, reparations, and Czech independence.

The Fourteen Points Address was Wilson's shield and standard all during the Paris Peace Conference that met from January 18 through June 28, 1919, to hammer out a treaty for Germany. Forces beyond his control prevented complete vindication of the points, notably those concerning the colonial settlement, reparations, and disarmament. But the Versailles Treaty honored the Fourteen Points more in the observance than in the breach, and Wilson was certain that the new League of Nations, to which was entrusted enforcement of the Treaty, would go far toward redeeming broken pledges to Germany, as, indeed, it did.

The Fourteen Points Address has shown enduring vitality and power in changing historical circumstances since 1919. It was not only Wilson's greatest speech, but one of the few really notable pronouncements of the twentieth century. Idealists, antiwar groups, and Germans appealed under the Fourteen Points' authority for revision of the Versailles Treaty. The ideals and general objectives enunciated in the address fell out of sight or into obloquy in the United States in the wake of an isolationist upsurge in the 1930's. So-called realists in the 1940's and 1950's condemned its alleged romanticism about the possibilities of a world order based on justice and good will. But Wilson's address remains today, as it has been since it was first uttered, a goad and challenge to its critics and a charter of world liberty to men who treasure its hope of a new world organized for peace and the advancement of mankind.

Henry Cabot Lodge
Speech on the League of Nations
1919

EDITED BY JOHN A. GARRATY

When Henry Cabot Lodge rose to address the Senate on August 12, 1919, the United States was in the midst of a "Great Debate" over its future foreign policy. Should it join the new League of Nations that President Wilson had hammered into shape at the Versailles Peace Conference, or should the nation retain its traditional aloofness from the kind of "permanent alliances" that George Washington had warned against in his hallowed Farewell Address? Ardent internationalists, of course, favored joining the League. If the bloody battles of the World War were not to be repeated, some international organization would have to be created to settle disputes and preserve the peace, they argued. But certain "irreconcilables" were dead set against any involvement in European affairs. Between these extremes stood the majority of the people, willing to see the country assume its responsibilities as a world power, but uneasy about committing themselves irrevocably to a supranational organization.

Senator Lodge belonged in this middle group. However, his position was unusual. He was a Republican (an extremely partisan one) and also Senate Majority Leader and chairman of the Foreign Relations Committee. His political instincts, highly refined by years of experience, told him that Wilson must not be allowed to monopolize the credit for having devised a scheme for preserving world peace. He had also the task of shaping a strategy that all Republicans, isolationists as well as interna-

782

tionalists, could accept. His position was further complicated on the one hand by his personal dislike of Wilson, and on the other by his belief that America should play an important role in world affairs. He therefore took the position that the League should be accepted with "reservations" which, by limiting American obligations, would make it impossible for the League or any of its members to involve the nation in important international commitments without the consent of Congress.

This speech was Lodge's first full-dress statement of his position in the Senate. He prepared for it with extreme care, writing out every word and delivering it, as one observer noted, in a manner "studiously, if not painfully devoid of accentuation or emphasis." Seldom did he even raise his eyes from his manuscript.

Nonetheless, his carefully measured phrases, appealing to the mood of the audience, unleashed a storm of applause from the packed galleries. A group of Marines, just returned from France, pounded their helmets enthusiastically against the gallery railing; men and women cheered, whistled, waved handkerchiefs and hats. It was minutes before order could be restored, and when a Democratic Senator attempted to reply to Lodge's arguments, his remarks were greeted with boos and hisses.

I OBJECT in the strongest possible way to having the United States agree, directly or indirectly, to be controlled by a league which may at any time, and perfectly lawfully and in accordance with the terms of the covenant, be drawn in to deal with internal conflicts in other countries, no matter what those conflicts may be. We should never permit the United States to be involved in any internal conflict in another country, except by the will of her people expressed through the Congress which represents them.

With regard to wars of external aggression on a member of the league, the case is perfectly clear. There can be no genuine dispute whatever about the meaning of the first clause of article 10. In the first place, it

The address is reprinted here from the *Congressional Record, Proceedings and Debates of the First Session of the Sixty-sixth Congress of the United States of America*, Vol. LVIII, Part 4 (Washington, D.C.: Government Printing Office, 1919), August 12, 1919, pp. 3778–84. One line of type inadvertently omitted there has been restored in brackets.

differs from every other obligation in being individual and placed upon each nation without the intervention of the league. Each nation for itself promises to respect and preserve as against external aggression the boundaries and the political independence of every member of the league. . . .

It is, I repeat, an individual obligation. It requires no action on the part of the league, except that in the second sentence the authorities of the league are to have the power to advise as to the means to be employed in order to fulfill the purpose of the first sentence. But that is a detail of execution, and I consider that we are morally and in honor bound to accept and act upon that advice. The broad fact remains that if any member of the league suffering from external aggression should appeal directly to the United States for support the United States would be bound to give that support in its own capacity and without reference to the action of other powers, because the United States itself is bound, and I hope the day will never come when the United States will not carry out its promises. If that day should come, and the United States or any other great country should refuse, no matter how specious the reasons, to fulfill both in letter and spirit every obligation in this covenant, the United States would be dishonored and the league would crumble into dust, leaving behind it a legacy of wars. If China should rise up and attack Japan in an effort to undo the great wrong of the cession of the control of Shantung to that power, we should be bound under the terms of article 10 to sustain Japan against China, and a guaranty of that sort is never involved except when the question has passed beyond the stage of negotiation and has become a question for the application of force. I do not like the prospect. It shall not come into existence by any vote of mine. . . .

Any analysis of the provisions of this league covenant, however, brings out in startling relief one great fact. Whatever may be said, it is not a league of peace; it is an alliance, dominated at the present moment by five great powers, really by three, and it has all the marks of an alliance. The development of international law is neglected. The court which is to decide disputes brought before it fills but a small place. The conditions for which this league really provides with the utmost care are political conditions, not judicial questions, to be reached by the executive council and the assembly, purely political bodies without any trace of a judicial character about them. Such being its machinery, the control being in the hands of political appointees whose votes will be controlled by interest and expedience it exhibits that most marked characteristic of an alliance —that its decisions are to be carried out by force. Those articles upon which the whole structure rests are articles which provide for the use of force; that is, for war. This league to enforce peace does a great deal for enforcement and very little for peace. It makes more essential provisions looking to war than to peace for the settlement of disputes. . . .

Taken altogether, these provisions for war present what to my mind is the gravest objection to this league in its present form. We are told that of course nothing will be done in the way of warlike acts without the assent of Congress. If that is true let us say so in the covenant. But as it stands there is no doubt whatever in my mind that American troops and American ships may be ordered to any part of the world by nations other than the United States, and that is a proposition to which I for one can never assent. It must be made perfectly clear that no American soldiers, not even a corporal's guard, that no American sailors, not even the crew of a submarine, can ever be engaged in war or ordered anywhere except by the constitutional authorities of the United States. To Congress is granted by the Constitution the right to declare war, and nothing that would take the troops out of the country at the bidding or demand of other nations should ever be permitted except through congressional action. The lives of Americans must never be sacrificed except by the will of the American people expressed through their chosen Representatives in Congress. This is a point upon which no doubt can be permitted. American soldiers and American sailors have never failed the country when the country called upon them. They went in their hundreds of thousands into the war just closed. They went to die for the great cause of freedom and of civilization. They went [at their country's bidding and because their country summoned them] to service. We were late in entering the war. We made no preparation, as we ought to have done, for the ordeal which was clearly coming upon us; but we went and we turned the wavering scale. It was done by the American soldier, the American sailor, and the spirit and energy of the American people. They overrode all obstacles and all shortcomings on the part of the administration or of Congress and gave to their country a great place in the great victory. It was the first time we had been called upon to rescue the civilized world. Did we fail? On the contrary, we succeeded, succeeded largely and nobly, and we did it without any command from any league of nations. When the emergency came, we met it and we were able to meet it because we had built up on this continent the greatest and most powerful Nation in the world, built it up under our own policies, in our own way, and one great element of our strength was the fact that we had held aloof and had not thrust ourselves into European quarrels; that we had no selfish interest to serve. We made great sacrifices. We have done splendid work. I believe that we do not require to be told by foreign nations when we shall do work which freedom and civilization require. I think we can move to victory much better under our own command than under the command of others. Let us unite with the world to promote the peaceable settlement of all international disputes. Let us try to develop international law. Let us associate ourselves with the other nations for these purposes. But let us retain in our own hands and in our own control the lives of the youth of the land. Let no American be sent into battle except by the constituted authorities of his own country and by the will of the people of the United States.

Those of us, Mr. President, who are either wholly opposed to the league, or who are trying to preserve the independence and the safety of the United States by changing the terms of the league, and who are endeavoring to make the league, if we are to be a member of it, less certain to promote war instead of peace have been reproached with selfishness in our outlook and with a desire to keep our country in a state of isolation. So far as the question of isolation goes, it is impossible to isolate the United States. I well remember the time, 20 years ago, when eminent Senators and other distinguished gentlemen who were opposing the Philippines and shrieking about imperialism sneered at the statement made by some of us, that the United States had become a world power. I think no one now would question that the Spanish war marked the entrance of the United States into world affairs to a degree which had never obtained before. It was both an inevitable and an irrevocable step, and our entrance into the war with Germany certainly showed once and for all that the United States was not unmindful of its world responsibilities. We may set aside all this empty talk about isolation. Nobody expects to isolate the United States or to make it a hermit Nation, which is a sheer absurdity. But there is a wide difference between taking a suitable part and bearing a due responsibility in world affairs and plunging the United States into every controversy and conflict on the face of the globe. By meddling in all the differences which may arise among any portion or fragment of humankind we simply fritter away our influence and injure ourselves to no good purpose. We shall be of far more value to the world and its peace by occupying, so far as possible, the situation which we have occupied for the last 20 years and by adhering to the policy of Washington and Hamilton, of Jefferson and Monroe, under which we have risen to our present greatness and prosperity. The fact that we have been separated by our geographical situation and by our consistent policy from the broils of Europe has made us more than any one thing capable of performing the great work which we performed in the war against Germany and our disinterestedness is of far more value to the world than our eternal meddling in every possible dispute could ever be.

Now, as to our selfishness, I have no desire to boast that we are better than our neighbors, but the fact remains that this Nation in making peace with Germany had not a single selfish or individual interest to serve. All we asked was that Germany should be rendered incapable of again breaking forth, with all the horrors, incident to German warfare, upon an unoffending world, and that demand was shared by every free nation and indeed by humanity itself. For ourselves we asked absolutely nothing. We have not asked any government or governments to guarantee our boundaries or our political independence. We have no fear in regard to either. We have sought no territory, no privileges, no advantages, for ourselves. That is the fact. It is apparent on the face of the treaty. I do not mean to reflect upon a single one of the powers with which we have been associated in the war against Germany, but there is not one of them which has not sought individual advantages for their own national benefit. I do not criticize their desires at all. The services and sacrifices of England and France and Belgium and Italy are beyond estimate and beyond praise. I am glad they should have what they desire for their own welfare and safety. But they all receive under the peace territorial and commercial benefits. We are asked to give, and we in no way seek to take. Surely it is not too much to insist that when we are offered nothing but the opportunity to give and to aid others we should have the right to say what sacrifices we shall make and what the magnitude of our gifts shall be. In the prosecution of the war we gave unstintedly American lives and American treasure. When the war closed we had 3,000,000 men under arms. We were turning the country into a vast workshop for war. We advanced ten billions to our allies. We refused no assistance that we could possibly render. All the great energy and power of the Republic were put at the service of the good cause. We have not been ungenerous. We have been devoted to the cause of freedom, humanity, and civilization everywhere. Now we are asked, in the making of peace, to sacrifice our sovereignty in important respects, to involve ourselves almost without limit in the affairs of other nations and to yield up policies and rights which we have maintained throughout our history. We are asked to incur liabilities to an unlimited extent and furnish assets at the same time which no man can measure. I think it is not only our right but our duty to determine how far we shall go. Not only must we look carefully to see where we are being led into endless disputes and entanglements, but we must not forget that we have in this country millions of people of foreign birth and parentage.

Our one great object is to make all these people Americans so that we may call on them to place America first and serve America as they have done in the war just closed. We cannot Americanize them if we are continually thrusting them back into the quarrels and difficulties of the countries from which they came to us. We shall fill this land with political disputes about the troubles and quarrels of other countries. We shall have a large portion of our people voting not on American questions and not on what concerns the United States but dividing on issues which concern foreign countries alone. That is an unwholesome and perilous condition to force upon this country. We must avoid it. We ought to reduce to the lowest possible point the foreign questions in which we involve ourselves. Never forget that this league is primarily— I might say overwhelmingly—a political organization, and I object strongly to having the politics of the United States turn upon disputes where deep feeling is aroused but in which we have no direct interest. It will all tend to delay the Americanization of our great population, and it is more important not only to the United States but to the peace of the world to make all these people good Americans than it is to determine that some piece of territory should belong to one European country rather than to another. For this reason I wish to limit strictly our interference in the affairs of Europe and of Africa. We have interests of our own in Asia and in the Pacific which we must guard upon our own account, but the less we undertake to play the part of umpire and thrust ourselves into European conflicts the better for the United States and for the world.

It has been reiterated here on this floor, and reiterated to the point of weariness, that in every treaty there is some sacrifice of sovereignty. That is not a universal truth by any means, but it is true of some treaties and it is a platitude which does not require reiteration. The question and the only question before us here is how much of our sovereignty we are justified in sacrificing. In what I have already said about other nations putting us into war I have covered one point of sovereignty which ought never to be yielded—the power to send American soldiers and sailors everywhere, which ought never to be taken from the American people or impaired in the slightest degree. Let us beware how we palter with our independence. We have not reached the great position from which we were able to come down into the field of battle and help to save the world from tyranny by being guided by others. Our vast power has all been built up and gathered together by ourselves alone. We forced our way upward from the days of the Revolution, through a world often hostile and always indifferent. We owe no debt to anyone except to France in that Revolution, and those policies and those rights on which our power has been founded should never be lessened or weakened. It will be no service to the world to do so and it will be of intolerable injury to the United States. We will do our share. We are ready and anxious to help in all ways to preserve the world's peace. But we can do it best by not crippling ourselves.

I am as anxious as any human being can be to have the United States render every possible service to the civilization and the peace of mankind, but I am certain we can do it best by not putting ourselves in leading strings or subjecting our policies and our sovereignty to other nations. The independence of the United States is not only more precious to ourselves but to the world than any single possession. Look at the United States to-day. We have made mistakes in the past. We have had shortcomings. We shall make mistakes in the future and fall short of our own best hopes. But none the less is there any country to-day on the face of the earth which can compare with this in ordered liberty, in peace, and in the largest freedom? I feel that I can say this without being accused of undue boastfulness, for it is the simple fact, and in making this treaty and taking on these obligations all that we do is in a spirit of unselfishness and in a desire for the good of mankind. But it is well to remember that we are dealing with nations every one of which has a direct individual interest to serve, and there is grave danger in an unshared idealism. Contrast the United States with any country on the face of the earth to-day and ask yourself whether the situation of the United States is not the best to be found. I will go as far as anyone in world service, but the first step to world service is the maintenance of the United States. You may call me selfish if you will, conservative or reactionary, or use any other harsh adjective you see fit to apply, but an

American I was born, an American I have remained all my life. I can never be anything else but an American, and I must think of the United States first, and when I think of the United States first in an arrangement like this I am thinking of what is best for the world, for if the United States fails the best hopes of mankind fail with it. I have never had but one allegiance—I cannot divide it now. I have loved but one flag and I cannot share that devotion and give affection to the mongrel banner invented for a league. Internationalism, illustrated by the Bolshevik and by the men to whom all countries are alike provided they can make money out of them, is to me repulsive. National I must remain, and in that way I like all other Americans can render the amplest service to the world. The United States is the world's best hope, but if you fetter her in the interests and quarrels of other nations, if you tangle her in the intrigues of Europe, you will destroy her power for good and endanger her very existence. Leave her to march freely through the centuries to come as in the years that have gone. Strong, generous, and confident, she has nobly served mankind. Beware how you trifle with your marvelous inheritance, this great land of ordered liberty, for if we stumble and fall freedom and civilization everywhere will go down in ruin.

We are told that we shall "break the heart of the world" if we do not take this league just as it stands. I fear that the hearts of the vast majority of mankind would beat on strongly and steadily and without any quickening if the league were to perish altogether. If it should be effectively and beneficiently changed the people who would lie awake in sorrow for a single night could be easily gathered in one not very large room but those who would draw a long breath of relief would reach to millions.

We hear much of visions and I trust we shall continue to have visions and dream dreams of a fairer future for the race. But visions are one thing and visionaries are another, and the mechanical appliances of the rhetorician designed to give a picture of a present which does not exist and of a future which no man can predict are as unreal and shortlived as the steam or canvas clouds, the angels suspended on wires and the artificial lights of the stage. They pass with the moment of effect and are shabby and tawdry in the daylight. Let us at least be real. Washington's entire honesty of mind and his fearless look into the face of all facts are qualities which can never go out of fashion and which we should all do well to imitate.

Ideals have been thrust upon us as an argument for the league until the healthy mind which rejects cant revolts from them. Are ideals confined to this deformed experiment upon a noble purpose, tainted, as it is, with bargains and tied to a peace treaty which might have been disposed of long ago to the great benefit of the world if it had not been compelled to carry this rider on its back? "Post equitem sedet atra cura," Horace tells us, but no blacker care ever sat behind any rider than we shall find in this covenant of doubtful and disputed interpretation as it now perches upon the treaty of peace.

No doubt many excellent and patriotic people see a coming fulfill-ment of noble ideals in the words "league for peace." We all respect and share these aspirations and desires, but some of us see no hope, but rather defeat, for them in this murky covenant. For we, too, have our ideals, even if we differ from those who have tried to establish a monopoly of idealism. Our first ideal is our country, and we see her in the future, as in the past, giving service to all her people and to the world. Our ideal of the future is that she should continue to render that service of her own free will. She has great problems of her own to solve, very grim and perilous problems, and a right solution, if we can attain to it, would largely benefit mankind. We would have our country strong to resist a peril from the West, as she has flung back the German menace from the East. We would not have our politics distracted and embit-tered by the dissensions of other lands. We would not have our country's vigor exhausted or her moral force abated, by everlasting meddling and muddling in every quarrel, great and small, which afflicts the world. Our ideal is to make her ever stronger and better and finer, because in that way alone, as we believe, can she be of the greatest service to the world's peace and to the welfare of mankind.

Of course, Lodge's speech alone did not account for the rejection of the League of Nations by the Senate or for the fact that the American people as a whole, in the years between World Wars I and II, firmly opposed the idea of surrendering any part of their sovereignty to an international organization. But his basic point, so clearly and forcefully expressed in the speech, was the controlling consideration in American foreign-policy

discussions at all levels during the twenties and thirties. This fact does not mean that the United States isolated itself from the rest of the world. The nation participated actively in international affairs and in doing so accepted obligations and made commitments of various sorts to other nations. Lodge himself, for example, was a delegate to the Washington Disarmament Conference, and put his name freely to treaties restricting the size of the Navy and accepting other limits on American freedom of action. However, these treaties were separately considered and ratified by the Senate in the traditional manner. But even so imaginary a surrender of sovereignty as would have been involved in American membership in the World Court was rejected. And as, in critical situations, the members of the League repeatedly proved unwilling to employ forceful means of preventing aggression by the dictators, Americans were further strengthened in the conviction that the position outlined by Lodge was sound.

Then, when World War II erupted with all its horrors, people began once again to consider employing some form of international organization as a means of preventing war. The result was the Charter of the United Nations. In the drafting of that Charter much consideration was given to Lodge's arguments against the League. Time had shown that these arguments reflected a widespread feeling in many nations besides the United States that national sovereignty ought not to be surrendered, no matter how desirable the objective. The influence of Lodge's thinking can be seen in many aspects of the organization of the United Nations, but especially in the veto granted to each of the great powers in the Security Council. The veto is the very antithesis of the principle behind Article 10 of the League, which Wilson called "the heart of the Covenant" and which Lodge, in his speech, so strongly opposed. It is important to remember that, while the Soviet Union has frequently abused the veto, the United States is as much against abolishing it as are the Russians.

Henry Cabot Lodge, Jr., grandson of the Senator and for many years United States Ambassador to the United Nations, summarized his grandfather's influence on the United Nations Charter in these words, written in 1953:

All the principal steps which have been taken since the end of World War II which relate to issues of peace and war specifically and categorically reserve the principle of national sovereignty and the principle of constitutional process. . . . [The Lodge Reservation to Article 10] simply preserved the power of Congress—a power which is jealously guarded today, which is completely safeguarded both in the United Nations Charter and in the Atlantic Pact, and which President Wilson was unwilling categorically to express at that time.

Speaking more generally, the historian Richard W. Leopold writes: "The obligations of the United States under the Charter resemble closely those it would have assumed under the Lodge reservations. Wilson intended the League to be a coercive type of body. . . . Lodge sought to transform the League into a noncoercive organization."

At the time of the League fight, and ever since, many high-minded believers in international cooperation have condemned Lodge bitterly, blaming him for the smashing of Wilson's bright hopes, and even for World War II. Partly Lodge deserved their opprobrium, because his personal hatred of the President and his partisan ambitions certainly added to his prejudice against the League. Yet in the long run Lodge taught his critics (and the lesson was clear in his great Senate speech) that no drafter of foreign policy can go beyond the limits of what the public will support and still remain successful. The idea of a world government is as attractive today as it was in 1919 and a good deal closer to reality, but it is not yet within our grasp. The United Nations, built to conform to the limitations of public support in each of the member nations, is a functioning and useful institution precisely because it recognizes the fact that men all over the world still place their own country first in their hearts, as Lodge did, and as he knew his countrymen did.

H. L. Mencken
Preface to "The American Language"
1919

EDITED BY THOMAS PYLES

By 1919, when The American Language was first published, Henry Louis Mencken was a well-known man. It is not surprising, if only from the sheer bulk of his production—and it usually had quality as well—that Mencken should have acquired a considerable reputation and influence as a literary critic, later enhanced by his brilliant editorship from 1924 to 1933 of the American Mercury, which with George Jean Nathan he founded. In the course of his zestful career he pole-axed many a sacred cow and deftly needled many a windbag, but the Preface to the first edition of The American Language reflects primarily his concern with the speech of what he liked to refer to as "this Great Republic."

Well before 1919, Mencken had written in the Baltimore Evening Sun and in The Smart Set, a magazine whose literary critic he was, on what he refers to in the Preface reprinted here as the "salient differences between the English of England and the English of America." His interest in the subject had been aroused in youth in the course of his work as a police reporter in his native Baltimore. As he himself testifies in the Preface to The American Language: Supplement One (1945), this interest was kindled specifically around 1905 by his discovery in Baltimore's Enoch Pratt Free Library of the riches to be unearthed in Dialect Notes, a journal which had been published since 1890 by the American Dialect Society. Thereafter, he tells us, "I was a steady customer of Dialect Notes," which in time sent him scurrying to earlier works on American

794

English. These, as he points out in the Preface of 1919, were few in number and poor in scholarship. He set out to do something better, and his success can be gauged, not alone by the four editions and the many printings of The American Language, which with its two supplements grew from 374 into more than 2,500 pages, but also and perhaps best by the universal respect in which it is held and by the influence which it has had upon the study of American English.

H. L. Mencken was not a trained linguist and never claimed to be one. Indeed, his formal education ended with his graduation from the Baltimore Polytechnic Institute, a public high school of high repute. Wisely fearing "the odium which attaches justly to those amateurs who 'because they speak, fancy they can speak about speech,'" he declared in the Preface to the fourth edition of The American Language (1936) that, until trained scholars appear, "I can only go on accumulating materials and arranging them as plausibly as possible"—a task which he performed superbly. He was, however, mistaken in his belief that his "inquiries and surmises will probably be of small value" to future scholars.

THE AIM of this book is best exhibited by describing its origin. I am, and have been since early manhood, an editor of newspapers, magazines and books, and a critic of the last named. These occupations have forced me into a pretty wide familiarity with current literature, both periodical and within covers, and in particular into a familiarity with the current literature of England and America. It was part of my daily work, for a good many years, to read the principal English newspapers and reviews; it has been part of my work, all the time, to read the more important English novels, essays, poetry and criticism. An American born and bred, I early noted, as everyone else in like case must note, certain salient differences between the English of

The Preface is reprinted here from the first edition of The American Language, by H. L. Mencken, by permission of Alfred A. Knopf, Inc. Copyright 1919 by Alfred A. Knopf, Inc. Renewed 1947 by H. L. Mencken. The typescript of the Preface, in the collection of the Enoch Pratt Free Library of Baltimore, shows that Mencken made no significant revision in his manuscript save for the insertion of *spoken and* before *written* in the fifth sentence of the opening paragraph. The change indicates that he had become quite aware of the priority of speech over writing, a rather sophisticated concept in those days.

England and the English of America as practically spoken and written—differences in vocabulary, in syntax, in the shades and habits of idiom, and even, coming to the common speech, in grammar. And I noted too, of course, partly during visits to England but more largely by a somewhat wide and intimate intercourse with English people in the United States, the obvious differences between English and American pronunciation and intonation.

Greatly interested in these differences—some of them so great that they led me to seek exchanges of light with Englishmen—I looked for some work that would describe and account for them with a show of completeness, and perhaps depict the process of their origin. I soon found that no such work existed, either in England or in America—that the whole literature of the subject was astonishingly meagre and unsatisfactory. There were several dictionaries of Americanisms, true enough, but only one of them made any pretension to scientific method, and even that one was woefully narrow and incomplete. The one more general treatise, the work of a man foreign to both England and America in race and education, was more than 40 years old, and full of palpable errors. For the rest, there was only a fugitive and inconsequential literature—an almost useless mass of notes and essays, chiefly by the minor sort of pedagogues, seldom illuminating, save in small details, and often incredibly ignorant and inaccurate. On the large and important subject of American pronunciation, for example, I could find nothing save a few casual essays. On American spelling, with its wide and constantly visible divergences from English usages, there was little more. On American grammar there was nothing whatever. Worse, an important part of the poor literature that I unearthed was devoted to absurd efforts to prove that no such thing as an American variety of English existed—that the differences I constantly encountered in English and that my English friends encountered in American were chiefly imaginary, and to be explained away by denying them.

Still intrigued by the subject, and in despair of getting any illumination from such theoretical masters of it, I began a collection of materials for my own information, and gradually it took on a rather formidable bulk. My interest in it being made known by various articles in the newspapers and magazines, I began also to receive contributions from other persons of the same fancy, both English and American, and gradually my collection fell into a certain order, and I saw the workings of general laws in what, at first, had appeared to be mere chaos. The

796

present book then began to take form—its preparation a sort of recreation from other and far different labor. It is anything but an exhaustive treatise upon the subject; it is not even an exhaustive examination of the materials. All it pretends to do is to articulate some of those materials—to get some approach to order and coherence into them, and so pave the way for a better work by some more competent man. That work calls for the equipment of a first-rate philologist, which I am surely not. All I have done here is to stake out the field, sometimes borrowing suggestions from other inquirers and sometimes, as in the case of American grammar, attempting to run the lines myself.

That it should be regarded as an anti-social act to examine and exhibit the constantly growing differences between English and American, as certain American pedants argue sharply—this doctrine is quite beyond my understanding. All it indicates, stripped of sophistry, is a somewhat childish effort to gain the approval of Englishmen—a belated efflorescence of the colonial spirit, often commingled with fashionable aspiration. The plain fact is that the English themselves are not deceived, nor do they grant the approval so ardently sought for. On the contrary, they are keenly aware of the differences between the two dialects, and often discuss them, as the following pages show. Perhaps one dialect, in the long run, will defeat and absorb the other; if the two nations continue to be partners in great adventures it may very well happen. But even in that case, something may be accomplished by examining the differences which exist today. In some ways, as in intonation, English usage is plainly better than American. In others, as in spelling, American usage is as plainly better than English. But in order to develop usages that the people of both nations will accept it is obviously necessary to study the differences now visible. This study thus shows a certain utility. But its chief excuse is its human interest, for it prods deeply into national idiosyncrasies and ways of mind, and that sort of prodding is always entertaining.

I am thus neither teacher, nor prophet, nor reformer, but merely inquirer. The exigencies of my vocation make me almost completely bilingual; I can write English, as in this clause, quite as readily as American, as in this here one. Moreover, I have a hand for a compromise dialect which embodies the common materials of both, and is thus free from offense on both sides of the water—as befits the editor of a magazine published in both countries. But that compromise dialect is the living speech of neither. What I have tried to do here is to make a

797

first sketch of the living speech of These States. The work is confessedly incomplete, and in places very painfully so, but in such enterprises a man must put an arbitrary term to his labors, lest some mischance, after years of diligence, take him from them too suddenly for them to be closed, and his laborious accumulations, as Ernest Walker says in his book on English surnames, be "doomed to the waste-basket by harassed executors."

If the opportunity offers in future I shall undoubtedly return to the subject. For one thing, I am eager to attempt a more scientific examination of the grammar of the American vulgar speech, here discussed briefly in Chapter VI. For another thing, I hope to make further inquiries into the subject of American surnames of non-English origin. Various other fields invite. No historical study of American pronunciation exists; the influence of German, Irish-English, Yiddish and other such immigrant dialects upon American has never been investigated; there is no adequate treatise on American geographical names. Contributions of materials and suggestions for a possible revised edition of the present book will reach me if addressed to me in care of the publisher at 220 West Forty-second Street, New York. I shall also be very grateful for the correction of errors, some perhaps typographical but others due to faulty information or mistaken judgment.

In conclusion I borrow a plea in confession and avoidance from Ben Jonson's pioneer grammar of English, published in incomplete form after his death. "We have set down," he said, "that that in our judgment agreeth best with reason and good order. Which notwithstanding, if it seem to any to be too rough hewed, let him plane it out more smoothly, and I shall not only not envy it, but in the behalf of my country most heartily thank him for so great a benefit; hoping that I shall be thought sufficiently to have done my part if in tolling this bell I may draw others to a deeper consideration of the matter; for, touching myself, I must needs confess that after much painful churning this only would come which here we have devised."

Baltimore, January 1, 1919.   MENCKEN.

Mencken's opinions on language, like those he expressed on other subjects, have given rise to much comment and controversy. One

wonders what he had in mind when he referred in the fourth paragraph of his Preface to British intonation as "plainly better" than American, or, for that matter, why he thought American spelling better than English, inasmuch as the differences affect comparatively few words. And one wonders also at an obtuseness not customary with him when in his fifth paragraph he contrasts the supposedly American "this here" with the supposedly British "this." What he is actually setting up for comparison in these examples is American folk usage with Standard English wherever spoken, which for no particularly good reason has always avoided "this here" used adjectivally. The fact is that "this here" is about as frequent in the nonstandard speech of England as in that of America, and the locution is condemned with equal vigor by schoolmasters and "marms" on both sides of the Atlantic. But Mencken's comparisons of humble American speech with Standard British English have been sufficiently stressed by other writers, to such an extent that he omitted from the fourth edition of his book "The Declaration of Independence in American" (beginning "When things get so balled up that the people of a country have got to cut loose from some other country, and go it on their own hook . . ."), even though he had plainly labeled this as a specimen of the American Vulgate.

Mencken was also to recant his faith, expressed in his first three editions, that "the American form of the English language was plainly departing from the parent stem"; instead, he had by 1936 come to the conclusion that British English was yielding to American example and that some of the differences which he had made so much of were beginning to disappear: British English would "on some not too remote tomorrow," he predicted, become "a kind of dialect of American"— which is, of course, about as fantastic as his earlier notion. (He doubtless had in mind only vocabulary items, like OK, blizzard, caucus, and a good many other terms of American origin which have indeed been naturalized in British English.) But these are venial errors to some extent forced upon Mencken by his title; later, when he would have preferred to change this title, it was too late. His faulty prognostications in no way lessened the influence of what was to all intents the earliest full-scale study of American English, appearing at a time when, as he implies in his Preface, there was little or no professional interest in the subject.

Since the publication of Mencken's work, the study of American English has gone on at a very lively rate, though Professor George Philip Krapp could say as late as 1925, in his English Language in America,

799

that "one may question whether even now the time is ripe for writing a history of the English language in America." There have nevertheless been a number of such attempts, with varying degrees of success. In addition, succeeding years have seen the publication of the first part of the monumental Linguistic Atlas of the United States and Canada, A Dictionary of American English, and A Dictionary of Americanisms, all works of the utmost importance in the study of American English. American Speech, the raciest of learned journals, was founded by Mencken, Kemp Malone, Louise Pound, and A. G. Kennedy in 1925. According to Professor Malone, "the idea was Mencken's." It has published scores of articles of the highest importance. The American Dialect Society, of which Mencken ultimately became a faithful member though he never contributed anything to its journal, continues to include the most distinguished linguistic scholars in the country. Dialect Notes is no longer published; its successor has since 1944 been called simply Publication of the American Dialect Society.

In its investigations of its own speech America has in recent years been far more active than the Mother Country has been in studying its vernacular. Much, if not all, of this activity can be attributed to what was in effect Mencken's linguistic declaration of independence—his recognition that the English of America is not a corruption, but a development, of British English as it was brought to this country by the early settlers. In view of Mencken's frequent jibes at professors and institutions of higher learning—though some of his best friends were professors—it is not without irony that his own work helped make the study of American English academically respectable.

It is true that Noah Webster had long before asserted the independence of what he also miscalled "the American language." But Webster's motives were not untainted by a rather unpleasant form of jingoism and a desire to promote the sales of his own books. Moreover, his humorless, heavily magisterial manner terrorized the linguistically insecure and antagonized the secure. Though Webster did little that inspired investigation by others, he was able to bulldoze a good many people into believing that he had spoken the final word on the English language. His greatest achievement has turned out to be the indoctrination of a rigorously authoritarian attitude toward language evincing itself in the phrase "according to Webster," which would have pleased self-righteous old Noah no end.

Mencken, as we have seen, never thought that he knew all the answers.

He was never too proud to admit and correct his mistakes. Furthermore, he was the master of as lively and readable a style as this country has ever known, even though its special brand of humor may have antagonized a great many sour and serious people. Best of all, he was, despite his satirical bent, a kindly and generous-hearted man, always interested in the encouragement of promising young people, who in their turn found him enormously attractive. He reserved his thunder for charlatans and frauds, mainly for those who played at being God.

The ideological drift since his day makes one hesitant to predict any renascence of interest in H. L. Mencken as a writer, critic, and commentator on nonlinguistic American life. But, even if he should be forgotten for everything else he wrote, his American Language is sure to live on as a monument of American linguistic scholarship.

Herbert Hoover
On American Individualism
1928

EDITED BY IRVIN G. WYLLIE

Carrying the fight to his opponent's home ground in the last days of the 1928 election campaign, Herbert Hoover invaded New York, the political stronghold of Alfred E. Smith. Hoover's task was to rally the New York business community through a review of Republican economic policy, and to discredit Smith by representing that his proposals in regard to public power and agriculture were dangerously socialistic. Persuaded that the United States was "being infected from the revolutionary caldrons of Europe," Hoover decided that the Republican Party should "draw the issue of the American system, as opposed to all forms of collectivism." Perhaps because they recalled that he had already developed this theme at some length in his book American Individualism (1922), his campaign managers advised him that the subject was not of great public interest and that harping on it might carry liabilities. But Hoover, sincerely believing that the Democrats represented a threat from the left and that the voters were entitled to a statement of his views on the principles and ideals underlying the conduct of government, refused to be diverted. "I felt that this infection was around and I dealt with it definitely in an address in New York on October 22, 1928."

Because radio always exposed him to the same national audience, Hoover felt that he needed ten days or two weeks between addresses in order to prepare something original. Altogether he invested two weeks in composing his Madison Square Garden address. He followed his usual custom of soliciting advice, suggestion, and criticism from colleagues, but from beginning to end the speech was his, written out "with my own hand." Hoover boasted that he had "never delivered a ghost-written public statement of importance," and that he had handwritten drafts of every major speech to prove it.

He could have used a ghost speaker at Madison Square Garden, where an enthusiastic crowd of 22,000, including 3,000 standees, assembled to hear him. Their enthusiasm barely survived his arrival. An eyewitness reported that an enlarged picture of the candidate, dominating the sports arena, conveyed an image "much more cheerful and jolly than that which sat upon his countenance when he appeared." Grim and unresponsive, he waited through four minutes of a tumultuous greeting before raising a hand and forcing a smile. At 9:08 P.M. he began reading in a low, rapid voice, blurring many words. He made no gestures, rarely looked up from his text, even on the few occasions when he was interrupted by applause. Having responded with hand and voice, the audience now responded with feet. Within half an hour after Hoover began, the standees had vanished and empty benches could be seen in the top gallery. Hoover, aware of the shuffling feet, increased his reading speed. When he finished at 10:03 P.M., at least 5,000 of his original audience had slipped away. Though he felt deeply about the principles he had expounded, he had been unable to stir his listeners, owing to his personal remoteness and tedious forensic style. A reporter for the Christian Science Monitor, sensing the significance of his central theme, put the best face on Hoover's performance when he described his language and delivery as those of "a learned teacher expounding to a gathering of other learned men and women the tenets of a great theme, a mighty project."

THIS CAMPAIGN now draws near a close. The platforms of the two parties defining principles and offering solutions of various national problems have been presented and are being earnestly considered by our people.

After four months' debate it is not the Republican Party which finds reason for abandonment of any of the principles it has laid down or of the views it has expressed for solution of the problems before the

---

Hoover entitled his speech "New York City." The text as reprinted here appeared in *The New Day: Campaign Speeches of Herbert Hoover, 1928* (Stanford University, Calif.: Stanford University Press, 1928), pp. 149–76.

country. The principles to which it adheres are rooted deeply in the foundations of our national life. The solutions which it proposes are based on experience with government and on a consciousness that it may have the responsibility for placing those solutions in action.

In my acceptance speech I endeavored to outline the spirit and ideals by which I would be guided in carrying that platform into adminis-tration. Tonight, I will not deal with the multitude of issues which have been already well canvassed. I intend rather to discuss some of those more fundamental principles and ideals upon which I believe the government of the United States should be conducted.

RECENT PROGRESS AS THE EFFECT OF REPUBLICAN POLICIES

The Republican Party has ever been a party of progress. I do not need to review its seventy years of constructive history. It has always reflected the spirit of the American people. Never has it done more for the advancement of fundamental progress than during the past seven and one-half years since we took over the government amidst the ruin left by war.

It detracts nothing from the character and energy of the American people, it minimizes in no degree the quality of their accomplishments to say that the policies of the Republican Party have played a large part in recuperation from the war and the building of the magnificent progress which shows upon every hand today. I say with emphasis that without the wise policies which the Republican Party has brought into action during this period, no such progress would have been possible.

CONFIDENCE RESTORED

The first responsibility of the Republican administration was to renew the march of progress from its collapse by the war. That task involved the restoration of confidence in the future and the liberation and stimulation of the constructive energies of our people. It discharged that task. There is not a person within the sound of my voice who does not know the profound progress which our country has made in this period. Every man and woman knows that American comfort, hope, and confidence for the future are immeasurably higher this day than they were seven and one-half years ago.

CONSTRUCTIVE MEASURES ADOPTED

It is not my purpose to enter upon a detailed recital of the great constructive measures of the past seven and one-half years by which this has been brought about. It is sufficient to remind you of the restoration

804

of employment to the millions who walked your streets in idleness; to remind you of the creation of the budget system; the reduction of six billions of national debt which gave the powerful impulse of that vast sum returned to industry and commerce; the four sequent reductions of taxes and thereby the lift to the living of every family; the enactment of adequate protective tariff and immigration laws which have safeguarded our workers and farmers from floods of goods and labor from foreign countries; the creation of credit facilities and many other aids to agriculture; the building up of foreign trade; the care of veterans; the development of aviation, of radio, of our inland waterways, of our highways; the expansion of scientific research, of welfare activities; the making of safer highways, safer mines, better homes; the spread of outdoor recreation; the improvement in public health and the care of children; and a score of other progressive actions.

DELICACY OF THE TASK

Nor do I need to remind you that government today deals with an economic and social system vastly more intricate and delicately adjusted than ever before. That system now must be kept in perfect tune if we would maintain uninterrupted employment and the high standards of living of our people. The government has come to touch this delicate web at a thousand points. Yearly the relations of government to national prosperity become more and more intimate. Only through keen vision and helpful co-operation by the government has stability in business and stability in employment been maintained during this past seven and one-half years. There always are some localities, some industries, and some individuals who do not share the prevailing prosperity. The task of government is to lessen these inequalities.

Never has there been a period when the Federal Government has given such aid and impulse to the progress of our people, not alone to economic progress but to the development of those agencies which make for moral and spiritual progress.

THE AMERICAN SYSTEM

But in addition to this great record of contributions of the Republican Party to progress, there has been a further fundamental contribution—a contribution underlying and sustaining all the others—and that is the resistance of the Republican Party to every attempt to inject the government into business in competition with its citizens.

After the war, when the Republican Party assumed administration of the country, we were faced with the problem of determination of the very nature of our national life. During one hundred and fifty years we have builded up a form of self-government and a social system which is peculiarly our own. It differs essentially from all others in the world. It is the American system. It is just as definite and positive a political and social system as has ever been developed on earth. It is founded upon a particular conception of self-government in which decentralized local responsibility is the very base. Further than this, it is founded upon the conception that only through ordered liberty, freedom, and equal opportunity to the individual will his initiative and enterprise spur on the march of progress. And in our insistence upon equality of opportunity has our system advanced beyond all the world.

SUSPENDED BY THE WAR

During the war we necessarily turned to the government to solve every difficult economic problem. The government having absorbed every energy of our people for war, there was no other solution. For the preservation of the state the Federal Government became a centralized despotism which undertook unprecedented responsibilities, assumed autocratic powers, and took over the business of citizens. To a large degree we regimented our whole people temporarily into a socialistic state. However justified in time of war, if continued in peacetime it would destroy not only our American system but with it our progress and freedom as well.

When the war closed, the most vital of all issues both in our own country and throughout the world was whether governments should continue their war-time ownership and operation of many instrumentalities of production and distribution. We were challenged with a peace-time choice between the American system of rugged individualism and a European philosophy of diametrically opposed doctrines—doctrines of paternalism and state socialism. The acceptance of these ideas would have meant the destruction of self-government through centralization of government. It would have meant the undermining of the individual initiative and enterprise through which our people have grown to unparalleled greatness.

RESTORED UNDER REPUBLICAN DIRECTION

The Republican Party from the beginning resolutely turned its face away from these ideas and these war practices. A Republican Congress

806

co-operated with the Democratic administration to demobilize many of our war activities. At that time the two parties were in accord upon that point. When the Republican Party came into full power it went at once resolutely back to our fundamental conception of the state and the rights and responsibilities of the individual. Thereby it restored confidence and hope in the American people, it freed and stimulated enterprise, it restored the government to its position as an umpire instead of a player in the economic game. For these reasons the American people have gone forward in progress while the rest of the world has halted, and some countries have even gone backward. If anyone will study the causes of retarded recuperation in Europe, he will find much of it due to stifling of private initiative on one hand, and overloading of the government with business on the other.

PROPOSALS NOW MENACING THIS SYSTEM

There has been revived in this campaign, however, a series of proposals which, if adopted, would be a long step toward the abandonment of our American system and a surrender to the destructive operation of governmental conduct of commercial business. Because the country is faced with difficulty and doubt over certain national problems —that is, prohibition, farm relief, and electrical power—our opponents propose that we must thrust government a long way into the businesses which give rise to these problems. In effect, they abandon the tenets of their own party and turn to state socialism as a solution for the difficulties presented by all three. It is proposed that we shall change from prohibition to the state purchase and sale of liquor. If their agricultural relief program means anything, it means that the government shall directly or indirectly buy and sell and fix prices of agricultural products. And we are to go into the hydro-electric power business. In other words, we are confronted with a huge program of government in business.

There is, therefore, submitted to the American people a question of fundamental principle. That is: shall we depart from the principles of our American political and economic system, upon which we have advanced beyond all the rest of the world, in order to adopt methods based on principles destructive of its very foundations? And I wish to emphasize the seriousness of these proposals. I wish to make my position clear; for this goes to the very roots of American life and progress.

807

CENTRALIZATION FATAL TO SELF-GOVERNMENT

I should like to state to you the effect that this projection of government in business would have upon our system of self-government and our economic system. That effect would reach to the daily life of every man and woman. It would impair the very basis of liberty and freedom not only for those left outside the fold of expanded bureaucracy but for those embraced within it.

Let us first see the effect upon self-government. When the Federal Government undertakes to go into commercial business it must at once set up the organization and administration of that business, and it immediately finds itself in a labyrinth, every alley of which leads to the destruction of self-government.

Commercial business requires a concentration of responsibility. Self-government requires decentralization and many checks and balances to safeguard liberty. Our government to succeed in business would need become in effect a despotism. There at once begins the destruction of self-government.

UNWISDOM OF GOVERNMENT IN BUSINESS

The first problem of the government about to adventure in commercial business is to determine a method of administration. It must secure leadership and direction. Shall this leadership be chosen by political agencies or shall we make it elective? The hard practical fact is that leadership in business must come through the sheer rise in ability and character. That rise can only take place in the free atmosphere of competition. Competition is closed by bureaucracy. Political agencies are feeble channels through which to select able leaders to conduct commercial business.

Government, in order to avoid the possible incompetence, corruption, and tyranny of too great authority in individuals entrusted with commercial business, inevitably turns to boards and commissions. To make sure that there are checks and balances, each member of such boards and commissions must have equal authority. Each has his separate responsibility to the public, and at once we have the conflict of ideas and the lack of decision which would ruin any commercial business. It has contributed greatly to the demoralization of our shipping business. Moreover, these commissions must be representative of different sections and different political parties, so that at once we have an entire blight upon co-ordinated action within their ranks which destroys any possibility of effective administration.

Moreover, our legislative bodies cannot in fact delegate their full authority to commissions or to individuals for the conduct of matters vital to the American people; for if we would preserve government by the people we must preserve the authority of our legislators in the activities of our government.

Thus every time the Federal Government goes into a commercial business, five hundred and thirty-one Senators and Congressmen become the actual board of directors of that business. Every time a state government goes into business one or two hundred state senators and legislators become the actual directors of that business. Even if they were supermen and if there were no politics in the United States, no body of such numbers could competently direct commercial activities; for that requires initiative, instant decision, and action. It took Congress six years of constant discussion to even decide what the method of administration of Muscle Shoals should be.

When the Federal Government undertakes to go into business, the state governments are at once deprived of control and taxation of that business; when a state government undertakes to go into business, it at once deprives the municipalities of taxation and control of that business. Municipalities, being local and close to the people, can, at times, succeed in business where federal and state governments must fail. We have trouble enough with log-rolling in legislative bodies today. It originates naturally from desires of citizens to advance their particular section or to secure some necessary service. It would be multiplied a thousandfold were the federal and state governments in these businesses.

The effect upon our economic progress would be even worse. Business progressiveness is dependent on competition. New methods and new ideas are the outgrowth of the spirit of adventure, of individual initiative, and of individual enterprise. Without adventure there is no progress. No government administration can rightly take chances with taxpayers' money.

There is no better example of the practical incompetence of government to conduct business than the history of our railways. During the war the government found it necessary to operate the railways. That operation continued until after the war. In the year before being freed from government operation they were not able to meet the demands for transportation. Eight years later we find them under private enterprise transporting fifteen per cent more goods and meeting every demand for service. Rates have been reduced by fifteen per cent and net earnings increased from less than one per cent on their valuation to about five per cent. Wages of employees have improved by thirteen per cent. The wages of railway employees are today one hundred and twenty-one per cent above pre-war, while the wages of government employees are today only sixty-five per cent above pre-war. That should be a sufficient commentary upon the efficiency of government operation.

DANGERS OF BUREAUCRACY

Let us now examine this question from the point of view of the person who may get a government job and is admitted into the new bureaucracy. Upon that subject let me quote from a speech of that great leader of labor, Samuel Gompers, delivered in Montreal in 1920, a few years before his death. He said:

I believe there is no man to whom I would take second position in my loyalty to the Republic of the United States, and yet I would not give it more power over the individual citizenship of our country. . . .

It is a question of whether it shall be government ownership or private ownership under control. . . . If I were in the minority of one in this convention, I would want to cast my vote so that the men of labor shall not willingly enslave themselves to government authority in their industrial effort for freedom. . . .

Let the future tell the story of who is right or who is wrong; who has stood for freedom and who has been willing to submit their fate industrially to the government.

I would amplify Mr. Gompers' statement. The great body of government employees which would be created by the proposals of our opponents would either comprise a political machine at the disposal of the party in power, or, alternatively, to prevent this, the government by stringent civil-service rules must debar its employees from their full political rights as free men. It must limit them in the liberty to bargain for their own wages, for no government employee can strike against his government and thus against the whole people. It makes a legislative body with all its political currents their final employer and master. Their bargaining does not rest upon economic need or economic strength but on political potence.

But what of those who are outside the bureaucracy? What is the effect upon their lives?

The area of enterprise and opportunity for them to strive and rise is at once limited.

The government in commercial business does not tolerate amongst its customers the freedom of competitive reprisals to which private business is subject. Bureaucracy does not tolerate the spirit of independence; it spreads the spirit of submission into our daily life and penetrates the temper of our people not with the habit of powerful resistance to wrong but with the habit of timid acceptance of irresistible might.

FATAL TO TRUE LIBERALISM

Bureaucracy is ever desirous of spreading its influence and its power. You cannot extend the mastery of the government over the daily working life of a people without at the same time making it the master of the people's souls and thoughts. Every expansion of government in business means that government in order to protect itself from the political consequences of its errors and wrongs is driven irresistibly without peace to greater and greater control of the nation's press and platform. Free speech does not live many hours after free industry and free commerce die.

It is a false liberalism that interprets itself into the government operation of commercial business. Every step of bureaucratizing of the business of our country poisons the very roots of liberalism—that is, political equality, free speech, free assembly, free press, and equality of opportunity. It is the road not to more liberty, but to less liberty. Liberalism should be found not striving to spread bureaucracy but striving to set bounds to it. True liberalism seeks all legitimate freedom first in the confident belief that without such freedom the pursuit of all other blessings and benefits is vain. That belief is the foundation of all American progress, political as well as economic.

Liberalism is a force truly of the spirit, a force proceeding from the deep realization that economic freedom cannot be sacrificed if political freedom is to be preserved. Even if governmental conduct of business could give us more efficiency instead of less efficiency, the fundamental objection to it would remain unaltered and unabated. It would destroy political equality. It would increase rather than decrease abuse and corruption. It would stifle initiative and invention. It would undermine the development of leadership. It would cramp and cripple the mental and spiritual energies of our people. It would extinguish equality and opportunity. It would dry up the spirit of liberty and progress. For these reasons primarily it must be resisted. For a hundred and fifty years liberalism has found its true spirit in the American system, not in the European systems.

FLEXIBILITY OF THE AMERICAN SYSTEM

I do not wish to be misunderstood in this statement. I am defining a general policy. It does not mean that our government is to part with one iota of its national resources without complete protection to the public interest. I have already stated that where the government is engaged in public works for purposes of flood control, of navigation, of irrigation, of scientific research or national defense, or in pioneering a new art, it will at times necessarily produce power or commodities as a by-product. But they must be a by-product of the major purpose, not the major purpose itself.

Nor do I wish to be misinterpreted as believing that the United States is free-for-all and devil-take-the-hindmost. The very essence of equality of opportunity and of American individualism is that there shall be no domination by any group or combination in this republic, whether it be business or political. On the contrary, it demands economic justice as well as political and social justice. It is no system of laissez faire.

I feel deeply on this subject because during the war I had some practical experience with governmental operation and control. I have witnessed not only at home but abroad the many failures of government in business. I have seen its tyrannies, its injustices, its destructions of self-government, its undermining of the very instincts which carry our people forward to progress. I have witnessed the lack of advance, the lowered standards of living, the depressed spirits of people working under such a system. My objection is based not upon theory or upon a failure to recognize wrong or abuse, but I know the adoption of such methods would strike at the very roots of American life and would destroy the very basis of American progress.

Our people have the right to know whether we can continue to solve our great problems without abandonment of our American system. I know we can. We have demonstrated that our system is responsive enough to meet any new and intricate development in our economic and business life. We have demonstrated that we can meet any economic problem and still maintain our democracy as master in its own house, and that we can at the same time preserve equality of opportunity and individual freedom.

PRACTICABILITY OF REGULATION

In the last fifty years we have discovered that mass production will produce articles for us at half the cost they required previously. We have seen the resultant growth of large units of production and distribution. This is big business. Many businesses must be bigger, for our tools are bigger, our country is bigger. We now build a single dynamo of a hundred thousand horsepower. Even fifteen years ago that would have been a big business all by itself. Yet today advance in production requires that we set ten of these units together in a row.

The American people from bitter experience have a rightful fear that great business units might be used to dominate our industrial life and by illegal and unethical practices destroy equality of opportunity.

Years ago the Republican administration established the principle that such evils could be corrected by regulation. It developed methods by which abuses could be prevented while the full value of industrial progress could be retained for the public. It insisted upon the principle that when great public utilities were clothed with the security of partial monopoly, whether it be railways, power plants, telephones, or what not, then there must be the fullest and most complete control of rates, services, and finances by government or local agencies. It declared that these businesses must be conducted with glass pockets.

As to our great manufacturing and distributing industries, the Republican Party insisted upon the enactment of laws that not only would maintain competition but would destroy conspiracies to destroy the smaller units or dominate and limit the equality of opportunity amongst our people.

One of the great problems of government is to determine to what extent the government shall regulate and control commerce and industry and how much it shall leave it alone. No system is perfect. We have had many abuses in the private conduct of business. That every good citizen resents. It is just as important that business keep out of government as that government keep out of business.

Nor am I setting up the contention that our institutions are perfect. No human ideal is ever perfectly attained, since humanity itself is not perfect.

The wisdom of our forefathers in their conception that progress can only be attained as the sum of the accomplishment of free individuals has been reinforced by all of the great leaders of the country since that day. Jackson, Lincoln, Cleveland, McKinley, Roosevelt, Wilson, and Coolidge have stood unalterably for these principles.

EFFECTIVENESS OF THE AMERICAN SYSTEM

And what have been the results of our American system? Our country has become the land of opportunity to those born without inheritance, not merely because of the wealth of its resources and industry but because of this freedom of initiative and enterprise. Russia has natural resources equal to ours. Her people are equally industrious, but she has not had the blessings of one hundred and fifty years of our form of government and of our social system.

By adherence to the principles of decentralized self-government, ordered liberty, equal opportunity, and freedom to the individual, our American experiment in human welfare has yielded a degree of well-being unparalleled in all the world. It has come nearer to the abolition of poverty, to the abolition of fear of want, than humanity has ever reached before. Progress of the past seven years is the proof of it. This alone furnishes the answer to our opponents, who ask us to introduce destructive elements into the system by which this has been accomplished.

Let us see what this system has done for us in our recent years of difficult and trying reconstruction and then solemnly ask ourselves if we now wish to abandon it.

POST-WAR RECOVERY

As a nation we came out of the war with great losses. We made no profits from it. The apparent increases in wages were at that time fictitious. We were poorer as a nation when we emerged from the war. Yet during these last eight years we have recovered from these losses and increased our national income by over one-third, even if we discount the inflation of the dollar. That there has been a wide diffusion of our gain in wealth and income is marked by a hundred proofs. I know of no better test of the improved conditions of the average family than the combined increase in assets of life and industrial insurance, building and loan associations, and savings deposits. These are the savings banks of the average man. These agencies alone have in seven years increased by nearly one hundred per cent to the gigantic sum of over fifty billions of dollars, or nearly one-sixth of our whole national wealth. We have increased in home ownership, we have expanded the investments of the average man.

In addition to these evidences of larger savings, our people are steadily increasing their spending for higher standards of living. Today there are almost nine automobiles for each ten families, where seven and one-half years ago only enough automobiles were running to average less than four for each ten families. The slogan of progress is changing from the full dinner pail to the full garage. Our people have more to eat, better things to wear, and better homes. We have even gained in elbow room, for the increase of residential floor space is over twenty-five per cent, with less than ten per cent increase in our number of people. Wages have increased, the cost of living has decreased. The job of every man and woman has been made more secure. We have in this short period decreased the fear of poverty, the fear of unemployment, the fear of old age; and these are fears that are the greatest calamities of humankind.

All this progress means far more than increased creature comforts. It finds a thousand interpretations into a greater and fuller life. A score of new helps save the drudgery of the home. In seven years we have added seventy per cent to the electric power at the elbows of our workers and further promoted them from carriers of burdens to directors of machines. We have steadily reduced the sweat in human labor. Our hours of labor are lessened; our leisure has increased. We have expanded our parks and playgrounds. We have nearly doubled our attendance at games. We pour into outdoor recreation in every direction. The visitors at our national parks have trebled and we have so increased the number of sportsmen fishing in our streams and lakes that the longer time between bites is becoming a political issue. In these seven and one-half years the radio has brought music and laughter, education and political discussion to almost every fireside.

Springing from our prosperity with its greater freedom, its vast endowment of scientific research, and the greater resources with which to care for public health, we have according to our insurance actuaries during this short period since the war lengthened the average span of life by nearly eight years. We have reduced infant mortality, we have vastly decreased the days of illness and suffering in the life of every man and woman. We have improved the facilities for the care of the crippled and helpless and deranged.

EDUCATIONAL PROGRESS

From our increasing resources we have expanded our educational system in eight years from an outlay of twelve hundred millions to twenty-seven hundred millions of dollars. The education of our youth has become almost our largest and certainly our most important activity. From our greater income and thus our ability to free youth from toil we have increased the attendance in our grade schools by fourteen per cent, in our high schools by eighty per cent, and in our institutions of higher learning by ninety-five per cent. Today we have more youth in these institutions of higher learning twice over than all the rest of the world put together. We have made notable progress in literature, in art, and in public taste.

We have made progress in the leadership of every branch of American life. Never in our history was the leadership in our economic life more distinguished in its abilities than today, and it has grown greatly in its consciousness of public responsibility. Leadership in our professions and in moral and spiritual affairs of our country was never of a higher order. And our magnificent educational system is bringing forward a host of recruits for the succession to this leadership.

I do not need to recite more figures and more evidence. I cannot believe that the American people wish to abandon or in any way to weaken the principles of economic freedom and self-government which have been maintained by the Republican Party and which have produced results so amazing and so stimulating to the spiritual as well as to the material advance of the nation.

SIGNIFICANCE TO NEW YORK CITY

Your city has been an outstanding beneficiary of this great progress and of these safeguarded principles. With its suburbs it has, during the last seven and one-half years, grown by over a million and a half of people until it has become the largest metropolitan district of all the world. Here you have made abundant opportunity not only for the youth of the land but for the immigrant from foreign shores. This city is the commercial center of the United States. It is the commercial agent of the American people. It is a great organism of specialized skill and leadership in finance, industry, and commerce which reaches every spot in our country. Its progress and its beauty are the pride of the whole American people. It leads our nation in its benevolences to charity, to education, and to scientific research. It is the center of art, music, literature, and drama. It has come to have a more potent voice than any other city in the United States.

But when all is said and done, the very life, progress, and prosperity of this city is wholly dependent on the prosperity of the 115,000,000 people who dwell in our mountains and valleys across the three thousand miles to the Pacific Ocean. Every activity of this city is sensitive to every evil and every favorable tide that sweeps this great nation of ours. Be there a slackening of industry in any place, it affects New York far more than any other part of the country. In a time of depression one-quarter of all the unemployed in the United States can be numbered in this city. In a time of prosperity the citizens of the great interior of our country pour into your city for business and entertainment at the rate of one hundred and fifty thousand a day. In fact, so much is this city the reflex of the varied interests of our country that the concern of every one of your citizens for national stability, for national prosperity, for national progress, for preservation of our American system is far greater than that of any other single part of our country.

UNFINISHED TASKS

We still have great problems if we would achieve the full economic advancement of our country. In these past few years some groups in our country have lagged behind others in the march of progress. I refer more particularly to those engaged in the textile, coal, and agricultural industries. We can assist in solving these problems by co-operation of our government. To the agricultural industry we shall need to advance initial capital to assist them to stabilize their industry. But this proposal implies that they shall conduct it themselves, and not the government. It is in the interest of our cities that we shall bring agriculture and all industries into full stability and prosperity. I know you will gladly co-operate in the faith that in the common prosperity of our country lies its future.

In bringing this address to a conclusion I should like to restate to you some of the fundamental things I have endeavored to bring out.

THE COMING DECISION FUNDAMENTAL

The foundations of progress and prosperity are dependent as never before upon the wise policies of government, for government now touches at a thousand points the intricate web of economic and social life.

Under administration by the Republican Party in the last seven and one-half years our country as a whole has made unparalleled progress and this has been in generous part reflected to this great city. Prosperity is no idle expression. It is a job for every worker; it is the safety and the safeguard of every business and every home. A continuation of the policies of the Republican Party is fundamentally necessary to the further advancement of this progress and to the further building up of this prosperity.

I have dwelt at some length on the principles of relationship between the government and business. I make no apologies for dealing with this subject. The first necessity of any nation is the smooth functioning of the vast business machinery for employment, feeding, clothing, housing, and providing luxuries and comforts to a people. Unless these basic elements are properly organized and function, there can be no progress in business, in education, literature, music, or art. There can be no advance in the fundamental ideals of a people. A people cannot make progress in poverty.

I have endeavored to present to you that the greatness of America has grown out of a political and social system and a method of control of economic forces distinctly its own—our American system—which has carried this great experiment in human welfare farther than ever before in all history. We are nearer today to the ideal of the abolition of poverty and fear from the lives of men and women than ever before in any land. And I again repeat that the departure from our American system by injecting principles destructive to it which our opponents propose will jeopardize the very liberty and freedom of our people, will destroy equality of opportunity not alone to ourselves but to our children.

THE NEW DAY

To me the foundation of American life rests upon the home and the family. I read into these great economic forces, these intricate and delicate relations of the government with business and with our political and social life, but one supreme end—that we reinforce the ties that bind together the millions of our families, that we strengthen the security, the happiness, and the independence of every home.

My conception of America is a land where men and women may walk in ordered freedom in the independent conduct of their occupations; where they may enjoy the advantages of wealth, not concentrated in the hands of the few but spread through the lives of all; where they build and safeguard their homes, and give to their children the fullest advantages and opportunities of American life; where every man shall be respected in the faith that his conscience and his heart direct him to follow; where a contented and happy people, secure in their liberties, free from poverty and fear, shall have the leisure and impulse to seek a fuller life.

Some may ask where all this may lead beyond mere material progress. It leads to a release of the energies of men and women from the dull drudgery of life to a wider vision and a higher hope. It leads to the opportunity for greater and greater service, not alone from man to man in our own land, but from our country to the whole world. It leads to an America, healthy in body, healthy in spirit, unfettered, youthful, eager— with a vision searching beyond the farthest horizons, with an open mind, sympathetic and generous. It is to these higher ideals and for these purposes that I pledge myself and the Republican Party.

The immediate effect of Hoover's delineation of American and un-American social principles was to harden partisan political sentiment. Senator George Norris of Nebraska, a Republican liberal and an advocate of public power, was so deeply offended that he declared immediately for Al Smith. "How any progressive in the United States can support him now, after his Madison Square Garden address . . . my God, I cannot conceive it," Norris asserted. Al Smith, stung by the socialism charge, answered two days later in Boston, declaring that Hoover had confused democratic social action with socialism. For a quarter of a century Republicans had opposed every measure for human betterment with the cry of socialism, with the result that "the people of the state of New York are sick and tired of listening to it." Franklin D. Roosevelt, campaigning to succeed Smith as governor, declared that if Smith was a socialist under Hoover's definition, he would declare himself to be one too. Democratic newspapers generally saw nothing but low partisanship in Hoover's high-sounding statement of principles. The Nashville Tennessean assailed him for knocking over a straw man, while the Birmingham Age-Herald dismissed the speech as "a diffuse dissertation on the horrors of state socialism," deriving from "warmed-over recollections of Leland Stanford courses in economics of the year '95." The Atlanta Constitution accused Hoover of trying to "out Hamilton Hamilton," and of naively claiming that the Republican Party was responsible for all progress, even in the arts and sciences, since March 4, 1921.

Republicans received Hoover's message as divine revelation, a reliable catechism of political faith. The Chicago Daily Tribune hailed it as one of the most important utterances by any public man in a generation. The Camden Courier Post praised the address for exposing the antidemocratic character of Democratic liberalism: "Herbert Hoover is the true liberal candidate in this campaign." Many other Republican newspapers also proclaimed their enthusiasm for Hoover's creed, calling it progressive but not radical, conservative but not reactionary. The New York Herald Tribune said the speech was profoundly constructive—an aid to progress, prosperity, and the cause of human liberty. The same newspaper also hailed the shift in betting odds following the speech; though less elevating than Hoover's sentiments, the bookmakers' reports were very gratifying. Wall Street betting brokers, who had previously quoted 6 to 5 odds on Smith to carry New York, kept the same odds, but now put Hoover on top.

After he became President, Hoover did much to guarantee that his Madison Square Garden address would have a partisan afterlife. He used it as a test for legislation, as in the case of the Muscle Shoals Bill of 1931, "to which piece of socialism I would not agree." He also used it to justify his limited response to mass unemployment, agricultural overproduction, bank failure, industrial collapse, and other problems of the depression years. It served as a ready defense for his unchanging view that the federal government's proper role was that of "umpire instead of a player in the economic game." After accepting the Republican presidential nomination in 1932, Hoover refurbished the old theme that the election was more than a contest between parties and men. "It is a contest between two philosophies of government." Returning to Madison Square Garden on October 31, 1932, he got additional mileage out of many of the arguments, ideas, and phrases that he had uttered there four years before. Later he attacked the economic planning of the New Deal which, in his view, involved "the pouring of a mixture of socialism and fascism into the American system." Whenever he returned to the political wars in the 1930's, he warned the people that the economic interventions of the New

Dealers were "more dangerous to free men than the depression itself." In his Memoirs, published in 1951–52, he quoted extensively from his 1928 address, for the instruction and benefit of posterity. "While campaign statements are of no great romantic interest," he declared, "the historian gleans something of economics, ideologies, and politics from them."

As Hoover and other partisans of his generation have passed from the political scene in recent years, it has been possible to view his first Madison Square Garden address as a serious and responsible analysis of the difficulty of preserving human liberty, guaranteeing equality of opportunity, and providing incentives to progress in societies in which government assumes the dominant role. The follies, failures, and crimes of modern totalitarian states have undermined blind faith in state action as the cure for every social ill, and underscored the propriety of concern for the welfare of the individual man, as against collective mankind. Only recently have Americans begun to acquire the comparative knowledge of the world that Hoover already possessed when he phrased his 1928 statement of faith. As an international businessman and American public servant, he had observed at first hand the operations of the managed economy. "I have seen its tyrannies, its injustices, its destructions of self-government, its undermining of the very instincts which carry our people forward to progress." Convinced by his experience abroad that America owed its distinctive character to individualism as a principle of social action, he became an unashamed individualist. His faith in American individualism was "confirmed and deepened by the searching experiences of seven years of service in the backwash and misery of war." Changing times have invested Hoover's utterances with a wisdom and credibility that they appeared to lack in 1928. The troubles of the contemporary world have helped to transform his originally partisan formulation into an appealing testimony to the American faith.

Sinclair Lewis
The American Fear of Literature
1930

EDITED BY MARK SCHORER

On November 5, 1930, Sinclair Lewis learned that he was the first American to win the Nobel Prize in Literature. The announcement brought on a storm of criticism from many of Lewis' American colleagues, none of it so bitter as that of the more conservative members of the American Academy of Arts and Letters, especially of that renowned protector of cultural gentility, the Reverend Henry Van Dyke. It is, in fact, a public utterance by Van Dyke that helps us date and place the composition of the address that Lewis was presently to deliver in Stockholm.

On the back of a telegram that he received on November 26, Lewis jotted down some random notes for that address, notes which indicate that up to this point he had prepared no text. On November 28, in a luncheon address delivered before a group of businessmen in Germantown, Pennsylvania, Van Dyke took occasion to remark that the award to Sinclair Lewis was an insult to the United States. "It shows," he declared, "the Swedish Academy knows nothing of the English language. They handed Lewis a bouquet, but they have given America a very backhanded compliment." Once, he continued, Americans were taught to honor traditions; today they only scoffed at them. Sinclair Lewis was among the great scoffers, and novels like Main Street and Elmer Gantry bore no relation to the best in American writing.

On the next day, November 29, Lewis was to sail for Sweden on the

Drottningholm. When he was interviewed on shipboard and asked to comment on Van Dyke's remarks, his face clouded, he hesitated, and then, almost as if his speech were at that moment taking shape in his mind, he said, "What can I say? Nothing. If I were to say what I think it would burn up the paper. . . . I am honored no less that American colleagues have attacked my work, and I am particularly honored that the attack came from where it did." The academicians might have been warned by the very restraint of those remarks.

The address was written during the long winter passage to Sweden on the Drottningholm. Arriving in Stockholm on the afternoon of December 9, Lewis cabled his publisher, Alfred Harcourt, on December 10 as follows:

HAVE YOU ARRANGED FOR PUBLICATION FULL TEXT MY ADDRESS NOBEL COMMITTEE NEXT FRIDAY. IF SO WHERE WHEN. OTHERWISE PLEASE TRY GET SUNDAY SECTIONS TIMES OR HERALD TRIBUNE. SPEECH AS IT WILL BE REPORTED PRESS CERTAIN CAUSE REPERCUSSIONS AND VERY IMPORTANT EXACT TEXT APPEARS SOMEWHERE AMERICA.

On that afternoon Lewis received his award. On the afternoon of December 12 he delivered his address and took his revenge: the American Academy and Henry Van Dyke had provided him not only with his theme but with his motive.

The entire address was cabled to the United States and, following what he presumed to be his author's wishes, Alfred Harcourt rushed the newspaper text into print, together with the ceremonial presentation remarks of Erik Axel Karlfeldt, the permanent secretary of the Swedish Academy; the two speeches were bound into a small pamphlet with the title Why Sinclair Lewis Got the Nobel Prize. But unfortunately the cablese was full of errors, a few of them rather appalling. Of the edition of 3,000 copies, it was possible to destroy 2,000, but 1,000 had been distributed and copies can still be come across today.

In London now, Lewis corrected his own text in two copies and appended a footnote to Dr. Karlfeldt's, thus correcting that gentleman's notions about sewage disposal in the United States, and on February 18, 1931, he sent one of these corrected copies to Donald Brace, Harcourt's partner, and explained that if he had added remarks, he had added them when he delivered the address as well. The corrected pamphlet was published by Harcourt, Brace and Company in an edition of 2,000 copies on April 2, 1931.

Six years later—two years after he had been inducted into the National Institute of Arts and Letters—Lewis moved into the parent body, the once-offensive American Academy of Arts and Letters.

MEMBERS OF THE SWEDISH ACADEMY; LADIES AND GENTLEMEN:

WERE I to express my feeling of honor and pleasure of having been awarded the Nobel Prize in Literature, I should be fulsome and perhaps tedious, and I present my gratitude with a plain "Thank you."

I wish, in this address, to consider certain trends, certain dangers, and certain high and exciting promises in present-day American literature. To discuss this with complete and unguarded frankness—and I should not insult you by being otherwise than completely honest, however indiscreet—it will be necessary for me to be a little impolite regarding certain institutions and persons of my own greatly beloved land.

But I beg of you to believe that I am in no case gratifying a grudge. Fortune has dealt with me rather too well. I have known little struggle, not much poverty, many generosities. Now and then I have, for my books or myself, been somewhat warmly denounced—there was one good pastor in California who upon reading my *Elmer Gantry* desired to lead a mob and lynch me, while another holy man in the State of Maine wondered if there was no respectable and righteous way of putting me in jail. And, much harder to endure than any raging condemnation, a certain number of old acquaintances among journalists, what in the galloping American slang we call the "I Knew Him When Club," have scribbled that since they know me personally, therefore I must be a rather low sort of fellow and certainly no writer. But if I have now and then received such cheering brickbats, still I, who have heaved a good many bricks myself, would be fatuous not to expect a fair number in return.

Lewis' corrected text is reproduced here from the revised pamphlet, *Why Sinclair Lewis Got the Nobel Prize* (New York: Harcourt, Brace and Company, 1931), except that one addition by Lewis, in the final paragraph, is not included here: "there are Michael Gold, who reveals the new frontier of the Jewish East Side, and William Faulkner, who has freed the South from hoop-skirts." This addition Lewis must have written into his galley proof, and it is also written into the second corrected copy of the original pamphlet, which Lewis later gave to his Hollywood friends, Mr. and Mrs. Jean Hersholt, who in turn gave it, with all the papers of Jean Hersholt, to the Library of Congress.

No, I have for myself no conceivable complaint to make, and yet for American literature in general, and its standing in a country where industrialism and finance and science flourish and the only arts that are vital and respected are architecture and the film, I have a considerable complaint.

I can illustrate by an incident which chances to concern the Swedish Academy and myself and which happened a few days ago, just before I took ship at New York for Sweden. There is in America a learned and most amiable old gentleman who has been a pastor, a university professor, and a diplomat. He is a member of the American Academy of Arts and Letters and no few universities have honored him with degrees. As a writer he is chiefly known for his pleasant little essays on the joy of fishing. I do not suppose that professional fishermen, whose lives depend on the run of cod or herring, find it altogether an amusing occupation, but from these essays I learned, as a boy, that there is something very important and spiritual about catching fish, if you have no need of doing so.

This scholar stated, and publicly, that in awarding the Nobel Prize to a person who has scoffed at American institutions as much as I have, the Nobel Committee and the Swedish Academy had insulted America. I don't know whether, as an ex-diplomat, he intends to have an international incident made of it, and perhaps demand of the American Government that they land Marines in Stockholm to protect American literary rights, but I hope not.

I should have supposed that to a man so learned as to have been made a Doctor of Divinity, a Doctor of Letters, and I do not know how many other imposing magnificences, the matter would have seemed different; I should have supposed that he would have reasoned, "Although personally I dislike this man's books, nevertheless the Swedish Academy has in choosing him honored America by assuming that the Americans are no longer a puerile backwoods clan, so inferior that they are afraid of criticism, but instead a nation come of age and able to consider calmly and maturely any dissection of their land, however scoffing."

I should even have supposed that so international a scholar would have believed that Scandinavia, accustomed to the works of Strindberg, Ibsen, and Pontoppidan, would not have been peculiarly shocked by a writer whose most anarchistic assertion has been that America, with all her wealth and power, has not yet produced a civilization good enough to satisfy the deepest wants of human creatures.

I believe that Strindberg rarely sang the "Star-Spangled Banner" or addressed Rotary Clubs, yet Sweden seems to have survived him.

I have at such length discussed this criticism of the learned fisherman not because it has any conceivable importance in itself, but because it does illustrate the fact that in America most of us—not readers alone but even writers—are still afraid of any literature which is not a glorification of everything American, a glorification of our faults as well as our virtues. To be not only a best-seller in America but to be really beloved, a novelist must assert that all American men are tall, hand-some, rich, honest, and powerful at golf; that all country towns are filled with neighbors who do nothing from day to day save go about being kind to one another; that although American girls may be wild, they change always into perfect wives and mothers; and that, geographically, America is composed solely of New York, which is inhabited entirely by millionaires; of the West, which keeps unchanged all the boisterous heroism of 1870; and of the South, where every one lives on a plantation perpetually glossy with moonlight and scented with magnolias.

It is not today vastly more true than it was twenty years ago that such novelists of ours as you have read in Sweden, novelists like Dreiser and Willa Cather, are authentically popular and influential in America. As it was revealed by the venerable fishing Academician whom I have quoted, we still most revere the writers for the popular magazines who in a hearty and edifying chorus chant that the America of a hundred and twenty million population is still as simple, as pastoral, as it was when it had but forty million; that in an industrial plant with ten thousand employees, the relationship between the worker and the manager is still as neighborly and uncomplex as in a factory of 1840, with five employees; that the relationships between father and son, between husband and wife, are precisely the same in an apartment in a thirty-story palace today, with three motor cars awaiting the family below and five books on the library shelves and a divorce imminent in the family next week, as were those relationships in a rose-veiled five-room cottage in 1880; that, in fine, America has gone through the revolutionary change from rustic colony to world-empire without having in the least altered the bucolic and Puritanic simplicity of Uncle Sam.

I am, actually, extremely grateful to the fishing Academician for having somewhat condemned me. For since he is a leading member of the American Academy of Arts and Letters, he has released me, has given me the right to speak as frankly of that Academy as he has spoken of me. And in any honest study of American intellectualism today, that curious institution must be considered.

Before I consider the Academy, however, let me sketch a fantasy which has pleased me the last few days in the unavoidable idleness of a rough trip on the Atlantic. I am sure that you know, by now, that the award to me of the Nobel Prize has by no means been altogether popular in America. Doubtless the experience is not new to you. I fancy that when you gave the award even to Thomas Mann, whose *Zauberberg* seems to me to contain the whole of intellectual Europe, even when you gave it to Kipling, whose social significance is so profound that it has been rather authoritatively said that he created the British Empire, even when you gave it to Bernard Shaw, there were countrymen of those authors who complained because you did not choose another.

And I imagined what would have been said had you chosen some American other than myself. Suppose you had taken Theodore Dreiser.

Now to me, as to many other American writers, Dreiser more than any other man, marching alone, usually unappreciated, often hated, has cleared the trail from Victorian and Howellsian timidity and gentility in American fiction to honesty and boldness and passion of life. Without his pioneering, I doubt if any of us could, unless we liked to be sent to jail, seek to express life and beauty and terror.

My great colleague Sherwood Anderson has proclaimed this leadership of Dreiser. I am delighted to join him. Dreiser's great first novel, *Sister Carrie*, which he dared to publish thirty long years ago and which I read twenty-five years ago, came to housebound and airless America like a great free Western wind, and to our stuffy domesticity gave us the first fresh air since Mark Twain and Whitman.

Yet had you given the Prize to Mr. Dreiser, you would have heard groans from America; you would have heard that his style—I am not exactly sure what this mystic quality "style" may be, but I find the word so often in the writings of minor critics that I suppose it must exist—you would have heard that his style is cumbersome, that his choice of words is insensitive, that his books are interminable. And certainly respectable scholars would complain that in Mr. Dreiser's world, men and women are often sinful and tragic and despairing, instead of being forever sunny and full of song and virtue, as befits authentic Americans.

And had you chosen Mr. Eugene O'Neill, who has done nothing much in American drama save to transform it utterly, in ten or twelve years, from a false world of neat and competent trickery to a world of splendor and fear and greatness, you would have been reminded that he has done something far worse than scoffing—he has seen life as not to be neatly arranged in the study of a scholar but as a terrifying, magnificent and often quite horrible thing akin to the tornado, the earthquake, the devastating fire.

And had you given Mr. James Branch Cabell the Prize, you would have been told that he is too fantastically malicious. So would you have been told that Miss Willa Cather, for all the homely virtue of her novels concerning the peasants of Nebraska, has in her novel, *The Lost Lady*, been so untrue to America's patent and perpetual and possibly tedious virtuousness as to picture an abandoned woman who remains, nevertheless, uncannily charming even to the virtuous, in a story without any moral; that Mr. Henry Mencken is the worst of all scoffers; that Mr. Sherwood Anderson viciously errs in considering sex as important a force in life as fishing; that Mr. Upton Sinclair, being a Socialist, sins against the perfectness of American capitalistic mass-production; that Mr. Joseph Hergesheimer is un-American in regarding graciousness of manner and beauty of surface as of some importance in the endurance of daily life; and that Mr. Ernest Hemingway is not only too young but, far worse, uses language which should be unknown to gentlemen; that he acknowledges drunkenness as one of man's eternal ways to happiness, and asserts that a soldier may find love more significant than the hearty slaughter of men in battle.

Yes, they are wicked, these colleagues of mine; you would have done almost as evilly to have chosen them as to have chosen me; and as a chauvinistic American—only, mind you, as an American of 1930 and not of 1880—I rejoice that they are my countrymen and countrywomen, and that I may speak of them with pride even in the Europe of Thomas Mann, H. G. Wells, Galsworthy, Knut Hamsun, Arnold Bennett, Feuchtwanger, Selma Lagerlöf, Sigrid Undset, Werner von Heidenstam, D'Annunzio, Romain Rolland.

It is my fate in this paper to swing constantly from optimism to pessimism and back, but so is it the fate of any one who writes or speaks of anything in America—the most contradictory, the most depressing, the most stirring, of any land in the world today.

Thus, having with no muted pride called the roll of what seem to me to be great men and women in American literary life today, and having indeed omitted a dozen other names of which I should like to boast were there time, I must turn again and assert that in our contemporary

American literature, indeed in all American arts save architecture and the film, we—yes, we who have such pregnant and vigorous standards in commerce and science—have no standards, no healing communication, no heroes to be followed nor villains to be condemned, no certain ways to be pursued and no dangerous paths to be avoided.

The American novelist or poet or dramatist or sculptor or painter must work alone, in confusion, unassisted save by his own integrity.

That, of course, has always been the lot of the artist. The vagabond and criminal François Villon had certainly no smug and comfortable refuge in which elegant ladies would hold his hand and comfort his starveling soul and more starved body. He, veritably a great man, destined to outlive in history all the dukes and puissant cardinals whose robes he was esteemed unworthy to touch, had for his lot the gutter and the hardened crust.

Such poverty is not for the artist in America. They pay us, indeed, only too well; that writer is a failure who cannot have his butler and motor and his villa at Palm Beach, where he is permitted to mingle almost in equality with the barons of banking. But he is oppressed ever by something worse than poverty—by the feeling that what he creates does not matter, that he is expected by his readers to be only a decorator or a clown, or that he is good-naturedly accepted as a scoffer whose bark probably is worse than his bite and who probably is a good fellow at heart, who in any case certainly does not count in a land that produces eighty-story buildings, motors by the million, and wheat by the billions of bushels. And he has no institution, no group, to which he can turn for inspiration, whose criticism he can accept and whose praise will be precious to him.

What institutions have we?

The American Academy of Arts and Letters does contain along with several excellent painters and architects and statesmen, such a really distinguished university-president as Nicholas Murray Butler, so admirable and courageous a scholar as Wilbur Cross, and several first-rate writers: the poets Edwin Arlington Robinson and Robert Frost, the free-minded publicist James Truslow Adams, and the novelists Edith Wharton, Hamlin Garland, Owen Wister, Brand Whitlock and Booth Tarkington.

But it does not include Theodore Dreiser, Henry Mencken, our most vivid critic, George Jean Nathan who, though still young, is certainly the dean of our dramatic critics, Eugene O'Neill, incomparably our best dramatist, the really original and vital poets, Edna St. Vincent Millay and Carl Sandburg, Robinson Jeffers and Vachel Lindsay and Edgar Lee Masters, whose *Spoon River Anthology* was so utterly different from any other poetry ever published, so fresh, so authoritative, so free from any gropings and timidities that it came like a revelation, and created a new school of native American poetry. It does not include the novelists and short-story writers, Willa Cather, Joseph Hergesheimer, Sherwood Anderson, Ring Lardner, Ernest Hemingway, Louis Bromfield, Wilbur Daniel Steele, Fannie Hurst, Mary Austin, James Branch Cabell, Edna Ferber, nor Upton Sinclair, of whom you must say, whether you admire or detest his aggressive Socialism, that he is internationally better known than any other American artist whosoever, be he novelist, poet, painter, sculptor, musician, architect.

I should not expect any Academy to be so fortunate as to contain all these writers, but one which fails to contain any of them, which thus cuts itself off from so much of what is living and vigorous and original in American letters, can have no relationship whatever to our life and aspirations. It does not represent literary America of today—it represents only Henry Wadsworth Longfellow.

It might be answered that, after all, the Academy is limited to fifty members; that, naturally, it cannot include every one of merit. But the fact is that while most of our few giants are excluded, the Academy does have room to include three extraordinarily bad poets, two very melodramatic and insignificant playwrights, two gentlemen who are known only because they are university presidents, a man who was thirty years ago known as a rather clever humorous draughtsman, and several gentlemen of whom—I sadly confess my ignorance—I have never heard.

Let me again emphasize the fact—for it is a fact—that I am not attacking the American Academy. It is a hospitable and generous and decidedly dignified institution. And it is not altogether the Academy's fault that it does not contain many of the men who have significance in our letters. Sometimes it is the fault of those writers themselves. I cannot imagine that grizzly-bear Theodore Dreiser being comfortable at the serenely Athenian dinners of the Academy, and were they to invite Mencken, he would infuriate them with his boisterous jeering. No, I am not attacking—I am reluctantly considering the Academy because it is so perfect an example of the divorce in America of intellectual life from all authentic standards of importance and reality.

Our universities and colleges, or gymnasia, most of them, exhibit the same unfortunate divorce. I can think of four of them, Rollins College in Florida, Middlebury College in Vermont, the University of Michigan, and the University of Chicago—which has had on its roll so excellent a novelist as Robert Herrick, so courageous a critic as Robert Morss Lovett—which have shown an authentic interest in contemporary creative literature. Four of them. But universities and colleges and musical emporiums and schools for the teaching of theology and plumbing and signpainting are as thick in America as the motor traffic. Whenever you see a public building with Gothic fenestration on a sturdy backing of Indiana concrete, you may be certain that it is another university, with anywhere from two hundred to twenty thousand students equally ardent about avoiding the disadvantage of becoming learned and about gaining the social prestige contained in the possession of a B.A. degree.

Oh, socially our universities are close to the mass of our citizens, and so are they in the matter of athletics. A great college football game is passionately witnessed by eighty thousand people, who have paid five dollars apiece and motored anywhere from ten to a thousand miles for the ecstasy of watching twenty-two men chase one another up and down a curiously marked field. During the football season, a capable player ranks very nearly with our greatest and most admired heroes—even with Henry Ford, President Hoover, and Colonel Lindbergh.

And in one branch of learning, the sciences, the lords of business who rule us are willing to do homage to the devotees of learning. However bleakly one of our trader aristocrats may frown upon poetry or the visions of a painter, he is graciously pleased to endure a Millikan, a Michelson, a Banting, a Theobald Smith.

But the paradox is that in the arts our universities are as cloistered, as far from reality and living creation, as socially and athletically and scientifically they are close to us. To a true-blue professor of literature in an American university, literature is not something that a plain human being, living today, painfully sits down to produce. No; it is something dead; it is something magically produced by superhuman beings who must, if they are to be regarded as artists at all, have died at least one hundred years before the diabolical invention of the typewriter. To any authentic don, there is something slightly repulsive in the thought that literature could be created by any ordinary human being, still to be seen walking the streets, wearing quite commonplace trousers and coat and looking not so unlike a chauffeur or a farmer. Our American professors like their literature clear and cold and pure and very dead.

I do not suppose that American universities are alone in this. I am aware that to the dons of Oxford and Cambridge, it would seem rather indecent to suggest that Wells and Bennett and Galsworthy and George Moore may, while they commit the impropriety of continuing to live, be compared to any one so beautifully and safely dead as Samuel Johnson. I suppose that in the universities of Sweden and France and Germany there exist plenty of professors who prefer dissection to understanding. But in the new and vital and experimental land of America, one would expect the teachers of literature to be less monastic, more human, than in the traditional shadows of old Europe.

They are not.

There has recently appeared in America, out of the universities, an astonishing circus called "the New Humanism." Now of course "humanism" means so many things that it means nothing. It may infer anything from a belief that Greek and Latin are more inspiring than the dialect of contemporary peasants to a belief that any living peasant is more interesting than a dead Greek. But it is a delicate bit of justice that this nebulous word should have been chosen to label this nebulous cult.

Insofar as I have been able to comprehend them—for naturally in a world so exciting and promising as this today, a life brilliant with Zeppelins and Chinese revolutions and the Bolshevik industrialization of farming and ships and the Grand Canyon and young children and terrifying hunger and the lonely quest of scientists after God, no creative writer would have time to follow all the chilly enthusiasms of the New Humanists—this newest of sects reasserts the dualism of man's nature. It would confine literature to the fight between man's soul and God, or man's soul and evil.

But, curiously, neither God nor the devil may wear modern dress, but must retain Grecian vestments. Oedipus is a tragic figure for the New Humanists; man, trying to maintain himself as the image of God under the menace of dynamos, in a world of high-pressure salesmanship, is not. And the poor comfort which they offer is that the object of life is to develop self-discipline—whether or not one ever accomplishes anything with this self-discipline. So this whole movement results in the not particularly novel doctrine that both art and life must be resigned and negative. It is a doctrine of the blackest reaction introduced into a stirringly revolutionary world.

Strangely enough, this doctrine of death, this escape from the complexities and danger of living into the secure blankness of the monastery, has become widely popular among professors in a land where one would have expected only boldness and intellectual adventure, and it has more than ever shut creative writers off from any benign influence which might conceivably have come from the universities.

But it has always been so. America has never had a Brandes, a Taine, a Goethe, a Croce.

With a wealth of creative talent in America, our criticism has most of it been a chill and insignificant activity pursued by jealous spinsters, ex-baseball-reporters, and acid professors. Our Erasmuses have been village schoolmistresses. How should there be any standards when there has been no one capable of setting them up?

The great Cambridge-Concord circle of the middle of the Nineteenth Century—Emerson, Longfellow, Lowell, Holmes, the Alcotts—were sentimental reflections of Europe, and they left no school, no influence. Whitman and Thoreau and Poe and, in some degree, Hawthorne, were outcasts, men alone and despised, berated by the New Humanists of their generation. It was with the emergence of William Dean Howells that we first began to have something like a standard, and a very bad standard it was.

Mr. Howells was one of the gentlest, sweetest, and most honest of men, but he had the code of a pious old maid whose greatest delight was to have tea at the vicarage. He abhorred not only profanity and obscenity but all of what H. G. Wells has called "the jolly coarseness of life." In his fantastic vision of life, which he innocently conceived to be realistic, farmers and seamen and factory-hands might exist, but the farmer must never be covered with muck, the seaman must never roll out bawdy chanteys, the factory-hand must be thankful to his good employer, and all of them must long for the opportunity to visit Florence and smile gently at the quaintness of the beggars.

So strongly did Howells feel this genteel, this New Humanistic philosophy that he was able vastly to influence his contemporaries, down even to 1914 and the turmoil of the Great War.

He was actually able to tame Mark Twain, perhaps the greatest of our writers, and to put that fiery old savage into an intellectual frock coat and top hat. His influence is not altogether gone today. He is still worshipped by Hamlin Garland, an author who should in every way have been greater than Howells but who under Howells' influence was changed from a harsh and magnificent realist into a genial and insignificant lecturer. Mr. Garland is, so far as we have one, the dean of

American letters today, and as our dean, he is alarmed by all of the younger writers who are so lacking in taste as to suggest that men and women do not always love in accordance with the prayer-book, and that common people sometimes use language which would be inappropriate at a women's literary club on Main Street. Yet this same Hamlin Garland, as a young man, before he had gone to Boston and become cultured and Howellized, wrote two most valiant and revelatory works of realism, *Main-Travelled Roads* and *Rose of Dutcher's Coolly*.

I read them as a boy in a prairie village in Minnesota—just such an environment as was described in Mr. Garland's tales. They were vastly exciting to me. I had realized in reading Balzac and Dickens that it was possible to describe French and English common people as one actually saw them. But it had never occurred to me that one might without indecency write of the people of Sauk Centre, Minnesota, as one felt about them. Our fictional tradition, you see, was that all of us in Midwestern villages were altogether noble and happy; that not one of us would exchange the neighborly bliss of living on Main Street for the heathen gaudiness of New York or Paris or Stockholm. But in Mr. Garland's *Main-Travelled Roads* I discovered that there was one man who believed that Midwestern peasants were sometimes bewildered and hungry and vile—and heroic. And, given this vision, I was released; I could write of life as living life.

I am afraid that Mr. Garland would not be pleased but acutely annoyed to know that he made it possible for me to write of America as I see it, and not as Mr. William Dean Howells so sunnily saw it. And it is his tragedy, it is a completely revelatory American tragedy, that in our land of freedom, men like Garland, who first blast the roads to freedom, become themselves the most bound.

But, all this time, while men like Howells were so effusively seeking to guide America into becoming a pale edition of an English cathedral town, there were surly and authentic fellows—Whitman and Melville, then Dreiser and James Huneker and Mencken—who insisted that our land had something more than tea-table gentility.

And so, without standards, we have survived. And for the strong young men, it has perhaps been well that we should have no standards. For, after seeming to be pessimistic about my own and much beloved land, I want to close this dirge with a very lively sound of optimism.

I have, for the future of American literature, every hope and every eager belief. We are coming out, I believe, of the stuffiness of safe, sane, and incredibly dull provincialism. There are young Americans today who are doing such passionate and authentic work that it makes me sick to see that I am a little too old to be one of them.

There is Ernest Hemingway, a bitter youth, educated by the most intense experience, disciplined by his own high standards, an authentic artist whose home is in the whole of life; there is Thomas Wolfe, a child of, I believe, thirty or younger, whose one and only novel, *Look Homeward, Angel,* is worthy to be compared with the best in our literary production, a Gargantuan creature with great gusto of life; there is Thornton Wilder, who in an age of realism dreams the old and lovely dreams of the eternal romantics; there is John Dos Passos, with his hatred of the safe and sane standards of Babbitt and his splendor of revolution; there is Stephen Benét who, to American drabness, has restored the epic poem with his glorious memory of old John Brown; and there are a dozen other young poets and fictioneers, most of them living now in Paris, most of them a little insane in the tradition of James Joyce, who, however insane they may be, have refused to be genteel and traditional and dull.

I salute them, with a joy in being not yet too far removed from their determination to give to the America that has mountains and endless prairies, enormous cities and lost farm cabins, billions of money and tons of faith, to an America that is as strange as Russia and as complex as China, a literature worthy of her vastness.

The immediate historic importance of Lewis' address in 1930 was the international recognition that the literature of the United States had, in spite of certain named obstacles, arrived at a state of maturity that made it the peer of any literature in Europe or of any other continent, and, more important, that America itself was a major power in the world as, twenty years before, Europe would have denied, and as, until Lewis stood up in Stockholm, she had been reluctant to concede.

Of those obstacles to literary maturity in the United States that Lewis named—academicism and gentility—one can only insist that, in 1930, he made too much. The extraordinary success of his own novels since the publication of Main Street ten years before would seem to demonstrate that for at least a decade American readers were as ready for self-criticism as the best American writers were prepared to give it. All through the decade of the twenties, the very writers whom Lewis named in his address as the déclassé were the most favorably received by any audience of critical consequence: Dreiser, Cather, Anderson, O'Neill, Mencken, Sinclair, Hemingway. Even those oddities, as they appear to us now, Cabell and Hergesheimer, were thought of indeed as among the liberators. It was a decade of liberation that climaxed a sporadic movement going back at least as far as 1900 and the suppression of the first publication of Dreiser's Sister Carrie. The remnants of academicism and gentility were, by the time that Sinclair Lewis made his address in Stockholm, remnants only.

Those remnants Lewis' address was probably instrumental in dispelling. The American Academy rapidly changed its character and was presently inviting all manner of experimental artists into its once stodgy fold. In the universities, the New Humanism was routed; the study not only of American literature but of the most contemporary American literature became, for better or worse, a major academic concern, and the close examination of American culture generally was presently a commonplace in most university curricula. How much of this may be attributed directly to Lewis's Nobel speech it is hard to say, and it is possible that once more, as he had done so often in his novels, Sinclair Lewis had anticipated by the smallest fraction of time a national mood that was ready for articulation.

Certainly the decade of the 1920's had freed American literature once and for all from timidity and chauvinism. A spokesman was still required to announce to the world that the event had taken place, and December 10, 1930, was an effectively round date for the world of international letters to have given the invitation to an American to make that declaration. "The American Fear of Literature" stands as probably our chief reminder that American literature is without fear.

Franklin D. Roosevelt
First Inaugural Address
1933

EDITED BY FRANK FREIDEL

In February, 1933, as the cruelest depression winter in American history began to draw toward a close, people looked forward expectantly to the event they hoped would bring an upturn in their own and the nation's fortunes. They awaited the inauguration on March 4 of the new Democratic President, Franklin D. Roosevelt. As the President-elect planned his Inaugural Address, economic machinery seemed to be slowing to a standstill. One-quarter of the wage-earners were unable to find work to support themselves or their families, and only one-quarter of these unemployed were receiving even paltry relief funds. A fourth of the farmers were losing or had lost their farms. For most of the remainder of the populace, whether located in the country or in the cities, incomes were appallingly inadequate. Every economic indicator pointed to disaster. Grain prices were the lowest since the reign of the first Queen Elizabeth; steel production, the bellwether of industry, slid to less than one-fifth of capacity. Already five thousand banks had succumbed to the long strain of the depression, and in February the banks had begun to close at such an alarming rate that, first in Michigan and then in almost every other state, the various governors proclaimed banking holidays or placed drastic restrictions on banking activities. Still people waited, and with incredibly little disorder. "Did you ever dream of anything like the docility of the American people under the crushing burden of these times?" William Allen White had inquired in January, 1933. "Why

don't they smash windows? Why don't they go and get it?" The answer
to White's query was that they were waiting to see what the Roosevelt
Administration could bring to them. If it had little to offer, then the
docility might give way to violence. One seasoned old senator remarked
privately, "We may be closer to revolution than we have ever been in our
lives."

Against this ominous backdrop Roosevelt worked upon his Inaugural
Address. On the surface all the portents were grim, but beneath the
surface the nation continued to possess economic resources and an
industrial and agricultural capacity so huge that, if properly employed,
they could provide for everyone a high standard of living. What the
economic system needed, Roosevelt and his advisers felt, was not
scrapping, but relatively minor reforms and a mild stimulus. The first
task was to restore public confidence. With a confident public and some
economic adjustments, prosperity could be attained.

It was in this spirit that Roosevelt outlined to his chief brain truster,
Professor Raymond Moley of Columbia University, the topics to be
covered in the Inaugural Address. Moley prepared a first draft on
February 12 and 13, then on February 26 and 27, while conferring with
Roosevelt at Hyde Park, he drafted a revision. At about nine o'clock on
Monday evening, February 27, Roosevelt seated himself at a card table in
the living room of his home at Hyde Park. Writing in a flowing hand on
lined yellow legal paper, Roosevelt, following Moley's draft, prepared his
own first version. By one-thirty in the morning Roosevelt had completed
his draft, almost as he would deliver it: one of the very few addresses for
which he prepared a complete draft in his own hand. When he had
finished with Moley's draft, Moley took it and threw it into the fire.

The ideas and phrasing in Roosevelt's address, as in most speeches,
came from many sources. The often quoted attack upon fear (inserted
after Roosevelt reached Washington) is at least as old as Francis Bacon.
Moley was responsible for the statement of the Good Neighbor Policy.
The biblically phrased indictment of bankers occurred to Roosevelt as he
sat in St. James Church, Hyde Park, on Sunday, February 26. Finally, as
Roosevelt sat in the Capitol waiting to take the oath of office, he added a
new first sentence to his reading copy, "This is a day of consecration."
When he delivered the address, he interpolated the word "national" into
his opening sentence. Whatever the origin of the concepts or the method
of their assemblage, the completed speech represented what Roosevelt
wanted to convey to the American people as he stood under the chilly

gray skies in front of the Capitol on March 4 and assumed his responsibilities as President. He wished to share with them his own vigor and optimism—and he succeeded in doing so.

THIS IS a day of national consecration.

I am certain that my fellow Americans expect that on my induction into the Presidency I will address them with a candor and a decision which the present situation of our Nation impels. This is preeminently the time to speak the truth, the whole truth, frankly and boldly. Nor need we shrink from honestly facing conditions in our country today. This great Nation will endure as it has endured, will revive and will prosper. So, first of all, let me assert my firm belief that the only thing we have to fear is fear itself—nameless, unreasoning, unjustified terror which paralyzes needed efforts to convert retreat into advance. In every dark hour of our national life a leadership of frankness and vigor has met with that understanding and support of the people themselves which is essential to victory. I am convinced that you will again give that support to leadership in these critical days.

In such a spirit on my part and on yours we face our common difficulties. They concern, thank God, only material things. Values have shrunken to fantastic levels; taxes have risen; our ability to pay has fallen; government of all kinds is faced by serious curtailment of income; the means of exchange are frozen in the currents of trade; the withered leaves of industrial enterprise lie on every side; farmers find no markets for their produce; the savings of many years in thousands of families are gone.

More important, a host of unemployed citizens face the grim problem of existence, and an equally great number toil with little return. Only a foolish optimist can deny the dark realities of the moment.

Yet our distress comes from no failure of substance. We are stricken by no plague of locusts. Compared with the perils which our forefathers conquered because they believed and were not afraid, we have still much to be thankful for. Nature still offers her bounty and human efforts have

---

The text comes from Franklin D. Roosevelt, *The Public Papers and Addresses* (New York: Random House, 1937), 1933 vol., pp. 11–16. The first sentence has been added from the reading copy of the address now at the Franklin D. Roosevelt Library, Hyde Park, New York.

multiplied it. Plenty is at our doorstep, but a generous use of it languishes in the very sight of the supply. Primarily this is because rulers of the exchange of mankind's goods have failed through their own stubbornness and their own incompetence, have admitted their failure, and have abdicated. Practices of the unscrupulous money changers stand indicted in the court of public opinion, rejected by the hearts and minds of men.

True they have tried, but their efforts have been cast in the pattern of an outworn tradition. Faced by failure of credit they have proposed only the lending of more money. Stripped of the lure of profit by which to induce our people to follow their false leadership, they have resorted to exhortations, pleading tearfully for restored confidence. They know only the rules of a generation of self-seekers. They have no vision, and when there is no vision the people perish.

The money changers have fled from their high seats in the temple of our civilization. We may now restore that temple to the ancient truths. The measure of the restoration lies in the extent to which we apply social values more noble than mere monetary profit.

Happiness lies not in the mere possession of money; it lies in the joy of achievement, in the thrill of creative effort. The joy and moral stimulation of work no longer must be forgotten in the mad chase of evanescent profits. These dark days will be worth all they cost us if they teach us that our true destiny is not to be ministered unto but to minister to ourselves and to our fellow men.

Recognition of the falsity of material wealth as the standard of success goes hand in hand with the abandonment of the false belief that public office and high political position are to be valued only by the standards of pride of place and personal profit; and there must be an end to a conduct in banking and in business which too often has given to a sacred trust the likeness of callous and selfish wrongdoing. Small wonder that confidence languishes, for it thrives only on honesty, on honor, on the sacredness of obligations, on faithful protection, on unselfish perform-ance; without them it cannot live.

Restoration calls, however, not for changes in ethics alone. This Nation asks for action, and action now.

Our greatest primary task is to put people to work. This is no unsolvable problem if we face it wisely and courageously. It can be accomplished in part by direct recruiting by the Government itself, treating the task as we would treat the emergency of a war, but at the same time, through this employment, accomplishing greatly needed projects to stimulate and reorganize the use of our natural resources.

Hand in hand with this we must frankly recognize the overbalance of population in our industrial centers and, by engaging on a national scale in a redistribution, endeavor to provide a better use of the land for those best fitted for the land. The task can be helped by definite efforts to raise the values of agricultural products and with this the power to purchase the output of our cities. It can be helped by preventing realistically the tragedy of the growing loss through foreclosure of our small homes and our farms. It can be helped by insistence that the Federal, State, and local governments act forthwith on the demand that their cost be drastically reduced. It can be helped by the unifying of relief activities which today are often scattered, uneconomical, and unequal. It can be helped by national planning for and supervision of all forms of transportation and of communications and other utilities which have a definitely public character. There are many ways in which it can be helped, but it can never be helped merely by talking about it. We must act and act quickly.

Finally, in our progress toward a resumption of work we require two safeguards against a return of the evils of the old order: there must be a strict supervision of all banking and credits and investments, so that there will be an end to speculation with other people's money; and there must be provision for an adequate but sound currency.

These are the lines of attack. I shall presently urge upon a new Congress, in special session, detailed measures for their fulfillment, and I shall seek the immediate assistance of the several States.

Through this program of action we address ourselves to putting our own national house in order and making income balance outgo. Our international trade relations, though vastly important, are in point of time and necessity secondary to the establishment of a sound national economy. I favor as a practical policy the putting of first things first. I shall spare no effort to restore world trade by international economic readjustment, but the emergency at home cannot wait on that accomplishment.

The basic thought that guides these specific means of national recovery is not narrowly nationalistic. It is the insistence, as a first consideration, upon the interdependence of the various elements in and parts of the United States—a recognition of the old and permanently important manifestation of the American spirit of the pioneer. It is the

841

way to recovery. It is the immediate way. It is the strongest assurance that the recovery will endure.

In the field of world policy I would dedicate this Nation to the policy of the good neighbor—the neighbor who resolutely respects himself and, because he does so, respects the rights of others—the neighbor who respects his obligations and respects the sanctity of his agreements in and with a world of neighbors.

If I read the temper of our people correctly, we now realize as we have never realized before our interdependence on each other; that we cannot merely take but we must give as well; that if we are to go forward, we must move as a trained and loyal army willing to sacrifice for the good of a common discipline, because without such discipline no progress is made, no leadership becomes effective. We are, I know, ready and willing to submit our lives and property to such discipline, because it makes possible a leadership which aims at a larger good. This I propose to offer, pledging that the larger purposes will bind upon us all as a sacred obligation with a unity of duty hitherto evoked only in time of armed strife.

With this pledge taken, I assume unhesitatingly the leadership of this great army of our people dedicated to a disciplined attack upon our common problems.

Action in this image and to this end is feasible under the form of government which we have inherited from our ancestors. Our Constitution is so simple and practical that it is possible always to meet extraordinary needs by changes in emphasis and arrangement without loss of essential form. That is why our constitutional system has proved itself the most superbly enduring political mechanism the modern world has produced. It has met every stress of vast expansion of territory, of foreign wars, of bitter internal strife, of world relations.

It is to be hoped that the normal balance of Executive and legislative authority may be wholly adequate to meet the unprecedented task before us. But it may be that an unprecedented demand and need for undelayed action may call for temporary departure from that normal balance of public procedure.

I am prepared under my constitutional duty to recommend the measures that a stricken Nation in the midst of a stricken world may require. These measures, or such other measures as the Congress may build out of its experience and wisdom, I shall seek, within my constitutional authority, to bring to speedy adoption.

But in the event that the Congress shall fail to take one of these two courses, and in the event that the national emergency is still critical, I shall not evade the clear course of duty that will then confront me. I shall ask the Congress for the one remaining instrument to meet the crisis—broad Executive power to wage a war against the emergency, as great as the power that would be given to me if we were in fact invaded by a foreign foe.

For the trust reposed in me I will return the courage and the devotion that befit the time. I can do no less.

We face the arduous days that lie before us in the warm courage of national unity; with the clear consciousness of seeking old and precious moral values; with the clean satisfaction that comes from the stern performance of duty by old and young alike. We aim at the assurance of a rounded and permanent national life.

We do not distrust the future of essential democracy. The people of the United States have not failed. In their need they have registered a mandate that they want direct, vigorous action. They have asked for discipline and direction under leadership. They have made me the present instrument of their wishes. In the spirit of the gift I take it.

In this dedication of a Nation we humbly ask the blessing of God. May He protect each and every one of us. May He guide me in the days to come.

To a weary nation and world, President Roosevelt's Inaugural Address delivered on that raw March day in 1933 seemed the first tentative ray of sunlight to break through the clouds of the depression. It brought promise of action, of a reversal of the slow, sickening drift into economic chaos. Instantly it enlisted the support of Congress. With few exceptions, senators and congressmen of both parties declared their approval. Senator Hiram Johnson of California, a Republican progressive who had long harassed President Hoover, like many others hailed Roosevelt's "real courage." "We have the new era," asserted Johnson, "and if we can judge from today, we have the new man." The American people were even more enthusiastic: nearly a half-million of them wrote to the White House in the next few days to express directly to Roosevelt himself their appreciation. One person wrote, "It seemed to give the people, as well as myself, a new hold upon life." Republican and Democratic newspapers alike acclaimed the address in superlatives. The Chicago Tribune declared that it "strikes the dominant note of courageous confidence." To the Nashville Banner it was proof "that, as every great epoch has called for a great leader, so never has the nation lacked the citizen to measure to the demands." Some newspapers such as these, which were subsequently to revise their estimates of Roosevelt, were for the moment eager to see Congress grant the President whatever authority he might desire.

In the crisis of the times, Roosevelt's firm assumption of leadership seemed to Americans the most encouraging aspect of his first Inaugural Address. In the perspective of the years that followed it came to assume another and even greater significance, the pronouncement of a decisive shift in the direction of national government and, indeed, of the national purpose. But even at the time, some newspapers, such as the Republican Deseret News of Salt Lake City and the Democratic News of Dayton, focused their approval upon Roosevelt's castigation of the "money-changers." The Dayton News declared, "This means the abandonment of the pivot on which American power has turned for twelve years past. Those were years of dependence upon a hierarchy of favorite interest. We gave them power; they were to return us prosperity. What we see now is the prosperity we got. Now for the laying of a broader base. Thus Roosevelt in the spirit of Lincoln calls the country to a right about face."

To a few critics like Edmund Wilson, Roosevelt's generalities were no more than flat-sounding empty verbiage, phrases which were no more than "the echoes of Woodrow Wilson's eloquence without Wilson's glow of life behind them." To the more optimistic observers these familiar phrases carried promise of a vital change. While the New Republic printed Edmund Wilson's pessimistic indictment, the Nation proclaimed, "Never in our national history has there been so dramatic a coincidence as this simultaneous transfer of power and the complete collapse of a system and of a philosophy. At that zero hour Roosevelt's words had something of the challenge, the symbolism, and the simplicity of a trumpet blast." In the light of the events that followed, the Inaugural Address was not so much what Edmund Wilson had seen in it and in the parade that followed—the weary symbol of the passing of an old order—as it was what the Nation had considered it to be—the exhilarating portent of a redirection of America "toward a goal such as Jefferson envisaged—a democracy based on full economic, as well as political, equality." For America this was the importance of the address.

For the world as well, Roosevelt's Inaugural Address was of serious purport. Radio carried it to Europe and even to Australia; it was widely read in Latin America. It came at a time when the German people in crisis had allowed Adolf Hitler and the Nazis to come to power, when democracies elsewhere seemed helpless to cope with the depression. Was the new American President joining the drive toward totalitarianism? Sitting by her husband, Mrs. Roosevelt was dismayed when the crowd broke into its most vociferous applause when the President warned that if Congress failed to act he would be forced to ask for wartime power. The press in Mussolini's Italy diagnosed the address as presaging a resort to Fascist techniques in the United States. Il Giornale d'Italia commented: "President Roosevelt's words are clear and need no comment to make even the deaf hear that not only Europe but the whole world feels the need of executive authority capable of acting with full powers of cutting short the purposeless chatter of legislative assemblies. This method of government may well be defined as Fascist."

The events that unfolded as the President and Congress fabricated the New Deal proved Mussolini's press wrong. To the world as a whole the address, far from being an endorsement of totalitarianism, was a proclamation that a democratic alternative could and would work—that the United States under the Presidency of Roosevelt could fight the depression and institute sweeping reforms without abandoning the traditional machinery of democracy. In the months and years that followed, the President and the nation demonstrated dramatically to all people everywhere that the crisis could be met with courage, humanitarianism, and vigor through a strengthening, rather than the destruction, of democracy. These were the factors which in the decades since its pronouncement have given a transcendent significance to Roosevelt's First Inaugural Address.

Franklin D. Roosevelt
"Quarantine" Address
1937

EDITED BY WILLIAM E. LEUCHTENBURG

In the late summer of 1937, Franklin Roosevelt decided to embark on a tour of the country to repair his political fortunes. Re-elected in November, 1936, by the greatest electoral margin of any President since James Monroe, he had seen his political strength dissipated only a short time later by his ill-starred attempt to reform the Supreme Court. The President was certain that Congress had misinterpreted the popular will, and he hoped that his forthcoming journey would demonstrate that the nation was still behind him. Moreover, after the fretful irritations of the abortive 168-day struggle over the Court bill, he sought to regain his good temper. He later told a crowd in Boise that he felt like Antaeus: "I regain strength by just meeting the American people."

Most of the President's attention was centered on domestic politics. Yet he could not ignore what was happening in the rest of the world. In a year's time, civil war had erupted in Spain, Hitler's legions had entered the Rhineland, and the governments of Germany, Italy, and Japan had moved closer to the creation of a common front against the democracies. In July, 1937, the very month the Court measure went down to defeat, Chinese and Japanese troops clashed at night at the Marco Polo Bridge just west of Peiping. As the Japanese drove into northern China and inflicted severe losses on civilians in Shanghai, the "China Incident" developed into full-scale undeclared war.

Both Secretary of State Cordell Hull and America's roving ambassador, Norman Davis, were deeply troubled by the rising danger of a new world war. They were even more disturbed by the growth of isolationist sentiment in America. Consequently, they called on the President to urge him to make an address on international cooperation during his transcontinental trip, "particularly in a large city where isolation was entrenched." Roosevelt consented, and asked his callers to prepare a draft.

Before the President departed for the West, Norman Davis sent him four memoranda. The first two, probably drafted with Hull, Roosevelt used almost in their entirety. These paragraphs discussed the chaos that Germany, Italy, and Japan were creating; stressed the fact that discord anywhere in the world jeopardized the security of the rest of the world; and urged peace-loving nations to concert their efforts to avert war.

The other two memoranda were drafted by Davis in New York and cleared with James Dunn in the State Department before being forwarded to the President. Roosevelt discarded passages in these two memoranda and improvised instead the striking "quarantine" section. (The metaphor may well have been suggested by a sentence in Davis' draft: "War is a contagion.") The President made one other significant revision. In place of Davis' ending, Roosevelt wrote four concluding sentences which stressed America's quest for peace. In its final form, the President's address did not differ substantially from the spirit of the four memoranda. Yet the President's revisions had momentous consequences. In the last four sentences, Roosevelt set down what he believed to be the theme of his speech: the need for positive endeavors to search for peace. It was the President's other improvisation, however—his vivid use of the "quarantine" analogy—which was to capture the attention of the world.

On the afternoon of October 5, 1937, before a crowd of 50,000 at the dedication of the Public Works Administration's Outer Drive Bridge in Chicago, President Roosevelt delivered the "Quarantine" Address.

I AM GLAD to come once again to Chicago and especially to have the opportunity of taking part in the dedication of this important project of civil betterment.

On my trip across the continent and back I have been shown many

The address is printed here from Franklin D. Roosevelt, *The Public Papers and Addresses*, edited by S. I. Rosenman, 13 vols. (New York: The Macmillan Company, 1938–50), VI, 406–11.

evidences of the result of common sense cooperation between municipalities and the Federal Government, and I have been greeted by tens of
thousands of Americans who have told me in every look and word that
their material and spiritual well-being has made great strides forward in
the past few years.

And yet, as I have seen with my own eyes, the prosperous farms, the
thriving factories and the busy railroads, as I have seen the happiness
and security and peace which covers our wide land, almost inevitably I
have been compelled to contrast our peace with very different scenes
being enacted in other parts of the world.

It is because the people of the United States under modern conditions
must, for the sake of their own future, give thought to the rest of the
world, that I, as the responsible executive head of the Nation, have
chosen this great inland city and this gala occasion to speak to you on a
subject of definite national importance.

The political situation in the world, which of late has been growing
progressively worse, is such as to cause grave concern and anxiety to all
the peoples and nations who wish to live in peace and amity with their
neighbors.

Some fifteen years ago the hopes of mankind for a continuing era of
international peace were raised to great heights when more than sixty
nations solemnly pledged themselves not to resort to arms in furtherance
of their national aims and policies. The high aspirations expressed in the
Briand-Kellogg Peace Pact and the hopes for peace thus raised have of
late given way to a haunting fear of calamity. The present reign of terror
and international lawlessness began a few years ago.

It began through unjustified interference in the internal affairs of
other nations or the invasion of alien territory in violation of treaties;
and has now reached a stage where the very foundations of civilization
are seriously threatened. The landmarks and traditions which have
marked the progress of civilization toward a condition of law, order and
justice are being wiped away.

Without a declaration of war and without warning or justification of
any kind, civilians, including vast numbers of women and children, are
being ruthlessly murdered with bombs from the air. In times of so-called
peace, ships are being attacked and sunk by submarines without cause or
notice. Nations are fomenting and taking sides in civil warfare in
nations that have never done them any harm. Nations claiming freedom
for themselves deny it to others.

848

Innocent peoples, innocent nations, are being cruelly sacrificed to a greed for power and supremacy which is devoid of all sense of justice and humane considerations.

To paraphrase a recent author [James Hilton in *Lost Horizon*] "perhaps we foresee a time when men, exultant in the technique of homicide, will rage so hotly over the world that every precious thing will be in danger, every book and picture and harmony, every treasure garnered through two millenniums, the small, the delicate, the defenseless—all will be lost or wrecked or utterly destroyed."

If those things come to pass in other parts of the world, let no one imagine that America will escape, that America may expect mercy, that this Western Hemisphere will not be attacked and that it will continue tranquilly and peacefully to carry on the ethics and the arts of civilization.

If those days come "there will be no safety by arms, no help from authority, no answer in science. The storm will rage till every flower of culture is trampled and all human beings are leveled in a vast chaos."

If those days are not to come to pass—if we are to have a world in which we can breathe freely and live in amity without fear—the peace-loving nations must make a concerted effort to uphold laws and principles on which alone peace can rest secure.

The peace-loving nations must make a concerted effort in opposition to those violations of treaties and those ignorings of humane instincts which today are creating a state of international anarchy and instability from which there is no escape through mere isolation or neutrality.

Those who cherish their freedom and recognize and respect the equal right of their neighbors to be free and live in peace, must work together for the triumph of law and moral principles in order that peace, justice and confidence may prevail in the world. There must be a return to a belief in the pledged word, in the value of a signed treaty. There must be recognition of the fact that national morality is as vital as private morality.

A bishop [Bishop Frank W. Sterett] wrote me the other day: "It seems to me that something greatly needs to be said in behalf of ordinary humanity against the present practice of carrying the horrors of war to helpless civilians, especially women and children. It may be that such a protest might be regarded by many, who claim to be realists, as futile, but may it not be that the heart of mankind is so filled with horror at the present needless suffering that that force could be mobilized in sufficient volume to lessen such cruelty in the days ahead. Even though it may take twenty years, which God forbid, for civilization to make effective its corporate protest against this barbarism, surely strong voices may hasten the day."

There is a solidarity and interdependence about the modern world, both technically and morally, which makes it impossible for any nation completely to isolate itself from economic and political upheavals in the rest of the world, especially when such upheavals appear to be spreading and not declining. There can be no stability or peace either within nations or between nations except under laws and moral standards adhered to by all. International anarchy destroys every foundation for peace. It jeopardizes either the immediate or the future security of every nation, large or small. It is, therefore, a matter of vital interest and concern to the people of the United States that the sanctity of international treaties and the maintenance of international morality be restored.

The overwhelming majority of the peoples and nations of the world today want to live in peace. They seek the removal of barriers against trade. They want to exert themselves in industry, in agriculture and in business, that they may increase their wealth through the production of wealth-producing goods rather than striving to produce military planes and bombs and machine guns and cannon for the destruction of human lives and useful property.

In those nations of the world which seem to be piling armament on armament for purposes of aggression, and those other nations which fear acts of aggression against them and their security, a very high proportion of their national income is being spent directly for armaments. It runs from thirty to as high as fifty percent. We are fortunate. The proportion that we in the United States spend is far less—eleven or twelve percent.

How happy we are that the circumstances of the moment permit us to put our money into bridges and boulevards, dams and reforestation, the conservation of our soil and many other kinds of useful works rather than into huge standing armies and vast supplies of implements of war.

I am compelled and you are compelled, nevertheless, to look ahead. The peace, the freedom and the security of ninety percent of the population of the world is being jeopardized by the remaining ten percent who are threatening a breakdown of all international order and law. Surely the ninety percent who want to live in peace under law and in accordance with moral standards that have received almost universal acceptance through the centuries, can and must find some way to make their will prevail.

The situation is definitely of universal concern. The questions involved relate not merely to violations of specific provisions of particular treaties; they are questions of war and peace, of international law and especially of principles of humanity. It is true that they involve definite violations of agreements, and especially of the Covenant of the League of Nations, the Briand-Kellogg Pact and the Nine Power Treaty. But they also involve problems of world economy, world security and world humanity.

It is true that the moral consciousness of the world must recognize the importance of removing injustices and well-founded grievances; but at the same time it must be aroused to the cardinal necessity of honoring sanctity of treaties, of respecting the rights and liberties of others and of putting an end to acts of international aggression.

It seems to be unfortunately true that the epidemic of world lawlessness is spreading.

When an epidemic of physical disease starts to spread, the community approves and joins in a quarantine of the patients in order to protect the health of the community against the spread of the disease.

It is my determination to pursue a policy of peace. It is my determination to adopt every practicable measure to avoid involvement in war. It ought to be inconceivable that in this modern era, and in the face of experience, any nation could be so foolish and ruthless as to run the risk of plunging the whole world into war by invading and violating, in contravention of solemn treaties, the territory of other nations that have done them no real harm and are too weak to protect themselves adequately. Yet the peace of the world and the welfare and security of every nation, including our own, is today being threatened by that very thing.

No nation which refuses to exercise forbearance and to respect the freedom and rights of others can long remain strong and retain the confidence and respect of other nations. No nation ever loses its dignity or its good standing by conciliating its differences, and by exercising great patience with, and consideration for, the rights of other nations.

War is a contagion, whether it be declared or undeclared. It can engulf states and peoples remote from the original scene of hostilities.

We are determined to keep out of war, yet we cannot insure ourselves against the disastrous effects of war and the dangers of involvement. We are adopting such measures as will minimize our risk of involvement, but we cannot have complete protection in a world of disorder in which confidence and security have broken down.

If civilization is to survive the principles of the Prince of Peace must be restored. Trust between nations must be revived.

Most important of all, the will for peace on the part of peace-loving nations must express itself to the end that nations that may be tempted to violate their agreements and the rights of others will desist from such a course. There must be positive endeavors to preserve peace.

America hates war. America hopes for peace. Therefore, America actively engages in the search for peace.

President Roosevelt's Quarantine Address has a special place in the folklore of the 1930's. In this speech, it has been claimed, Roosevelt proposed nothing less than the abandonment of the isolationism of the past two decades in favor of American participation in a system of collective security. Unhappily, it has been noted, the President's appeal to "quarantine the aggressors" raised such a storm of protest that Roosevelt was compelled to retreat. Shackled by public opinion, which lacked the President's awareness of the threat posed by the Axis, Roosevelt thereafter found himself powerless to use the influence of the United States either to curb Fascist aggression or to avert a second world war. Such is the traditional view of the Quarantine Address.

Writers who have advanced this interpretation have been compelled to explain why, on the very day after the President's Chicago oration, Roosevelt "retreated." When reporters pressed him on what he meant by "quarantine," Roosevelt expostulated: "Look, 'sanctions' is a terrible word to use. They are out of the window." Newspapermen were bewildered by what seemed to be an abrupt volte-face. When they persisted in trying to discern the meaning of the speech, Roosevelt admonished them to look at the final sentence of his address: "Therefore, America actively engages in the search for peace."

Both memoirists and historians have explained the President's "retreat" as a response to the intensely unfavorable reaction to his speech.

"This bold effort to awaken public opinion overshot the mark, for its rash phrases frightened people who feared the country might be dragged into a new cauldron of battle," Allan Nevins has written. "It had a bad press." Cordell Hull recalled: "The reaction against the quarantine idea was quick and violent. As I saw it, this had the effect of setting back for at least six months our constant educational campaign intended to create and strengthen public opinion toward international cooperation." Roosevelt's speech writer, Samuel Rosenman, has observed: "The President was attacked by a vast majority of the press. . . . Telegrams of denunciation came in at once. . . . 'It's a terrible thing,' he once said to me, having in mind I'm sure, this occasion, 'to look over your shoulder when you are trying to lead—and to find no one there.'"

It is true that both the isolationist press and isolationist leaders in Congress denounced the President's speech. Hearst's San Francisco Examiner pleaded: "Don't Stick Out Your Neck, Uncle!" When the Philadelphia Inquirer conducted a telegraphic poll of Congress, it found better than 2-to-1 opposition to cooperation with the League of Nations in sanctions against Japan. Representative Hamilton Fish of New York assailed the speech as the "most provocative, inflammatory and dangerous ever delivered by any President," and Senator Gerald Nye of North Dakota cried: "Once again we are baited to thrill to a call to save the world." Roosevelt received little public support from his own lieutenants, and some of his diplomats were dismayed. After seeing "Gone with the Wind," Ambassador to Japan Joseph Grew noted that this was "precisely the way I felt" in response to Roosevelt's address.

But is this unfavorable public reaction an adequate explanation for Roosevelt's retreat? His statements at the press conference were made before much of the response, especially letters to the White House, could have been assessed. He could hardly have expected a favorable reception from the Hearst press or from senators like Nye. The Inquirer's poll diminishes in importance when it is noted that only forty-nine congressmen commented. If senators like Nye disliked the address, the chairman of the Senate Foreign Relations Committee, Key Pittman, who often opposed the Administration's proposals for international cooperation, announced that he favored the "ostracism" of Japan by economic action. The President had, too, the backing of Republican Henry Stimson, who had been Hoover's Secretary of State. Moreover, an entry in a contemporary diary suggests that Hull's recollection that he was disconcerted by the "quarantine" reference is in error. J. Pierrepont Moffat, chief of the State Department's Division of European Affairs, was in Hull's office when the ticker reported Roosevelt's address; "The Secretary," he noted, "was delighted at the speech."

There is an even more compelling reason for doubting the familiar version. Historians have remarked on the popular indignation expressed in the torrent of hostile letters and wires directed to the White House. Yet an examination of the White House files (now at the Franklin D. Roosevelt Library at Hyde Park) reveals that the letters and telegrams the President received were overwhelmingly favorable.

Moreover, again contrary to the traditional exegesis, most of the press response to the Quarantine Address was favorable. The New York Times of October 6 printed excerpts from editorials under the headline "Roosevelt Speech Widely Approved." The anti-Administration New York Herald Tribune ran a survey of newspaper opinion under the banner "Press Accepts Roosevelt Talk As Vital Step." Time observed that the press had "produced more words of approval, some enthusiastic and some tempered, than have greeted any Roosevelt step in many a month." Even the Chicago Tribune commented that the response to the address must have been "gratifying" to the internationalists. The very newspapers the President was most likely to read supported him warmly: journals such as the New York Times, the Baltimore Sun, the Washington Post, and the Washington Evening Star. The Star, often critical of Roosevelt, wrote: "Not since Woodrow Wilson's message to Congress in April, 1917, have more prescient words fallen from the lips of the President of the United States."

The anti-Roosevelt writer David Lawrence thought Roosevelt's address "penetrating and incisive," and Westbrook Pegler commented, "Roosevelt May Have Said Just What Was Needed to Avert New World War." The President received the anticipated support in the southern press. More striking is the endorsement he received from Pacific Coast newspapers like the San Francisco Chronicle and the Portland Oregonian, which had opposed him in 1936, and, in the "isolationist" Middle West, from such journals as the Indianapolis Star, the Cleveland Plain Dealer, and the Cincinnati Enquirer. Roosevelt himself confided to Colonel House: "I thought, frankly, that there would be more criticism."

If the response to the speech was largely affirmative, why, then, did Roosevelt "retreat" so quickly? This is much more debatable. The answer would appear to be that the President did not "retreat," because he had never really advanced, or at least not very far. The crux of the problem is

what Roosevelt meant by "quarantine." It has always been supposed that
he meant the use of some kind of sanctions, and there is impressive
evidence to support this belief. Harold Ickes noted in his diary that
Roosevelt in September, 1937, contemplated proposing joint action of
the "peace-loving nations" to cut off all trade with future aggressors.
Sumner Welles has written that Roosevelt used the word "quarantine"
to connote an embargo on Japan enforced by the American and British
fleets. In December, 1937, the President argued at a Cabinet meeting
that economic sanctions could be effective. "We don't call them
economic sanctions; we call them quarantines," he observed. Joseph
Alsop and Robert Kintner, who had access to restricted documents,
concluded that Roosevelt intended by "quarantine" to suggest a strong
form of sanctions: total nonintercourse with an aggressor.

Yet there is persuasive reason for doubting that Roosevelt intended his
Quarantine Address to mark a new departure in foreign policy that would
embrace collective action to impose sanctions. His letters and memoranda in 1937 indicate that his thinking was not that sharply defined. He
was disturbed by the drift toward war, and felt called on to do something
to prevent it, but he was not sure what specific action to recommend. He
toyed with different ideas at different times—a new world peace conference, an economic embargo, perhaps even a naval blockade.

But he had not yet reached the conviction that the aggressors could be
deterred only by military or economic coercion. He seems still to have
hoped that the dictators could be swayed by the threat of disapproval. In
many respects a nineteenth-century moralist, Roosevelt had a gentleman's dismay at the violation of treaties and a gentleman's faith that fear
of ostracism might deter men from violating the code. His first step
would be to alert the American people to the peril they faced, and to
point out to them that isolation and neutrality were inadequate responses. Beyond this, he would impress on the world the distinction
between the peace-loving and the aggressor states, and the need for the
peace-loving states to take joint action. By joint action, he seems to have
meant a warning to future war-makers that they would be ostracized if
they broke the peace. Ostracism would take the form of breaking off
diplomatic relations and of joint expressions of condemnation; if these
did not suffice, economic measures might be considered. But it was not
any specific program so much as the need to take common counsel in
search of peace that Roosevelt stressed. After his speech, Roosevelt went
directly to the house of Cardinal Mundelein. Subsequently, Mundelein

gave a lucid report to the Apostolic Delegate to the United States on the President's thinking: "His plan does not contemplate either military or naval action against the unjust aggressor nation, nor does it involve 'sanctions' as generally understood but rather a policy of isolation, severance of ordinary communications in a united manner by all the governments of the pact."

Roosevelt's intentions were obscured by his unfortunate choice of the word "quarantine." It seemed natural for the President to use a medical metaphor; he often conceived of himself as Dr. Roosevelt attending to the ills of a sick society. But, in employing the term "quarantine," he appeared to be serving notice on Japan of an imminent embargo. When, on the very next day, the League of Nations censured Japan, Roosevelt's address seemed to be an episode in a concert of powers against Tokyo, although the President had, in fact, made no commitment to Geneva. After his speech, the President was nonplussed by the attention focused on the word "quarantine." He confided to Norman Davis that he regarded "quarantine" as a much milder term than "ostracism" or similar synonyms.

Neither friend nor foe comprehended the intent of Roosevelt's address. His critics were certain he sought to achieve "peace through war," his friends wondered why the President did not follow up his Chicago speech with specific recommendations. By the time the President spoke, thought had become polarized between isolationists, who believed that any questioning of their assumptions implied a commitment to collective security, and internationalists, who assumed that any departure from isolation carried with it an acceptance of sanctions. Each found in the President's speech what he expected to find.

Roosevelt himself believed, or professed to believe, that the speech had achieved its main purpose: the education of the nation. He wrote Nicholas Murray Butler: "Much can be accomplished by the iteration of moralities even though the tangible results seem terrifically slow." He had no doubt that the meaning of the speech lay not in the interpretation that was given to his "quarantine" image, but rather in the modest conclusion he had interpolated: "There must be positive endeavors to preserve peace. America hates war. America hopes for peace. Therefore, America actively engages in the search for peace."

Albert Einstein
Letter to Franklin D. Roosevelt
1939

EDITED BY DONALD FLEMING

On August 2, 1939, Albert Einstein wrote a letter to President Roosevelt; this letter drafted the atom for war. Less than a year before, nuclear physics was still the standing illustration of intellectual curiosity for its own sake. The situation began to be transformed when the Germans Otto Hahn and Fritz Strassmann announced in January, 1939, that bombardment of uranium by neutrons appeared to produce the much lighter element barium. This conclusion, as they said, played such havoc with accepted notions in physics that they hesitated to believe it themselves. From her exile in Sweden, Hahn's former associate Lise Meitner, driven from Germany in 1938 as a Jew, promptly concluded that Hahn had indeed split uranium into two lighter elements—a process which she and her physicist-nephew Otto Frisch compared with "fission" in bacteria. Meitner and Frisch surmised, and Frisch speedily demonstrated, that fission ought to be accompanied by a tremendous release of energy according to Einstein's formula $E = mc^2$. Frédéric Joliot-Curie in Paris and, almost simultaneously, Enrico Fermi and Leo Szilard in the United States made the further demonstration that fission of uranium liberated additional neutrons. That discovery was a lever for moving the world. If neutrons on splitting uranium kept breeding more neutrons to split more uranium, a chain reaction would result. Two possibilities loomed, later succinctly described as the "bomb" and the "boiler"— explosive chain reactions for war, or controlled reactions for industry.

Yet Hahn and those who repeated his experiments did not get a chain reaction. The question became why not. This was one of the points that Fermi discussed with Niels Bohr when the latter attended a conference in the United States in January, 1939, and told the Americans what Meitner and Frisch had deduced. Bohr's solution to the puzzle turned upon the existence of two principal isotopes of uranium—238, overwhelmingly predominant, and 235, of which an ordinary sample would yield only 0.7 per cent. Bohr argued on theoretical grounds that ordinary "slow" neutrons would split 235 but merely be absorbed by 238. The chain reaction would be choked off by the scarcity of appropriate targets. The situation was further complicated by the fact that the neutrons liberated on fission of 235 were "fast" and therefore less adapted to keep the reaction going. Fermi and others, however, had shown in 1935 that fast neutrons could be "moderated," i.e., slowed down, by passing through hydrogenous substances like water and paraffin; and carbon was another moderator. The inference was that by interspersing even ordinary uranium with a moderating substance, fast neutrons could be slowed down and the chain reaction maintained. The line of reasoning was tenuous. If, alternatively, the separation of pure 235 from 238 was contemplated, that was an almost inconceivable feat in 1939.

Even if all the links of the argument held and all the strategies proved workable in the laboratory, to turn these academic triumphs into actual bombs or power plants would be the greatest achievement in the history of technology. There was no assurance that the problems could be solved, either in theory or in practice; they could not even be tackled without diverting men and resources from other more immediately promising research, as on radar; and at best the anticipated war might be over before the scientists had anything tangible to show for their labors—even before any politicians would blindly stake them out of the public funds.

When the doubts inside the scientific community and the general incomprehension without are added together, the wonder becomes that the bomb did materialize in time to play a part in the war. This was undoubtedly the doing of the refugee scientists from the continent of Europe—men who had seen their own countries succumb to Hitler and who now turned to make a last stand by the side of the decent but appallingly innocent Anglo-Saxons who had never known utter defeat and did not really believe it could happen to them. The refugees knew better. They were desperately afraid that Hitler, with the still considerable resources of German science and German industry, would get the atomic bomb and gain the final victory.

Somehow the refugees must shake the democracies awake to this terrible new menace before it was too late. The Italian refugee Fermi talked with people in the Navy Department in March, 1939, but they were not impressed by his presentation. His English was halting and the legend has it that some of his interrogators dismissed him as a "crazy wop." By summer Fermi and the Hungarian refugee Szilard, with the latter's compatriots Edward Teller and Eugene Wigner, were in despair as they tried to think how to attract the notice of somebody in authority. Szilard knew the most famous refugee of all, Albert Einstein, and he knew the Dowager Queen of the Belgians. The least Szilard could do was to get Einstein to warn the Queen to keep the uranium of the Belgian Congo out of German hands. Einstein was willing, but before he could send a letter to the Queen, Szilard met an economist with Lehman Brothers named Alexander Sachs. Sachs told him to forget about the Queen. Einstein was the one man whose name was a big trumpet to catch the ear of Franklin D. Roosevelt. Sachs had an entree to the White House and undertook to deliver a letter from Einstein to the President personally. Though dated August 2, the letter was not in fact delivered till October 11. In the meantime the war had come.

Albert Einstein
Old Grove Road
Nassau Point
Peconic, Long Island
August 2, 1939

F. D. Roosevelt
President of the United States
White House
Washington, D. C.

SIR:

Some recent work by E. Fermi and L. Szilard, which has been communicated to me in manuscript, leads me to expect that the element uranium may be turned into a new and important source of energy in the immediate future. Certain aspects of the situation seem to call for watchfulness and, if necessary, quick action on the part of the Adminis-

---

The letter as reprinted here appeared in Otto Nathan and Heinz Norden, eds., *Einstein on Peace* (New York: Simon and Schuster, 1960), pp. 294–96.

tration. I believe, therefore, that it is my duty to bring to your attention the following facts and recommendations.

In the course of the last four months, it has been made probable—through the work of Joliot in France as well as Fermi and Szilard in America—that it may become possible to set up nuclear chain reactions in a large mass of uranium, by which vast amounts of power and large quantities of new radium-like elements would be generated. Now it appears almost certain that this could be achieved in the immediate future.

This new phenomenon would also lead to the construction of bombs, and it is conceivable—though much less certain—that extremely powerful bombs of a new type may thus be constructed. A single bomb of this type, carried by boat or exploded in a port, might very well destroy the whole port together with some of the surrounding territory. However, such bombs might very well prove to be too heavy for transportation by air.

The United States has only very poor ores of uranium in moderate quantities. There is some good ore in Canada and the former Czechoslovakia, while the most important source of uranium is the Belgian Congo.

In view of this situation you may think it desirable to have some permanent contact maintained between the Administration and the group of physicists working on chain reactions in America. One possible way of achieving this might be for you to entrust with this task a person who has your confidence and who could perhaps serve in an unofficial capacity. His task might comprise the following:

a) To approach Government Departments, keep them informed of the further developments, and put forward recommendations for Government action, giving particular attention to the problem of securing a supply of uranium ore for the United States.

b) To speed up the experimental work which is at present being carried on within the limits of the budgets of University laboratories, by providing funds, if such funds be required, through his contacts with private persons who are willing to make contributions for this cause, and perhaps also by obtaining the cooperation of industrial laboratories which have the necessary equipment.

I understand that Germany has actually stopped the sale of uranium from the Czechoslovakian mines which she has taken over. That she should have taken such early action might perhaps be understood on the ground that the son of the German Under-Secretary of State, von Weizsäcker, is attached to the Kaiser Wilhelm Institut in Berlin, where some of the American work on uranium is now being repeated.

Yours very truly,

A. EINSTEIN

Some time after Einstein wrote the letter to Roosevelt, he said in exculpation that he had merely been used as a mailbox by Szilard. At the time neither Einstein nor any of the other refugee scientists had any hesitation in setting the wheels in motion. They were not, after all, proposing to use the bomb, but merely to have the means of calling Hitler's bluff if he got it and tried atomic blackmail, and they thought the odds were in his favor. They were sure that scientists on the other side had already set the same wheels in motion under worse auspices.

For a long time, the only thing Szilard and Fermi worried about was their failure to get the wheels moving fast enough on their side. Roosevelt did set up a committee on uranium immediately after his interview with Sachs, and a year's contract for research was actually let on November 1, 1939—for $6,000. Though other research was financed by universities and foundations, really sizable government contracts did not come till autumn, 1940. At mid-summer, 1941, there was still no crash program to build an atomic bomb. The refugee scientists had failed to convey their own sense of urgency to the Americans. Technically, the United States was still at peace. The situation might well have been transformed in the wake of Pearl Harbor. But if the decisive commitment had been delayed even a few months beyond December 7, 1941, the war might have been over before the bomb was ready.

In fact, the great decision to go all out on the bomb was taken on December 6. The refugees who got to America had failed to communicate their urgency; but Hitler had seeded England with his enemies too. They included some of the most brilliant nuclear scientists—above all, Otto Frisch, Rudolf Peierls, and two leading members of Joliot-Curie's team, Hans Halban and Lew Kowarski. All of these men were rigorously excluded by British security regulations from participating in the sensitive military research already in progress. Conversely, they were almost alone in having the leisure to speculate on other matters. Radar they

861

could not touch; the only thing they were free to occupy themselves with was working out the atomic bomb. They were severely confined in the name of security to the most explosive security issue of the war. They demonstrated, in collaboration with the great English nuclear physicists Sir James Chadwick (the discoverer of the neutron) and G. P. Thomson, that the bomb could probably be built in time to affect the war. Their optimistic report of July, 1941, and the detailed case they made to American scientists who visited England in the fall, played a major, perhaps critical, part in the American decision to make a big push on the eve of Pearl Harbor rather than later. It does not follow that Einstein's letter of August, 1939, served no purpose. The decision of December 6, 1941, would have been comparatively empty if the Americans had had no base to build upon.

In the spring of 1945, when the bomb was almost ready for testing, the grim ironies began to pile up. The refugees' target, Hitler, was already beaten without the bomb; the Germans, incredibly, had made no real progress toward building one; and the only possible target was a country —Japan—that had never been in the running, and still less in the minds of the European refugees. Leo Szilard began frantically distributing petitions to stave off the consequences of his own initiative, but it was too late. Einstein, for his part, on learning of Hiroshima cried out, "Oh, weh!" He, the great enemy of war, had brought flaming death upon hundreds of thousands of Japanese to whom neither he nor his counselors had given a moment's thought when they were drafting the letter to Roosevelt. The Japanese took Hitler's medicine.

Wendell L. Willkie
One World
1943

EDITED BY MAX LERNER

One World was Wendell Willkie's prime contribution to World War II, its fighting aims, its coalition strategy, and its postwar settlements. The 1940 Republican candidate for the Presidency, who had seemed to waver during the campaign on the issue of interventionism or isolationism, was actually a strong interventionist despite his German ancestry and his Indiana-Ohio Midwest roots. After his defeat in the election he remained a figure with considerable personal and political following and with hopes for success in the next presidential contest, as well as with a deep commitment to the struggle against a fascism which threatened what he held dear—personal and economic freedom. While the bombs were still falling, he paid a sympathetic visit to London early in 1941 and was enthusiastically received. He was a leader in the successful battle at home for Lend-Lease aid to Britain.

After the entrance of both Russia and America into the war, Willkie was restless about what role he could play. When he received a cable in July, 1942, from three American war reporters in Russia's wartime capital at Kuibishev—Maurice Hindus, Eddie Gilmore, and Ben Robertson—urging him to make a good-will visit to beleaguered Russia, he eagerly agreed. After securing some broad commissions from President Roosevelt, he set off on August 26 in a converted bomber for a round-the-world trip, accompanied by Joseph Barnes and Gardner Cowles, Jr., both of them his friends, both from the Office of War Information. The trip took fifty days and covered 31,000 miles on five continents, with stops at the Middle Eastern, Russian, and Chinese war fronts. Aside from showing that the Allies still dominated the world's airways even at the *low ebb of their fortunes in the war, the aim was to carry the tidings of America's massive war-production effort around the world, and to dramatize to America's allies the unity of the two major parties in their determination to win the war. But Willkie was not content to stop there. Speaking for himself, in a statement at Moscow, he called for a second front, and added that American military leaders "will need some public prodding." At Chungking he called for "an end to the empire of nations over other nations," and a timetable to give the colonial peoples a chance to "work out and train governments of their own choosing." Both statements stirred worldwide controversy.*

After a striking popular response to a radio broadcast he delivered after his return to America, Willkie decided to put into book form what he had seen on his trip and learned from it. Working from notes and outlines submitted by Barnes and Cowles as well as from his own recollections, Willkie spent every morning from nine to noon for six weeks on the book, at the apartment of Irita Van Doren, a close friend and his literary adviser. His publishers, Simon and Schuster, had suggested as a title One War, One Peace, One World; in the end Willkie cut it down, at the suggestion of one of the editors, Tom Bevans, to One World. The book was published April 8, 1943, and was an immediate and resounding success, reaching the figure of a million copies in print in seven weeks, and going into many editions later. With his basic themes of Allied unity in war and peacemaking, and the recognition of new forces everywhere demanding freedom, Willkie struck a strong and deep contemporary chord.

M<small>Y SECOND</small> memory of Alexandria is of a dinner that night at the home of Admiral Harwood, hero of the epic fight of the *Exeter* against the *Graf Spee* in South American waters, and now commander of the British Navy in the eastern Mediter-

---

These excerpts from *One World* have been reprinted from the original edition (New York: Simon and Schuster, 1943). They comprise roughly one-eighth of the total book. The sequence of chapters follows the stages of the flight, with emphasis on the Middle Eastern, Russian, and Chinese fronts, and on the subsurface revolutionary changes that Willkie felt at work in each. The present excerpts, omitting some preliminary pages on the first leg of the trip, plunge into what Willkie found at El Alamein, in Egypt. The excerpts end with the crucial passages of two concluding chapters on "What We Are Fighting For" and "One World."

ranean. He invited to dine with us ten of his compatriots in the naval, diplomatic, or consular service in Alexandria. We discussed the war in the detached, almost impersonal way in which the war is discussed all over the world by officers engaged in fighting it, and then the conversation turned to politics. I tried to draw out these men, all of them experienced and able administrators of the British Empire, on what they saw in the future, and especially in the future of the colonial system and of our joint relations with the many peoples of the East.

What I got was Rudyard Kipling, untainted even with the liberalism of Cecil Rhodes. I knew that informed Englishmen in London and all over the British Commonwealth were working hard on these problems, that many of them, for example, were trying to find a formula which will go farther toward self-government than the older concept of "trusteeship." But these men, executing the policies made in London, had no idea that the world was changing. The British colonial system was not perfect in their eyes; it seemed to me simply that no one of them had ever thought of it as anything that might possibly be changed or modified in any way. The Atlantic Charter most of them had read about. That it might affect their careers or their thinking had never occurred to any of them. That evening started in my mind a conviction which was to grow strong in the days that followed it in the Middle East: that brilliant victories in the field will not win for us this war now going on in the far reaches of the world, that only new men and new ideas in the machinery of our relations with the peoples of the East can win the victory without which any peace will be only another armistice. . . .

. . . One senses a ferment in these lands, a groping of the long-inert masses, a growing disregard of restrictive religious rites and practices. In every city I found a group—usually a small group—of restless, energetic, intellectual young people who knew the techniques of the mass movement that had brought about the revolution in Russia and talked about them. They knew also the history of our own democratic development. In their talk with me they seemed to be weighing in their minds the course through which their own intense, almost fanatical, aspirations should be achieved. Likewise I found in this part of the world, as I found in Russia, in China, everywhere, a growing spirit of fervid nationalism, a disturbing thing to one who believes that the only hope of the world lies in the opposite trend. . . .

I shall . . . never forget my visit with General de Gaulle. I was met at the airport at Beirut, received by an elaborately uniformed color guard and band, and whisked several miles to the house where the general was living—a great white structure, surrounded by elaborate and formal gardens, where guards saluted at every turn. We talked for hours in the general's private room, where every corner, every wall, held busts, statues, and pictures of Napoleon. The conversation continued through an elaborate dinner and went on late into the night, as we sat out on a beautiful starlit lawn.

Frequently the general, in describing his struggle of the moment with the British as to whether he or they should dominate Syria and the Lebanon, would declare dramatically, "I cannot sacrifice or compromise my principles." "Like Joan of Arc," his aide added. When I referred to my great interest in the Fighting French movement, he corrected me sharply. "The Fighting French are not a movement. The Fighting French are France itself. We are the residuary legatees of all of France and its possessions." When I reminded him that Syria was but a mandated area under the League of Nations, he said, "Yes, I know. But I hold it in trust. I cannot close out that mandate or let anyone else do so. That can be done only when there is a government again in France. In no place in this world can I yield a single French right, though I am perfectly willing to sit with Winston Churchill and Franklin Roosevelt and consider ways and means by which French rights and French territories can be momentarily and temporarily used in order to help drive the Germans and the collaborators from the control of France.

"Mr. Willkie," he continued, "some people forget that I and my associates represent France. They apparently do not have in mind France's glorious history. They are thinking in terms of its momentary eclipse.". . .

After a few formal speeches, the dinner [given by the Syrian Prime Minister, Nuri el-Said, at his Bagdad home] became a concert, and the concert became an exhibition of Arab dancing girls, and this in turn became a Western ball with English nurses and American soldiers up from Basra on the Persian Gulf and Iraqi officers dancing under an Arabian sky. No man could have sat through that evening and preserved any notion that the East and the West will never meet, or that Allah is determined to keep the Arabs a desert folk, ruled by foreigners from across the seas.

The next day, flying from Bagdad to Teheran, I was thinking over the events of the night before. And I became aware of certain sober undercurrents that had been beneath the gaiety, the same undercurrents I had noticed before in talking with students, newspapermen, and soldiers throughout the Middle East. It all added up to the conviction that these newly awakened people will be followers of some extremist leader in this generation if their new hunger for education and opportunity for a release from old restrictive religious and governmental practice is not met by their own rulers and their foreign overlords. The veil, the fez, the sickness, the filth, the lack of education and modern industrial development, the arbitrariness of government, all commingled in their minds to represent a past imposed upon them by a combination of forces within their own society and the self-interest of foreign domination. Again and again I was asked: does America intend to support a system by which our politics are controlled by foreigners, however politely, our lives dominated by foreigners, however indirectly, because we happen to be strategic points on the military roads and trade routes of the world? Or, they would say, to put it your way: because we are strategic points which must be held to prevent Axis or some other non-democratic domination of the key military roads and trade routes of the world? Because our canals, our seas, and our countries are necessary to the control of the eastern Mediterranean and constitute the road to Asia?

I know this problem can be oversimplified in its statement and is not susceptible of easy answers. I know that the retention of points such as Suez, the eastern Mediterranean, and the roads through Asia Minor to the East obviously, if our Western democracy is not to be threatened by hostile forces, must be kept in both friendly and stabilized hands. Likewise, I know there is much historical and even present-day justification for the current "protective" colonial system. Pragmatically, however, in view of the ferment which is going on, it is a question whether that system can be maintained. Idealistically, we must face the fact that the system is completely antipathetic to all the principles for which we claim we fight. Furthermore, the more we preach those principles, the more we stimulate the ferment that endangers the system.

I know all this. But I am here reporting what is in the minds of Prime Ministers, Foreign Ministers, awakened intellectual groups to be found in every city of the Middle East, and even vaguely in the minds of uneducated masses. Somehow, with a new approach and a patient wisdom, the question must be answered or a new leader will arise with a fierce fanaticism who will coalesce these discontents. And the result will

867

be of necessity either the complete withdrawal of outside powers with a complete loss of democratic influence or complete military occupation and control of the countries by those outside powers.

If we believe in the ends we proclaim and if we want the stirring new forces within the Middle East to work with us toward those ends, we must cease trying to perpetuate control by manipulation of native forces, by playing off one against the other for our own ends. . . .

. . . I had not sufficiently taken into account, in appraising modern Russia, that it is ruled by and composed almost entirely of people whose parents had no property, no education, and only a folk heritage. That there is hardly a resident of Russia today whose lot is not as good as or better than his parents' lot was prior to the revolution. The Russian individual, like all individuals, naturally finds some good in a system that has improved his own lot, and has a tendency to forget the ruthless means by which it has been brought about. This may be difficult for an American to believe or like. But it was plainly the explanation among all sorts of people, everywhere, and it was clearly expressed during a stimulating evening I spent in Moscow when I was trying to put a group of intelligent modern Russians on the spot to defend their system.

But I had not gone to Russia to remember the past. Besides my concrete assignments for the President, I had gone determined to find an answer for myself to the actual problems posed for our generation of Americans by the simple fact that the Soviet Union, whether we like it or not, exists.

Some of these answers I believe I found, at least to my own satisfaction. I can sum up the three most important in a few sentences.

First, Russia is an effective society. It works. It has survival value. The record of Soviet resistance to Hitler has been proof enough of this to most of us, but I must admit in all frankness that I was not prepared to believe before I went to Russia what I now know about its strength as a going organization of men and women.

Second, Russia is our ally in this war. The Russians, more sorely tested by Hitler's might even than the British, have met the test magnificently. Their hatred of Fascism and the Nazi system is real and deep and bitter. And this hatred makes them determined to eliminate Hitler and exterminate the Nazi blight from Europe and the world.

Third, we must work with Russia after the war. At least it seems to me that there can be no continued peace unless we learn to do so.

Those conclusions were reinforced by what I saw and heard in various parts of the Soviet Union. I saw one portion of the Russian front, close enough to know something at first hand of what the Red Army has done. I saw a good many of the factories behind the front, where the Soviet workers have fooled too many of our experts by keeping up a steady flow of supplies to the fighting men. And I saw collective farms. Behind the factories and the farms, I saw and talked with the Soviet newspapermen and writers who have given all Russians the strangely exalted feeling of being in a crusade. Behind the journalists, I saw the Kremlin, having talked twice at great length with Mr. Stalin, and observed something of how power is really exercised under the dictatorship of the proletariat. Finally, behind all these, I saw the Russian people from one end of Russia to the other, and if my sampling of the 200,000,000 was absurdly small, it had the advantage of being chosen entirely by chance. . . .

In Moscow I had two long talks with Joseph Stalin. Much of what was said I am not at liberty to report. But about the man himself there is no reason to be cautious. He is one of the significant men of this generation.

At his invitation I called on him one evening at 7:30. He apparently has most of his conferences at night. His office was a fair-sized room about eighteen by thirty-five feet. On its walls hung pictures of Marx and Engels and Lenin, and profiles of Lenin and Stalin together, the same pictures that you see in practically every schoolhouse, public building, factory, hotel, hospital, and home in Russia. Often you find in addition the picture of Molotov. In an anteroom visible from the office was a huge globe some ten feet in diameter.

Stalin and Molotov were standing to welcome me at the far end of a long oak conference table. They greeted me simply and we talked for some three hours—about the war, about what would come after, about Stalingrad and the front, about America's position, the relationship of Great Britain, the United States, and Russia, and about many other important and unimportant subjects.

A few days later I spent some five hours sitting next to Stalin, through the numerous courses of a state dinner which he gave for me; later while we all drank coffee at little tables in another room, and finally through a private showing of a motion picture of the siege and defense of Moscow.

It was at this dinner, incidentally, that we toasted the interpreters. We had toasted our respective countries and leaders; we had toasted the Russian people and the American people and our hopes for future collaboration; we had toasted each other. Finally it occurred to me that the only people really working at that dinner were the interpreters who were kept bobbing up and down to translate. So I proposed a toast to them. Later, I said to Mr. Stalin, "I hope I didn't step out of line in suggesting that we toast the interpreters." And he replied, "Not at all, Mr. Willkie, we are a democratic country."

Stalin, I should judge, is about five feet four or five, and gives the appearance of slight stockiness. I was surprised to find how short he is; but his head, his mustache, and his eyes are big. His face, in repose, is a hard face, and he looked tired in September—not sick, as is so often reported, but desperately tired. He had a right to be. He talks quietly, readily, and at times with a simple, moving eloquence. When he described to me Russia's desperate situation as to fuel, transportation, military equipment, and man power, he was genuinely dramatic.

He has, I would say, a hard, tenacious, driving mind. He asked searching questions, each of them loaded like a revolver, each of them designed to cut through to what he believed to be the heart of the matter that interested him. He pushes aside pleasantries and compliments and is impatient of generalities.

When he asked me about my trips through various factories, he wanted detailed reports, department by department, not general judgments as to their operating methods and efficiency. When I asked him about Stalingrad, he developed for me logically not alone its geographical and military importance, but the moral effect on Russia, Germany, and particularly the Middle East, of the successful or unsuccessful defense. He made no predictions as to Russia's ability to hold it and he was quite definite in his assertion that neither love of homeland nor pure bravery could save it. Battles were won or lost primarily by numbers, skill, and matériel.

He told me again and again that his propaganda was deliberately designed to make his people hate the Nazis, but it was obvious that he himself had a certain bitter admiration for the efficiency by which Hitler had transplanted to Germany as much as ninety-four per cent of the working population from some of the conquered Russian territory, and

870

he respected the completely professional training of the German Army, particularly its officers. He discounted, just as Winston Churchill did to me two years before in England, the notion that Hitler was but a tool in the hands of abler men. He did not think we should count upon an early internal collapse in Germany. He said that the way to defeat Germany was to destroy its army. And he believed that one of the most effective methods of destroying faith in Hitler's invincibility throughout Europe was in continuous air-raid bombings of German cities and of German-held docks and factories in the conquered countries.

When we talked of the causes of the war and the economic and political conditions that would face the world after it was over, his comprehension was broad, his detailed information exact, and the cold reality of his thinking apparent. Stalin is a hard man, perhaps even a cruel man, but a very able one. He has few illusions.

His admiration for the effectiveness of American production methods would more than satisfy the National Association of Manufacturers. But he does not understand the indirections and some of the restraints of the democratic methods of waging war. He wondered, for instance, why the democracies should not insist upon using certain bases for war purposes that would be of great value to them, particularly if the nations that owned them were unco-operative and not able to defend them.

Quite contrary to general report, Stalin has great respect for Winston Churchill; he almost said it to me—the respect of one great realist for another.

On the personal side Stalin is a simple man, with no affectations or poses. He does not seek to impress by any artificial mannerisms. His sense of humor is a robust one, and he laughs readily at unsubtle jokes and repartee. Once I was telling him of the Soviet schools and libraries I had seen—how good they seemed to me. And I added, "But if you continue to educate the Russian people, Mr. Stalin, the first thing you know you'll educate yourself out of a job."

He threw his head back and laughed and laughed. Nothing I said to him, or heard anyone else say to him, through two long evenings, seemed to amuse him as much.

Strange as it may seem, Stalin dresses in light pastel shades. His well-known tunic is of finely woven material and is apt to be a soft green or a delicate pink; his trousers a light-tannish yellow or blue. His boots are black and highly polished. Ordinary social pleasantries bother him a little. As I was leaving him after my first talk, I expressed appreciation of the time he had given me, the honor he conferred in talking so candidly. A little embarrassed, he said:

"Mr. Willkie, you know I grew up a Georgian peasant. I am unschooled in pretty talk. All I can say is I like you very much."

Inevitably, Stalin's simple ways have set a fashion of a kind for other Soviet leaders. Especially in Moscow and in Kuibishev, there is an absence of flamboyance about Russian leaders that is remarkable. They all dress simply. They talk little and listen well. A surprising number of them are young, in their thirties. It would be my guess, which I could not prove or document, that Stalin likes a pretty heavy turnover of young people in his immediate entourage in the Kremlin. It is his way, I think, of keeping his ear to the ground.

Among the other leaders I met and talked to at any great length were Viacheslav Molotov, the Foreign Minister, Andrei Vishinsky and Solomon Lozovsky, his assistants, Marshal Voroshilov, the former Commissar of Defense, Anastasia Mikoyan, Commissar of Supply and head of the Soviet foreign-trade apparatus. Each of these is an educated man, interested in the foreign world, completely unlike in manner, appearance, and speech the uncouth, wild Bolshevik of our cartoons.

In Kuibishev, at a dinner given for me by Mr. Vishinsky, who was the chief state prosecutor in all the grim treason trials of four and five years ago, I caught myself studying his white hair, his professor's face, and his quiet, almost studious manner, and wondering if this could possibly be the same man who had purged some of the oldest heroes of the Russian Revolution on charges of murder and betrayal of their country.

Whenever the talk of these men ran to the peace, to what the world must be prepared to do after the war is over, they talked with statesmanship and real understanding.

Since I have returned to the United States, Mr. Stalin has defined the program, as he sees it, of the Anglo-American-Soviet coalition in the European war. These are the goals he calls for:

"Abolition of racial exclusiveness, equality of nations and integrity of their territories, liberation of enslaved nations and restoration of their sovereign rights, the right of every nation to arrange its affairs as it wishes, economic aid to nations that have suffered and assistance to them in attaining their material welfare, restoration of democratic liberties, the destruction of the Hitlerite regime."

We may ask: does Stalin mean what he says? Some will point out that only two years ago Russia was in an alliance of expediency with

Germany. I make no defense of expediency, military, political, temporary, or otherwise. For I believe the moral losses of expediency always far
outweigh the temporary gains. And I believe that every drop of blood
saved through expediency will be paid for by twenty drawn by the sword.
But a Russian, feeling that by the German alliance his country was
buying time, might well remind the democracies of Munich, and of the
seven million tons of the best grade of scrap iron the United States
shipped to Japan between 1937 and 1940.

Perhaps we can better measure the good faith of Stalin's statement in
the light of the millions of Russians who have already died defending
their fatherland and of the sixty million who have become slaves of the
Nazis; in those other millions of Russian men and women who are
working feverishly sixty-six hours a week in factories and mines to forge
and produce instruments of war for the fighters at the front; and in the
effort that went into the almost miraculous movement of great factories,
hundreds of miles, that they might operate, uninterrupted, beyond Nazi
reach. For it is in the attitude of the people that we may find the best
interpretation of Stalin's purpose.

Many among the democracies fear and mistrust Soviet Russia. They
dread the inroads of an economic order that would be destructive of
their own. Such fear is weakness. Russia is neither going to eat us nor
seduce us. That is—and this is something for us to think about—that is,
unless our democratic institutions and our free economy become so frail
through abuse and failure in practice as to make us soft and vulnerable.
The best answer to Communism is a living, vibrant, fearless democracy
—economic, social, and political. All we need to do is to stand up and
perform according to our professed ideals. Then those ideals will be
safe.

No, we do not need to fear Russia. We need to learn to work with her
against our common enemy, Hitler. We need to learn to work with her
in the world after the war. For Russia is a dynamic country, a vital new
society, a force that cannot be bypassed in any future world. . . .

I arrived in Chungking late in the afternoon, at an airport some miles
from the city. Long before our automobiles had reached the city, the
road on either side was lined with people. Before we reached the middle
of the city, the crowds stood packed from curb to store front. Men,
women, young boys and girls, bearded old gentlemen, Chinese with
fedora hats, others with skullcaps, coolies, porters, students, mothers

nursing their children, well dressed and poorly dressed—they packed eleven miles of road over which our cars slowly moved on our way to the guesthouse in which we were to stay. On the other side of the Yangtze River, they stood and waited. On all the hills of Chungking, which must be the world's hilliest city, they stood and smiled and cheered and waved little paper American and Chinese flags.

Any man who has run for President of the United States is used to crowds. But not to this one. I could discount it in my mind as much as I wished, but to no avail. The paper flags waved by the people were all of the same size, suggesting that the hospitable and imaginative Mayor of Chungking, Dr. K. C. Wu, had had a hand in planning this demonstration. It was perfectly clear that not all these people, many of whom were barefoot or dressed in rags, had any clear idea of who I was or why I was there. The firecrackers which were exploding on every street corner, I told myself, are an old Chinese passion, anyway.

But in spite of all my efforts to discount it, this scene moved me profoundly. There was nothing synthetic or fake about the faces I looked at. They were seeing, in me, a representative of America and a tangible hope of friendship and help that might be forthcoming. It was a mass demonstration of good will. And it was an impressive show of the simple strength, in people and in emotions, which is China's greatest national resource.

I had seen a crowd like this one, but a little smaller, on my arrival in Lanchow, far into the northwest. I was later to see another, as impressive as any, which waited for hours in the rain on the streets of Sian, capital of Shensi province, because our plane was late. They never failed to move me deeply. It is impossible in a short trip through a country as big as China to make as many close and personal friendships as one would like, those relationships through which one generally comes to know the spirit and the ideas of a foreign people. But these crowds of Chinese people gave me a sure and lasting feeling that my surface impressions of China were backed by something no one could misread in those thousands of faces.

The Chinese I came to know well were, inevitably, leaders in one field or another. Some of them I will describe later in this account, and in high terms. But I know no praise high enough for the anonymous people of China. . . .

Possibly no other country on our side in this war is so dominated by the personality of one man as China. His name is Chiang Kai-shek, although he is universally referred to in China as "The Generalissimo," sometimes affectionately shortened to "Gissimo."

I had a number of long talks with the Generalissimo, as well as family breakfasts and other meals alone with him and Mme Chiang.

One late afternoon we drove to the Chiangs' country place, high on the steep bank of the Yangtze River. . . . Across the front of the simple frame house was a large porch where we sat looking out to the hills of Chungking. In the river below, a number of small boats moved in the swift current, carrying the Chinese farmer and his produce downstream to market. It had been a hot day in Chungking but here a pleasant breeze was blowing, and as Mme Chiang served us tea, the Generalissimo and I began to talk. . . .

We discussed the past and his administration's aim to change China from an almost exclusively agricultural society into a modern industrial one. He hoped in the change to retain the best of the old traditions and to avoid the social dislocations of large-scale Western industrial development by the establishment of a great number of widely distributed small plants. He was sure that in the teachings of Dr. Sun, the father of the republic, concerning a combined agricultural and industrial society he would find the way. But he was eager to discuss the question with someone from the West and he asked me many questions. I explained to him that the social problems created by mass production in America and the large industrial combinations which he wanted to avoid had not arisen, as he seemed to think, solely because of desire for power and the building of individual fortunes, though these elements undoubtedly contributed. In part, at least, they arose because of economic requirements: mass production greatly lowers costs.

I gave him the illustration of the automobile, which he hoped to see manufactured at low cost in China to fill Chinese roads. I pointed out to him that an automobile manufactured in a small plant would cost five times as much as an automobile manufactured on an assembly line under scientific management in a large plant. That it is impossible to have some of the products that make for a high standard of living at prices within the reach of the great masses of the people, if they must be produced exclusively in small plants. That every thoughtful American knew that in many instances we have created large industrial combinations unnecessarily. That for our social and economic good we should

875

give the utmost encouragement and preference to the small industries. But that in certain industries, in order to maintain our standard of living, it was necessary to have large-scale production. I told him that we recognized the social, economic, and almost non-democratic maladjustments created by the collection of thousands of workers under single factory roofs, with the consequent possibility of unemployment of whole communities at one time. That we regretted the stratification of large groups of our population into a permanent employee class which this system produced, and the reduction of the opportunity for individual men to become owners of their own businesses. I also told the Generalissimo that we had not as yet found all the answers. But we did know that the solution did not consist in breaking up necessary large units into inefficient small ones.

I reminded him that there was an experiment going on much closer to him than any in the Western world, the Communist one in Russia, and that part of its success was due to the mass-production technique of using large groups for the accomplishment of a particular purpose.

He suggested that perhaps he could find the solution in having necessary large units partly owned by government and partly by private capital.

The discussion went on for hours. Then Mme Chiang, who had been acting as interpreter for us, with pleasant but firm feminine authority, said: "It's ten o'clock and you men haven't had anything to eat. Come on now; we must drive into town and get at least a bite. You can finish this some other time."

At other times we did talk more of this, and of many other things. We talked of India, of the whole East, of its aspirations, of its purposes, of how it should fit into a world-wide order, of military strategy, of Japan and its resources, of Pearl Harbor and the fall of Singapore and their profound psychological effect on the attitude of the East toward the West. We talked of the growing spirit of intense, almost fanatical nationalism which I had found developing in the countries of the Middle East, in Russia and now in China, of how such a spirit might upset the possibility of world co-operation. We talked of Russia and of Chiang's relationship to the Communists within China, of Great Britain and her policy in the East, of Franklin Roosevelt and Winston Churchill and Joseph Stalin.

In fact, the six days I was with the Generalissimo were filled with talk. . . .

876

Millions have already died in this war and many thousands more will go before it is over. Unless Britons and Canadians and Russians and Chinese and Americans and all our fighting allies, in the common co-operation of war, find the instrumentalities and the methods of co-operative effort after the war, we, the people, have failed our time and our generation. . . .

The statement of Mr. Stalin [a statement of Russian war aims on November 6, 1942, emphasizing "the liberation of enslaved nations and the restoration of their sovereign rights" and "the right of every nation to arrange its affairs as it wishes"] and the Atlantic Charter seem to me to have a common fallacy. They forecast the re-creation of western Europe in its old divisions of small nations, each with its own individual political, economic, and military sovereignty. It was this outmoded system that caused millions in Europe to be captivated by Hitler's proposed new order. For even with Hitler tyranny they at least saw the hope of the creation of an area large enough so that the economics of the modern world could successfully function. They had come to realize through bitter experience that the restricted areas of trade imposed by the high walls of a multitude of individual nationalisms, with the consequent manipulations of power politics, made impoverishment and war inevitable.

The re-creation of the small countries of Europe as political units, *yes*; their re-creation as economic and military units, *no*, if we really hope to bring stabilization to western Europe both for its own benefit and for the peace and economic security of the world. . . .

If our withdrawal from world affairs after the last war was a contributing factor to the present war and to the economic instability of the past twenty years—and it seems plain that it was—a withdrawal from the problems and responsibilities of the world after this war would be sheer disaster. Even our relative geographical isolation no longer exists.

At the end of the last war, not a single plane had flown across the Atlantic. Today that ocean is a mere ribbon, with airplanes making regular scheduled flights. The Pacific is only a slightly wider ribbon in the ocean of the air, and Europe and Asia are at our very doorstep.

America must choose one of three courses after this war: narrow nationalism, which inevitably means the ultimate loss of our own liberty; international imperialism, which means the sacrifice of some other nation's liberty; or the creation of a world in which there shall be an equality of opportunity for every race and every nation. I am convinced the American people will choose, by overwhelming majority, the last of these courses. To make this choice effective, we must win not only the war, but also the peace, and we must start winning it now.

To win this peace three things seem to me necessary—first, we must plan now for peace on a world basis; second, the world must be free, politically and economically, for nations and for men, that peace may exist in it; third, America must play an active, constructive part in freeing it and keeping its peace.

When I say that peace must be planned on a world basis, I mean quite literally that it must embrace the earth. Continents and oceans are plainly only parts of a whole, seen, as I have seen them, from the air. England and America are parts. Russia and China, Egypt, Syria and Turkey, Iraq and Iran are also parts. And it is inescapable that there can be no peace for any part of the world unless the foundations of peace are made secure throughout all parts of the world.

This cannot be accomplished by mere declarations of our leaders, as in an Atlantic Charter. Its accomplishment depends primarily upon acceptance by the peoples of the world. For if the failure to reach international understanding after the last war taught us anything it taught us this: even if war leaders apparently agree upon generalized principles and slogans while the war is being fought, when they come to the peace table they make their own interpretations of their previous declarations. So unless today, while the war is being fought, the people of the United States and of Great Britain, of Russia and of China, and of all the other United Nations, fundamentally agree on their purposes, fine and idealistic expressions of hope such as those of the Atlantic Charter will live merely to mock us as have Mr. Wilson's Fourteen Points. The Four Freedoms will not be accomplished by the declarations of those momentarily in power. They will become real only if the people of the world forge them into actuality.

When I say that in order to have peace this world must be free, I am only reporting that a great process has started which no man—certainly not Hitler—can stop. Men and women all over the world are on the march, physically, intellectually, and spiritually. After centuries of ignorant and dull compliance, hundreds of millions of people in eastern Europe and Asia have opened the books. Old fears no longer frighten them. They are no longer willing to be Eastern slaves for Western profits. They are beginning to know that men's welfare throughout the world is interdependent. They are resolved, as we must be, that there is no more place for imperialism within their own society than in the society of nations. The big house on the hill surrounded by mud huts has lost its awesome charm.

Our Western world and our presumed supremacy are now on trial. Our boasting and our big talk leave Asia cold. Men and women in Russia and China and in the Middle East are conscious now of their own potential strength. They are coming to know that many of the decisions about the future of the world lie in their hands. And they intend that these decisions shall leave the peoples of each nation free from foreign domination, free for economic, social, and spiritual growth.

Economic freedom is as important as political freedom. Not only must people have access to what other peoples produce, but their own products must in turn have some chance of reaching men all over the world. There will be no peace, there will be no real development, there will be no economic stability, unless we find the method by which we can begin to break down the unnecessary trade barriers hampering the flow of goods. Obviously, the sudden and uncompromising abolition of tariffs after the war could only result in disaster. But obviously, also, one of the freedoms we are fighting for is freedom to trade. I know there are many men, particularly in America, where our standard of living exceeds the standard of living in the rest of the world, who are genuinely alarmed at such a prospect, who believe that any such process will only lessen our own standard of living. The reverse of this is true.

Many reasons may be assigned for the amazing economic development of the United States. The abundance of our national resources, the freedom of our political institutions, and the character of our population have all undoubtedly contributed. But in my judgment the greatest factor has been the fact that by the happenstance of good fortune there was created here in America the largest area in the world in which there were no barriers to the exchange of goods and ideas.

And I should like to point out to those who are fearful one inescapable fact. In view of the astronomical figures our national debt will assume by the end of this war, and in a world reduced in size by industrial and transportation developments, even our present standard of living in America cannot be maintained unless the exchange of goods flows more freely over the whole world. It is also inescapably true that to raise the standard of living of any man anywhere in the world is to raise the standard of living by some slight degree of every man everywhere in the world.

Finally, when I say that this world demands the full participation of a self-confident America, I am only passing on an invitation which the peoples of the East have given us. They would like the United States and the other United Nations to be partners with them in this grand adventure. They want us to join them in creating a new society of independent nations, free alike of the economic injustices of the West and the political malpractices of the East. But as partners in that great new combination they want us neither hesitant, incompetent, nor afraid. They want partners who will not hesitate to speak out for the correction of injustice anywhere in the world.

Our allies in the East know that we intend to pour out our resources in this war. But they expect us now—not after the war—to use the enormous power of our giving to promote liberty and justice. Other peoples, not yet fighting, are waiting no less eagerly for us to accept the most challenging opportunity of all history—the chance to help create a new society in which men and women the world around can live and grow invigorated by independence and freedom.

Long after Wendell Willkie's struggle with the TVA and the details of his campaign for the Presidency have become footnotes to a history of the New Deal era, his "one world" will remain as his most enduring achievement. As a phrase it has become part of the language, and part also of the current hopes of people who have never heard of Willkie.

One World appeared just when the Allied fortunes of war were changing, and to some extent it helped change them by reassuring the Allies about American war and postwar aims. It also helped to overcome the distrust of Russian aims in a reading public which included the intellectuals of both major parties. It thus had considerable impact (questionable from the vantage point of the present) in winning public acceptance for later American military and diplomatic decisions which had far-reaching political consequences: the holding back of American armies from Berlin, the Yalta decision on Poland, the willingness to allow the Soviet armies to occupy the East European capitals, the premature withdrawal of American troops from Europe.

It is true that Stalin attacked some of Willkie's own speeches and positions, and that Willkie ruefully asked the British ambassador to Russia, Sir Archibald Clark Kerr, to find out from Stalin what was troubling him. Willkie, like Roosevelt, thought of himself as a realist toward the Russians. He would have been horrified, had he lived, to see the ruthlessness of Russian expansionism in the last months of the war and the years immediately following it. Yet the book had its autonomous existence. What counted was not Willkie's intention but his theme that the world was stirring out of feudalism and nationalism, and that there were overriding postwar purposes that went beyond differences in political institutions and viewpoints. This seemed to give sanction to the new antifeudal postwar "people's democracies" in Eastern Europe and later to the success of the Communist revolution in China. Willkie's "one world" was thus a prelude to the more naïve formulation by Henry Wallace of the "century of the common man."

Although Roosevelt, Stalin, and Churchill had not yet agreed on their idea of a United Nations in 1943, Willkie's book anticipated them. There was in it a strong strain of Wilsonian idealist internationalism, not surprising when one remembers that Willkie was one of the "Newton Baker Boys" at the 1924 Democratic Convention, when Baker fought for a stronger position on the League of Nations. In fact it was One World, even more than the Atlantic Charter, that was the real analogue to Wilson's Fourteen Points, except that it did not have official sanction. Roosevelt was caught, during and after the war, between a distrust of British imperialism and a distrust of Wilsonian idealism. The Four Freedoms plus the Concert of Powers (which was how he saw the United Nations) was as far as he was willing to go in his postwar formulation. Not only was Willkie against British imperialism, but he hit at the nationalism and militarism which he saw as the root of the decay of the Old Order. Curiously he saw both de Gaulle and Chiang Kai-shek as new rather than as old figures, despite their nationalism and militarism. To the extent that the book crystallized British opinion it may have added to the British feeling in 1945 that Churchill was a great war captain but not a peace leader, which led to his electoral defeat. In the age of nuclear weapons, which started two years after the book was published (the Manhattan Project was already under way), Willkie's conviction that national sovereignty could not organize world order was to prove a crucial insight. The idea of "one world" needed only another step to become the basis of the movement for a policing force against aggression, and for the development of a body of world law.

The book, more than any other of its day, foreshadowed the "revolution of rising expectations" which, along with nuclear technology, has dominated the postwar world. Willkie was not a sharp thinker. He did not see the contradiction between his harshness about nationalism and militarism in the old Europe and his acceptance of both in the new Middle East, Russia, and China. He looked for the new energies in people as diverse as de Gaulle, Stalin, Chiang Kai-shek, Chou En-lai, Nuri el-Said. All he knew was that people were stirring everywhere, and that something was coming to birth in them very different from what had dominated the old order of things. Whatever his blurrings there were perceptive insights in the book which expressed—and evoked—the inner spirit of the new national-identity revolutions of our time. His hopes for a reformed Chinese social system under Chiang never materialized, but in its place came a stern new Communist empire which spoke in the name of anticolonialism. In Asia and Africa the Bandung anticolonialist movement was the first of a series which used for their own anti-Western purposes Willkie's idea of a surge of popular aspirations cutting across national boundaries. The French, Dutch, and Portuguese, as well as the British, were to discover the truth of Willkie's warning that unless the West recognized the validity of the new revolutions they would come under less welcome direction. The timetable that Willkie asked for, in the withdrawal of colonialist power, was foreshortened by the event, and in some places—like the Congo and Kenya—the retreat came before authentic self-governing forces could be shaped for a multiracial society. Governments based on the rule of force rather than law, and in many cases on inverse racism, would have shocked Willkie. Yet it can be said of few of his contemporaries as it can of him, that so much of history has marched to the rhythm of his words.

George C. Marshall
The Marshall Plan
1947

EDITED BY HANS J. MORGENTHAU

The Marshall Plan, as formulated in the Commencement Address which Secretary of State George C. Marshall delivered at Harvard University on June 5, 1947, owes its existence to the Truman Doctrine. The Marshall Plan and the Truman Doctrine are, in the words of President Truman, "two halves of the same walnut." On March 12, 1947, President Truman declared before a joint session of Congress, "It must be the policy of the United States to support free peoples who are resisting attempted subjugation by armed minorities or by outside pressure. . . . I believe that our help should be primarily through economic and financial aid which is essential to economic stability and orderly political processes." Two developments appeared to make an authoritative elaboration of the Truman Doctrine necessary: the widespread interpretation of the Truman Doctrine primarily in terms of ideological warfare and military defense, and the rapidly deteriorating economic and political situation in Europe. This elaboration was to take the form of a proposal for the economic reconstruction of all of Europe, east and west alike.

This proposal was made in considerable detail in the address which Under Secretary of State Dean G. Acheson gave on May 8, 1947, before the Delta Council in Cleveland, Mississippi. Acheson's address was intended as preparation for an authoritative statement of policy by Marshall. On May 29, 1947, Marshall decided to make this statement in the form of a Commencement Address at Harvard; he had tentatively accepted an invitation to be present. He asked Charles E. Bohlen, his special assistant, to draft the speech. Bohlen drew primarily upon two documents supplied respectively by George F. Kennan, head of the Policy Planning Staff of the Department of State, and William L. Clayton, Under Secretary of State for Economic Affairs. Marshall had asked Kennan on April 28 to develop within two weeks recommendations for an American foreign aid policy for Europe. Kennan submitted the recommendations on May 23. Clayton had returned on May 19 to Washington after a stay of six weeks in Europe. He brought with him a memorandum stressing the economic devastation of Europe and outlining a policy of American aid, and gave it on May 27 to Acheson, who in turn sent it the same day to Marshall.

Bohlen's draft, incorporating verbatim passages from both documents, was checked by Acheson and Clayton before it was submitted to Marshall. Twice—once in his office and again on the plane that took him to Cambridge on June 4—Marshall rewrote the next-to-last paragraph, stressing the need for European initiative. After reading the text of the address as printed here, which is the official version, Marshall added extemporaneously three sentences emphasizing "the vast importance to our people to reach some general understanding rather than to react to the passions and prejudices of the moment."

I NEED not tell you gentlemen that the world situation is very serious. That must be apparent to all intelligent people. I think one difficulty is that the problem is one of such enormous complexity that the very mass of facts presented to the public by press and radio make it exceedingly difficult for the man in the street to reach a clear appraisement of the situation. Furthermore, the people of this country are distant from the troubled areas of the earth and it is hard for them to comprehend the plight and consequent reactions of the long-suffering peoples, and the effect of those reactions on their governments in connection with our efforts to promote peace in the world.

In considering the requirements for the rehabilitation of Europe, the physical loss of life, the visible destruction of cities, factories, mines, and

The text is reprinted from U.S. Department of State *Bulletin*, Vol. XVI, No. 415 (June 15, 1947), pp. 1159–60.

railroads was correctly estimated, but it has become obvious during recent months that this visible destruction was probably less serious than the dislocation of the entire fabric of European economy. For the past 10 years conditions have been highly abnormal. The feverish preparation for war and the more feverish maintenance of the war effort engulfed all aspects of national economies. Machinery has fallen into disrepair or is entirely obsolete. Under the arbitrary and destructive Nazi rule, virtually every possible enterprise was geared into the German war machine. Long-standing commercial ties, private institutions, banks, insurance companies, and shipping companies disappeared, through loss of capital, absorption through nationalization, or by simple destruction. In many countries, confidence in the local currency has been severely shaken. The breakdown of the business structure of Europe during the war was complete. Recovery has been seriously retarded by the fact that two years after the close of hostilities a peace settlement with Germany and Austria has not been agreed upon. But even given a more prompt solution of these difficult problems, the rehabilitation of the economic structure of Europe quite evidently will require a much longer time and greater effort than had been foreseen.

There is a phase of this matter which is both interesting and serious. The farmer has always produced the foodstuffs to exchange with the city dweller for the other necessities of life. This division of labor is the basis of modern civilization. At the present time it is threatened with breakdown. The town and city industries are not producing adequate goods to exchange with the food-producing farmer. Raw materials and fuel are in short supply. Machinery is lacking or worn out. The farmer or the peasant cannot find the goods for sale which he desires to purchase. So the sale of his farm produce for money which he cannot use seems to him an unprofitable transaction. He, therefore, has withdrawn many fields from crop cultivation and is using them for grazing. He feeds more grain to stock and finds for himself and his family an ample supply of food, however short he may be on clothing and the other ordinary gadgets of civilization. Meanwhile people in the cities are short of food and fuel. So the governments are forced to use their foreign money and credits to procure these necessities abroad. This process exhausts funds which are urgently needed for reconstruction. Thus a very serious situation is rapidly developing which bodes no good for the world. The modern system of the division of labor upon which the exchange of products is based is in danger of breaking down.

The truth of the matter is that Europe's requirements for the next three or four years of foreign food and other essential products—principally from America—are so much greater than her present ability to pay that she must have substantial additional help or face economic, social, and political deterioration of a very grave character.

The remedy lies in breaking the vicious circle and restoring the confidence of the European people in the economic future of their own countries and of Europe as a whole. The manufacturer and the farmer throughout wide areas must be able and willing to exchange their products for currencies the continuing value of which is not open to question.

Aside from the demoralizing effect on the world at large and the possibilities of disturbances arising as a result of the desperation of the people concerned, the consequences to the economy of the United States should be apparent to all. It is logical that the United States should do whatever it is able to do to assist in the return of normal economic health in the world, without which there can be no political stability and no assured peace. Our policy is directed not against any country or doctrine but against hunger, poverty, desperation, and chaos. Its purpose should be the revival of a working economy in the world so as to permit the emergence of political and social conditions in which free institutions can exist. Such assistance, I am convinced, must not be on a piecemeal basis as various crises develop. Any assistance that this Government may render in the future should provide a cure rather than a mere palliative. Any government that is willing to assist in the task of recovery will find full cooperation, I am sure, on the part of the United States Government. Any government which maneuvers to block the recovery of other countries cannot expect help from us. Furthermore, governments, political parties, or groups which seek to perpetuate human misery in order to profit therefrom politically or otherwise will encounter the opposition of the United States.

It is already evident that, before the United States Government can proceed much further in its efforts to alleviate the situation and help start the European world on its way to recovery, there must be some agreement among the countries of Europe as to the requirements of the situation and the part those countries themselves will take in order to give proper effect to whatever action might be undertaken by this Government. It would be neither fitting nor efficacious for this Government to undertake to draw up unilaterally a program designed to place

Europe on its feet economically. This is the business of the Europeans. The initiative, I think, must come from Europe. The role of this country should consist of friendly aid in the drafting of a European program and of later support of such a program so far as it may be practical for us to do so. The program should be a joint one, agreed to by a number, if not all, European nations.

An essential part of any successful action on the part of the United States is an understanding on the part of the people of America of the character of the problem and the remedies to be applied. Political passion and prejudice should have no part. With foresight, and a willingness on the part of our people to face up to the vast responsibility which history has clearly placed upon our country, the difficulties I have outlined can and will be overcome.

Marshall's speech, outlining a course of action which then became official policy as the European Recovery Program, had an immediate galvanizing effect in Europe. The effect was comparable to that of American intervention in the two world wars. America had put its enormous resources in the scale of Western Europe, and victory was certain. The economic and political recovery of Europe can well be said to have begun the day after that speech.

The speech also laid the foundation for the division of Europe at the line of military demarcation of 1945 and for the economic unification of Western Europe. It was the distinct novelty of Marshall's proposal that it offered aid to Europe as a whole rather than to individual nations. The rejection of that aid by the members of Soviet bloc made inevitable their economic dependence on the Soviet Union, their separate and slow economic development, and, hence, the division of Europe on economic as well as military and political lines. On the other hand, the collective approach to economic recovery on the part of the United States required a corresponding approach on the part of the nations of Western Europe. A few weeks after Marshall's speech the Committee for European Economic Cooperation was formed, and in quick succession other European organizations, seeking economic, political, and military unification, came into being.

The speech thus stands as a symbol of American generosity, foresight, and wisdom in action. However, it is exactly by dint of the soundness of its philosophy, proved in action, that the speech came to be regarded as a prescription universally applicable. What the Marshall Plan had achieved in Europe, it was widely believed, could be accomplished elsewhere by similar means. The Marshall Plan became the inspiration and the model for the foreign aid policies of the United States in the 1950's and the early 1960's.

Yet not only was the philosophy of the Marshall Plan less applicable to conditions elsewhere, but that philosophy itself, in the process of being made universal, changed. The collective approach to a group of nations in similar conditions of economic distress was transformed into piece-meal aid to individual nations. The emphasis of the Marshall Plan on economic reconstruction rather than on ideological warfare and military defense was reversed. Finally, the requirements of effective cooperation among the recipient nations, and of their initiative rather than unilateral action by the United States, were largely lost sight of. It is only in the Alliance for Progress of 1961, a kind of Marshall Plan for Latin America, that these three elements of the Marshall Plan have been—at least in theory—restored.

Perhaps the highest tribute to the practical wisdom of the Marshall Plan is that it proved to be a mere temporary emergency program. It made itself superfluous through its success.

Harry S Truman
The Point IV Program
1949

EDITED BY HERBERT FEIS

The imposition of Communist control over Czechoslovakia in early 1948, by conspiracy and threat, jolted Americans toward the conclusion that the international Communist movement would not restrain itself. This opinion was confirmed by the Russian attempt to force the democracies to submit to its terms by blockading Berlin. The Communist parties in Western Europe were concurrently grasping for power. The main formal Western European allies were impelled by these events to conclude a military pact which was the forerunner of the North Atlantic Treaty.

The American government and people by this time had also begun to display their resistant will and strength. Greece and Turkey were being protected from an imminent threat of civil war provoked by the Communists. A good start had been made in uplifting the economies and spirits of the countries of Western Europe by the Marshall Plan. The purpose of the Soviet blockade of Berlin was being defeated by our air lift. These were some of the encouraging signs of what could be achieved by courageous and assertive leadership.

American attention turned to the dangers besetting Latin America and the more distant areas of the world—the Far East, the Middle East, and Africa. The Communists in China were on their way to victory and control of the whole vast mainland of that country. Korea and the Philippines were being given emergency economic assistance. India and

Pakistan, angrily arguing over Kashmir, were both in trouble. Indonesia was in the last stages of its struggle for independence from the Netherlands. In Africa, independence movements were increasingly successful, and the new nations that were coming into existence had little experience, capital, or technical knowledge.

Meanwhile, the economic efforts of many countries were restricted by what was called the "dollar gap." Almost all countries sought to procure more American products than they could pay for in dollars. This condition, it was thought at the time, was going to last indefinitely. It was hoped that by transmitting some of our technical knowledge to them their plight would be eased.

Such were the circumstances behind the "Point IV" proposal which was enunciated by President Harry S Truman in his Inaugural Address of January 20, 1949.

The proffer that was made in Point IV had been looking for influential sponsors in the State Department and the White House. But the memoranda of its first active advocate, Benjamin Hardy, a member of the Office of Public Affairs of the State Department, had not gained effective attention. When the Policy Planning staff, then under the direction of Paul Nitze, proposed modest extension of the kinds of technical assistance then being given Latin America be extended to all countries, the Bureau of the Budget turned down the suggestion.

Hardy turned to friends in the White House for support. Clark Clifford, eager to have new ideas to give the Inaugural Address life and appeal, took up the idea at once. He and the members of his staff—particularly David Lloyd and George Elsey—shaped the form and language of the proposal for inclusion in the Inaugural Address. Nitze and Charles Bohlen, then counselor of the State Department, believed that what had been favored as a modest practical effort, to be expanded with experience, was being blown up too dramatically for political effect. They feared that the expectations aroused could not be satisfied, since Congress would not provide for the purpose the large sums implicitly promised. But the President was enthusiastically for the bold version of Clifford and his staff. He approved its inclusion in the Inaugural Address.

☆

I N THE coming years, our program for peace and freedom will emphasize four major courses of action: . . .

Fourth—we must embark on a bold new program for making the benefits of our scientific advances and industrial progress available for the improvement and growth of underdeveloped areas. More than half the people of the world are living in conditions approaching misery. Their food is inadequate. They are victims of disease. Their economic life is primitive and stagnant. Their poverty is a handicap and a threat both to them and to more prosperous areas.

For the first time in history, humanity possesses the knowledge and the skill to relieve the suffering of these people.

The United States is preeminent among nations in the development of industrial and scientific techniques. The material resources which we can afford to use for the assistance of other peoples are limited. But our imponderable resources in technical knowledge are constantly growing and are inexhaustible.

I believe that we should make available to peace-loving peoples the benefits of our store of technical knowledge in order to help them realize their aspirations for a better life. And, in cooperation with other nations, we should foster capital investment in areas needing development.

Our aim should be to help the free peoples of the world, through their own efforts, to produce more food, more clothing and more materials for housing, more mechanical power to lighten their burdens.

We invite other countries to pool their technological resources in this undertaking. Their contributions will be warmly welcomed. This should be a cooperative enterprise in which all nations work together through the United Nations and its specialized agencies wherever practicable. It must be a world-wide effort for the achievement of peace, plenty, and freedom.

With the cooperation of business, private capital, agriculture, and labor in this country, this program can greatly increase the industrial

The Point IV Program is reprinted here from President Truman's Inaugural Address, January 20, 1949. Following the outline of the program are excerpts from the "Message of the President to the Congress Recommending the Enactment of Legislation to Authorize an Expanded Program of Technical Assistance for the Underdeveloped Areas of the World," which President Truman delivered on June 24, 1949. Both the address and the message appeared in the *Congressional Record, Proceedings and Debates of the 81st Congress First Session,* Vol. 95— Parts 1 & 6 (Washington, D.C.: Government Printing Office, 1949), January 20, and June 24, 1949, pp. 477–78, and 8397–99.

activity in other nations and can raise substantially their standards of living.

Such new economic developments must be devised and controlled to benefit the peoples of the areas in which they are established. Guaranties to the investor must be balanced by guaranties in the interest of the people whose resources and whose labor go into these developments.

The old imperialism—exploitation for foreign profit—has no place in our plans. What we envisage is a program of development based on the concepts of democratic fair-dealing. . . .

Only by helping the least fortunate of its members to help themselves can the human family achieve the decent, satisfying life that is the right of all people.

Democracy alone can supply the vitalizing force to stir the peoples of the world into triumphant action, not only against their human oppressors, but also against their ancient enemies—hunger, misery, and despair. . . .

[From President Truman's message to Congress, June 24, 1949:]

In order to enable the United States, in cooperation with other countries, to assist the peoples of economically underdeveloped areas to raise their standards of living, I recommend the enactment of legislation to authorize an expanded program of technical assistance for such areas, and an experimental program for encouraging the outflow of private investment beneficial to their economic development. These measures are the essential first steps in an undertaking which will call upon private enterprise and voluntary organizations in the United States, as well as the Government, to take part in a constantly growing effort to improve economic conditions in the less-developed regions of the world.

The grinding poverty and the lack of economic opportunity for many millions of people in the economically underdeveloped parts of Africa, the Near and Far East, and certain regions of Central and South America, constitute one of the greatest challenges of the world today. In spite of their age-old economic and social handicaps, the peoples in these areas have in recent decades been stirred and awakened. The spread of industrial civilization, the growing understanding of modern concepts of government, and the impact of two World Wars have changed their lives and their outlook. They are eager to play a greater part in the community of nations.

All these areas have a common problem. They must create a firm economic base for the democratic aspirations of their citizens. Without such an economic base, they will be unable to meet the expectations which the modern world has aroused in their peoples. If they are frustrated and disappointed, they may turn to false doctrines which hold that the way of progress lies through tyranny. . . .

The major effort in such a program must be local in character; it must be made by the people of the underdeveloped areas themselves. It is essential, however, to the success of their effort that there be help from abroad. In some cases the peoples of these areas will be unable to begin their part of this great enterprise without initial aid from other countries.

The aid that is needed falls roughly into two categories. The first is the technical, scientific, and managerial knowledge necessary to economic development. This category includes not only medical and educational knowledge, and assistance and advice in such basic fields as sanitation, communications, road building and governmental services, but also, and perhaps most important, assistance in the survey of resources and in planning for long-range economic development.

The second category is production goods—machinery and equipment—and financial assistance in the creation of productive enterprises. The under-developed areas need capital for port and harbor development, roads and communications, irrigation and drainage projects, as well as for public utilities and the whole range of extractive, processing, and manufacturing industries. Much of the capital required can be provided by these areas themselves, in spite of their low standards of living. But much must come from abroad.

The two categories of aid are closely related. Technical assistance is necessary to lay the groundwork for productive investment. Investment, in turn, brings with it technical assistance. In general, however, technical surveys of resources and of the possibilities of economic development must precede substantial capital investment. Furthermore, in many of the areas concerned, technical assistance in improving sanitation, communications, or education is required to create conditions in which capital investment can be fruitful.

This country, in recent years, has conducted relatively modest programs of technical cooperation with other countries. . . . Through these various activities we have gained considerable experience in rendering technical assistance to other countries. What is needed now is to expand and integrate these activities and to concentrate them particularly on the economic development of underdeveloped areas.

Much of the aid that is needed can be provided most effectively through the United Nations. . . . In addition to our participation in this work of the United Nations, much of the technical assistance required can be provided directly by the United States to countries needing it. A careful examination of the existing information concerning the under-developed countries shows particular need for technicians and experts with United States training in plant and animal diseases, malaria and typhus control, water supply and sewer systems, metallurgy and mining, and nearly all phases of industry.

It has already been shown that experts in these fields can bring about tremendous improvements. For example, the health of the people of many foreign communities has been greatly improved by the work of United States sanitary engineers in setting up modern water-supply systems. The food supply of many areas has been increased as the result of the advice of United States agricultural experts in the control of animal diseases and the improvement of crops. These are only examples of the wide range of benefits resulting from the careful application of modern techniques to local problems. The benefits which a comprehensive program of expert assistance will make possible can only be revealed by studies and surveys undertaken as a part of the program itself. . . .

All countries concerned with the program should work together to bring about conditions favorable to the flow of private capital. To this end we are negotiating agreements with other countries to protect the American investor from unwarranted or discriminatory treatment under the laws of the country in which he makes his investment. . . .

Many of these conditions of instability in under-developed areas which deter foreign investment are themselves a consequence of the lack of economic development which only foreign investment can cure. Therefore, to wait until stable conditions are assured before encouraging the outflow of capital to under-developed areas would defer the attainment of our objectives indefinitely. It is necessary to take vigorous action now to break out of this vicious circle.

Since the development of underdeveloped economic areas is of major importance in our foreign policy, it is appropriate to use the resources of the Government to accelerate private efforts toward that end. . . .

The enactment of these two legislative proposals, the first pertaining to technical assistance and the second to the encouragement of foreign investment, will constitute a national endorsement of a program of major importance in our efforts for world peace and economic stability. Nevertheless, these measures are only the first steps. We are here embarking on a venture that extends far into the future. We are at the beginning of a rising curve of activity—private, governmental, and international—that will continue for many years to come. It is all the more important, therefore, that we start promptly. . . .

Before the peoples of these areas we hold out the promise of a better future through the democratic way of life. It is vital that we move quickly to bring the meaning of that promise home to them in their daily lives.

Congress settled down to long hearings on the proposed legislation to give effect to Point IV. The atomic bomb set off by the Soviet government in the summer of 1949 undoubtedly helped overcome resistance to the program. At last, in June, 1950, the Act for International Development was passed, with a small allocation of funds to finance the first year of the program. Concurrently, the American government in 1950 made its first substantial pledge of funds for the expanded Technical Assistance Program of the United Nations. It set about at the same time to increase the lending and insurance capacity of the Export-Import Bank. During the same year the countries of the British Commonwealth, led by Great Britain, inaugurated a greatly expanded "Colombo Plan" for Cooperative Economic Development in South and Southeast Asia, including India and Pakistan. In sum, the Western democratic world, led by the United States and the British Commonwealth, during these two years (1949–50) definitely committed themselves to make an effort to assist poor peoples everywhere to better their living conditions, prolong their life, and ease the burden of their work.

During the next decade the United States demonstrated its willingness to open almost the whole lexicon of technical knowledge to the rest of the world. It and other leading industrial countries no longer waited for seekers of information about methods and processes of production to come to them. They began to purvey it on an ever-larger scale through books and articles. They displayed and demonstrated their new devices at fairs. They sought out purchasers of licenses and patent rights, and when the needy countries could not afford to pay, the aiding countries handed these over free or as a charge against the future. They established missions in the industrial and political capitals of the poorer countries to study local needs and wants and the best possible uses of technical knowledge. They responded willingly to requests for experts to give instruction in the new methods. The subsequent experience contains many significant achievements—dimmed by failure of results to match anticipations and realize potentialities. It has also brought a clearer and graver appreciation of the obstacles to the diffusion of technology among the poorer peoples.

When Point IV was first announced, the American government did not intend to provide large sums of capital out of the public treasury—sums comparable to those being given to our associates in Europe under the Marshall Plan. It was conceived that if the technical innovations were of evident value, private capital would be available from both local and foreign sources.

But only sparse amounts of private capital have thus far been ventured in the poorer countries; the only really substantial investments have been in the development of natural resources—especially oil and minerals, for which there was a reliable foreign market. Capital was not attracted into those fields of activity which were prerequisites for increasing industrial productivity. For the prospects of profit have been poor, and government controls and impositions severe, and involvement in local political issues inevitable. Even had private capital been more venturesomely disposed, many poorer countries would have wanted to retain government ownership or control of enterprise in these fields. They did not want foreign private capitalists to have as important a part in their national life as they almost inevitably would have had if engaged in basic branches of production. This reservation has caused them to seek the capital from various national governments and from the multinational agencies such as the International Bank for Reconstruction and Development, the Inter-American Bank, and the United Nations, which, however, has little capital to lend or give. The American government has been impelled to make up for the lack of private capital, domestic and foreign, by making large loans and grants, mounting in recent years to almost $2 billion—for technical aid, economic development, social progress, financial stability. But now American legislation and appropriations are again being reshaped with the intention of inducing or compelling the poorer countries to court private capital more and public treasuries less.

These are some of the sobering lessons that have been learned since the ideal of Point IV was propounded. Probably the wish for the benefits of technology is so strong and commanding that it will prevail more often than not over human and natural deficiencies. The American people and their associates in world affairs will continue to make a great effort to see that they do prevail. Point IV may well be elevated again to its original conception.

William Faulkner
Speech on Acceptance of the Nobel Prize
1950

EDITED BY RICHARD ELLMANN

The award to William Faulkner of the Nobel Prize for Literature in November, 1950, aroused more approval than has been accorded many of these awards. By that year Faulkner had published twenty books, which were widely known in Europe and Asia as well as in the United States. Americans noted that he was the first writer from the South to win the prize and praised his intimate knowledge of his own region.

This famous localism was in danger of being misunderstood. Some of his readers interpreted him too narrowly as a portrayer of a dying culture who recognized only with reluctance and disappointment the encroachments of a new century upon a feudal past. Others took his subject matter, in which lynching, rape, and murder figure prominently, for a rustic variation, in a Mississippi accent, of the conditions which Theodore Dreiser and other naturalists had berated in northern cities.

While Faulkner usually made no complaint when he was described as a southern naturalist or anything else, he did remark on one occasion with a little impatience, "I try to tell the truth of man. The area is incidental. That's just all I know." The other criticism, that he was stiffened in a backward look, devoted to reviewing what was dead, was equally far from the truth, though he waited a long time to say so explicitly.

All his life Faulkner had avoided speeches, and insisted that he not be taken as a man of letters. "I'm just a farmer who likes to tell stories," he once said. Because of his known aversion to making formal pronouncements, there was much interest, when he traveled to Stockholm to receive the prize on December 10, 1950, in what he would say in the speech that custom obliged him to deliver. Faulkner evidently wanted to set right the misinterpretation of his own work as pessimistic. But beyond that, he recognized that, as the first American novelist to receive the prize since the end of World War II, he had a special obligation to take the changed situation of the writer, and of man, into account.

I FEEL that this award was not made to me as a man but to my work—a life's work in the agony and sweat of the human spirit, not for glory [and least of all for profit,] but to make out of the material of the human spirit something which was not there before; so this award is only mine in trust. It will not be hard to find a dedication for the money part of it to commemorate with the purpose and the significance of its origin but I would like to do the same with the acclaim too by using this fine moment as a pinnacle from which I might be listened to by the young man or young woman, already dedicated to the same anguish and sweat, who will some day stand here where I am standing.

Our tragedy today is a general and universal physical fear so long sustained by now that we can even bear it. There are no longer problems of the spirit. There is only the question: When will I be blown up? Because of this, the young man or woman writing today has forgotten the problems of the human heart in conflict with itself which alone can make good writing because only that is worth writing about, worth the agony and the sweat.

He must learn them again, he must teach himself that the basest of all things is to be afraid, and teaching himself that, forget it forever

The speech is reprinted here from the official record of the Nobel Prize ceremonies, Les Prix Nobel en 1950 (Stockholm: Imprimerie Royale, P. A. Norstedt & Söner, 1951), pp. 71–72. Bracketed words, added by the editor, are the significant variations made by Faulkner from the original text. Most of the versions which have appeared in this country include Faulkner's changes made in the manuscript which he supplied his publishers after delivering the address. The Nobel Prize Speech (New York: The Spiral Press, 1951) was the first impression inscribed by Faulkner for his editor. An amended version also appeared in The Faulkner Reader: Selections from the Works of William Faulkner (New York: Random House, 1954). For reference to other versions see, James B. Meriwether, The Literary Career of William Faulkner: A Bibliographical Study (Princeton: Princeton University Library, 1961), p. 49.

leaving no room in his workshop for anything but the old verities and truths of the heart, the old universal truths lacking which any story is ephemeral and doomed—love and honor and pity and pride and compassion and sacrifice. Until he does so, he labors under a curse. He writes not of love but of lust, of defeats in which nobody loses anything of value, of victories without hope and, worst of all, without pity or compassion. His griefs grieve on no universal bones, leaving no scars. He writes not of the heart but of the gland.

Until he relearns these things, he will write as though he stood among and watched the end of man. I do not believe in the end of man. It is easy enough to say that man is immortal simply because he will endure: that when the last ding-dong of doom has clanged and faded from the last worthless rock hanging tideless in the last red and dying evening, that even then there will still be one more sound: that of his puny inexhaustible voice still talking. I believe more than this. I believe man will not merely endure, he will prevail. He is immortal, not because he, alone among creatures, has an inexhaustible voice but because he has a soul, a spirit, capable of compassion and sacrifice and endurance. The poet's, the writer's duty is to write about these things. It is his privilege to help man endure by lifting his heart, by reminding him of courage and honor and hope and pride and compassion and pity [and sacrifice which have been the glory of his past]. The poet's voice need not merely be the record of man, it can be one of the props to help him endure and prevail.

This speech, after having been printed by the Nobel Prize authorities in 1950, went into a succession of reprintings in newspapers, magazines, and pamphlets. Its special strength comes from the fact that a great writer uttered it in response to the threat, then only five years old, of atomic destruction. Faulkner might have argued on rational grounds that the extinction of man was unlikely, but he preferred to assert his position as a creative artist, at once undeceived and unvanquished.

Faulkner derives his authority from the fact that the business of the writer is to bring into being what has never existed before. In so defining his own occupation and character, he gives the lie to the notion that the writer is either a graveyard ghost enthralled by time past, on the one hand, or on the other, a photographer of disrupted living conditions of the present. Although he never says so directly, he regards the writer as a kind of rebel against the inhibiting forces of the external world, who denies the mechanical denier and affirms continued human experience by prolonging its creation in his own fiction. The special quality which Faulkner celebrates in the creative process is compassion, and this quality, which all men share in their degree, will help to bring them to something better.

In his earlier work Faulkner had stressed the importance of simply enduring. He liked to use that verb intransitively, to embody patient persistence, as in the case of the Negroes in The Sound and the Fury. That "they endured" is his highest praise. But in his novel A Fable, published in the year of his Nobel Prize speech and closely related to it in thought, Faulkner said that "man and his folly" will do more than endure; "they will prevail." In Stockholm he reaffirmed, in the characteristic rhythms of his prose, that man's voice was inexhaustible, and added that the creative writer had the specific task of disburdening man of the curse of fear which now seems to immobilize him.

Faulkner's proud assertion, "I do not believe in the end of man," is one of those statements which assume their moral force because the speaker has encompassed all the agony which might have prompted an opposite view. It is this sense of the moral depths out of which the words have been wrung that gives Faulkner's speech its defiant grandeur and capacity of its own for enduring.

The United States Supreme Court
Brown v. Board of Education of Topeka
1954

EDITED BY HARRY W. JONES

The United States Supreme Court decision in the case of Brown v. Board of Education of Topeka was a long time on the way. "All men are created equal," the framers of the Declaration had proclaimed as self-evident truth in 1776, and Lincoln at Gettysburg had reaffirmed this as the distinctive proposition of American national dedication. In 1868, the Fourteenth Amendment had written the proposition plainly into the Constitution of the United States: "nor shall any State . . . deny to any person within its jurisdiction the equal protection of the laws."

On what theory, then, was it maintained until 1954 that racial segregation in the public schools is consistent with the Fourteenth Amendment? The argument in defense of the constitutionality of school segregation proceeded from an 1896 decision, Plessy v. Ferguson (163 U.S. 537), in which the Supreme Court held that a Louisiana statute requiring separate accommodations for white and colored railway passengers was not a denial of the equal protection of the laws. Distinctions based on color are constitutionally permissible, the Court ruled over the passionate dissent of the first Justice Harlan, if the separate accommodations provided for "white" persons and "colored" persons are, in other respects, equal in quality. Over the years, this "separate but equal" doctrine became an accepted gloss on the Fourteenth Amendment and was extended by analogy from railroad accommodations to other facilities and, most importantly, to the public schools.

The erosion away of "separate but equal" began in 1938, when the

Supreme Court held, in Missouri ex rel. Gaines v. Canada (305 U.S. 337), that the equal protection of the laws had been denied to a qualified Negro applicant who had been refused admission to the University of Missouri Law School and had been offered, instead, a money grant sufficient to pay his law-school tuition at some state university outside Missouri. In the fifteen years between the Gaines decision and the argument in Brown v. Board of Education, three other cases, all involving public higher education, were decided by the Supreme Court in favor of the respective Negro applicants. In each instance, however, the stated theory of the decision was that the separate educational facilities provided for Negroes in the state concerned were not genuinely "equal" in dignity and educational quality. The central question remained: is "separate but equal" a contradiction in terms? Can segregated schools and colleges be "equal" in a constitutional sense?

During its 1952–53 term, the Supreme Court heard argument in five separate cases challenging the constitutionality of racial segregation in the public schools of Kansas, South Carolina, Virginia, Delaware, and the District of Columbia. The five cases remained undecided throughout the term, and, on June 8, 1953, they were ordered restored to the Court's docket and assigned for reargument together during the 1953–54 term. The Court's order invited the Attorney General of the United States to take part in the argument and stated five questions that counsel in the cases were requested "to discuss particularly." From the stated questions, it was clear that the Court was now ready to face the issue squarely: Does segregation in the public schools violate the Fourteenth Amendment?

The long-awaited argument began on December 7, 1953, and continued for three days. The constitutional points at issue were argued eloquently and in depth by gifted advocates including, for the South, John W. Davis, acknowledged leader of the Supreme Court bar, and, for the desegregation forces, Thurgood Marshall, then chief counsel of the NAACP (later a judge of the Court of Appeals of the United States and then Solicitor General). Assistant Attorney General J. Lee Rankin appeared for the United States and spoke in general support of the desegregation position. The Attorneys General of southern states defended the constitutionality of the school laws of their states. No case in Supreme Court history was ever presented more exhaustively by the advocates for both sides, or weighed more carefully by the members of the Court.

The three-day argument was concluded on December 9. Tension grew as five months passed without a decision, and the Court approached the end of the 1953–54 term. On Monday, May 17, 1954, the decision at last came down. It was unanimous. For once, there was no dissent, not even a separate concurring opinion. Chief Justice Earl Warren's Brown opinion is precisely what the report declares it to be, "the opinion of the Court." Warren of California, Black of Alabama, Reed of Kentucky, Frankfurter of Massachusetts, Douglas of Connecticut, Jackson of New York, Burton of Ohio, Clark of Texas, and Minton of Indiana—Democrats and Republicans, "liberals" and "conservatives"—agreed that "in the field of public education, the doctrine of 'separate but equal' has no place."

T HESE cases come to us from the States of Kansas, South Carolina, Virginia, and Delaware. They are premised on different facts and different local conditions, but a common legal question justifies their consideration together in this consolidated opinion.

In each of the cases, minors of the Negro race, through their legal representatives, seek the aid of the courts in obtaining admission to the public schools of their community on a nonsegregated basis. In each instance, they had been denied admission to schools attended by white children under laws requiring or permitting segregation according to race. This segregation was alleged to deprive the plaintiffs of the equal protection of the laws under the Fourteenth Amendment. In each of the cases other than the Delaware case, a three-judge federal district court denied relief to the plaintiffs on the so-called "separate but equal" doctrine announced by this Court in *Plessy v. Ferguson*, 163 U.S. 537. Under that doctrine, equality of treatment is accorded when the races are provided substantially equal facilities, even though these facilities be separate. In the Delaware case, the Supreme Court of Delaware adhered to that doctrine, but ordered that the plaintiffs be admitted to the white schools because of their superiority to the Negro schools.

The plaintiffs contend that segregated public schools are not "equal" and cannot be made "equal," and that hence they are deprived of the equal protection of the laws. Because of the obvious importance of the

_____

The decision is reprinted from 347 U.S. 483.

question presented, the Court took jurisdiction. Argument was heard in the 1952 Term, and reargument was heard this Term on certain questions propounded by the Court.

Reargument was largely devoted to the circumstances surrounding the adoption of the Fourteenth Amendment in 1868. It covered exhaustively consideration of the Amendment in Congress, ratification by the states, then existing practices in racial segregation, and the views of proponents and opponents of the Amendment. This discussion and our own investigation convince us that, although these sources cast some light, it is not enough to resolve the problem with which we are faced. At best, they are inconclusive. The most avid proponents of the post-War Amendments undoubtedly intended them to remove all legal distinctions among "all persons born or naturalized in the United States." Their opponents, just as certainly, were antagonistic to both the letter and the spirit of the Amendments and wished them to have the most limited effect. What others in Congress and the state legislatures had in mind cannot be determined with any degree of certainty.

An additional reason for the inconclusive nature of the Amendment's history, with respect to segregated schools, is the status of public education at that time. In the South, the movement toward free common schools, supported by general taxation, had not yet taken hold. Education of white children was largely in the hands of private groups. Education of Negroes was almost non-existent, and practically all of the race were illiterate. In fact, any education of Negroes was forbidden by law in some states. Today, in contrast, many Negroes have achieved outstanding success in the arts and sciences as well as in the business and professional world. It is true that public school education at the time of the Amendment had advanced further in the North, but the effect of the Amendment on Northern States was generally ignored in the congressional debates. Even in the North, the conditions of public education did not approximate those existing today. The curriculum was usually rudimentary; ungraded schools were common in rural areas; the school term was but three months a year in many states; and compulsory school attendance was virtually unknown. As a consequence, it is not surprising that there should be so little in the history of the Fourteenth Amendment relating to its intended effect on public education.

In the first cases in this Court construing the Fourteenth Amendment, decided shortly after its adoption, the Court interpreted it as proscribing all state-imposed discriminations against the Negro race.

The doctrine of "separate but equal" did not make its appearance in this Court until 1896 in the case of *Plessy* v. *Ferguson, supra,* involving not education but transportation. American courts have since labored with the doctrine for over half a century. In this Court, there have been six cases involving the "separate but equal" doctrine in the field of public education. In *Cumming* v. *Board of Education of Richmond County,* 175 U.S. 528, and *Gong Lum* v. *Rice,* 275 U.S. 78, the validity of the doctrine itself was not challenged. In more recent cases, all on the graduate school level, inequality was found in that specific benefits enjoyed by white students were denied to Negro students of the same educational qualifications. *Missouri ex rel. Gaines* v. *Canada,* 305 U.S. 337; *Sipuel* v. *Board of Regents of University of Oklahoma,* 332 U.S. 631; *Sweatt* v. *Painter,* 339 U.S. 629; *McLaurin* v. *Oklahoma State Regents,* 339 U.S. 637. In none of these cases was it necessary to re-examine the doctrine to grant relief to the Negro plaintiff. And in *Sweatt* v. *Painter, supra,* the Court expressly reserved decision on the question whether *Plessy* v. *Ferguson* should be held inapplicable to public education.

In the instant cases, that question is directly presented. Here, unlike *Sweatt* v. *Painter,* there are findings below that the Negro and white schools involved have been equalized, or are being equalized, with respect to buildings, curricula, qualifications and salaries of teachers, and other "tangible" factors. Our decision, therefore, cannot turn on merely a comparison of these tangible factors in the Negro and white schools involved in each of the cases. We must look instead to the effect of segregation itself on public education.

In approaching this problem, we cannot turn the clock back to 1868 when the Amendment was adopted, or even to 1896 when *Plessy* v. *Ferguson* was written. We must consider public education in the light of its full development and its present place in American life throughout the Nation. Only in this way can it be determined if segregation in public schools deprives these plaintiffs of the equal protection of the laws.

Today, education is perhaps the most important function of state and local governments. Compulsory school attendance laws and the great expenditures for education both demonstrate our recognition of the importance of education to our democratic society. It is required in the performance of our most basic public responsibilities, even service in the armed forces. It is the very foundation of good citizenship. Today it is a principal instrument in awakening the child to cultural values, in preparing him for later professional training, and in helping him to adjust normally to his environment. In these days, it is doubtful that any child may reasonably be expected to succeed in life if he is denied the opportunity of an education. Such an opportunity, where the state has undertaken to provide it, is a right which must be made available to all on equal terms.

We come then to the question presented: Does segregation of children in public schools solely on the basis of race, even though the physical facilities and other "tangible" factors may be equal, deprive the children of the minority group of equal educational opportunities? We believe that it does.

In *Sweatt* v. *Painter, supra,* in finding that a segregated law school for Negroes could not provide them equal educational opportunities, this Court relied in large part on "those qualities which are incapable of objective measurement but which make for greatness in a law school." In *McLaurin* v. *Oklahoma State Regents, supra,* the Court, in requiring that a Negro admitted to a white graduate school be treated like all other students, again resorted to intangible considerations: ". . . his ability to study, to engage in discussions and exchange views with other students, and, in general, to learn his profession." Such considerations apply with added force to children in grade and high schools. To separate them from others of similar age and qualifications solely because of their race generates a feeling of inferiority as to their status in the community that may affect their hearts and minds in a way unlikely ever to be undone. The effect of this separation on their educational opportunities was well stated by a finding in the Kansas case by a court which nevertheless felt compelled to rule against the Negro plaintiffs:

Segregation of white and colored children in public schools has a detrimental effect upon the colored children. The impact is greater when it has the sanction of the law; for the policy of separating the races is usually interpreted as denoting the inferiority of the negro group. A sense of inferiority affects the motivation of a child to learn. Segregation with the sanction of law, therefore, has a tendency to [retard] the educational and mental development of negro children and to deprive them of some of the benefits they would receive in a racial[ly] integrated school system.

Whatever may have been the extent of psychological knowledge at the time of *Plessy* v. *Ferguson,* this finding is amply supported by modern authority. Any language in *Plessy* v. *Ferguson* contrary to this finding is rejected.

907

We conclude that in the field of public education the doctrine of "separate but equal" has no place. Separate educational facilities are inherently unequal. Therefore, we hold that the plaintiffs and others similarly situated for whom the actions have been brought are, by reason of the segregation complained of, deprived of the equal protection of the laws guaranteed by the Fourteenth Amendment. This disposition makes unnecessary any discussion whether such segregation also violates the Due Process Clause of the Fourteenth Amendment.

Because these are class actions, because of the wide applicability of this decision, and because of the great variety of local conditions, the formulation of decrees in these cases presents problems of considerable complexity. On reargument, the consideration of appropriate relief was necessarily subordinated to the primary question—the constitutionality of segregation in public education. We have now announced that such segregation is a denial of the equal protection of the laws. In order that we may have the full assistance of the parties in formulating decrees, the cases will be restored to the docket, and the parties are requested to present further argument on Questions 4 and 5 previously propounded by the Court for the reargument this Term. The Attorney General of the United States is again invited to participate. The Attorneys General of the states requiring or permitting segregation in public education will also be permitted to appear as *amici curiae* upon request to do so by September 15, 1954, and submission of briefs by October 1, 1954.

On May 17, 1954, seventeen southern and border states maintained segregated elementary and secondary schools. In four other states, as in Kansas, school segregation was permitted to school districts on a local-option basis. How were the offending states to be brought into compliance with the constitutional principle established in Brown v. Board of Education?

Questions 4 and 5, referred to in the last paragraph of the Brown opinion, concerned the ways and means by which the Court's substantive decision might be implemented. On May 31, 1955, a year after its original Brown ruling, the Supreme Court announced a second unanimous decision, this one directed to the manner in which "relief is to be afforded" to the plaintiffs in the several cases. The Court took approving notice of the progress that had already occurred in Kansas, Delaware, and several other states, and in the District of Columbia, where steps to end school segregation were taken on the day immediately following the decision in the Brown case and its District of Columbia counterpart, Bolling v. Sharpe (347 U.S. 497 [1954]). No such progress had taken place in Virginia and South Carolina, however, and the cases from these two states were remanded to the District Courts, with instructions to enter such decrees as might be required to assure that the plaintiff Negro children would be admitted to schools, on a racially nondiscriminatory basis, "with all deliberate speed."

Has school desegregation gone forward "with all deliberate speed" in the southern and border states where racially separate public schools were required by local law at the time of the Brown decisions? By 1965, ten years after the Supreme Court's implementing decision in the Brown cases, approximately one out of nine of the three million Negro children who live in these seventeen states were attending school with white children. This was measurable progress, although hardly "speed" even by the most deliberate of standards, but almost all of the gain had been registered in the border states. Whereas, by 1965, 60 per cent of border-state Negro children were in biracial schools, only 2 per cent of the Negro children were attending biracial schools in the nine southern (once Confederate) states. It was evident, however, that the next decade would see a stepping-up of progress toward school desegregation, partly because of changed social attitudes, partly in response to federal court orders requiring desegregation of specific school districts, and partly under the influence of federal legislation providing for the withholding of grants in aid of education from state educational systems that continued to maintain segregation in their schools.

Racial segregation in the schools is not, of course, a phenomenon unique to the South; it exists, factually if not formally, in the North, Midwest, and West as well. Since children are normally assigned to schools nearest their homes, racial discrimination in housing, particularly in urban areas, is inevitably accompanied by racial segregation in the schools. Private elementary and secondary schools, which have increased greatly since World War II, contribute to school segregation in the North, although some of these schools, most notably the Roman Catholic parochial schools, have made determined efforts to achieve substantial integration. Brown v. Board of Education was but the first step toward the desegregation of American education. Difficult problems of racial discrimination in housing and employment will have to be solved before genuinely integrated schools become a fact of American life.

Brown v. Board of Education was a school case, and conceivably its holding might have been limited by later Supreme Court rulings to situations involving racial segregation in schools and colleges. The decision, however, became a landmark case in American constitutional law, and its influence as a judicial precedent was extended far beyond the area of segregation in the schools. In successive decisions since 1955, the Supreme Court and other federal courts have drawn on the analogy of the Brown decision to invalidate many other forms of state-enforced racial segregation, at public beaches and bathhouses, on municipal golf courses, on local buses, and in public parks and theaters. It is clear enough from the consistent trend of the Court's decisions that the "separate but equal" doctrine retains no vitality in any area of regulation of public service.

One limitation should be noted on the future reach of the Brown precedent. The "equal protection" clause of the Fourteenth Amendment applies, in terms, only to "State" action. Racially discriminatory conduct of individual private citizens is not within the ban of the Fourteenth Amendment unless sponsored or in some way supported by state or local public authority. But such individual discriminatory conduct can be made unlawful by specific act of Congress, and this is the great significance of the Civil Rights Act of 1964. In the long-range strategy of the civil rights movement, legislation and political action are fully as important as constitutional litigation. The Supreme Court, very promptly and by unanimous vote, upheld the validity of the challenged "public accommodations" provisions of the Civil Rights Act of 1964, and there appears to be no serious question concerning the constitutionality of the Voting Rights Act, passed by Congress in 1965. Both in its direct effect and in its indirect influence as the first great breakthrough in the campaign for racial equality, Brown v. Board of Education has become one of the three or four leading cases in American constitutional history.

However far-reaching the influence of Brown v. Board of Education may be for constitutional jurisprudence generally, the crucial problem remains that of securing effective desegregation of the public schools. The intransigent refusal of southern political leaders to give even grudging assent to the principle of equality declared in the school cases created a grave crisis in American constitutional morality. Compulsory school-attendance laws were suspended in several southern states, provisions requiring the maintenance of free public schools were deleted from state constitutions, and state legislatures enacted a variety of schemes designed to evade the constitutional requirement that their schools be desegregated. Such legalistic evasions as these were only part of the pattern of resistance. Segregationist spokesmen characterized the Brown decision as "usurpation" and "mere fiat" and flatly denied the Supreme Court's constitutional authority to decide the case as it did. Notions of "nullification" and "interposition" were withdrawn from the museum of ancient constitutional curiosities and heard again. Outright defiance of specific federal court decrees occurred, as at Little Rock in 1958 and at Oxford, Mississippi, in 1962, and two successive Presidents of the United States had to make the painful decision to use troops to enforce the orders of the federal courts.

Will enforced desegregation be worth its heavy cost in strife and disaffection? The issue must be seen in historical perspective. For the historic American injustice to the Negro, the United States has already suffered the penance of an appalling civil war. The account is far from settled. The nation is paying still in racial estrangement, in the flight of the Negro from the South to northern industrial cities, and in the increasing but understandable bitterness with which Negro intellectuals of the younger generation tend to appraise the declared aspirations of American society. Conceivably it is too late, even now, to achieve a genuine fellowship of reconciliation among Americans of various shades of pigmentation. But, at least, Justice Harlan's protest in Plessy v. Ferguson has become a principle of the American legal order: "Our constitution is color-blind and neither knows nor tolerates classes among citizens." In a free and responsible society, the maintenance of just law can exert a powerful force for public education. If our Constitution is color-blind, perhaps there is reason to hope that, some day, American culture and American society will be color-blind, too.

John F. Kennedy
Inaugural Address
1961

EDITED BY JAMES MACGREGOR BURNS

President-elect John F. Kennedy wrote most of his Inaugural Address early in January, 1961, at his father's home in Palm Beach, Florida. He wrote it in the open air, under a warm sun, on yellow legal-sized paper, with draft material spread out on a low glass coffee table beside him. The speech was the product of long and extensive labors by a large number of public men. Assembling of materials had begun the previous November under the direction of Kennedy's aide, Theodore Sorensen. Ideas, paragraphs, even whole drafts came from Adlai Stevenson, Walter Lippmann, Kenneth Galbraith, Chester Bowles, Billy Graham, and others. Kennedy had asked Sorensen to study all past inaugural addresses, especially Lincoln's, to see what could be learned from them. Kennedy told his aide that he wanted a short, eloquent, nonpartisan, optimistic speech that would focus on foreign policy and would shun cold-war stereotypes on the one hand and, on the other, "weasel words" that could be mistaken for weakness by the Communists. Many of the most evocative phrases, such as the passing of the torch to a new generation of Americans, came from earlier campaign talks. The most quoted sentence —"Ask not what you can do . . ."—had a much earlier origin: in a passage from Rousseau that Kennedy had jotted down in 1945, and in his nomination acceptance speech in Los Angeles in 1960. Concerned that people would expect of him a Rooseveltian "Hundred Days" of miracles, he instructed Sorensen: "Let's put in that this won't all be finished in a

*hundred days or a thousand." The concept of the "thousand days" had
been contributed early in the presidential campaign by a political
scientist who knew of Kennedy's distaste for the F.D.R. parallel and who
computed that in four years there would be about one thousand working
days. Kennedy continued to work on his address on his flight to
Washington three days before the Inaugural, and at his house in
Georgetown, where he kept a copy by his side at odd moments so that he
could continue to rework it. He was changing words as late as the
morning of Inaugural Day.*

VICE PRESIDENT JOHNSON, MR. SPEAKER, MR. CHIEF JUSTICE,
PRESIDENT EISENHOWER, VICE PRESIDENT NIXON, PRESIDENT
TRUMAN, REVEREND CLERGY, FELLOW CITIZENS:

WE OBSERVE today not a victory of a party but a celebration of
freedom—symbolizing an end as well as a beginning—signi-
fying renewal as well as change. For I have sworn before you
and Almighty God the same solemn oath our forebears prescribed nearly
a century and three quarters ago.

The world is very different now. For man holds in his mortal hands
the power to abolish all forms of human poverty and all forms of human
life. And yet the same revolutionary beliefs for which our forebears
fought are still at issue around the globe—the belief that the rights of
man come not from the generosity of the state but from the hand of
God.

We dare not forget today that we are the heirs of that first revolution.
Let the word go forth from this time and place, to friend and foe alike,
that the torch has been passed to a new generation of Americans—born
in this century, tempered by war, disciplined by a hard and bitter peace,
proud of our ancient heritage—and unwilling to witness or permit the
slow undoing of those human rights to which this Nation has always
been committed, and to which we are committed today at home and
around the world.

Let every nation know, whether it wishes us well or ill, that we shall

---

The address is reprinted here as it appeared in the *Congressional Record, Proceedings and Debates of the 87th Congress, 1st Session*, Vol. 107, Part 1 (Washington, D.C.: Government Printing Office, 1961), January 20, 1961, pp. 1012–13.

pay any price, bear any burden, meet any hardship, support any friend, oppose any foe to assure the survival and success of liberty.

This much we pledge—and more.

To those old allies whose cultural and spiritual origins we share, we pledge the loyalty of faithful friends. United, there is little we cannot do in a host of cooperative ventures. Divided, there is little we can do—for we dare not meet a powerful challenge at odds and split asunder.

To those new states whom we welcome to the ranks of the free, we pledge our word that one form of colonial control shall not have passed away merely to be replaced by a far more iron tyranny. We shall not always expect to find them supporting our view. But we shall always hope to find them strongly supporting their own freedom—and to remember that, in the past, those who foolishly sought power by riding the back of the tiger ended up inside.

To those peoples in the huts and villages of half the globe struggling to break the bonds of mass misery, we pledge our best efforts to help them help themselves, for whatever period is required—not because the Communists may be doing it, not because we seek their votes, but because it is right. If a free society cannot help the many who are poor, it cannot save the few who are rich.

To our sister republics south of our border, we offer a special pledge— to convert our good words into good deeds—in a new alliance for progress—to assist free men and free governments in casting off the chains of poverty. But this peaceful revolution of hope cannot become the prey of hostile powers. Let all our neighbors know that we shall join with them to oppose aggression or subversion anywhere in the Americas. And let every other power know that this hemisphere intends to remain the master of its own house.

To that world assembly of sovereign states, the United Nations, our last best hope in an age where the instruments of war have far outpaced the instruments of peace, we renew our pledge of support—to prevent it from becoming merely a forum for invective—to strengthen its shield of the new and the weak—and to enlarge the area in which its writ may run.

Finally, to those nations who would make themselves our adversary, we offer not a pledge but a request: that both sides begin anew the quest for peace, before the dark powers of destruction unleashed by science engulf all humanity in planned or accidental self-destruction.

We dare not tempt them with weakness. For only when our arms are sufficient beyond doubt can we be certain beyond doubt that they will never be employed.

But neither can two great and powerful groups of nations take comfort from our present course—both sides overburdened by the cost of modern weapons, both rightly alarmed by the steady spread of the deadly atom, yet both racing to alter that uncertain balance of terror that stays the hand of mankind's final war.

So let us begin anew—remembering on both sides that civility is not a sign of weakness, and sincerity is always subject to proof. Let us never negotiate out of fear. But let us never fear to negotiate.

Let both sides explore what problems unite us instead of belaboring those problems which divide us. Let both sides, for the first time, formulate serious and precise proposals for the inspection and control of arms—and bring the absolute power to destroy other nations under the absolute control of all nations.

Let both sides seek to invoke the wonders of science instead of its terrors. Together let us explore the stars, conquer the deserts, eradicate disease, tap the ocean depths and encourage the arts and commerce.

Let both sides unite to heed in all corners of the earth the command of Isaiah—to "undo the heavy burdens and to let the oppressed go free."

And if a beach-head of cooperation may push back the jungle of suspicion, let both sides join in a new endeavor; not a new balance of power, but a new world of law, where the strong are just and the weak secure and the peace preserved.

All this will not be finished in the first one hundred days. Nor will it be finished in the first one thousand days, nor in the life of this Administration, nor even perhaps in our lifetime on this planet. But let us begin.

In your hands, my fellow citizens, more than mine, will rest the final success or failure of our course. Since this country was founded, each generation of Americans has been summoned to give testimony to its national loyalty. The graves of young Americans who answered the call to service surround the globe.

Now the trumpet summons us again—not as a call to bear arms, though arms we need—not as a call to battle, though embattled we are —but a call to bear the burden of a long twilight struggle, year in and year out, "rejoicing in hope, patient in tribulation"—a struggle against the common enemies of man: tyranny, poverty, disease and war itself.

Can we forge against these enemies a grand and global alliance, North and South, East and West, that can assure a more fruitful life for all mankind? Will you join in that historic effort?

In the long history of the world, only a few generations have been granted the role of defending freedom in its hour of maximum danger. I do not shrink from this responsibility—I welcome it. I do not believe that any of us would exchange places with any other people or any other generation. The energy, the faith, the devotion which we bring to this endeavor will light our country and all who serve it—and the glow from that fire can truly light the world.

And so, my fellow Americans: Ask not what your country can do for you—ask what you can do for your country.

My fellow citizens of the world: Ask not what America will do for you, but what together we can do for the freedom of man.

Finally, whether you are citizens of America or citizens of the world, ask of us here the same high standards of strength and sacrifice which we ask of you. With a good conscience our only sure reward, with history the final judge of our deeds, let us go forth to lead the land we love, asking His blessing and His help, but knowing that here on earth God's work must truly be our own.

Kennedy's Inaugural Address kindled a tremendous immediate response, set the tone and style of the whole Administration to come, and presaged both the triumph and the tragedy of the thirty-four months ahead. The speech immensely moved the throng shivering in the cold of the Capitol Plaza, the millions watching television, and countless Americans and foreigners huddled around radios overseas. The President's summons to new beginnings, to sustained effort, to higher standards of strength and sacrifice, to a long twilight struggle was cited again and again in the conduct of affairs in Washington. And in the end his Administration was just a beginning; he was given only a thousand days to do his work, if we count—as we must—every day as a working day.

The address reflected Kennedy's main concern with foreign affairs and forecast some of his memorable foreign policies. He urged a host of cooperative ventures with our older allies—and later he issued a new "Declaration of Interdependence" and gained passage of a major trade-expansion bill. He spoke to the new states and to the people in the huts and villages—and followed up with expanded political and economic efforts in Asia and Africa and with a Peace Corps. He made a special pledge to our sister republics to the South—and soon proclaimed the Alliance for Progress. He called the United Nations our last best hope in an age of unrest—and gave to it the most beloved leader of his party. He warned of the dangers of arms escalation in itself—and took the potential momentous "first step" in proposing the partial nuclear test ban treaty and gaining its approval by the Senate.

Kennedy indicated almost nothing about domestic policy in his Inaugural, and this too was prophetic. The exception was his reference to "those human rights to which this nation has always been committed, and to which we are committed today at home and around the world." Nothing in his speech forecast his efforts to obtain expanded social welfare, medicare, general federal aid to education, and the other natural extensions of the New Deal and Fair Deal. Was this an early hint that while he was long and deeply committed in campaign speeches and party promises to a New Frontier at home as well as abroad, he would give priority to his foreign-policy goals when he felt he had to make a choice? Later he deferred even civil-rights commitments until he won passage of the Trade Expansion Act.

What will be the "afterlife" of John Kennedy's Inaugural Address? One can speculate that its main importance in the long run may be much like that of the Kennedy Administration as a whole—more a matter of tone and style than of substance. This is not to underestimate the concrete achievements of the Kennedy Administration, which were considerable, especially in light of the roadblocks to action in Congress and in some of the agencies. But Kennedy's "radical rhetoric," as compared to his moderately liberal domestic proposals and fairly conservative fiscal policies, had in itself a profound influence in focusing men's hopes and in raising—perhaps inflating—their expectations. In the long run the most significant sentence might be his appeal to explore the stars, conquer the deserts, eradicate disease, tap the ocean depths and encourage the arts and commerce. In short, the speech, like Franklin Roosevelt's Inaugural, was in itself a decisive political act that had immense possibilities for influencing later politicians and publics. Especially in the more comfortable days of the future, when people will seem torpid and their affairs seem to be drifting, Presidents will evoke memories of the vibrant young leader who summoned his country and his world to a long twilight struggle against the common enemies of man.

Lyndon B. Johnson
Address on Voting Rights
1965

EDITED BY OSCAR HANDLIN

Six years of inaction after the school desegregation decision of 1954 touched off the Negro revolution. The awareness that normal political procedures would not, in the South, secure an early redress of ancient grievances drew the disadvantaged colored people into direct action—sit-ins, boycotts, and demonstrations—that challenged the legitimacy of government itself. The movement gained rapid momentum after 1960 and brought measurable results in some parts of the nation. Above all, these dramatic incidents were eloquent appeals to the conscience of Americans, committed to the ideal of equality, even if only in the abstract.

Nevertheless, the hard-core resistance in the southern states remained intransigent. By the end of 1964 there were few signs that either Alabama or Mississippi was about to alter its attitudes toward race. There were ominous indications that this defiance might actually take more overt, forceful forms. The 87 per cent of the vote that Barry Goldwater gained in Mississippi was a measure of the distance that separated that state from the rest of the nation.

In the 1950's, neither John F. Kennedy nor Lyndon B. Johnson had stood in the forefront of the civil rights struggle. By 1963, both were aware of the issues at stake. When President Kennedy that year gave official recognition to the March on Washington, he clearly affirmed the commitment of the federal government to the cause of Negro equality.

President Johnson, for whom principle and necessity blended, assumed the burden with the office. Altogether apart from his need to earn the loyalty of Negro voters in the northern cities, he viewed equality as a goal that conformed to his emerging concept of the Great Society.

By 1964, the right to the ballot had become central. That year only about 7½ per cent of the southerners registered as voters were Negro, although Negroes constituted 20 per cent of the voting-age population. Disenfranchisement perpetuated demagoguery in the politics of the Deep South and left control of the rural counties to local court-house groups callous toward the welfare of minorities and willing to tolerate violence, even murder, directed against dissidents. The refusal of juries to convict whites guilty of crimes against Negroes outraged Americans everywhere.

In these circumstances, Negroes unwilling to acquiesce in the loss of their rights had to turn to nonpolitical, extralegal means. The hard line of the Mississippi Freedom Democratic Party in the Democratic Convention of 1964 showed the danger of further drifting. Only if the Negroes were assured the full rights of citizenship could they be persuaded to act as citizens. Lyndon Johnson proposed to provide such assurance, in part, by means of a voting-rights bill which he presented to a joint session of Congress in a speech delivered on March 15, 1965. The concept of federal intervention to protect civil rights was not novel; it had roots in the Fifteenth Amendment. President Johnson's address was fresh not in its ideas, but in its ringing determination to make those ideas effective.

MR. SPEAKER, MR. PRESIDENT, MEMBERS OF THE CONGRESS:

I SPEAK tonight for the dignity of man and the destiny of democracy. I urge every member of both parties, Americans of all religions and of all colors, from every section of this country, to join me in that cause.

At times history and fate meet at a single time in a single place to shape a turning point in man's unending search for freedom. So it was at

---

The address is reprinted here as it appeared in the *Congressional Record, Proceedings and Debates of the 89th Congress, 1st Session,* Vol. 111, No. 47 (Washington, D.C.: Government Printing Office, 1965), March 15, 1965, pp. 4924–26.

Lexington and Concord. So it was a century ago at Appomattox. So it was last week in Selma, Alabama.

There, long-suffering men and women peacefully protested the denial of their rights as Americans. Many were brutally assaulted. One good man, a man of God, was killed.

There is no cause for pride in what has happened in Selma. There is no cause for self-satisfaction in the long denial of equal rights of millions of Americans.

But there is cause for hope and for faith in our democracy in what is happening here tonight.

For the cries of pain and the hymns and protests of oppressed people, have summoned into convocation all the majesty of this great government of the greatest nation on earth.

Our mission is at once the oldest and the most basic of this country: to right wrong, to do justice, to serve man.

In our time we have come to live with the moments of great crisis. Our lives have been marked with debate about great issues, issues of war and peace, issues of prosperity and depression. But rarely in any time does an issue lay bare the secret heart of America itself. Rarely are we met with a challenge, not to our growth or abundance, or our welfare or our security, but rather to the values and the purposes and the meaning of our beloved nation.

The issue of equal rights for American Negroes is such an issue. And should we defeat every enemy, and should we double our wealth and conquer the stars and still be unequal to this issue, then we will have failed as a people and as a nation.

For with a country as with a person, "What is a man profited, if he shall gain the whole world, and lose his own soul?"

There is no Negro problem. There is no Southern problem. There is no Northern problem. There is only an American problem. And we are met here tonight as Americans, not as Democrats or Republicans, we are met here as Americans to solve that problem.

This was the first nation in the history of the world to be founded with a purpose. The great phrases of that purpose still sound in every American heart, North and South: "All men are created equal"—"government by consent of the governed"—"give me liberty or give me death." Those are not just clever words. Those are not just empty theories. In their name Americans have fought and died for two centuries, and tonight around the world they stand there as guardians of our liberty, risking their lives.

Those words are a promise to every citizen that he shall share in the dignity of man. This dignity cannot be found in a man's possessions. It cannot be found in his power or in his position. It really rests on his right to be treated as a man equal in opportunity to all others. It says that he shall share in freedom, he shall choose his leaders, educate his children, provide for his family according to his ability and his merits as a human being.

To apply any other test—to deny a man his hopes because of his color or race, or his religion, or the place of his birth—is not only to do injustice, it is to deny America and to dishonor the dead who gave their lives for American freedom.

Our fathers believed that if this noble view of the rights of man was to flourish, it must be rooted in democracy. The most basic right of all was the right to choose your own leaders. The history of this country in large measure is the history of expansion of that right to all of our people.

Many of the issues of civil rights are very complex and most difficult. But about this there can and should be no argument. Every American citizen must have an equal right to vote. There is no reason which can excuse the denial of that right. There is no duty which weighs more heavily on us than the duty we have to ensure that right.

Yet the harsh fact is that in many places in this country men and women are kept from voting simply because they are Negroes.

Every device of which human ingenuity is capable has been used to deny this right. The Negro citizen may go to register only to be told that the day is wrong, or the hour is late, or the official in charge is absent. And if he persists and if he manages to present himself to the registrar, he may be disqualified because he did not spell out his middle name or because he abbreviated a word on the application. And if he manages to fill out an application he is given a test. The registrar is the sole judge of whether he passes this test. He may be asked to recite the entire constitution, or explain the most complex provisions of state laws. And even a college degree cannot be used to prove that he can read and write.

For the fact is that the only way to pass these barriers is to show a white skin.

Experience has clearly shown that the existing process of law cannot overcome systematic and ingenious discrimination. No law that we now have on the books—and I have helped to put three of them there—can ensure the right to vote when local officials are determined to deny it.

In such a case our duty must be clear to all of us. The Constitution says that no person shall be kept from voting because of his race or his color. We have all sworn an oath before God to support and to defend that Constitution. We must now act in obedience to that oath.

Wednesday I will send to Congress a law designed to eliminate illegal barriers to the right to vote.

The broad principle of that bill will be in the hands of the Democratic and Republican leaders tomorrow. After they have reviewed it, it will come here formally as a bill. I am grateful for this opportunity to come here tonight at the invitation of the leadership to reason with my friends, to give them my views and to visit with my former colleagues.

I have had prepared a more comprehensive analysis of the legislation which I have intended to transmit to the clerks tomorrow, but which I will submit to the clerks tonight; but I want to really discuss with you now briefly the main proposals of this legislation.

This bill will strike down restrictions to voting in all elections— Federal, State, and local—which have been used to deny Negroes the right to vote.

This bill will establish a simple, uniform standard which cannot be used however ingenious the effort to flout our Constitution.

It will provide for citizens to be registered by officials of the United States government, if the state officials refuse to register them.

It will eliminate tedious, unnecessary lawsuits which delay the right to vote.

Finally, this legislation will ensure that properly registered individuals are not prohibited from voting.

I will welcome the suggestions from all of the members of Congress. I have no doubt that I will get some on ways and means to strengthen this law and to make it effective. But experience has plainly shown that this is the only path to carry out the command of the Constitution.

To those who seek to avoid action by their national government in their own communities, who want to and who seek to maintain purely local control over elections, the answer is simple.

Open your polling places to all your people.

Allow men and women to register and vote whatever the color of their skin.

Extend the rights of citizenship to every citizen of this land.

There is no constitutional issue here. The command of the Constitution is plain.

There is no moral issue. It is wrong to deny any of your fellow Americans the right to vote in this country.

There is no issue of states rights or national rights. There is only the struggle for human rights.

I have not the slightest doubt what will be your answer.

But the last time a President sent a civil rights bill to the Congress it contained a provision to protect voting rights in Federal elections. That civil rights bill was passed after eight long months of debate. And when that bill came to my desk from the Congress for my signature, the heart of the voting provision had been eliminated.

This time, on this issue, there must be no delay, or no hesitation or no compromise with our purpose.

We cannot, we must not refuse to protect the right of every American to vote in every election that he may desire to participate in. And we ought not, we must not wait another eight months before we get a bill. We have already waited a hundred years and more and the time for waiting is gone.

So I ask you to join me in working long hours, nights, and weekends if necessary, to pass this bill. And I don't make that request lightly. Far from the window where I sit with the problems of our country, I recognize that from outside this chamber is the outraged conscience of a nation, the grave concern of many nations and the harsh judgment of history on our acts.

But even if we pass this bill, the battle will not be over. What happened in Selma is part of a far larger movement which reaches into every section and state of America. It is the effort of American Negroes to secure for themselves the full blessings of American life.

Their cause must be our cause too. Because it is not just Negroes, but really it is all of us, who must overcome the crippling legacy of bigotry and injustice. And we shall overcome.

As a man whose roots go deeply into Southern soil I know how agonizing racial feelings are. I know how difficult it is to reshape the attitudes and the structure of our society.

But a century has passed, more than a hundred years, since the Negro was freed. And he is not fully free tonight.

It was more than a hundred years ago that Abraham Lincoln, the great President of the Northern party, signed the Emancipation Proclamation, but emancipation is a proclamation and not a fact.

A century has passed, more than a hundred years since equality was promised. And yet the Negro is not equal.

A century has passed since the day of promise. And the promise is unkept.

The time of justice has now come. I tell you that I believe sincerely that no force can hold it back. It is right in the eyes of man and God that it should come. And when it does, I think that day will brighten the lives of every American.

For Negroes are not the only victims. How many white children have gone uneducated, how many white families have lived in stark poverty, how many white lives have been scarred by fear because we wasted our energy and our substance to maintain the barriers of hatred and terror.

So I say to all of you here and to all in the nation tonight, that those who appeal to you to hold on to the past do so at the cost of denying you your future.

This great, rich, restless country can offer opportunity and education and hope to all—all black and white, all North and South, sharecropper, and city dweller. These are the enemies—poverty, ignorance, disease. They are enemies, not our fellow man, not our neighbor, and these enemies too, poverty, disease and ignorance, we shall overcome.

Now let none of us in any section look with prideful righteousness on the troubles in another section or the problems of our neighbors. There is really no part of America where the promise of equality has been fully kept. In Buffalo as well as in Birmingham, in Philadelphia as well as in Selma, Americans are struggling for the fruits of freedom.

This is one nation. What happens in Selma or in Cincinnati is a matter of legitimate concern to every American. But let each of us look within our own hearts and our own communities, and let each of us put our shoulder to the wheel to root out injustice wherever it exists.

As we meet here in this peaceful historic chamber tonight, men from the South, some of whom were at Iwo Jima, men from the North who have carried Old Glory to far corners of the world and brought it back without a stain on it, men from the East and West are all fighting together without regard to religion, or color, or region, in Vietnam, men from every region fought for us across the world twenty years ago. And now in these common dangers and these common sacrifices the South made its contribution of honor and gallantry no less than any other region of the great Republic. In some instances, a great many of them more. And I have not the slightest doubt that good men from everywhere in this country, from the Great Lakes to the Gulf of Mexico, from the Golden Gate to the harbors along the Atlantic, will rally now together in this cause to vindicate the freedom of all Americans. For all of us owe this duty; and I believe all of us will respond to it.

Your President makes that request of every American.

The real hero of this struggle is the American Negro. His actions and protests, his courage to risk safety and even to risk his life, have awakened the conscience of this nation. His demonstrations have been designed to call attention to injustice, designed to provoke change, designed to stir reform. He has called upon us to make good the promise of America. And who among us can say that we would have made the same progress were it not for his persistent bravery, and his faith in American democracy.

For at the real heart of battle for equality is a deep seated belief in the democratic process. Equality depends not on the force of arms or tear gas but depends upon the force of moral right—not on recourse to violence but on respect for law and order.

There have been many pressures upon your President and there will be others as the days come and go, but I pledge you tonight that we intend to fight this battle where it should be fought, in the courts, and in the Congress, and in the hearts of men.

We must preserve the right of free speech and the right of free assembly. But the right of free speech does not carry with it as has been said, the right to holler fire in a crowded theater. We must preserve the right to free assembly but free assembly does not carry with it the right to block public thoroughfares to traffic.

We do have a right to protest, and a right to march under conditions that do not infringe the Constitutional rights of our neighbors. I intend to protect all those rights as long as I am permitted to serve in this Office.

We will guard against violence, knowing it strikes from our hands the very weapons with which we seek progress—obedience to law, and belief in American values.

In Selma as elsewhere we seek and pray for peace. We seek order. We seek unity. But we will not accept the peace of stifled rights, or the order imposed by fear, or the unity that stifles protest. For peace cannot be purchased at the cost of liberty.

In Selma tonight—and we had a good day there—as in every city, we are working for just and peaceful settlement. We must all remember that after this speech I am making tonight, after the police and the FBI and the marshals have all gone, and after you have promptly passed this bill, the people of Selma and the other cities of the nation must still live and work together. And when the attention of the nation has gone elsewhere they must try to heal the wounds and to build a new community. This cannot be easily done on a battleground of violence as the history of the South itself shows. It is in recognition of this that men of both races have shown such an outstandingly impressive responsibility in recent days, last Tuesday, again today.

The bill that I am presenting to you will be known as a civil rights bill. But, in a larger sense, most of the program I am recommending is a civil right. Its object is to open the city of hope to all people of all races, because all Americans just must have the right to vote. And we are going to give them that right.

All Americans must have the privileges of citizenship regardless of race. And they are going to have those privileges of citizenship regardless of race.

But I would like to caution you and remind you that to exercise these privileges takes much more than just legal right. It requires a trained mind and a healthy body. It requires a decent home, and the chance to find a job, and the opportunity to escape from the clutches of poverty.

Of course people cannot contribute to the nation if they are never taught to read or write, if their bodies are stunted from hunger, if their sickness goes untended, if their life is spent in hopeless poverty just drawing a welfare check.

So we want to open the gates to opportunity. But we are also going to give all our people, black and white, the help that they need to walk through those gates.

My first job after college was as a teacher in Cotulla, Texas, in a small Mexican-American school. Few of them could speak English and I couldn't speak much Spanish. My students were poor and they often came to class without breakfast, hungry, and they knew even in their youth that pain of prejudice. They never seemed to know why people disliked them. But they knew it was so. Because I saw it in their eyes. I often walked home late in the afternoon after the classes were finished, wishing there was more that I could do. But all I knew was to teach them the little that I knew, hoping that it might help them against the hardships that lay ahead.

Somehow you never forget what poverty and hatred can do when you see its scars on the hopeful face of a young child.

I never thought then in 1928 that I would be standing here in 1965. It never even occurred to me in my fondest dreams that I might have the chance to help the sons and daughters of those students and to help people like them all over this country. But now I do have that chance and I let you in on a secret, I mean to use it. And I hope that you will use it with me.

This is the richest and most powerful country which ever occupied this globe. The might of past empires is little compared to ours.

But I do not want to be the President who built empires, or sought grandeur, or extended dominion. I want to be the President who educated young children to the wonders of their world. I want to be the President who helped to feed the hungry and to prepare them to be taxpayers instead of taxeaters. I want to be the President who helped the poor to find their own way and who protected the right of every citizen to vote in every election. I want to be the President who helped to end hatred among his fellow men and who prompted love among the people of all races and all regions and all parties. I want to be the President who helped to end war among the brothers of this earth.

And so at the request of your beloved Speaker and Senator from Montana, the Majority Leader, the Senator from Illinois, the Minority Leader, Mr. McCulloch and other leaders of both parties, I came here tonight not as President Roosevelt came down one time in person to veto a bonus bill, not as President Truman came down one time to urge the passage of a railroad bill, but I came down here to ask you to share this task with me and to share it with the people that we both work for. I want this to be the Congress, Republicans and Democrats alike, which did all those things for all these people.

Beyond this great chamber, out yonder, the fifty states are the people we serve. Who can tell what deep and unspoken hopes are in their hearts tonight as they sit there and listen. We all can guess, from our own lives, how difficult they often find their own pursuit of happiness. How many problems each little family has. They look most of all to themselves for their futures. But I think that they also look to each of us.

927

Above the pyramid on the great seal of the United States it says—in Latin—"God has favored our undertaking."

God will not favor everything that we do. It is rather our duty to divine His will. But I cannot help believing that He truly understands and that He really favors the undertaking that we begin here tonight.

President Johnson's call for action to "overcome the crippling legacy of bigotry and injustice" mobilized the means for enacting the most drastic voting-rights legislation since Reconstruction. Events outside Washington emphasized the urgency of his appeal. A week after he spoke, the Selma march drew together representatives of every sector of American opinion; and a few days later, the murder of one of the marchers showed the danger of the Alabama situation. The prominence of the clergy in the Selma demonstration exerted a particularly powerful impact on opinion. Vigorous expressions of support from throughout the country sustained the pressure for passage of the law in the months of debate that followed.

Senators Mansfield and Dirksen, the majority and minority leaders of the Senate, together with sixty-six bipartisan cosponsors, introduced the bill which embodied the President's views and on which the Justice Department had worked for some time. An impressive demonstration of unity, however, was not in itself enough to carry the day. The defenders of the southern status quo had often before shown the capacity for blocking action by parliamentary maneuver and the filibuster when the odds were against them. But this time it was clear at the outset that evasive tactics would not be effective. The Senate imposed a fifteen-day limit on the Judiciary Committee's hearings and proceeded to act with unaccustomed speed. Indeed, while some amendments were offered in the committee and from the floor, the most controversial were those in which supporters of the bill attempted to extend its provisions by banning the poll tax.

The debate opened on April 22 and continued for about a month. Pressure from the President and from the Senate leaders averted the threat of a filibuster. On May 25, the Senate imposed closure of further debate by a vote of 70 to 30. The fate of the measure was then clear. The Senate passed the Act by a vote of 77 to 19; and on July 9, the House passed its own version by a vote of 333 to 85. A conference committee ironed out the differences between the two houses and the President's signature made the voting-rights bill law on August 6, 1965.

The long-term consequences were not immediately apparent. Some states—notably Alabama, Arkansas, and Mississippi—relaxed their restrictions on voting rights even before passage of the law. The specter of federal intervention was enough to persuade them to ease access to the registration rolls. A variety of civil-rights groups labored through the summer and fall to help Negroes, long deprived of the ballot, prepare to exercise the rights of citizenship. The number of Negro voters registered rose steadily.

The number of such candidates for office also increased. By the spring of 1966, for instance, Negroes were running in the Democratic primaries of every Alabama county, evidence of their potential political strength. Furthermore, white aspirants even in the Deep South were taking a much more moderate position on race issues than formerly.

The new law was far from a cure-all, however. Much depended upon the quality of leadership and the total political situation in the localities in which the law was applied. It was not enough to register the Negroes; it was also necessary to get them to vote and to help them understand the issues on which they cast their ballots. In communities like Atlanta, Georgia, where a basis for collaboration and effective action existed, Negroes were able to make their weight felt at once. Elsewhere, the election of 1965 still found the Negro vote a negligible factor. The voting-rights law put the instruments of democratic political action within reach of the Negro; how they would be used remained to be seen.

Acknowledgments

The preparation of this volume within five years would have been impossible without the friendly collaboration not only of the eighty-three chapter-editors who have been generous, scrupulous, and patient in their efforts to distil much learning into a few words, but of many others too numerous to list by name.

The general editor has been lucky to have as his right hand Mrs. Ann B. Congdon of Cleveland Heights, Ohio, who has handled much of the correspondence with authors, and whose editorial skill, discriminating judgment, eye for detail, and passion for precision have added immensely to the life and style of this volume. Her help has been invaluable.

In preparing the manuscript for the press and in settling countless questions of fact, the general editor has greatly benefited from the resourcefulness and historical imagination of Mr. Stanley K. Schultz, a postgraduate student in the Department of History at the University of Chicago.

Thanks are due to Miss Isabel Garvey of Yarmouth Port, Massachusetts, for the copious and detailed subject index. The phrase index, which has required a special feeling for the classic or the familiar (or should-be familiar) phrase and an understanding of the context of the documents and their promise of new meanings, is the work of Mrs. Lila Weinberg of Chicago.

The general editor wishes to thank his wife, Ruth F. Boorstin, who, as usual, has been unstinting in her editorial and other assistance.

The following chapter-editors wish to give special thanks to these individuals and institutions: Lawrence W. Towner, to the Massachusetts Historical Society; Edmund S. Morgan, to Philip A. Hennessey, Clerk of the Courts, Salem, Massachusetts; Ralph L. Ketcham, to the Cornell University Library; L. H. Butterfield, to Harold R. Manakee, Director, the Maryland Historical Society; Robert E. Spiller, to the Harvard College Library; Barbara M. Solomon, to Miss Alma Lutz, Boston, Massachusetts, and the Women's Archives, Radcliffe College; William G. McLoughlin, to Roger E. Stoddard, Assistant Curator, the Harris Collection, Brown University Library; Matthew Josephson, to the United States Park Service, Edison Laboratory, West Orange, New Jersey; Lon L. Fuller, to Mark De Wolfe Howe; Thomas

931

Pyles, to the Enoch Pratt Free Library, Baltimore, Maryland; William E. Leuchtenburg, to the Franklin D. Roosevelt Library, Hyde Park, New York. The general editor wishes to give to Dr. L. H. Butterfield special acknowledgment for his generosity in sharing with the general editor his unpublished researches in connection with his editing of the letter from John Adams to Hezekiah Niles.

The University of Chicago Press wishes to thank the following for permission to reprint their versions of the material indicated: The Princeton University Press: The Declaration of Independence; The Rutgers University Press: Abraham Lincoln's Second Annual Message to Congress, and his Second Inaugural Address; The University of North Carolina Press: The Ballad of John Henry; Trustees Under the Will of Mary Baker Eddy: Excerpts from *Science and Health*; The Catholic University of America Press: "The Question of the Knights of Labor"; Time, Inc.: Quotation from *Life* Magazine, November 11, 1957, reprinted in the Introduction to "Cheapest Supply House on Earth"; The Macmillan Company: Excerpt from Vachel Lindsay's poem "Bryan, Bryan, Bryan, Bryan"; Charles Scribner's Sons: Theodore Roosevelt's Speech on "The New Nationalism"; The Pilgrim Press: Excerpts from *For God and the People: Prayers of the Social Awakening*; Harper & Row, Publishers: The paragraph from Frederick W. Taylor's *The Principles of Scientific Management* beginning "At the works of the Bethlehem Steel Company"; the Estate of Calvin Coolidge and Houghton Mifflin Company: "Have Faith in Massachusetts"; Alfred A. Knopf, Inc.: The Preface to *The American Language*; The Estate of Herbert Hoover: The speech entitled here "On American Individualism"; The Estate of Sinclair Lewis: The speech entitled here "The American Fear of Literature"; Random House, Inc.: Franklin D. Roosevelt's First Inaugural Address; The Macmillan Company: Franklin D. Roosevelt's "Quarantine" Address; The Estate of Albert Einstein: Einstein's Letter to Franklin D. Roosevelt; The Wendell L. Willkie Fund: Excerpts from *One World*; Elsevier Publishing Company, Amsterdam: William Faulkner's speech on acceptance of the Nobel Prize.

Index of Authors, Titles, and Editors

The authors of documents are in Roman type (with birth and death dates in parentheses); editors' names are in small capital letters; and titles are italicized.

General Index

Abbott, Lyman, 465

Abolitionists, 357, 358, 380; and Emancipation Proclamation, 410; Garrison, and the *Liberator*, 276–81; and Mexican War, 317; Thoreau as, 317–40

Abrams v. United States, 665–71

Abundance: public education as way to, 344–48; as theme in promotional literature, 32–47

Acheson, Dean G., 883, 884

Adamic, Louis, 462

Adams, Charles Francis, on James Otis, 237

Adams, Charles Francis, Jr., on Lincoln, 425

Adams, Charles Kendall, 523

Adams, Herbert Baxter, 523

Adams, James Truslow, 829

Adams, John, 109, 208; on Body-Politic, 5–6; and Declaration of Independence, 66, 67, 71, 72, 73; on meaning of American Revolution, 227–38

Adams, John Quincy, 209, 263; on Mayflower Compact, 6; and Monroe Doctrine, 255, 256; on public lands, 539–40

Adams, Samuel, 71, 73, 229 (note), 231–36 (*passim*), 238

Adler, Dankmar, 561

Advertising: to attract immigrants, *see* Promotional literature; of Sears, Roebuck and Company, 551–59; by Wanamaker, 630–31, 632, 637, 638

Agassiz, Louis, quoted by Holmes, 596

Agrarianism, 346–47; Bryan's "Cross of Gold" speech as expression of, 573–83, 584; and People's Party Platform of 1892, 513–21

Agriculture (*see also* Farmers): in depression of 1930's, 837, 838; European, after World War II, 885; Hoover and, 802, 805, 807, 817, 820; Jackson on, 268; manufacturing in relation to, Hamilton on, 178–81, 187; parity price levels, 583; Roosevelt, F. D., on, 841; as theme in promotional literature, 33, 37–38, 41–42, 46

Agriculture, Department of, 395, 720

Alabama: Indian sovereignty a question in, 270–72; Montgomery, 339, 340; Selma, 920, 923–28 (*passim*)

Albany Congress of 1754, 532

Alcoholic beverages (*see also* Prohibition): drunkard theme in Stanton address on divorce bill, 369, 371, 374; in Pennsylvania, *c.* 1698, 36, 40

Alcott, Bronson, 338; and Louisa May Alcott, Sinclair Lewis on, 833

Alden, John, 3, 6

Allen, William Francis, 523

Allerton, Isaac, 3

Allerton, John, 3

Alliance for Progress, 888, 914, 917

Alliances: avoidance of, 193, 205–06, 208, 209, 215, 217; and League of Nations, 782, 784–85; power to contract, 71

Alsop, Joseph, on "Quarantine" Address, 855

American Academy of Arts and Letters, and Nobel Prize address of Sinclair Lewis, 822–36

American character: arraignments of, 658–59; Bill of Rights and, 160; contempt for the unsuccessful, 585–90; economic abundance and, 46–47; frontier in formation of, 546–47, 548, 549; idealism of, expressed by Lincoln, 424, 426; practical genius in, 496; surrender terms at Appomattox as symbol of, 431; Washington's First Inaugural Address as expression of, 176

American Dream, Edison's career as enactment of, 496

811; of the seas, 776, 779; worldwide, 878–80

—individual: big business and, 771; Emerson's focus on, 287, 294, 298–300, 301; Holmes on, 596; Stevenson on, 414–15; unlimited, 584, 589

—of religion, 121, 153–54, 155, 157, 159, 167; effect on women, 357; and elective office, 219–26; religious test for federal office, 142, 143, 432–33

—of speech, 121, 155, 157, 167, 301, 925; Holmes on, 159, 665, 666–69; Hoover on, 811

Frémont, John C., 394–95

Friends, Society of. *See* Quakers

Freneau, Philip, 300

Frisch, Otto, 857, 858, 861

Frontier: in American history, 522–50; boaster of, 442; civil compacts of, 5; effect on women's status, 357; land speculators on, 386–87, 391–92; outrages against Indians, exemplified in Logan's Speech, 60–64; promotional literature and, 45

Frost, Robert, 829

Frugality. *See* Thrift

Full Employment Act, 191

Fuller, Edward, 3

Fuller, Samuel, 3

Fursenko, A. A., 629

Galbraith, Kenneth, 912

Galsworthy, John, 828, 832

Gandhi, Mohandas K., 338–39

Gantt, Henry, 748

Gardiner, Richard, 3

Garfield, James Randolph, 709

Garland, Hamlin, 829, 833–34

Garretson, Austin B., 769

Garrison, William Lloyd, prospectus for the *Liberator*, 276–81

General welfare (*see also* Public good; Public welfare): Constitution on, 85, 94; Coolidge on, 752–53; Jackson on, 269; neglect of doctrine c. 1890–1937, 315; prayer for, 732–33

George III, 6, 65, 432; denounced in Declaration of Independence, 67, 69–70, 72

George, Henry, 522

Georgia, Indian sovereignty a question in, 270–72

German immigrants, 461–62, 523, 526, 537, 538

Germany: Fourteen Points Address directed to, 772–81; Monroe Doctrine used against, 260, 261; and "Quarantine" Address, 846–56

Gerry, Elbridge, 71, 122, 130, 142, 154

Gerrymandering, 683

Gettysburg Address, 86, 176, 416–17, 418, 419–21

Ghost-writing, for Presidents, 170–71, 192–93, 264

Gibbons, James, Cardinal, memorial on Knights of Labor, 477–92

Gibson, Bob, 445

Gibson, John, 60, 62, 63

Gilbert, Cass, 571

Gilbreth, Frank, 739

Gilman, Nicholas, 144

Gilmore, Eddy, 558, 863

Gitlow v. New York, 157

Gladstone, William, 499, 510

Glen, James, on South Carolina trade, 537–38

God: as America's guide, 628; Civil War as judgment of, 424, 425; invoked by Franklin at Federal Convention, 77; invoked in Mayflower Compact, 3, 7; Lincoln's faith in, 423; named in 1868 oath of office, 435; Nature's God, 68, 229; New Humanism and, Sinclair Lewis on, 832; pragmatic conception of, 697, 704, 705; Puritans' covenant with, 21–23; teacher as prophet of, 619; Washington's appeal to and terms for, 172–75 (*passim*), 195, 203

Gold, Michael, 824 (note)

Gold standard, Bryan's "Cross of Gold" speech on, 579–82

Goldman, Emma, 339

Goldwater, Barry, 918

Gompers, Samuel, 755; quoted by Hoover, 810

Good Neighbor Policy, 838, 842

Goodman, John, 3

Gorelik, S. B., 629

Gorham, Nathaniel, 80–81, 84, 144

Gospel of Wealth, of Andrew Carnegie, 498–512, 584–85, 589–90

Government: American, Thoreau on, 318–19, 321, 325, 335; in business, Hoover on, 805–13, 818, 820–21; by compact, 1–7; corruption in, *see* Corruption in government; decentralized self-government, Hoover on, 806, 808, 814; least is best, 275, 318; limited, Americans first to set up, 73; of Plymouth Colony, 4–5

—representative: Coolidge on, 752, 753; Plunkitt of Tammany Hall on, 679; and special interests, 723–24

—republican form of, 123; America's destiny to preserve, 174; guaranteed to states by Constitution, 125, 128–29; Jefferson on, 213–15; public education necessary to, 348–51, 356; symbolized in Statue of Liberty, 460, 461

—source of authority in: compact between people and ruler, 6–7; consent of the

Madison, James, 76, 81, 82, 151, 256; and
Bill of Rights, 152, 154, 159–60; and
Confederation debt, 150; on congressional supremacy over states, 140; at
Constitutional Convention, 84, 89, 103,
105, 114, 122, 130, 131, 144, 433; as
defender of states' rights, 148, 149; as
ghost-writer for Washington, 171, 192;
on language of ideas, 73; on Louisiana
Purchase, 545; as nationalist, 140–41,
146; on republican government, 123
Magna Carta, 153, 165
Majority: government by, Jackson on, 263,
265–66, 273; right of, to embody opinion
in law, 662; will of, Coolidge on, 753;
will of, Jefferson on, 213, 215, 216–17
"Malefactors of great wealth," 589
Malone, Kemp, 800
Manifest Destiny, 25, 26
Manifest Destiny, by Albert K. Weinberg,
629
Mann, Horace, and common school educa-
tion, 341–56
Mann, Thomas, 827, 828
Manning, Henry Edward, Cardinal, on
working population, 485, 486
Mansfield, Mike, 928
Manufacturing: effect of Centennial Exhi-
bition of 1876 on, 634; Hamilton's report
on, 177–91; improved standard of living
from, 500–01; Jackson on, 268; of Penn-
sylvania, c. 1698, 44
Marble, Manton, 419
Marbury v. Madison, 119
"March of the Flag, The," speech by Al-
bert J. Beveridge, 621–29
March on Washington, 918
Margeson, Edmund, 3
Marriage: and divorce, Elizabeth Cady
Stanton on, 366–79; as theme in promo-
tional literature, 42, 44–45, 46; women's
legal status in, in 19th century, 357, 361,
367, 368
Marshall, Charles, 427, 428
Marshall, George C., and Marshall Plan,
426, 883–88, 889, 896
Marshall, John, 99–100, 119, 147–48, 149,
157, 217; opinion in *M'Culloch v. Mary-
land*, 86, 99, 239–54
Marshall, Thurgood, 903
Martin, Christopher, 3
Martin, Luther, 61, 63, 77, 81, 123, 124,
141
Maryland: *M'Culloch v.*, 86, 99, 239–54;
religion and public office in, 224
Mason, George, 90, 122, 130, 131, 142,
541; and Bill of Rights, 152, 153, 154
Mason, Stephen C., on Bishops' Program of
Social Reconstruction, 491

Massachusetts: Constitution of 1780, 5–6;
disestablishment in, 223; *Have Faith in*,
by Coolidge, 751–56; Pilgrims, and May-
flower Compact, 1–7; Puritans and their
ideals of a Christian community, 8–25;
Revolutionary heroes of, 228–38; witch
trials, 26–30
Masters, Edgar Lee, 830
Materialism, and ideal of economic abun-
dance, 46–47
Matthews, Lois K., on civil compacts, 5
Maximilian, Archduke of Austria, 259
Mayflower Compact, 1–7
Mayhew, Jonathan, 73, 231, 234–35, 238
Mecom, Benjamin, 57
Medicine, practice of, in Pennsylvania c.
1698, 36, 41
Meiklejohn, Alexander, 755
Meitner, Lise, 857, 858
Mellon, Richard B., 770
"Melting pot": America's first, 46
Melville, Herman, 834
Mencken, H. L., 828, 829, 830, 834, 836;
on American language, 794–801; on Coo-
lidge, 756
Merchandising, 551–59, 630–40
Mercy: duty of, Puritan concept, 11, 12–16
Metternich, on Monroe Doctrine, 259
Mexico: Monroe Doctrine and, 259; Tho-
reau's protest against war with, 317–40
Michelson, Albert A., 831
Michigan, University of, 831
Middle East, Willkie on, 864–68, 879, 882
Middle region, 540–41
Middlebury College, 831
Middleton, Arthur, 71
Midwest: in American literature, 834; racial
discrimination in, 909–10
Mies van der Rohe, Ludwig, 572
Mifflin, Thomas, 144
Mikoyan, Anastasia, 872
Mill, John Stuart, 687
Millay, Edna St. Vincent, 830
Millikan, Robert A., 831
Milton, John: on freedom of speech, 669;
on marriage, 375, 379
Miner's frontier, 527–32 (*passim*)
Mining, in Pennsylvania, advertised in
1698, 39
Minority: election of a President by, Jack-
son on, 266; danger from, 199–200; pro-
tection of, 213, 217, 584; morality of,
and promulgation of law, 133–34; Tho-
reau on, 319, 325, 327
Minority groups: civil discrimination
against, 223–26; 14th Amendment and,
169; movement to raise status of, 462
Minton, Sherman, 904
Mission. *See* American mission
Moffat, J. Pierrepont, 853–54

Rural America: in American literature, Sinclair Lewis on, 826; machine government in, and "class struggle" with immigrant America, 682–85; protests of, against industrial-urban society, 513–21, 573–83, 584
Rush, Benjamin, 71, 227
Rush, Richard, 256
Russell, Horace, 465
Russell, William E., 576
Russia: Bolshevik revolution, and Fourteen Points Address, 772–81; Jewish refugees from, 459; and Monroe Doctrine, 255–59, 261; rejection of Marshall Plan aid by Soviet bloc, 887; Sears, Roebuck catalogues as propaganda in, 558–59; Willkie's view of, 864, 868–73, 877–82 (passim)
Rutledge, Edward, 71
Rutledge, John, 84, 122, 131, 144
Ryan, John A., 491

Sachs, Alexander, 859, 861
Sage, Russell, 465
St. Louis, municipal corruption in, 649–50
Salem witch trials, 26–30
Salesmanship: in propaganda literature, 31–47; of Sears, 551–59; of Wanamaker, 630–40; world of, Sinclair Lewis on, 832
Salt, significance on frontier, 533–34
Saltonstall, Richard, 8
San Francisco Committee of Vigilance of 1851, 5
Sandburg, Carl, 830; on Gettysburg Address, 421; on John Henry, 443
Sankey, Ira D., 631
"Saunders, Richard," 49, 57
Scaife, Roger L., 755
Schenck v. United States, 159
Schiller, F. C. S., 692–93
Scholar, American: Emerson on, 282–301; and literature, Sinclair Lewis on, 822–36
Schuyler, Georgina, 460, 462
Science, 820, 825, 829, 831; atomic bomb development, 857–62; Franklin and, 59, 78; freedom of inquiry in, 301; pragmatism related to philosophy of, 688, 689–93, 701–02, 707; in school curriculum, 614–15
Scientific management, 738–50, 767, 875
Scopes trial, 583
Scott, Senator, quoted by Turner, 540
Searches and seizures, 155–56, 168
Sears, Richard Warren, and Sears, Roebuck and Company, 551–59, 639
Secessionist movements: from Massachusetts Bay Colony, 5; of South, 396–98, 403, 423–24; in South Carolina in 1832, 274
Secret ballot, 519, 521

Sectionalism: in drafting of Constitution, 90; in free-silver issue, 574, 575; frontier vs., 540–41; southern, and doctrine of state sovereignty, 148–49; Washington's warnings against, 171, 173, 198–99, 208
Securities Act of 1933, 770
Securities Exchange Commission, 770
Security. See National security
Sedition Act of 1798, 668
Seditious speech, 670
Seeger, Charles, 445
Segregation, racial: "separate but equal" concept, 475; Supreme Court decisions on, 120, 149–50, 169, 902–11, 918; Thoreau's influence in movement against, 339–40
"Self-evident" truths, 68, 72–73, 360, 364
Sellers, William, 745
Selma, Ala., 920, 923–28 (passim)
Senate, U.S.: Constitution on, 89, 91–96, 131; election of members, 91, 96, 133, 135–36, 520, 521; performance of, 101–02
Seneca Falls Declaration of Sentiments and Resolutions, 357–65
"Separate but equal" concept, 169, 475, 902–11
Separation of powers, 89, 114: points of contact between branches of government, 98, 118; Washington's warning against encroachment, 201–02
Sewall, Samuel, 28–29
Seward, Frederick, 411
Seward, William H., 162, 163, 259, 410, 411, 413, 416, 625
Sex: in American literature, 828, 834, 900; double standard in, 368–69; symbolized in "Ballad of John Henry," 438–41, 444, 445
Shapiro, Irwin, 443
Shaw, Albert, on American fortunes, 510
Shaw, George Bernard, 511, 827
Shaw, Lemuel, opinion in Commonwealth v. Hunt, 302–16
Shay, Frank, 443
Shays' Rebellion, 84
Shelley v. Kraemer, 169
Sherman, Roger, 66, 71; at Constitutional Convention, 103, 104, 119, 122, 131, 144
Sherman, William Tecumseh, 422, 429–30, 465; Henry W. Grady on, 469, 470, 472, 476
Sherman Act. See Antitrust Act of 1890
Shopping centers, 639
Sidney, Philip, 66
Siegmeister, Elie, 445
Silver (see also Free silver), demonetization of, 515, 516
Simeoni, Giovanni, Cardinal, 477, 490
Sinclair, Upton, 339, 589, 828, 830

Skyscrapers, 560–72

Slack, Ann, 57

Slave trade: Constitution on, 90, 95; denounced by Jefferson, 67

Slavery (see also Abolitionists): abolition of, 161–62, 163–64; as cause of Civil War, 400, 407, 413, 424, 425; colonization of freed slaves proposed by Lincoln, 403–04; Constitution and, 90, 131; Emancipation Proclamation, 161, 395, 407, 408, 409–15, 471, 924; escaped slaves, Constitution on, 125; Fugitive Slave Acts, 127, 394; Jefferson's attitude toward, 67, 74; Lincoln's plan for compensated emancipation, 161, 395, 398–407; New South's attitude toward, 471, 472, 473; relation to westward expansion, 525, 538, 539, 542; Thoreau's protest against, 317–40

Slums, 584–85, 682–83, 727; battle against, 641–48

Small, Albion W., 620

Smith, Alfred E., 225, 683, 684–85, 802, 819, 820

Smith, F. Hopkinson, 465

Smith, Gerrit, 367

Smith, James, 71

Smith, John, 530; Henry W. Grady on, 467

Smith, T. V., 82

Smith, Theobald, 831

Smith Act of 1940, 670

Social Christianity, 727–37

Social contract theory of government, 6, 73

Social evolution, 749; exemplified on frontier, 523–50

Social legislation, 589–90; Bryan on, 581, 584, 588; contempt for, 588, 590; and Hamilton's paternalistic theories, 191; and New Nationalism of Theodore Roosevelt, 709–26; rooted in Puritan sense of community, 24–25; Supreme Court decisions on, 100, 120, 166–67, 661–64

Social security, 25

Socialism: Carnegie on, 502; of 1890's, 522; fear of, Holmes on, 600, 663; Hoover on state socialism in America, 802, 806, 807, 819–20; Plunkitt of Tammany Hall on, 679; of Populists, 521

Sombart, Werner, on Thomas A. Edison, 494

Sorensen, Theodore, 912

Soule, George, 3

South: agrarian protest in, 513; "Battle Hymn of the Republic" in, 383; demand for free silver, 573; vs. free-homestead policy, 387; "frontier hypothesis" on, 537, 540, 541; in literature, 824 (note), 826, 898; Negro struggle for equality in, 918, 920, 928; New South, 463–76; Reconstruction, 120, 162–63, 425, 430–31;

resistance to desegregation, 910–11; state-sovereignty doctrine, 148–49; Thoreau's Civil Disobedience in, 339–40; "white primary" in, 169

South America. See Latin America

South Carolina, nullification doctrine in, 274

Soviet Union. See Russia

Spangenberg, Augustus G., quoted by Turner, 533–34

Spanish America. See Latin America

Spanish-American War, 384, 549; imperialist aftermath of, 621–29, 786

Special interests, Theodore Roosevelt vs., 714–20, 724

Speech. See Freedom of speech

Speed, Joshua, on Gettysburg Address, 420

Spencer, Herbert, 499, 508, 599, 619, 662, 664

"Spoils System," and civil service reform, 274, 543, 678–82, 683–84

Spotswood, Alexander, 526: on frontier, 537

Spraight, Richard Dobbs, 144

Spreckels, Rudolph, 659

Springfield Agreement of 1636, 5

Square deal, of Theodore Roosevelt, 715

Stalin, Joseph, Willkie and, 869–73, 877, 880–81, 882

Standard of living: and free exchange of goods, 879–80; Hoover on, 815–16; improvement in, as theme in promotional literature, 39–42, 46–47; improvement through merchandising, 551–59, 630–40; mass production and, 875–76; of rich and of poor, Carnegie on, 500–01

Standish, Myles, 3; Henry W. Grady on, 467

Stanford, Leland, 509

Stanton, Edwin M., on Gettysburg Address, 420

Stanton, Elizabeth Cady, 358–59, 365; address on New York divorce bill, 366–79

Stanton, Henry B., 358, 367

Staples, Sam, 317, 318

States: constitutional provisions concerning, 122–29; new, admission of, 122–23, 125, 127–28; political control over cities, 682–84; social legislation enacted by, 166–67, 661–64; Supreme Court decisions on relations among, 126–29

States' rights: Bill of Rights (U.S.) and, 157–58, 167–68; Civil War amendments and, 132; constitutional limitations on, 96; federal power over state laws, 119, 140–41, 143, 146–49; internal improvement legislation vs., 541; interposition of state sovereignty against federal power, 148–49, 911; Jackson on, 269–70; Jefferson and, 148, 215, 218; M'Culloch v.

957

Index of Words and Phrases

Abandon quiet life, 39
Ability to govern themselves, people's, 645
Abolish it, duty to, 375
Absolute power to destroy other nations, 915
Absolutism all the same, benevolent absolutism is, 760
   contrast between political liberty and industrial, 759
   experience with political, 765
Abstain from all violence, 412
Abuse it, power and proneness to, 202
Abused books, among the worst, 287
Abuses, arraignment of all, 215
   long train of, 66, 68
Accumulation, laws of, will be left free, 509
Achieved by loss of blood and treasure, 257
Acquiescence, absolute, 215
Acquisition, foreign capital is a precious, 184
Action, government supreme within sphere of, 243
   he turns toward, 690
   is a resource, 291
   is with the scholar subordinate, 290
Activity, our criticism a chill and insignificant, 833
Adequacy, he turns toward, 690
Administer to produce beneficial results, 507
Administration, duties of civil, 172
   has come, day of enlightened, 550
   in the life of this, 915
   of government, 195
   of justice depends on opinions of jurists, 369
   of your affairs, 216
   revolutionary, is not good government, 651
Adoration, offerings of man's, 222

Adultery of husband ought not be noticed, 368–69
Advance, no money in, 556
   of American settlement westward, 524
Advantage, considerations of social, 600
   national need before sectional, 722
   to a country, 180
Advantages authorize them to aspire, opulence to which, 181
   monopoly of, 185
   of so peculiar a situation, 193
   why forego, 205
Advice, we may give, 56
Advise people, 593
Affection for England as Mother-Country, 230
Afford to lose a customer, we can't, 555
Afraid, basest of all things is to be, 899
Age does not endow all with virtue, 468
   for, save while you may, 56
   must write its own books, each, 287
   of introversion, 296
Ages, intended to endure for, 247
   remain for, 568
Aggrandizement is gone, day of, 776
Aggression, against force and selfish, 776
Aggressive and oracular speech, 456
Agitator, silence the, 436
Agony of the human spirit, 899
Agreement, my, has nothing to do with right of majority, 662
Agricultural, country which is merely, 186
Allegiance, are absolved from all, 71
   I will bear true, 435
   was dissolved, 229
Allegory in which virtue was personified, 171
Alliances for extraordinary emergencies, 206
   occasional, 193
   permanent, 193
   temporary, 193

Creative talent, wealth of, 833
Creator, any other earthly work of the, 343
  endowed by their, 68, 278
Creature, in the veins of any living, 62
Credit, full faith and, 124
Creditors are a superstitious sect, 55
  have better memories, 55
  whack the stuffing out of the, 588
Crises, in all municipal, 654
Criticism has been insignificant activity,
  833
Criticize the inevitable, waste of time to,
  500
Cross of gold, 520, 582
Crowd, given the, you have the slum, 643
Crown of thorns, 582
Crucify mankind upon cross of gold, 582
Cruel as well as unconstitutional, 153
Cruelty, circumstances of, 70
Cultivated and inhabited districts, 180
Culture, best thing a man can do for his,
  328
Currency, contraction of, 588
Curse, fond pride of dress is sure a very, 54
  of bigness, 758
Customer, we can't afford to lose a, 555

Damage, want of care does more, 52
Danger, clear and imminent, 666
  clear and present, 665, 669
  contemplation of her, 280
  defending freedom in hour of, 916
  in an unshared idealism, 789
  is that (they) look with indifference, 604
  prepare for, 203
Dangers of invasion from without, exposed
  to, 69
Dead, hasten resurrection of the, 279
  literature is, 831
  patriotism is, 645
  shall not have died in vain, 418
Deadness and dullness, next to, 617
Death, he only leaves wealth at, 505
  opinions fraught with, 668
  slumbering in moral, 280
  to localism, mobility is, 542
Debt, first vice is running in, 55
  of gratitude, 195
  oppressive, is bane of enterprise, 270
  rather go to bed supperless than rise in,
  56
Debtor who borrowed money, 588
Debtors, better memories than, 55
Debts, industry pays, 51
  who can't pay his, 588
Deceit, women wine game and, 53
Decentralized self-government, principles
  of, 814
Decision, language of judicial, 599

will depend on judgment more subtle,
  663
Decisions, right to assist in making, 761
Declaration of Independence, our intellectual, 300
Dedicate this nation to policy of the good
  neighbor, 842
Defeat every enemy, should we, 920
Defend, committing us to a cause reason
  could not, 471
  Constitution of the United States, 107,
  435
Defending freedom in its hour of danger,
  916
Defense, dread and love shall be wall of,
  299
  make preparation for our, 257
  means of, 186
  of cause holy as liberty, 575
  provide for the common, 94
Defensive, man on the, 587
  posture, on a respectable, 206
Deference for public opinion, 204
Definite difference it will make at definite
  instants, 690
Degradations of others, to endure the, 214
Deity, most acceptable to the, 222
Deliberations, tranquil, 173
Demagogue, expect to be called a, 754
Demand in this war, what we, 776
  popular, 110
Demands of the social situations, 609
Democracy a success, can make, 651
  answer to communism is a fearless, 873
  destiny of, 919
  faith in American, 925
  frontier individualism promoted, 542
  last improvement possible in government,
  337
  social justice is result of, 761
  striving for, 766
  will not come by gift, industrial, 765
Democratic corruption, Tammany corrup-
  tion is, 656
  idea is to make masses prosperous, 581,
  588
Democratization in ownership, 763
Demoralized, people are, 515
Denying future, do so at cost of, 924
Depart from it, he will not, 351
Dependence, our day of, 300
Dependent on the states, 252
  upon conduct of race, 344
Depends, making of a contract, 598
Deplores volcanic abyss like that which
  church, 484
Depravity, not evidence of, 369
Descendants, enough room for our, 214
Designs in this spirit, man who, 566

Desire material improvement, however
    much we may, 761
    suppress the first, 54
Desirous of being a good neighbor, 333
Despised, new things (are not) to be, 468
Despotic government, corrupted people
    need, 79
    political intolerance as, 213
Despotism, can only end in, 79
    erected on happy commonwealth, 302
    hateful paths of, 75
    party domination a frightful, 201
Destinies, advancing rapidly to, 212
Destiny, a greater England with a nobler,
    622
    in league with our, 625
    interweaving our, 205
    of democracy, 919
    of man, 599
    of the Republican model of government,
    174
Destroy other nations, absolute power to,
    915
    power to tax involves power to, 239, 251
    power to tax is not power to, 254
Destroys foundation for peace, 850
Destruction of all ages, undistinguished, 70
    of American rights, 153
    of these ends, when government be-
    comes, 68
Determination, opportunity for independ-
    ent, 777
    to give America a literature worthy of her
    vastness, 835
Development continually beginning over
    again, 525
    determination of her own political, 777
    inequality of, 370
    of manhood, 761
    of men, striving for the, 766
    of our law, 600
    of race, higher, 374
    of race, moral, 595
Devotion we bring to this endeavor, 916
Devil, neither God nor the, 832
Dictate any mode of belief, right to, 222
Dictionary, life is our, 291
Die, fasting, he that lives upon hope will,
    51
    for liberty and country, 420
    I know I must, 28
Died in vain, these dead shall not have, 418
Dies, he is born he acts he, 575
    rich dies disgraced, man who, 510
Difference between honest and dishonest
    graft, 673
    of purpose between Almighty and men,
    425
    there can be no, anywhere that doesn't
    make a difference elsewhere, 690

Difficulty, occasion piled high with, 406
Dignity of his calling, teacher should
    realize, 619
    of man, 919, 921
Diligence and patience, 52
    is mother of good luck, 51
Direction, they have asked for, 843
Disadvantages of a new undertaking, 182
Disagreement my, has nothing to do with
    right of majority, 662
Disbursements to prepare for danger, 203
Discipline of life, 613
    they have asked for, 843
Disciplined by a hard and bitter peace, 913
Discontent of the literary class, 297
Discoveries, increased, 347, 356
Discovery, meeting ground of scientific, 494
    of natural resources, 550
Discriminations, derived from local, 197
Disease, struggle against, 915
Disgraced, man who dies rich dies, 510
Dishonest graft and honest, distinction be-
    tween, 673
    Tammany is honestly, 655
Dishonor, honor or, 406
Disinterestedness of more value than med-
    dling, 787
Dispute, eternal meddling in every, 787
Dissension, spirit of revenge natural to
    party, 201
Dissolved, political connection to be, 71
Distance cuts no figure, 554
Distinction between honest and dishonest
    graft, 673
    between morality and law, 595
Distinctions in society, factitious, 347
Distribution, laws of, left free, 509
    of stock harmful, ownership through, 763
Distrust, look with, 604
    mutual ignorance breeds mutual, 501
Disturb arrangement originally made, 336
Disturbances, redeemed from unsupport-
    able, 379
    to peace and contentment, 379
Diversification of industry, 180
Divided in purpose, we cannot be, 778
    little we can do, 914
Divorce, revision of laws on, 368
    speech, women respond to, 377
Divorced, different parts of our country can-
    not be, 396–97
Doctrinaire, but I am not, 758
Doctrine, certainly of their, 78
    of separate but equal, 904
    our policy not directed against any, 886
Doctrines of paternalism and state social-
    ism, 806
    of the wisest writers, 73
    that had no place in common law, 663
Dogma enclosed within definite lines, 595

Hero of this struggle is the Negro, 925
Heroes, blood of our, 215
    football player ranks with our greatest, 831
Hill, city upon a, 9, 22
History, American, has been history of colonization, 524
    frontier gone and with its going closed first period of American, 547
    harsh judgment of, 923
    land which has no, 529
    of America central feature of history of world, 711
    of moral development of race, 595
    of the world, 916
    study of law is study of, 601
Hoe and spade, virtue in, 292
Hold what you get, 56
Homage to the Great Author, 173
Home, life in the, 612
    you cannot rob a child of its, 646
Homeless, send these, to me, 459
Homes, greatness of a city measured by its, 647
Homicidal, unrestrained passions are, 351
Honest and dishonest, distinction between, 673
Honor, mutually pledge our sacred, 71
    office of profit and, 51
    or dishonor, 406
Honorable in what we give and what we preserve, 406
    no man more, 10
Honors it has conferred upon me, 195
Hope, he that lives upon, 51
    of earth, the last best, 161, 406–7
    rejoicing in, 915
    this government the world's best, 214
    United Nations our last best, 914
Hoping for better times, 51
Horizon, narrow our, 507
Horse, for want of a, 53
Hostile, through a world often, 789
    to republican liberty, 198
Hostilities, remote from original scene of, 851
Hour, throw not away an, 52
House of another, let not him pull down the, 714
Human heart, one throb of the, 642
    ideal perfectly attained, no, 813
    institution, if marriage is a, 369
    race, benign parent of, 175
    race, brethren of the, 265
    rights, struggle for, 923
    rights, witness slow undoing of those, 913
    spirit, agony of the, 899
    welfare, experiment in, 814, 818
Humanity and justice of this government, 272

cause of, 575
church should be on side of, 486
is not perfect, 813
recovered its rights, in cabin of Mayflower, 6
sad music of, 155
stages in the advance of, 714
Hunger looks in, at the workingman's house, 51
    our policy is against, 886
Hungry, if ever he entered, 62
Husband and wife are one, 368
Hypocrisy is not a Tammany vice, 655
Hypocrites, bribed into, 222
    persecution can render men, 222

Idea, it is a mistaken, 374
    one single definite, 247
    truth happens to an, 698
Ideal be high, let the state, 588
    is to our country, our first, 791
    perfectly attained, no human, 813
Idealism, there is danger in an unshared, 789
Ideals, perform according to our professed, 873
Ideas, exchange of goods and, 879
    include many different, 73
    look with distrust upon, 604
    of government, there are two, 581, 588
    true, are those we can assimilate, 698
    ultimate good reached by free trade in, 668
Idle, be ashamed that a master catch you, 51
    who here need not lie, 44
    why stand we, 65
Idleness, trouble springs from, 52
    we are taxed by our, 50
Idolizers of state authority, 115
Ignorance breeds mutual distrust, mutual, 501
    fear springs from, 294
    substitution of knowledge for, 770
Ignorant compliance, centuries of, 878
Illusions, blinded by their old, 448
Illustrious, his progenitors had been, 232
    more, than any kingdom, 296
Image is instrument of instruction, 616
Images which he forms, 616
Imagination, true excitant of his, 565
Imitation of life of Christ, 507
Immoral becomes unmoral, 324
Immortal, man is, 900
Immunities, privileges and, 167
Imperfect man, lot of, 215
    our best work most, 507
Imperfection in midst of, 454
Imperialism, international, sacrifice of some other nation's liberty, 877

INDEX OF WORDS AND PHRASES

988